T0340100

NETWORKING GAMES

NETWORKING GAMES

Network Forming Games and Games on Networks

VLADIMIR V. MAZALOV
JULIA V. CHIRKOVA
Russian Academy of Sciences
Karelia, Petrozavodsk, Russian Federation

ACADEMIC PRESS

An imprint of Elsevier

Academic Press is an imprint of Elsevier
125 London Wall, London EC2Y 5AS, United Kingdom
525 B Street, Suite 1650, San Diego, CA 92101, United States
50 Hampshire Street, 5th Floor, Cambridge, MA 02139, United States
The Boulevard, Langford Lane, Kidlington, Oxford OX5 1GB, United Kingdom

Copyright © 2019 Elsevier Inc. All rights reserved.

No part of this publication may be reproduced or transmitted in any form or by any means, electronic or mechanical, including photocopying, recording, or any information storage and retrieval system, without permission in writing from the publisher. Details on how to seek permission, further information about the Publisher's permissions policies and our arrangements with organizations such as the Copyright Clearance Center and the Copyright Licensing Agency, can be found at our website: www.elsevier.com/permissions.

This book and the individual contributions contained in it are protected under copyright by the Publisher (other than as may be noted herein).

Notices

Knowledge and best practice in this field are constantly changing. As new research and experience broaden our understanding, changes in research methods, professional practices, or medical treatment may become necessary.

Practitioners and researchers must always rely on their own experience and knowledge in evaluating and using any information, methods, compounds, or experiments described herein. In using such information or methods they should be mindful of their own safety and the safety of others, including parties for whom they have a professional responsibility.

To the fullest extent of the law, neither the Publisher nor the authors, contributors, or editors, assume any liability for any injury and/or damage to persons or property as a matter of products liability, negligence or otherwise, or from any use or operation of any methods, products, instructions, or ideas contained in the material herein.

Library of Congress Cataloging-in-Publication Data
A catalog record for this book is available from the Library of Congress

British Library Cataloguing-in-Publication Data
A catalogue record for this book is available from the British Library

ISBN: 978-0-12-816551-5

For information on all Academic Press publications
visit our website at https://www.elsevier.com/books-and-journals

Working together
to grow libraries in
developing countries

www.elsevier.com • www.bookaid.org

Publisher: Candice Janco
Acquisition Editor: Scott J. Bentley
Editorial Project Manager: Michael Lutz
Production Project Manager: Paul Prasad Chandramohan
Designer: Matthew Limbert

Typeset by VTeX

CONTENTS

PREFACE

The book is dedicated to game-theoretic models in communication and information networks. This research field forms a modern direction of game theory, which originated with the appearance of new technologies such as the Internet, mobile communications, distributed and cloud computing, social networks, etc. A basic knowledge of mathematical analysis, algebra, and probability theory is a necessary prerequisite for reading.

The book is addressed to under- and postgraduates and to experts in the field of operations research, information technology, and modeling of social systems and processes.

Some of the problems considered remain unsolved and can be the subject of independent research. As a matter of fact, our primary goal is to stimulate further investigations for interested readers. The list of references at the end of the book will guide them through relevant publications.

For many years, the authors have been enjoying the opportunity to discuss the derived results with Russian colleagues L.A. Petrosyan, V.V. Zakharov, N.V. Zenkevich, A.Yu. Garnaev, A.A. Sedakov (St. Petersburg State University), A.A. Vasin (Moscow State University), D.A. Novikov (Trapeznikov Institute of Control Sciences, Russian Academy of Sciences), and A.B. Zhizhchenko (Steklov Mathematical Institute, Russian Academy of Sciences) and with foreign colleagues M. Sakaguchi (Osaka University), B. Monin (University of Paderborn), K.E. Avrachenkov (INRIA Sophia Antipolis), A.V. Gurtov (Linköping University), and A.S. Lukyanenko (Aalto University, Helsinki). They all have our deep and sincere appreciation. We also express gratitude to colleagues A.N. Rettieva, A.Yu. Kondratjev, N.N. Nikitina, B.T. Tsynguev, and A.V. Shchiptsova from Institute of Applied Mathematical Research (Karelian Research Center, Russian Academy of Sciences) for helpful remarks. Finally, we thank A.Yu. Mazurov (Alekseev Nizhny Novgorod State Technical University) for his thorough translation, permanent feedback, and positive contribution to the English version of the book.

Results presented in this work were obtained in the IAMR KarRS RAS and supported by the Russian Foundation for Basic Research (project nos. 16-51-55006, 16-01-00183), the Russian Science Foundation (project no. 17-11-01079) and by the Shandong Province of China "Double-Hundred Talent Plan (no. WST2017009)".

INTRODUCTION

Network games, or games on networks, are games defined over graphs. This branch of game theory originated with the appearance of new information technologies, in the first place the Internet, mobile communications, distributed and cloud computing, and social networks. All users of a network are linked by (information and communication) channels, which leads to different problems such as the choice of data routes or channels, the definition of signal levels and quality, the establishment of links to neighbor nodes, and others. For example, in routing games the players choose data channels of limited capacity. As a result, jamming occurs in networks, causing interesting effects and even paradoxes such as the well-known Braess paradox.

Network games can be divided into two classes, namely, (1) network formation games in which the players establish links to each other based on personal interests and (2) games on formed networks. In addition, there exists a combined two-stage setting of such games where a network is formed at the first stage and the agents located at different nodes of this network play with each other at the second stage.

The recent years have been remarkable for a technological breakthrough in the analysis of the virtual information world. In terms of game theory, all participants of the Internet and mobile communication networks are interacting players who receive and transmit information by appropriate data channels. Each player pursues individual interests, acquiring some information or complicating this process. The players need high-capacity channels, and the channel distribution problem arises naturally in the case of numerous players. Game-theoretic methods are of assistance here.

Owing to the development of the Internet, information transmission techniques were changed accordingly, and new decision-making systems were designed. Novel approaches were suggested in the field of artificial intelligence, resource allocation, computational resource optimization, and the number of such approaches is still rapidly growing. The global control of the Internet turns out to be impossible. We may speak about distributed control of the network where each user manages his traffic to maximize his utility or the amount of information or to minimize delays. In this context, we mention a series of problems such as optimal routing, equilibrium design in global large-scale networks, the existence of pure strategy equilibria, resource allocation, negotiations in networks, energy balance control and its efficiency in wireless networks, multiagent systems, learning capabilities of agents, and decision support in telecommunication networks. The same class of problems includes boosting the performance of multiprocessor computers. These problems can be solved using noncooperative game theory methods.

Control of distributed resources is a key problem for smart grids, that is, intelligent power networks. They consist of autonomous segments that are power consumers and suppliers simultaneously. Modern information and communication networks and technologies are actively used to design, create, and operate smart grids. Similar problems arise during organization of computer networks for physical objects with embedded technologies that interact with each other, the so-called Internet of Things (IoT).

As such systems contain very many agents, an efficient approach is to employ game theory methods. Here one should consider the behavioral specifics of the agents.

The market of high-performance computing is undergoing changes due to widespread use of desktop grids, a promising class of computer systems. They have a considerable advantage over traditional high-performance computer systems in terms of scalability and peak performance, whereas computational resources are provided on voluntary basis. Note that the owners of computational nodes pursue personal interests, like system administrator, the owners of computational tasks, and so on. Optimal control of the computational process must satisfy the interests of all participants. Therefore, game theory methods find direct application to desktop grids for control of their computational resources. For example, hierarchical games are an appropriate modeling framework for telecommunication systems in which the administrator or resource provider interacts with lower-level users.

For a given control system, it is important to measure quantitatively the efficiency of its decentralized setup in comparison with the case of optimal centralized control. Based on the results of such a comparative study, we may give recommendations on structural redesign of the system. A good characteristic is the so-called price of anarchy suggested in 1999 by E. Koutsoupias and C.H. Papadimitriou. In fact, the book pays much attention to calculation of the price of anarchy.

Many novel statements of game-theoretic problems are associated with the appearance of social networks. The users of such networks organize and join communities, thereby forming different topology graphs. Their structural analysis plays a major role, but another important problem for such networks is to assess the results of game-theoretic interaction in equilibrium.

All these problems are considered in the book. A series of results belong to the authors. The book can be used as a textbook on operations research and game theory. We also recommend it as a guide for independent investigations.

CHAPTER 1

Nash Equilibrium

Contents

For network games, a primary tool of analysis is game-theoretic methods. The central role is played by the concept of equilibrium. The basic notions of game theory include Players, Strategies, and Payoffs. In the sequel, the players are denoted by $\{1, 2, \ldots, n\}$. In network games, players can be programs, mobile phones, or members of social networks. Strategies can be the choice of a path in a graph, the level of a signal, the formation of links in a graph. A normal-form game is organized in the following way. Each player i chooses a certain strategy x_i from a set X_i, $i = 1, 2, \ldots, n$. As a result, player i obtains a payoff $H_i(x_1, x_2, \ldots, x_n)$ or bears a cost $C_i(x_1, x_2, \ldots, x_n)$, $i = 1, 2, \ldots, n$. In the former case, each player seeks to maximize his payoff; in the latter, to minimize his cost.

1.1 NASH EQUILIBRIUM

Let us introduce the main definitions for the n-player games.

Definition 1. A normal-form n-player game is an object

$$\Gamma = \; < N, \{X_i\}_{i \in N}, \{H_i\}_{i \in N} >,$$

where $N = \{1, 2, \ldots, n\}$ denotes the set of players, X_i is a strategy set of player i, and $H_i : \prod_{i=1}^{n} X_i \to R$ gives a payoff function of player i, $i = 1, \ldots, n$.

In such a game, player i chooses a strategy $x_i \in X_i$ without any information about the choice of his opponents. Player i is interested to maximize his payoff $H_i(x_1, \ldots, x_n)$, which actually depends on the strategies of all players. A set of strategies of all players is called a strategy profile of a game. Any subset $S \subset N$ is called a coalition in a game. We denote by x_S the strategy profile of the players belonging to a coalition S.

Networking Games
https://doi.org/10.1016/B978-0-12-816551-5.00007-1
Copyright © 2019 Elsevier Inc.
All rights reserved.

For a given strategy profile $x = (x_1, \ldots, x_n)$, the notation

$$(x_{-i}, x_i') = (x_1, \ldots, x_{i-1}, x_i', x_{i+1}, \ldots, x_n),$$

indicates that player i changed his strategy from x_i to x_i', whereas the other players use the same strategies as before. Similarly, denote by

$$(x_{-S}, x_S')$$

the strategy profile in which only the players from a coalition S changed their strategies.

The concept of a Nash equilibrium is the main solution principle for n-player games.

Definition 2. A Nash equilibrium in a game Γ is a strategy profile $x^* = (x_1^*, \ldots, x_n^*)$ in which any player $i \in N$ satisfies the conditions

$$H_i(x_{-i}^*, x_i) \leq H_i(x^*) \ \forall x_i. \tag{1.1}$$

The strategies that enter a Nash equilibrium are called optimal.

This definition means that any player decreases his payoff by changing his strategy in a Nash equilibrium. Therefore, none of the players benefits by a unilateral deviation from a Nash equilibrium. Of course, the situation can be different if two or more players deviate from a Nash equilibrium simultaneously.

Definition 3. A strategy profile $x^* = (x_1^*, \ldots, x_n^*)$ is called a strong Nash equilibrium in a game Γ if, for any coalition $S \subset N$ and any strategy profile x_S, there exists at least one player $i \in S$ such that

$$H_i(x_{-S}^*, x_S) \leq H_i(x^*).$$

Remark. The games with the cost functions of players can be considered by analogy to the games with their payoff functions. In this case, instead of payoff maximization, we are concerned with cost minimization. The cost functions of players will be denoted as $C_i(x_1, \ldots, x_n)$, $i \in N$. For example, the setup with the cost functions of players arises in load balancing games and routing games.

1.2 COOPERATION AND COMPETITION

Under cooperation, it is possible achieve a solution that maximizes the total payoff of all players. A strategy profile x_{OPT} yielding the maximum of the total payoff

$$H(x_1, \ldots, x_n) = \sum_{i \in N} H_i(x_1, \ldots, x_n)$$

is called the cooperative solution.

Definition 4. A Nash equilibrium x_{WNE} is called worst-case if, for any other Nash equilibrium x,

$$H(x) \geq H(x_{WNE}).$$

A useful characteristic for comparing the total income under cooperation and competition is the well-known price of anarchy pioneered by Koutsoupias and Papadimitriou [50].

Definition 5. Let x_{WNE} and x_{OPT} be the worst-case Nash equilibrium and cooperative solution, respectively. Then the ratio

$$PoA = \frac{H(x_{WNE})}{H(x_{OPT})}$$

is called the price of anarchy.

This characteristic can be adopted to identify whether a system needs some regulation.

In the games with the cost functions of players instead of their payoff functions, the price of anarchy is defined as the ratio

$$PoA = \frac{C(x_{WNE})}{C(x_{OPT})},$$

where the cooperative solution minimizes the total cost

$$C(x_1, \ldots, x_n) = \sum_{i \in N} C_i(x_1, \ldots, x_n),$$

whereas in the worst-case Nash equilibrium x_{WNE}, the total cost takes the maximum value over all Nash equilibria. Obviously, in this case, we have $PoA \geq 1$, and the greater this ratio, the higher the system cost (also known as the social cost) in the unregulated state.

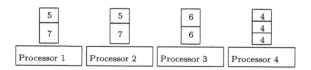

Figure 1.1 The optimal profile

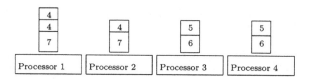

Figure 1.2 The Nash equilibrium

1.3 EXAMPLES OF LOAD BALANCING GAMES

Consider $n = 4$ identical processors and nine jobs of different volumes given by the vector $w = (7, 7, 6, 6, 5, 5, 4, 4, 4)$. Assume that the execution time of jobs is the load of a processor. Obviously, the optimal allocation of these jobs among the processors has the form as in Fig. 1.1.

The execution time of all jobs at each processor is the same (OPT=12).

Now, imagine that the jobs represent players choosing an appropriate processor for execution. Then the strategy profile presented in Fig. 1.2 is another solution that forms a Nash equilibrium. Indeed, if, for example, the job of volume 7 moves from processor 1 with load 15 to processor 2, then the load of the latter makes up 18. If the job of volume 4 moves from processor 1 to processor 2, then the load of the latter increases, also reaching 15.

Consequently, in this Nash equilibrium the social cost is 15. The price of anarchy constitutes

$$PoA = 15/12 = 1.25.$$

Note that this allocation represents a Nash equilibrium yet not a strong Nash equilibrium. More specifically, there exists a coalition of the form (7, 4, 4, 5, 5) that improves the situation for each member. Assume that the job of volume 7 from processor 1 changes places with the job of volume 5 from processor 3 and also both jobs of volume 4 from processor 1 change places with the job of volume 5 from processor 4. This leads to the strategy profile presented in Fig. 1.3, in which all the mentioned players reduced their execution times. The new strategy profile is a strong Nash equilibrium.

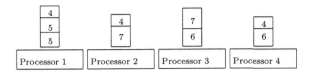

Figure 1.3 The strong Nash equilibrium

The social cost in this equilibrium makes up 14 and the strong price of anarchy is

$$SPoA = 14/12 = 1.166.$$

1.4 CONVEX GAMES

Nash equilibria may not exist. However, there is a class of games that always have a Nash equilibrium, the so-called convex games.

Definition 6. A function $H(x)$ is called concave (convex) on a set $X \subseteq R^n$ if for any $x, y \in X$ and $\alpha \in [0, 1]$, we have $H(\alpha x + (1 - \alpha)y) \geq (\leq)\alpha H(x) + (1 - \alpha)H(y)$.

This definition directly implies that the concave functions also satisfy the inequality

$$H(\sum_{i=1}^{p} \alpha_i x_i) \geq \sum_{i=1}^{p} \alpha_i H(x_i)$$

for any convex combination of points $x_i \in X$, $i = 1, \ldots, p$, where $\alpha_i \geq 0$, $i = 1, \ldots, p$, and $\sum \alpha_i = 1$.

As a matter of fact, the Nash theorem [64] is a central result on the existence of equilibria in such games. Let us prove it for the case of two players. Prior to doing so, we will establish an auxiliary statement, which can be treated as an alternative definition of a Nash equilibrium.

Lemma 1. *A Nash equilibrium exists in a game* $\Gamma = < I, II, X, Y, H_1, H_2 >$ *if and only if there is a set of strategies* (x^*, y^*) *such that*

$$\max_{x,y}\left\{H_1(x, y^*) + H_2(x^*, y)\right\} = H_1(x^*, y^*) + H_2(x^*, y^*). \qquad (1.2)$$

Proof. Necessity. Let a Nash equilibrium (x^*, y^*) exist in the game under consideration. By Definition 2, for an arbitrary pair of strategies (x, y), we have

$$H_1(x, y^*) \leq H_1(x^*, y^*), \quad H_2(x^*, y) \leq H_2(x^*, y^*).$$

Summing up these inequalities yields

$$H_1(x, y^*) + H_2(x^*, y) \leq H_1(x^*, y^*) + H_2(x^*, y^*) \qquad (1.3)$$

for arbitrary strategies x, y of the players, and formula (1.2) is immediate.

Sufficiency. Assume that there exists a pair (x^*, y^*) that satisfies (1.2) and hence (1.3). By letting $x = x^*$ and subsequently $y = y^*$ in inequality (1.3), we arrive at conditions (1.1) defining a Nash equilibrium. $\qquad \square$

This lemma allows to use conditions (1.2) or (1.3) instead of equilibrium check based on (1.1).

Theorem 1. *Consider a two-player game* $\Gamma = < I, II, X, Y, H_1, H_2 >$. *Let the strategy sets* X, Y *be compact convex sets in space* R^n, *and also let the payoffs* $H_1(x, y)$, $H_2(x, y)$ *be continuous functions that possess concavity in* x *and* y, *respectively. Then the game always has a Nash equilibrium.*

Proof. To establish this result, we apply the *ex contrario* principle. Assume that there is no Nash equilibrium in the game. In this case, by Lemma 1, for any pair of strategies (x, y), it is always possible to find a pair (x', y') that violates condition (1.3), that is,

$$H_1(x', y) + H_2(x, y') > H_1(x, y) + H_2(x, y).$$

Consider the sets

$$S_{(x',y')} = \left\{ (x, y) : H_1(x', y) + H_2(x, y') > H_1(x, y) + H_2(x, y) \right\},$$

which in fact form open sets owing to the continuity of the functions $H_1(x, y)$ and $H_2(x, y)$. The whole space of strategies $X \times Y$ is covered by the sets $S_{(x',y')}$, that is, $\bigcup\limits_{(x',y') \in X \times Y} S_{(x',y')} = X \times Y$. Using the compactness of $X \times Y$, we can extract a finite subcovering

$$\bigcup\limits_{i=1,\dots,p} S_{(x_i, y_i)} = X \times Y.$$

For each $i = 1, \dots, p$, denote

$$\varphi_i(x, y) = \left[H_1(x_i, y) + H_2(x, y_i) - (H_1(x, y) + H_2(x, y)) \right]^+, \qquad (1.4)$$

where $a^+ = \max\{a, 0\}$. All the functions $\varphi_i(x, y)$ are nonnegative, and by the definition of $S_{(x_i, y_i)}$ at least one of them is positive. Hence it appears that $\sum_{i=1}^{p} \varphi_i(x, y) > 0 \ \forall (x, y)$.

Now, introduce a mapping $\varphi(x, y) : X \times Y \to X \times Y$ of the form

$$\varphi(x, y) = \left(\sum_{i=1}^{p} \alpha_i(x, y) x_i, \sum_{i=1}^{p} \alpha_i(x, y) y_i \right),$$

where

$$\alpha_i(x, y) = \frac{\varphi_i(x, y)}{\sum_{i=1}^{p} \varphi_i(x, y)}, \quad i = 1, \ldots, p, \quad \sum_{i=1}^{p} \alpha_i(x, y) = 1.$$

The functions $H_1(x, y)$ and $H_2(x, y)$ are continuous, and therefore the same property applies to the mapping $\varphi(x, y)$. In addition, by assumption the sets X and Y are convex, and hence the convex combinations $\sum_{i=1}^{p} \alpha_i x_i \in X$ and $\sum_{i=1}^{p} \alpha_i y_i \in Y$. Thus $\varphi(x, y)$ is the mapping of the convex compact set $X \times Y$ into itself. The Brouwer fixed point theorem states that this mapping has a fixed point $(\bar{x}, \bar{y})$ such that $\varphi(\bar{x}, \bar{y}) = (\bar{x}, \bar{y})$, or

$$\bar{x} = \sum_{i=1}^{p} \alpha_i(\bar{x}, \bar{y}) x_i, \quad \bar{y} = \sum_{i=1}^{p} \alpha_i(\bar{x}, \bar{y}) y_i.$$

Recall that the functions $H_1(x, y)$ and $H_2(x, y)$ are concave in x and y, respectively. So, we naturally arrive at

$$
\begin{aligned}
H_1(\bar{x}, \bar{y}) + H_2(\bar{x}, \bar{y}) &= H_1\left(\sum_{i=1}^{p} \alpha_i x_i, \bar{y}\right) + H_2\left(\bar{x}, \sum_{i=1}^{p} \alpha_i y_i\right) \\
&\geq \sum_{i=1}^{p} \alpha_i H_1(x_i, \bar{y}) + \sum_{i=1}^{p} \alpha_i H_2(\bar{x}, y_i).
\end{aligned}
\tag{1.5}
$$

On the other hand, by definition the functions $\alpha_i(x, y)$ and $\varphi_i(x, y)$ have the same domain of positivity. For positive functions $\varphi_i(\bar{x}, \bar{y})$ (note that at least one such function surely exists), we have the following inequality (see (1.4)):

$$H_1(x_i, \bar{y}) + H_2(\bar{x}, y_i) > H_1(\bar{x}, \bar{y}) + H_2(\bar{x}, \bar{y}). \tag{1.6}$$

For the indexes j such that $\alpha_j(\bar{x}, \bar{y}) = 0$,

$$\alpha_j(\bar{x}, \bar{y})\left(H_1(x_j, \bar{y}) + H_2(\bar{x}, y_j)\right) > \alpha_j(\bar{x}, \bar{y})\left(H_1(\bar{x}, \bar{y}) + H_2(\bar{x}, \bar{y})\right). \quad (1.7)$$

Multiplying (1.6) by $\alpha_i(\bar{x}, \bar{y})$ and summing up the result with (1.7) over all indexes $i, j = 1, \ldots, p$ give the final inequality

$$\sum_{i=1}^{p} \alpha_i H_1(x_i, \bar{y}) + \sum_{i=1}^{p} \alpha_i H_2(\bar{x}, y_i) > H_1(\bar{x}, \bar{y}) + H_2(\bar{x}, \bar{y}),$$

which obviously contradicts formula (1.5). Hence there exists a Nash equilibrium in convex games, and the proof is finished. □

CHAPTER 2

Congestion Games

Contents

A congestion game represents a routing game on a graph in which players choose an appropriate route, striving to avoid "bottlenecks" that hamper traffic flows. Theory of potential games is a good tool to find equilibria in such systems. Therefore, we first dwell on the methods of potential games and then pass to an analysis of congestion games.

2.1 POTENTIAL GAMES

Games with potentials were studied by Shapley and Monderer [62]. Consider a normal-form n-player game $\Gamma = < N, \{X_i\}_{i \in N}, \{H_i\}_{i \in N} >$. Assume that there exists a function $P : \prod_{i=1}^{n} X_i \rightarrow R$ such that, for any $i \in N$,

$$H_i(x_{-i}, x_i') - H_i(x_{-i}, x_i) = P(x_{-i}, x_i') - P(x_{-i}, x_i) \tag{2.1}$$

for arbitrary $x_{-i} \in \prod_{j \neq i} X_j$ and any strategies $x_i, x_i' \in X_i$. If such a function exists, it is called the **potential** of the game Γ, whereas the game itself is called a **potential game**.

Traffic jamming. Suppose that companies *I* and *II*, each possessing two trucks, have to deliver some cargo from point A to point B. These points are connected by two roads (see Fig. 2.1), and one road allows a two-times higher speed of motion than the other. Moreover, assume that the trip time on any road is proportional to the number of trucks moving on it. Fig. 2.1 also indicates the trip times depending on the number of moving trucks on each road.

Therefore, as their strategies the players choose the allocation of their trucks between the roads, that is, the admissible strategies are the combina-

Copyright © 2019 Elsevier Inc.
All rights reserved.

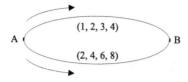

Figure 2.1 Traffic jamming

tions $(2, 0), (1, 1), (0, 2)$. For each player, the cost function is the total trip time of his trucks. The payoff matrix takes the form

$$
\begin{array}{c@{\qquad}c@{\qquad}c}
 & (2, 0) & (1, 1) & (0, 2)
\end{array}
$$
$$
\begin{array}{c}
(2, 0) \\
(1, 1) \\
(0, 2)
\end{array}
\left(
\begin{array}{ccc}
(-8, -8) & (-6, -5) & (-4, -8) \\
(-5, -6) & (-6, -6) & (-7, -12) \\
(-8, -4) & (-12, -7) & (-16, -16)
\end{array}
\right).
$$

Obviously, the game under consideration possesses three pure strategy equilibria as follows. These are the strategy profiles in which (a) the trucks of one player move on road 1 whereas the other player chooses different roads for his trucks and (b) both players chooses different roads for their trucks.

This game has the potential

$$
P = \begin{array}{c}
(2, 0) \\
(1, 1) \\
(0, 2)
\end{array}
\left(
\begin{array}{ccc}
13 & 16 & 13 \\
16 & 16 & 10 \\
13 & 10 & 1
\end{array}
\right).
$$

Choice of data centers. Assume that each of two cloud operators (see Fig. 2.2) may conclude a contract to utilize the capacity resources of one or two of three data centers available. The resources of data centers 1, 2, and 3 are 2, 4, and 6, respectively. If both operators choose the same data center, then they equally share its resources. The payoff of each player is the sum of the obtained resources at each segment minus the rent cost of the resources provided by a data center (let this cost be 1).

Therefore, as their strategies the players choose appropriate data centers for cooperation, that is, the admissible strategies are $(1), (2), (3), (1, 2), (1, 3), (2, 3)$. The payoff matrix takes the form

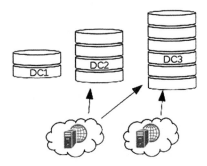

Figure 2.2 Choice of data centers

$$
\begin{array}{c c c c c c c}
 & (1) & (2) & (3) & (1,2) & (1,3) & (2,3) \\
(1) & (0,0) & (1,3) & (1,5) & (0,3) & (0,5) & (1,8) \\
(2) & (3,1) & (1,1) & (3,5) & (1,2) & (3,6) & (1,6) \\
(3) & (5,1) & (5,3) & (2,2) & (5,4) & (2,3) & (2,5) \\
(1,2) & (3,0) & (2,1) & (4,5) & (1,1) & (3,5) & (2,6) \\
(1,3) & (5,0) & (6,3) & (3,2) & (5,3) & (2,2) & (3,5) \\
(2,3) & (8,1) & (6,1) & (5,2) & (6,2) & (5,3) & (3,3)
\end{array}.
$$

There exist three pure strategy equilibria in this game, namely, (a) both operators choose data centers 2 and 3, and (b) one of the operators chooses data centers 1 and 3, whereas the other chooses data centers 2 and 3. The potential can be defined by

$$
P=
\begin{array}{c c c c c c c}
 & (1) & (2) & (3) & (1,2) & (1,3) & (2,3) \\
(1) & 1 & 4 & 6 & 4 & 6 & 9 \\
(2) & 4 & 4 & 8 & 5 & 9 & 9 \\
(3) & 6 & 8 & 7 & 9 & 8 & 10 \\
(1,2) & 4 & 5 & 9 & 5 & 9 & 10 \\
(1,3) & 6 & 9 & 8 & 9 & 8 & 11 \\
(2,3) & 9 & 9 & 10 & 10 & 11 & 11
\end{array}.
$$

Theorem 2. *Let an n-player game $\Gamma =< N, \{X_i\}_{i \in N}, \{H_i\}_{i \in N} >$ have a potential P. Then a Nash equilibrium in the game Γ is a Nash equilibrium in the game $\Gamma' =< N, \{X_i\}_{i \in N}, \{P\}_{i \in N} >$, and vice versa. In addition, there always exists at least one pure strategy equilibrium in the game Γ.*

Proof. The first statement of this theorem follows directly from the definition of a potential. Indeed, by (2.1) the inequality

$$H_i(x^*_{-i}, x_i) \leq H_i(x^*) \ \forall x_i$$

coincides with the inequality

$$P(x^*_{-i}, x_i) \leq P(x^*) \ \forall x_i.$$

In other words, if x^* is a Nash equilibrium in the game Γ, then it is also the same in the game Γ', and vice versa.

Now, demonstrate that the game Γ' always has a pure strategy equilibrium. As x^* choose a pure strategy profile that maximizes the potential $P(x)$ over the set $\prod_{i=1}^{n} X_i$. Then, $P(x) \leq P(x^*)$ for any $x \in \prod_{i=1}^{n} X_i$; in particular, this is the case with respect to each argument, that is,

$$P(x^*_{-i}, x_i) \leq P(x^*) \ \forall x_i.$$

Hence, x^* is a Nash equilibrium in the game Γ', *ergo* in the game Γ.   □

Consequently, if a game allows a potential, then it always has a pure strategy equilibrium. This fact has been illustrated by the examples of traffic jamming and the choice of data centers.

The Cournot oligopoly. Consider the Cournot oligopoly, a game in which the payoff functions of the players have the form

$$H_i(x) = (p - b\sum_{j=1}^{n} x_j)x_i - c_i x_i, \ \ i = 1, \ldots, n.$$

This game is potential, too. The potential represents the function

$$P(x_1, \ldots, x_n) = \sum_{j=1}^{n}(p - c_j)x_j - b\left(\sum_{j=1}^{n} x_j^2 + \sum_{1 \leq i < j \leq n} x_i x_j\right). \quad (2.2)$$

Indeed, the functions $H_i(x)$ and $P(x)$ are quadratic in the variable q_i, and their derivatives coincide:

$$\frac{\partial H_i}{\partial x_i} = \frac{\partial P}{\partial x_i} = p - c_i - 2bx_i - b\sum_{j \neq i} x_j, \ i = 1, \ldots, n. \quad (2.3)$$

Hence, the functions $H_i(x)$ and $P(x)$ possess the same values in each variable x_i (to some constant), that is,

$$H_i(x_{-i}, x_i) - H_i(x_{-i}, x_i') = P(x_{-i}, x_i) - P(x_{-i}, x_i') \ \forall x_i.$$

Therefore, function (2.2) is a potential in the oligopoly model. By Theorem 2 an equilibrium can be calculated through maximization of function (2.2). The first-order necessary optimality conditions

$$\frac{\partial P}{\partial x_i} = p - c_i - 2bx_i - b \sum_{j \neq i} x_j = 0, \ i = 1, \ldots, n,$$

lead to expressions (2.2), which yield an equilibrium in the oligopoly model.

A game without potential. Note that a game may have no potential, even if a pure strategy equilibrium exists. Get back to the example of traffic jamming (see Fig. 2.1). Under the same assumptions, let the cost functions of the players be defined by the maximal trip time of their trucks on both roads. In this case, the payoff matrix becomes

$$
\begin{array}{cccc}
 & (2,0) & (1,1) & (0,2) \\
(2,0) & \left(\begin{array}{ccc} (-4,-4) & (-3,-3) & (-2,-4) \\
(1,1) & (-3,-3) & (-4,-4) & (-6,-6) \\
(0,2) & (-4,-2) & (-6,-6) & (-8,-8) \end{array}\right).
\end{array}
$$

The modified game possesses two pure strategy equilibria. These are the strategy profiles in which the trucks of one player move on the first road whereas the other player chooses different roads for his trucks. Nevertheless, the game has no potential. For proving this fact, assume on the contrary that a potential P exists. Then definition (2.1) implies

$$P(1, 1) - P(3, 1) = H_1(1, 1) - H_1(3, 1) = -4 - (-4) = 0,$$
$$P(1, 1) - P(1, 2) = H_2(1, 1) - H_2(1, 2) = -4 - (-3) = -1.$$

As a result,

$$P(3, 1) - P(1, 2) = -1. \tag{2.4}$$

On the other hand,

$$P(1, 2) - P(3, 2) = H_1(1, 2) - H_1(3, 2) = -3 - (-6) = 3,$$

and

$$P(3, 1) - P(3, 2) = H_2(3, 1) - H_2(3, 2) = -2 - (-6) = 4,$$

which gives

$$P(3, 1) - P(1, 2) = 1.$$

This relationship contradicts (2.4), and thus the game possesses no potential. Interestingly, in contrast to the earlier example, here the cost functions are not in the additive form.

2.2 CONGESTION GAMES

Congestion games were pioneered by Rosenthal [72]. As a matter of fact, the term "congestion game" has the following origin. In such games, payoff functions depend only on the number of players choosing identical strategies. This class comprises routing games of transition between two points (trip time depends on the number of automobiles on a given route segment). The choice of data centers is also a congestion game: the amount of resources received by a player from a data center depends on the number of other players choosing this data center.

Definition 7. A symmetric congestion game is an n-player game $\Gamma = < N, M, \{S_i\}_{i \in N}, \{c_i\}_{i \in N} >$, where $N = \{1, \ldots, n\}$ denotes the set of players, and $M = \{1, \ldots, m\}$ is a finite set of some objects for strategy formation. The strategy of player i is the choice of a certain subset from M. Denote b S_i, $i = 1, \ldots, n$, the set of all admissible strategies of player i. Each object $j \in M$ is associated with a function $c_j(k), 1 \leq k \leq n$, which describes the payoff of each player k who chose strategies containing j. This function depends on the total number k of such players only.

Assume that the players chose strategies $s = (s_1, \ldots, s_n)$. Each s_i represents a set of objects from M. Then the payoff function of player i is defined by the total payoff on each object, that is,

$$H_i(s_1, \ldots, s_n) = \sum_{j \in s_i} c_j(k_j(s_1, \ldots, s_n)),$$

where $k_j(s_1, \ldots, s_n)$ gives the number of players whose strategies incorporate object j, $i = 1, \ldots, n$.

Theorem 3. *A symmetric congestion game is potential and hence always possesses a pure strategy equilibrium.*

Proof. Consider the function

$$P(s_1, \ldots, s_n) = \sum_{j \in \cup_{i \in N} s_i} \left(\sum_{k=1}^{k_j(s_1, \ldots, s_n)} c_j(k) \right)$$

and demonstrate that this is a potential of the game. Let us verify conditions (2.1). On the one hand,

$$H_i(s_{-i}, s_i') - H_i(s_{-i}, s_i) = \sum_{j \in s_i'} c_j(k_j(s_{-i}, s_i')) - \sum_{j \in s_i} c_j(k_j(s_{-i}, s_i)).$$

For all $j \in s_i \cap s_i'$, the payoffs c_j in the first and second sums are the same. Therefore,

$$H_i(s_{-i}, s_i') - H_i(s_{-i}, s_i) = \sum_{j \in s_i' \setminus s_i} c_j(k_j(s) + 1) - \sum_{j \in s_i \setminus s_i'} c_j(k_j(s)).$$

Next, find

$$P(s_{-1}, s_i') - P(s_{-1}, s_i) = \sum_{j \in \cup_{l \neq i} s_l \cup s_i'} \left(\sum_{k=1}^{k_j(s_{-i}, s_i')} c_j(k) \right) - \sum_{j \in \cup_{l \in N} s_l} \left(\sum_{k=1}^{k_j(s_{-i}, s_i)} c_j(k) \right).$$

Under $j \notin s_i \cup s_i'$, the corresponding summands in these expressions coincide, which leads to

$$P(s_{-1}, s_i') - P(s_{-1}, s_i) = \sum_{j \in s_i \cup s_i'} \left(\sum_{k=1}^{k_j(s_{-i}, s_i')} c_j(k) - \sum_{k=1}^{k_j(s_{-i}, s_i)} c_j(k) \right)$$

$$= \sum_{j \in s_i' \setminus s_i} \left(\sum_{k=1}^{k_j(s_{-i}, s_i')} c_j(k) - \sum_{k=1}^{k_j(s_{-i}, s_i)} c_j(k) \right) + \sum_{j \in s_i \setminus s_i'} \left(\sum_{k=1}^{k_j(s_{-i}, s_i')} c_j(k) - \sum_{k=1}^{k_j(s_{-i}, s_i)} c_j(k) \right).$$

In the case $j \in s_i' \setminus s_i$, we have $k_j(s_{-i}, s_i') = k_j(s) + 1$. If $j \in s_i \setminus s_i'$, then $k_j(s_{-i}, s_i') = k_j(s) - 1$. Consequently,

$$P(s_{-1}, s_i') - P(s_{-1}, s_i)$$

$$= \sum_{j \in s_i' \setminus s_i} \left(\sum_{k=1}^{k_j(s)+1} c_j(k) - \sum_{k=1}^{k_j(s)} c_j(k) \right) + \sum_{j \in s_i \setminus s_i'} \left(\sum_{k=1}^{k_j(s)-1} c_j(k) - \sum_{k=1}^{k_j(s)} c_j(k) \right)$$

$$= \sum_{j \in s_i' \setminus s_i} c_j(k_j(s) + 1) - \sum_{j \in s_i \setminus s_i'} c_j(k_j(s)),$$

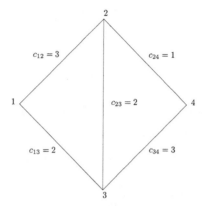

Figure 2.3 A network of four nodes

which exactly matches the expression for $H_i(s_{-i}, s_i') - H_i(s_{-i}, s_i)$. The proof of Theorem 3 is finished. □

An example of potential routing game. Consider players 1–4 who intend to send traffic of unit volume from node 1 to node 4 through a network illustrated in Fig. 2.3. The capacities c_{ij}, $i,j = 1, \ldots, 4$, of the edges are also indicated in the figure. Assume that the transmission time on an edge (i, j) is k/c_{ij} if this edge contains k players. For each player, the payoff function is the total transmission time on the whole route with the minus sign.

The players can choose the following routes as their strategies: $s_1 = \{(1, 2)(2, 4)\}$, $s_2 = \{(1, 3)(3, 4)\}$, $s_3 = \{(1, 2)(2, 3), (3, 4)\}$, $s_4 = \{(1, 3)(3, 2), (2, 4)\}$. For example, in the strategy profile (s_1, s_2, s_3, s_4), edge $(1, 2)$ is chosen by two players (players 1 and 3), and edge $(2, 4)$ also by two players (players 1 and 4). Therefore, the payoff of player 1 in this strategy profile makes up

$$H_1(s_1, s_2, s_3, s_4) = -\left(\frac{2}{3} + \frac{2}{1}\right) = -2.666.$$

Let us calculate the potential for different strategy profiles:
$P(s_1, s_2, s_3, s_4) = -(\frac{1+2}{3} + \frac{1+2}{1} + \frac{1+2}{2} + \frac{1+2}{2} + \frac{1+2}{3}) = -8;$
$P(s_1, s_1, s_2, s_2) = (\frac{1+2}{3} + \frac{1+2}{1} + \frac{1+2}{2} + \frac{1+2}{2} + \frac{1+2}{3}) = -6.5;$
$P(s_1, s_2, s_2, s_3) = (\frac{1+2}{3} + \frac{1}{1} + \frac{1+2}{2} + \frac{1}{2} + \frac{1+2+3}{3}) = -6.$
The potential achieves maximum in the strategy profile (s_1, s_2, s_2, s_3), which is hence a Nash equilibrium.

Consequently, symmetric congestion games always have at least one pure strategy equilibrium. There may exist a mixed strategy equilibrium as well. However, the existence of pure strategy equilibria is of crucial importance for applications. Note also that such equilibria exist owing to the additive form of the payoff functions and their homogeneity in symmetric games. In what follows, we consider the case of player-specific congestion games where the payoffs of different players can have different forms. Our analysis will be confined to the consideration of simple strategies in which each player chooses only one object from the set $M = \{1, \ldots, m\}$ [61].

2.3 PLAYER-SPECIFIC CONGESTION GAMES

Definition 8. A player-specific congestion game is an n-player game $\Gamma = < N, M, \{c_{ij}\}_{i \in N, j \in M} >$, where $N = \{1, \ldots, n\}$ denotes the set of players, and $M = \{1, \ldots, m\}$ gives a finite set of objects. The strategy of player i is the choice of some object from M. Therefore, M can be interpreted as the strategy set of the players. The payoff function of player i who chooses strategy j is defined by $c_{ij} = c_{ij}(k_j)$, where k_j is the number of players using strategy j, $0 \leq k_j \leq n$. For the time being, c_{ij} are supposed to be nonincreasing functions. In other words, the more players choose a given strategy, the smaller is the payoff.

Denote by $s = (s_1, \ldots, s_n)$ the strategy profile composed of the strategies chosen by all players. Each strategy profile s corresponds to the **congestion vector** $k = (k_1, \ldots, k_m)$, where k_j is the number of players choosing strategy j. Then the payoff function of player i takes the form

$$H_i(s_1, \ldots, s_n) = c_{is_i}(k_{s_i}), \ i = 1, \ldots, n.$$

We will be concerned with the pure strategy profiles only. For the games under consideration, the definition of a pure strategy Nash equilibrium can be reformulated in the following way. In an equilibrium s^*, any player i does not benefit by deviating from his optimal strategy s_i^*, and so, the optimal strategy payoff $c_{is_i^*}(k_{s_i^*})$ is not smaller than the payoff from joining the players who use any other strategy j, that is, $c_{ij}(k_j + 1)$.

Definition 9. A Nash equilibrium in a game $\Gamma = < N, M, \{c_{ij}\}_{i \in N, j \in M} >$ is a strategy profile $s^* = (s_1^*, \ldots, s_n^*)$ in which the following conditions hold for any player $i \in N$:

$$c_{is_i^*}(k_{s_i^*}) \geq c_{ij}(k_j + 1) \ \forall j \in M. \tag{2.5}$$

Now, we present another constructive concept proposed by Shapley and Monderer. It will serve to establish the existence of equilibrium in congestion games.

Definition 10. Suppose that a game $\Gamma = < N, M, \{c_{ij}\}_{i \in N, j \in M} >$ has a sequence of strategy profiles $s(t), t = 0, 1, \ldots$, such that (a) each profile differs from the preceding one in a single component and (b) the payoff of a player who changed his strategy is strictly greater. Such a sequence is called an improvement sequence. If any improvement sequence in Γ is finite, then we say that this game satisfies the Final Improvement Property (FIP).

Clearly, if an improvement sequence is finite, then the terminal strategy profile represents a Nash equilibrium, as it satisfies conditions (2.5). However, for some games with a Nash equilibrium, the FIP fails. In such games, improvement sequences can be infinite and have cyclic repetitions. This fact follows from the finiteness of the strategy sets.

Nevertheless, the games Γ with the two-element strategy sets M always possess the FIP.

Theorem 4. *A player-specific congestion game* $\Gamma = < N, M, \{c_{ij}\}_{i \in N, j \in M} >$, *where* $M = \{1, 2\}$, *always possesses a pure strategy Nash equilibrium.*

Proof. We are going to demonstrate that a congestion game with two strategies has the FIP. Suppose on the contrary that this is not the case. In other words, there exists an infinite improvement sequence $s(0), s(1), \ldots$. Extract its cyclic subsequence $s(0), \ldots, s(T)$, that is, $s(0) = s(T)$ and $T > 1$. In this chain, each strategy profile $s(t), t = 1, \ldots, T$, corresponds to a congestion vector $k(t) = (k_1(t), k_2(t)), t = 0, \ldots, T$. Obviously, $k_2 = n - k_1$. Find the element with the maximal value $k_2(t)$. Without loss of generality, we believe that this element is $k_2(1)$ (otherwise, just renumber the elements of the sequence using its cyclic character). Then $k_1(1) = n - k_2(1)$ is the minimal element in the chain, and so, at the initial time, some player i switches from strategy 1 to strategy 2, that is,

$$c_{i2}(k_2(1)) > c_{i1}(k_1(1) + 1). \tag{2.6}$$

Since $s(t), t = 0, \ldots, T$, is an improvement sequence, the monotonous property of the payoff function implies

$$c_{i2}(k_2(1)) \leq c_{i2}(k_2(t)), \ t = 0, \ldots, T.$$

On the other hand,

$$c_{i1}(k_1(1) + 1) \geq c_{i1}(k_1(t) + 1), \ t = 0, \ldots, T.$$

In combination with (2.6), this leads to the inequality $c_{i2}(k_2(t)) > c_{i1}(k_1(t) + 1)$, $t = 0, \ldots, T$, that is, player i strictly follows strategy 2. However, at the initial time $t = 0$, *ergo* at the time $t = T$, he applied strategy 1.

The resulting contradiction argues that a congestion game with two strategies has the FIP. Consequently, such a game possesses a pure strategy equilibrium. □

Let us emphasize a relevant aspect. The proof of Theorem 4 relies on that the maximal congestion of strategy 1 corresponds to the minimal congestion of strategy 2. Generally speaking, this fails even for the games with three strategies. The congestion games with three and more strategies may not satisfy the FIP.

A congestion game without the FIP. Consider a two-player congestion game with three strategies and the payoff matrix

$$\begin{pmatrix} (0, 4) & (5, 6) & (5, 3) \\ (4, 5) & (3, 1) & (4, 3) \\ (2, 5) & (2, 6) & (1, 2) \end{pmatrix}.$$

This game has the infinite cyclic improvement sequence

$$(1, 1) \to (3, 1) \to (3, 2) \to (2, 2) \to (2, 3) \to (3, 1) \to (1, 1).$$

Therefore, it does not satisfy the FIP. Still, there exist two (!) pure strategy equilibria, namely, the profiles $(1, 2)$ and $(2, 1)$.

To establish the existence of equilibrium in the class of pure strategies in the general case, we introduce a stronger solution improvement condition. More specifically, assume that each player in an improvement sequence chooses the best reply under a given strategy profile, which yields his maximal payoff. If there are several best replies, then the player chooses one of them. Such an improvement sequence will be called a best-reply sequence.

Definition 11. Suppose that a game $\Gamma = < N, M, \{c_{ij}\}_{i \in N, j \in M} >$ has a sequence of strategy profiles $s(t)$, $t = 0, 1, \ldots$, such that (a) each profile differs from the preceding one in a single component and (b) the payoff of a player who changed his strategy is strictly greater, yielding him the maximal payoff in this strategy profile. Such a sequence is called a best-reply sequence. If any best-reply sequence in the game Γ is finite, then we say that this game satisfies the Final Best-Reply Property (FBRP).

Evidently, any best-reply sequence represents an improvement sequence. The converse statement is false. Now, we prove the basic result.

Theorem 5. *A player-specific congestion game* $\Gamma =< N, M, \{c_{ij}\}_{i\in N, j\in M} >$ *always possesses a pure strategy Nash equilibrium.*

Proof. Let us apply mathematical induction by the number of players. Basis: for $n = 1$, the statement becomes trivial, as the player chooses the best strategy from M. Inductive step: show that if the statement is true for $n - 1$ players, then it also true for n players.

Consider an n-player game $\Gamma =< N, M, \{c_{ij}\}_{i\in N, j\in M} >$. First, eliminate player n from further analysis. In the reduced game Γ' with $n - 1$ players and m strategies, the inductive hypothesis implies that there exists an equilibrium $s' = (s_1(0), \ldots, s_{n-1}(0))$. Denote by $k'(0) = (k'_1(0), \ldots, k'_m(0))$ the corresponding congestion vector. Then $c_{is_i(0)}(k'_{s_i(0)}) \geq c_{ij}(k'_j + 1)$ for all $j \in M, i = 1, \ldots, n-1$. Revert to the game Γ and let player n choose the best reply (the strategy $j(0) = s_n(0)$). Consequently, just one component changes in the congestion vector $k' = (k'_1, \ldots, k'_m)$ (component $j(0)$ increases by 1).

Now, construct the best-reply sequence. The initial term of the sequence takes the form $s(0) = (s_1(0), \ldots, s_{n-1}(0), s_n(0))$. The corresponding congestion vector will be denoted by $k(0) = (k_1(0), \ldots, k_m(0))$. In the strategy profile $s(0)$, the payoffs possibly decreased only for the players with the strategy $j(0)$; the other players obtain the same payoff and do not benefit by modifying their strategy. Suppose that player i_1 (actually applying the strategy $j(0)$) can guarantee a greater payoff using another strategy. If such a player does not exist, then an equilibrium in the game Γ is achieved. Choose his best reply $j(1)$ and denote by $s(1)$ the new strategy profile. In the corresponding congestion vector $k(1)$, component $j(0)$ (component $j(1)$) decreased (increased, respectively) by 1. In the new strategy profile $s(1)$, the payoffs can be improved only by the players applying the strategy $j(1)$. The other players have the same payoffs in comparison with the original strategy profile. Assume that player i_2 can improve his payoff. Choose his best reply $j(2)$ and continue the described procedure.

Therefore, we have constructed the best-reply sequence $s(t)$. It corresponds to a sequence of congestion vectors $k(t)$ in which any component $k_j(t)$ either equals the initial value $k'_j(0)$ or exceeds it by 1. The last situation occurs if at the time $t-1$ player i_t switches to the strategy $j(t)$. In other cases, the number of players employing the strategy $j \neq j(t)$ is $k'_j(0)$. Note that each player can switch to another strategy just once. Indeed, imagine that, at the time $t-1$, player i_t switches to the strategy j; then at the time t, this strategy is used by the maximal number of players. Hence, at the subsequent times the number of the players with this strategy remains the same or even goes down (accordingly, the number of the players choosing other strategies is the same or goes up). Owing to the monotonic payoff functions, player i_t cannot obtain a greater payoff. Since the game involves a finite number of players, the resulting best-reply sequence is finite: $s(t), t = 1, 2, \ldots, T$, where $T \leq n$.

There may exist several best-reply sequences of this form. Among them, take the one $s(t), t = 1, \ldots, T$, with the maximal value T. Finally, demonstrate that the last strategy profile $s(T) = (s_1(T), \ldots, s_n(T))$ is a Nash equilibrium.

As mentioned earlier, the players deviating from their original strategies would not increase their payoffs in the strategy profile $s(T)$, and so, consider the players who fix their strategies during the time period T. Suppose that there is a player among them who belongs to the group with the strategy $j(T)$. If he improves his payoff, then we could extend the best-reply sequence to the time $T + 1$. However, this contradicts the maximality of T. Suppose that there is a player among them who belongs to the group with a strategy $j \neq j(T)$. The number of players in this group is the same as at the initial time (see the discussion above), and this player cannot increase his payoff as well.

Therefore, we have argued that, in the strategy profile $s(T) = (s_1(T), \ldots, s_n(T))$, any player $i = 1, \ldots, n$ satisfies the conditions

$$c_{is_i(T)}(k_{s_i(T)}(T)) \geq c_{ij}(k_j(T) + 1) \ \forall j \in M.$$

Consequently, $s(T)$ forms a Nash equilibrium for n players. The proof of Theorem 5 is finished. $\qquad\qquad\Box$

2.4 CONGESTION GAMES WITH STRATEGY SET CONSTRAINT

In Section 2.2, we have considered the n-player congestion games $\Gamma = \ <N, M, \{S_i\}_{i \in N}, \{c_{ij}\}_{i \in N} >$ in which the strategy set S_i of player i represents the set of all the subsets of the set M, that is, $S_i = 2^M$. It is of definite interest to consider the games with certain constraints imposed on the strategy set. For example, in routing games the admissible strategies are paths in a graph.

Assume that n players can choose objects from a set $M = \{1, 2, \ldots, m\}$. The strategy of player i is a set of objects $s_i = (j_1, \ldots, j_l)$ from the set M, where $s_i \in S_i$, $i = 1, \ldots, n$. For each object j chosen, player i obtains a payoff $c_{ij}(k_j)$, where k_j is the number of players who chose this object. As before, designates as $(k_1, \ldots, k_m)$ the associated congestion vector. Let $c_{ij}(k)$ be a nonincreasing function taking values in R. Note that $c_{ij}(k)$ may have negative values.

Denote by $s_i \in S_i$ the strategy of player i. Then the payoff of player i is the sum of all payoffs for the chosen objects $j \in s_i$, that is,

$$V_i = \sum_{j \in s_i} c_{ij}(k_j), \quad i = 1, \ldots, n.$$

As established earlier, the congestion games in which the strategy set is the set of all subsets (see Section 2.2) or simply the set M (see Section 2.3) always possess a pure strategy equilibrium. However, the following examples show that the existence of a pure strategy equilibrium depends on the structure of S_i, $i = 1, \ldots, n$.

Example 1. Consider two players choosing a certain number of objects from three objects, that is, $n = 2$ and $m = 3$, and the strategy sets are

$$S_1 = \{\{1, 2\}, \{3\}\}, \quad S_2 = \{\{1\}, \{2, 3\}\}.$$

For each of the objects, the payoffs of player I are given by

$$(1, 0) \quad (7, 2) \quad (6, 5),$$

where the first value in parentheses corresponds to the payoff of player I if an appropriate object is chosen by him only, and the second value to the payoff of player I if the object is chosen by both players. By analogy the payoffs of player II are described by

$$(7, 3) \quad (5, 4) \quad (5, 1).$$

The resulting bimatrix game has the form

$$\begin{array}{cc} & \begin{array}{cc} (1) & (2, 3) \end{array} \\ \begin{array}{c} (1, 2) \\ (3) \end{array} & \begin{pmatrix} (7, 3) & (3, 9) \\ (6, 7) & (5, 6) \end{pmatrix} \end{array}.$$

Obviously, this game possesses no pure strategy equilibrium.

Example 2. Again, consider the case $n = 2, m = 3$ with the same payoffs as in Example 1 and the modified strategy set

$$S_1 = \{\{1, 2\}, \{1, 3\}, \{2, 3\}\}, \quad S_2 = \{\{1, 2\}, \{1, 3\}, \{2, 3\}\}.$$

For these strategies, the bimatrix game takes the form

$$
\begin{array}{cccc}
 & (1, 2) & (1, 3) & (2, 3) \\
(1, 2) & (2, 7) & (7, 8) & (3, 9) \\
(1, 3) & (6, 8) & (5, 4) & (6, 6) \\
(2, 3) & (8, 11) & (12, 8) & (7, 5)
\end{array}.
$$

It possesses the pure strategy equilibrium $(8, 11)$.

The examples illustrate that the existence of a pure strategy equilibrium depends on the structure of the strategy set of all players.

To obtain sufficient conditions for the existence of an equilibrium, modify the original game Γ as follows. Introduce the set of new objects

$$M^- = \{-m, \ldots, -1\}, M^+ = \{m + 1, \ldots, 2m\},$$
$$M' = M^- \cup M \cup M^+ = \{-m, \ldots, -1, 1, \ldots, 2m\}.$$

They will be used in the proofs further. Let $c_{ij}(k) = 0$ for $j \in M^+$ and $c_{ij}(k) = c$ for $j \in M^-$, where c takes a sufficiently small value so that

$$c < \min\{(c_{ij}(k))^- \mid 1 \leq i \leq n, 1 \leq j \leq m, 1 \leq k \leq n\}.$$

Now, define the new strategy set S_i' of the players as the set of all $s_i' \subset M'$ such that $|s_i'| = m$ and there exists $s_i \in S_i$ satisfying the conditions $s_i' \cap M \subset s_i$ and

$$|s_i \setminus s_i'| \leq |s_i' \cap M^-|.$$

Denote by Γ' the new game constructed in this way.

The games Γ and Γ' are equivalent. All payoffs vanish on the set M^+, and hence each player can choose the same number m of objects. None of the players benefits by choosing the objects from the set M^-, and this feature allows us to add a new player without changing the payoffs of other players.

Definition 12. For a fixed strategy profile $s = (s_1, \ldots, s_n)$, we say that player i is satisfied with object $j \in s_i$ if, for any other object j' such that

$$s_i' = s_i \cup \{j'\} \setminus \{j\} \in S_i',$$

the payoff of player i from the strategy s_i' is not greater than that from the strategy s_i.

Obviously, $s = (s_1, \ldots, s_n)$ forms a **Nash equilibrium** in the game Γ if each player is satisfied with all his objects.

As easily observed, if $s' = (s_1', \ldots, s_n')$ is a Nash equilibrium in the game Γ', then $s = (s_1' \cap M, \ldots, s_1' \cap M)$ is an equilibrium in the game Γ.

Theorem 6. *Assume that the set S_i', $i = 1, \ldots, n$, satisfies the following condition:*

(A'): for any $s_i, s_i' \in S_i'$, there exists a bijection

$$f : s_i \to s_i'$$

such that

1) f is an identity transformation into $s_i \cap s_i'$;
2) for $j \in s_i \setminus s_i'$,

$$s_i \cup \{f(j)\} \setminus \{j\} \in S_i'.$$

Then the game Γ_n' has a pure strategy equilibrium.

Proof. Note that condition (A') allows us to increase the payoff by replacing one of the objects with another. Again, we use mathematical induction by the number of players n to prove the existence of a pure strategy equilibrium.

Basis: for $n = 1$, the statement becomes trivial, as the player chooses the strategy $s_1' \in S_1'$ that maximizes $\sum_{j \in s' \cap M} c_{1j}^+$.

Inductive step: show that if the statement is true for $n - 1$ players, then it also true for n players. Suppose $(s_1, \ldots, s_{n-1})$ forms an equilibrium in the game Γ_{n-1}'. Consequently, $s_i \cap M^- = \emptyset$ for all players $i = 1, \ldots, n - 1$. Let $s_n = M^-$. This leads to the strategy profile $s(0) = (s_1, \ldots, s_n)$ in the game Γ_n'. For this strategy profile, each of the players $i = 1, \ldots, n - 1$ is satisfied with his objects whereas new player n is not satisfied with any object. In particular, player n is not satisfied with object $j_0 = -1$. Assume that player n replaces it with object $j_1 \in M$ that belongs to his admissible strategy and maximizes his payoff. Denote by $s(1)$ the new strategy profile.

Now, player n is satisfied with object j_1. Players $1, \ldots, n - 1$ are satisfied with all objects $j \neq j_1$. Suppose player $i_1 \in \{1, \ldots, n - 1\}$ is not satisfied with object j_1, choosing object j_2 that belongs to his admissible strategy and maximizes his payoff.

Continuing the best-reply procedure as the described procedure, we construct the sequence $\{s(k), j_k, i_k\}$ of strategy profiles, objects, and players. Assume that we have found $s(l)$, j_l for $l \leq k$ and i_l for $l \leq k - 1$. Consider player i_k who is not satisfied with object j_k (if such a player does not exist, then the current strategy profile is an equilibrium). Fix the strategies of all other players. Suppose player i_k obtains the maximal payoff by replacing object j_k with object j_{k+1} and the new strategy is admissible. The new strategy profile $s(k + 1)$ has the property

$$s_{i_k}(k + 1) = s_{i_k}(k) \cup \{j_{k+1}\} \setminus \{j_k\}.$$

Show that if player i_k is satisfied with object j in the strategy profile $s(k)$, then he is also satisfied with this object in the strategy profile $s(k + 1)$. Assume on the contrary that the payoff of player i_k increases from replacing object j with the new object j' at step $(k + 1)$. As a result, the strategy

$$s_{i_k}(k + 2) = s_{i_k}(k) \cup \{j_{k+1}, j'\} \setminus \{j_k, j\}$$

is admissible for this player. Let

$$f : s_{i_k}(k) \to s_{i_k}(k + 2)$$

be a bijection defined by condition (A'). Then

$$f(\{j_k, j\}) = \{j_{k+1}, j'\}.$$

Note that $f(j) \neq j'$ (otherwise, in the strategy profile $s(k)$ the payoff would increase from replacing object j with object j', which contradicts the condition that player i_k is satisfied with object j). Hence, $f(j_k) = j'$ and $f(j) = j_{k+1}$. It follows that the strategies

$$s_{i_k}(k) \cup \{j'\} \setminus \{j_k\}, \quad s_{i_k}(k) \cup \{j_{k+1}\} \setminus \{j\}$$

are admissible for this player, and so, in the strategy profile $s(k)$ the payoff of player i_k increases from replacing object j with j_{k+1}. This contradicts the assumption that player i_k is satisfied with object j at step k.

Thus, in the strategy profile $s(k)$, all the players $1, \ldots, n - 1$ are satisfied with all the objects except for object j_k. At the same time, player i_k is satisfied with object j_{k+1} in the strategy profiles s_l for $l > k$. Indeed, he is satisfied with this object in the strategy profile s_{k+1} and in the strategy $s_l, l \geq k+1$, and the congestion vector that corresponds to this object is not greater than before. For the other objects, the congestion vector may increase only. All the pairs (i_k, j_k) are hence different. The procedure converges to a finite strategy profile s_T due to the finiteness of the problem.

In the terminal strategy profile s_T, players $1, \ldots, n - 1$ are satisfied with all objects, but player n is satisfied with object -1 only and not satisfied with the other $m - 1$ objects. Applying the same arguments to the strategy profile s_T and object -2 and subsequently to the objects $\{-3, \ldots - m\}$, we construct an equilibrium strategy profile for n players in m steps. The proof of Theorem 6 is finished. $\qquad\square$

Now, get back to the original game Γ_n and find sufficient conditions for an equilibrium in this game. Condition (A') is equivalent to the following condition.

(A): Let $s_i, s_i' \in S_i, |s_i| \leq |s_i'|$. Then there exist injections

$$f, g : s_i \to s_i'$$

such that

1) f are g identity transformations on $s_i \cap s_i'$;
2) for $j \in s_i \setminus s_i'$, we have the inclusions

$$s_i \cup \{f(j)\} \setminus \{j\} \in S_i$$

and

$$s_i' \cup \{j\} \setminus \{g(j)\} \in S_i;$$

3) for $j \in s_i' \setminus f(s_i)$ and $j \in s_i' \setminus g(s_i)$, we have the inclusions $s_i \cup \{j\} \in S_i$ and $s_i' \setminus \{j\} \in S_i$, respectively.

Theorem 6, together with the equivalence of conditions (A) and (A'), leads to the following result.

Theorem 7. *Assume that each strategy set $S_i, i = 1, \ldots, n$, satisfies condition (A). Then there exists a pure strategy equilibrium in the game Γ_n.*

Condition (A) allows us to modify the admissible strategy profiles s in order to increase payoffs as the result of replacing one object with another or adding or removing an object.

Example 3. The set $S = 2^M$ of all subsets of the set M satisfies condition (A).

Example 4. The set S of all subsets s of the set M such that $|s| = l, l = 1, \ldots, m$, satisfies condition (A).

Example 5. For the set M, consider a partition $M = M_1 \cup \cdots \cup M_k$ in which $M_i \cap M_j = \emptyset$, and also integer numbers b_l, t_l such that

$$0 \le b_l \le t_l \le |M_l|, \quad l = 1, \ldots, k.$$

Then the set S composed of all $s \subset M$ such that

$$b_l \le |s \cap M_l| \le t_l \ \forall l$$

satisfies condition (A). We further establish this fact rigorously.

Let $s, s' \in S$ and $|s| \le |s'|$. Define f as the identity transformation on $s \cap s'$. Denote by L the set of numbers l obeying the inequality

$$|s \cap M_l| \le |s' \cap M_l|$$

and by L' the set of numbers l obeying the inequality

$$|s \cap M_l| > |s' \cap M_l|.$$

For $l \in L$, define f as an injection from $(s \setminus s') \cap M_l$ into $(s' \setminus s) \cap M_l$. For $l \in L'$, find in $(s \setminus s') \cap M_l$ a subset S_l of the same dimension as $(s' \setminus s) \cap M_l$. Define f as an injection of S_l into $(s' \setminus s) \cap M_l$. Further, define f as an injective mapping of

$$\bigcup_{l \in L'} (((s \setminus s') \cap M_l) \setminus S_l)$$

into

$$\bigcup_{l \in L} (((s' \setminus s) \cap M_l) \setminus f((s \setminus s') \cap M_l))$$

(this is possible, since $|s| \le |s'|$). Let $g = f$. Then condition (A) holds obviously.

Example 6. Let $m = 5$ and

$$S = \{\{1, 2\}, \{1, 3\}, \{2, 4\}, \{3, 4\},$$
$$\{1, 5\}, \{2, 5\}, \{3, 5\}, \{4, 5\}\}.$$

The set S satisfies condition (A), but this example does not match Example 4.

CHAPTER 3

Routing Games

Contents

Routing games [28,29] form a modern branch of game theory. Their onrush development is connected with the expansion of the global information network (the Internet) and with the importance and complexity of cargo and passenger traffic problems in transportation networks. Such games are characterized by a large number of players acting independently (still, their individual payoffs depend on the behavior of all network participants).

The cost function of each player is defined as the execution time of his task or the transmission time of his data packet over a network. The payoff

Copyright © 2019 Elsevier Inc.
All rights reserved.
29

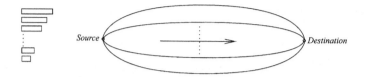

Figure 3.1 A network of parallel channels

function of each agent is defined as the volume of information transmitted by him or the capacity of his channel.

For this class of games, an important aspect is to compare the payoffs of the players with centralized (cooperative) behavior and their equilibrium payoffs in the noncooperative case. Such a comparative study answers the following question of principle: Should we organize management within a system (thereby bearing some cost)? If this sounds inefficient, the system has to be self-organized.

There exist two approaches to network games analysis. According to the first one, a player chooses a route to transmit his packet; note that a packet is treated as an unsplittable quantity. For these models, important results were established by Koutsoupias and Papadimitriou. Such models will be therefore called the KP-models. The second approach assumes that a packet can be divided into segments and transmitted through different routes. This approach utilizes the equilibrium concept suggested by Wardrop.

3.1 THE KP-MODEL OF OPTIMAL ROUTING WITH UNSPLITTABLE TRAFFIC. THE PRICE OF ANARCHY

We begin with an elementary information network representing m parallel channels (see Fig. 3.1).

Consider a system of n users (players). Player i $(i = 1, \ldots, n)$ intends to send traffic of some volume w_i through a channel. Each channel $l = 1, \ldots, m$ has a given capacity c_l. When traffic of a volume w is transmitted through a channel of a capacity c, the channel delay makes up w/c.

Each user pursues individual interests, endeavoring to occupy the minimal-delay channel. The pure strategy of player i is the choice of channel l for his traffic. Consequently, the vector $L = (l_1, \ldots, l_n)$ forms the pure strategy profile of all users, where l_i denotes the number of the channel chosen by user i. His mixed strategy represents a probabilistic distribution $p_i = (p_i^1, \ldots, p_i^m)$, where p_i^l is the probability of choosing channel l by user i.

The matrix P composed of the vectors p_i is the mixed strategy profile of the users.

In the case of pure strategies, the traffic delay for user i on channel l_i makes up $\lambda_i = \dfrac{\sum\limits_{k:l_k=l_i} w_k}{c_{l_i}}$.

Definition 13. A pure strategy profile $(l_1, \ldots, l_n)$ is called a Nash equilibrium if $\lambda_i = \min\limits_{j=1,\ldots,m} \dfrac{w_i + \sum\limits_{k \neq i:l_k=j} w_k}{c_j}$ for each user i.

In the case of mixed strategies, it is necessary to introduce the expected traffic delay of user i on channel l. This characteristic is defined by $\lambda_i^l = \dfrac{w_i + \sum\limits_{k=1,k\neq i}^{n} p_k^l w_k}{c_l}$. The minimal expected delay of user i equals $\lambda_i = \min\limits_{l=1,\ldots,m} \lambda_i^l$.

Definition 14. A strategy profile P is called a Nash equilibrium if, for each user i and any channel chosen by him, we have $\lambda_i^l = \lambda_i$ if $p_i^l > 0$ and $\lambda_i^l > \lambda_i$ if $p_i^l = 0$.

Definition 15. A mixed strategy equilibrium P is called a completely mixed Nash equilibrium if each user chooses each channel with a positive probability, that is, $p_i^l > 0$ for any $i = 1, \ldots, n$ and any $l = 1, \ldots, m$.

The value λ_i determines the minimum possible individual cost of user i to send his traffic. Pursuing personal goals, each user chooses the strategies that ensure this value of the expected delay. *Social cost* characterizes the total cost of the system incurred by the operation of all its channels. It is possible to consider the following types of the social cost $SC(w, c, L)$ for a pure strategy profile:

1. the linear social cost $LSC(w, c, L) = \sum\limits_{l=1}^{m} \dfrac{\sum\limits_{k:l_k=l} w_k}{c_l}$;

2. the quadratic social cost $QSC(w, c, L) = \sum\limits_{l=1}^{m} \dfrac{\left(\sum\limits_{k:l_k=l} w_k \right)^2}{c_l}$;

3. the maximal social cost $MSC(w, c, L) = \max\limits_{l=1,\ldots,m} \dfrac{\sum\limits_{k:l_k=l} w_k}{c_l}$.

Definition 16. The social cost for a mixed strategy profile P is the expected social cost $SC(w, c, L)$ for a random pure strategy profile L, that is,

$$SC(w, c, P) = E(SC(w, c, L)) = \sum_{L=(l_1,\ldots,l_n)} \left(\prod_{k=1}^{n} p_k^{l_k} \cdot SC(w, c, L) \right).$$

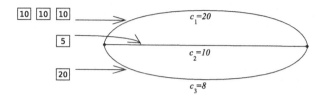

Figure 3.2 Worst-case Nash equilibrium with delay 2.5

Denote by $opt = \min_P SC(w, P)$ the optimal social cost. The global optimum in our model is yielded by social cost minimization. Generally, the global optimum is calculated through the exhaustive search of all admissible pure strategy profiles. However, in a series of cases, it represents the solution of a constrained social cost minimization problem in the continuous setup, with the mixed strategies of all users (the vector P) acting as the variables.

Definition 17. The price of anarchy is the ratio of the social cost in the worst-case Nash equilibrium and the optimal social cost:

$$PoA = \sup_{P\text{-equilibrium}} \frac{SC(w, P)}{opt}.$$

If sup applies to the equilibrium profiles composed of pure strategies only, then we mean the pure price of anarchy. In a similar fashion, an interested reader may define the mixed price of anarchy. The price of anarchy shows how much the social cost under centralized control differs from the social cost in the case of seeking for individual interests. Obviously, $PoA \geq 1$, and the deviation from 1 reflects the efficiency of centralized control.

3.2 PURE STRATEGY EQUILIBRIUM. BRAESS'S PARADOX

Consider several examples of the systems in which the behavior of users is restricted to the pure strategy profiles only. Choose the maximal social cost. Denote by $(w_{i_1}, \ldots, w_{i_k}) \to c_l$ a strategy profile in which traffic segments $w_{i_1}, \ldots, w_{i_k}$ belonging to users $i_1, \ldots, i_k \in \{1, \ldots, n\}$ are transmitted through the channel of capacity c_l.

Example 7. This example illustrates Braess's paradox occurring as one channel is eliminated from the system. Consider the following set of users and channels: $n = 5$, $m = 3$, $w = (20, 10, 10, 10, 5)$, $c = (20, 10, 8)$ (see Fig. 3.2). In this case, there exist several Nash equilibria. One of them

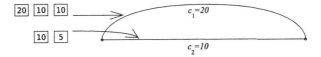

Figure 3.3 Reduced delay as the result of channel elimination

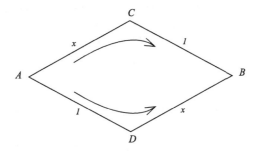

Figure 3.4 Uniform distribution of players between both routes in equilibrium

is the strategy profile

$$\{(10, 10, 10) \to 20, 5 \to 10, 20 \to 8)\}.$$

As easily verified, any deviation of a player from this profile increases his delay. However, the equilibrium in question maximizes the social cost:

$$MSC(w; c; (10, 10, 10) \to 20, 5 \to 10, 20 \to 8) = 2.5.$$

We will call this equilibrium the **worst-case equilibrium**.

Interestingly, the global optimum of the social cost is achieved in the strategy profile $(20, 10) \to 20, (10, 5) \to 10, 10 \to 8$, making up 1.5. Exactly this value represents the best-case pure strategy Nash equilibrium. If we remove channel 8 (see Fig. 3.3), then the worst-case social cost becomes

$$MSC(w; c; (20, 10, 10) \to 20, (10, 5) \to 10) = 2.$$

This strategy profile also forms the best-case pure strategy equilibrium and the global optimum.

Example 8 (Braess's paradox). This model was proposed by Braess in 1968 [13]. Consider a road network shown in Fig. 3.4. Assume that 60 automobiles move from point A to point B. The delay on the segments (C, B) and (A, D) does not depend on the number of automobiles and

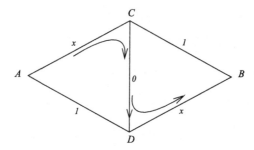

Figure 3.5 All players choose route *ACDB* in equilibrium

equal to 1 h. On the segments (A, C) and (D, B), the delay (measured in mins) is proportional to the number of moving automobiles. Obviously, here an equilibrium is the same number of automobiles distributed to the routes (A, C, B) and (A, D, B), that is, 30 automobiles per each route. In this case, for each automobile, the trip consumes 1.5 h.

Now, let the points C and D be connected by a speedway with zero delay for each automobile, as illustrated by Fig. 3.5. Then the automobiles that moved along the route (A, D, B) before benefit from choosing the route (A, C, D, B). This also applies to the automobiles that have chosen the route (A, C, B): now, they should move along the route (A, C, D, B) as well. Hence, the unique Nash equilibrium is the strategy profile in which all automobiles move along the route (A, C, D, B). However, each automobile spends 2 h for the trip.

Therefore, we observe a self-contradictory situation – the construction of a highway has actually increased the cost of each participant. In fact, this is Braess's paradox.

3.3 COMPLETELY MIXED EQUILIBRIUM IN THE PROBLEM WITH INHOMOGENEOUS USERS AND HOMOGENEOUS CHANNELS

In the current section, we study the system with identical-capacity channels. Assume that the capacity of each channel l is $c_l = 1$. Let us choose the linear social cost.

Lemma 2. *For a system with n users and m parallel channels of the same capacity, there exists a unique completely mixed Nash equilibrium such that, for any user i and channel l, the equilibrium probabilities are* $p_i^l = 1/m$.

Proof. By the definition of an equilibrium each player i has the same delay on all channels, that is,

$$\sum_{k \neq i} p_k^j w_k = \lambda_i, \ i = 1, \ldots, n, \ j = 1, \ldots, m.$$

First, sum up these equations over $j = 1, \ldots, m$ to get

$$\sum_{j=1}^{m} \sum_{k \neq i} p_k^j w_k = \sum_{k \neq i} w_k = m \lambda_i.$$

Hence it follows that

$$\lambda_i = \frac{1}{m} \sum_{k \neq i} w_k, \ i = 1, \ldots, n.$$

Second, sum up these equations over $i = 1, \ldots, n$ to obtain

$$\sum_{i=1}^{n} \sum_{k \neq i} p_k^j w_k = (n-1) \sum_{k=1}^{n} p_k^j w_k = \sum_{i=1}^{n} \lambda_i.$$

This yields

$$\sum_{k=1}^{n} p_k^j w_k = \frac{1}{n-1} \sum_{i=1}^{n} \lambda_i = \frac{1}{n-1} \cdot \frac{(n-1)W}{m} = \frac{W}{m},$$

where $W = w_1 + \cdots + w_n$. The equilibrium equations lead to

$$p_i^j w_i = \sum_{k=1}^{n} p_k^j w_k - \sum_{k \neq i} p_k^j w_k = \frac{W}{m} - \frac{1}{m} \sum_{k \neq i} w_k = \frac{w_i}{m},$$

and finally

$$p_i^j = \frac{1}{m}, \ i = 1, \ldots, n, \ j = 1, \ldots, m. \qquad \square$$

Denote by F the completely mixed equilibrium in this model and find the corresponding social cost:

$$LSC(w, F) = E\left(\sum_{l=1}^{m} \sum_{k:l_k=l} w_k\right) = \sum_{l=1}^{m} \sum_{k=1}^{n} E(w_k \cdot I_{l_k=l})$$

$$= \sum_{l=1}^{m} \sum_{k=1}^{n} w_k p_l^k = \sum_{k=1}^{n} w_k.$$

3.4 THE PRICE OF ANARCHY IN THE MODEL WITH PARALLEL CHANNELS AND UNSPLITTABLE TRAFFIC

In this section, we consider the system with m homogeneous parallel channels and n players under the maximal social cost $MSC(w, c, L)$. Without loss of generality, assume that the capacity c of all channels is 1 and $w_1 \geq w_2 \geq \cdots \geq w_n$. Let P be some Nash equilibrium. Denote by p_i^j the probability that player i chooses channel j and by M^j the expected traffic in channel j, $j = 1, \ldots, m$. Then

$$M^j = \sum_{i=1}^{n} p_i^j w_i. \tag{3.1}$$

In the Nash equilibrium P, the optimal strategy of player i is to employ only the channels j on which his delay $\lambda_i^j = w_i + \sum_{k=1, k \neq i}^{n} p_k^j w_k$ reaches the minimal value ($\lambda_i^j = \lambda_i$ if $p_i^j > 0$ and $\lambda_i^j > \lambda_i$ if $p_i^j = 0$). Reexpress the value λ_i^j as

$$\lambda_i^j = w_i + \sum_{k=1, k \neq i}^{n} p_k^j w_k = M^j + (1 - p_i^j) w_i. \tag{3.2}$$

Denote by S_i the support of the strategy of player i, that is, $S_i = \{j : p_i^j > 0\}$. We further write $S_i^j = 1$ if $p_i^j > 0$ and $S_i^j = 0$ otherwise. Suppose we know the supports $S_1, \ldots, S_n$ of the strategies of all players. In this case, the strategies themselves are defined by

$$M^j + (1 - p_i^j) w_i = \lambda_i, \quad S_i^j > 0, \quad i = 1, \ldots, n, \quad j = 1, \ldots, m.$$

Hence it follows that

$$p_i^j = \frac{M^j + w_i - \lambda_i}{w_i}. \tag{3.3}$$

By (3.1), for all $j = 1, \ldots, m$, we have

$$M^j = \sum_{i=1}^{n} S_i^j (M^j + w_i - \lambda_i).$$

Moreover, the equality $\sum_{j=1}^{m} p_i^j = 1$ holds for all players i, and therefore

$$\sum_{j=1}^{m} S_i^j(M^j + w_i - \lambda_i) = w_i, \quad i = 1, \dots, n.$$

Reexpress the social cost as the expected maximal traffic over all channels:

$$SC(w, P) = \sum_{j_1=1}^{m} \dots \sum_{j_n=1}^{m} \prod_{i=1}^{n} p_i^{j_i} \max_{l=1,\dots,m} \sum_{k:j_k=l} w_k. \tag{3.4}$$

Denote by $opt = \min_P SC(w, P)$ the optimal social cost.

Now, calculate the price of anarchy in this model. Recall that it represents the ratio of the social cost in the worst-case Nash equilibrium and the optimal social cost:

$$PoA = \sup_{P\text{-equilibrium}} \frac{SC(w, P)}{opt}.$$

Let P be some mixed strategy profile, and let q_i be the probability that player i chooses the maximal delay channel. Then

$$SC(w, P) = \sum_{i=1}^{n} w_i q_i.$$

In addition, introduce the probability that players i and k choose the same channel – the value t_{ik}. Consequently, the inequality $P(A \cup B) = P(A) + P(B) - P(A \cap B) \leq 1$ implies

$$q_i + q_k \leq 1 + t_{ik}.$$

Lemma 3. *The following condition holds in the Nash equilibrium P:*

$$\sum_{k \neq i} t_{ik} w_k = \lambda_i - w_i, \quad i = 1, \dots, n.$$

Proof. First, note that $t_{ik} = \sum_{j=1}^{m} p_i^j p_k^j$. In combination with (3.1), this yields

$$\sum_{k \neq i} t_{ik} w_k = \sum_{j=1}^{m} p_i^j \sum_{k \neq i} p_k^j w_k = \sum_{j=1}^{m} p_i^j (M^j - p_i^j w_i).$$

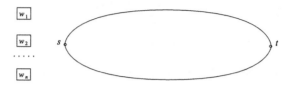

Figure 3.6 A two-channel network

By (3.3), $M^j - p_i^j w_i = \lambda_i - w_i$ if $p_i^j > 0$. Thus, we can write the last expression as

$$\sum_{k \neq i} t_{ik} w_k = \sum_{j=1}^{m} p_i^j (\lambda_i - w_i) = \lambda_i - w_i. \qquad \square$$

Lemma 4. *The following upper estimate is valid:*

$$\lambda_i \leq \frac{1}{m} \sum_{i=1}^{n} w_i + \frac{m-1}{m} w_i, \quad i = 1, \ldots, n.$$

Proof. The estimate follows immediately from the relationships

$$\lambda_i = \min_j \{M^j + (1 - p_i^j w_i)\} \leq \frac{1}{m} \sum_{j=1}^{m} \{M^j + (1 - p_i^j w_i)\}$$

$$= \frac{1}{m} \sum_{j=1}^{m} M^j + \frac{m-1}{m} w_i = \frac{1}{m} \sum_{i=1}^{n} w_i + \frac{m-1}{m} w_i. \qquad \square$$

Now, we can evaluate the price of anarchy in a two–channel network (see Fig. 3.6).

Theorem 8. *For the model with n inhomogeneous users and two homogeneous parallel channels, the price of anarchy is 3/2.*

Proof. Construct an upper estimate for the social cost $SC(w, P)$. Write this function as

$$SC(w, P) = \sum_{k=1}^{n} q_k w_k = \sum_{k \neq i} q_k w_k + q_i w_i = \sum_{k \neq i} (q_i + q_k) w_k - \sum_{k \neq i} q_i w_k + q_i w_i.$$

$$(3.5)$$

Since $q_i + q_k \leq 1 + t_{ik}$, we have

$$\sum_{k \neq i} (q_i + q_k) w_k \leq \sum_{k \neq i} (1 + t_{ik}) w_k.$$

In the case $m = 2$, Lemmas 3 and 4 imply

$$\sum_{k \neq i} t_{ik} w_k = c_i - w_i \leq \frac{1}{2} \sum_{k=1}^{n} w_k - \frac{1}{2} w_i = \frac{1}{2} \sum_{k \neq i}^{n} w_k.$$

Hence it appears that

$$\sum_{k \neq i} (q_i + q_k) w_k \leq \frac{3}{2} \sum_{k \neq i}^{n} w_k,$$

and the upper estimate for (3.5) takes the form

$$SC(w, P) \leq (\frac{3}{2} - q_i) \sum_{k=1}^{m} w_k + (2q_i - \frac{3}{2}) w_i.$$

Note that

$$OPT \geq \max\{w_1, \frac{1}{2} \sum_k w_k\}.$$

Indeed, if $w_1 \geq \frac{1}{2} \sum_k w_k$, then $w_1 \geq w_2 + \cdots + w_n$. The optimal strategy consists in sending the packet w_1 through one channel and the other packets through another channel; the corresponding delay makes up w_1. If $w_1 < \frac{1}{2} \sum_k w_k$, then the optimal strategy is to distribute each packet between the channels equiprobably, which leads to a delay of $\frac{1}{2} \sum_k w_k$.

Then, if some player i satisfies the inequality $q_i \geq 3/4$, then

$$SC(w, P) \leq (\frac{3}{2} - q_i) 2OPT + (2q_i - \frac{3}{2}) OPT = \frac{3}{2} OPT.$$

On the other hand, if all players i are such that $q_i < 3/4$, then

$$SC(w, P) = \sum_{k=1}^{m} q_k w_k \leq \frac{3}{4} \sum_k w_k \leq \frac{3}{2} OPT.$$

Therefore, all the Nash equilibria P obey the inequality $SC(w, P) \leq \frac{3}{2} OPT$, and so,

$$PoA = \sup_P \frac{SC(w, P)}{OPT} \leq \frac{3}{2}.$$

To derive a lower estimate, consider the system with two homogeneous channels and two players where $w_1 = w_2 = 1$. Obviously, the worst-case

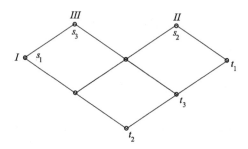

Figure 3.7 A symmetric network game with 10 channels

equilibrium is $p_i^j = 1/2$ for $i = 1, 2$ and $j = 1, 2$. The expected maximal load of the network makes up $1 \cdot 1/2 + 2 \cdot 1/2 = 3/2$. The value $OPT = 1$ is achieved when each channel sends a single packet. Thus, we have found a precise estimate for the price of anarchy in the system with two homogeneous channels.   □

3.5 THE PRICE OF ANARCHY IN THE MODEL WITH LINEAR SOCIAL COST AND UNSPLITTABLE TRAFFIC FOR AN ARBITRARY NETWORK

Up to this point, we have explored the networks with parallel channels. Now, switch to the network games with an arbitrary topology.

Consider the optimal routing problem as a noncooperative game $\Gamma = \langle N, G, Z, f \rangle$, where users (players) $N = (1, 2, \ldots, n)$ send their traffic via some channels of a network $G = (V, E)$. Here G is an undirected graph with a node set V and an edge set E (see Fig. 3.7). For each user i, there exists a set Z_i of routes from s_i to t_i via channels of G. Suppose the users send traffic of volume 1. Our analysis covers two types of such network games, viz., the symmetric games (in which all players have identical strategy sets Z_i) and the asymmetric ones (in which all players have different strategy sets).

Each channel $e \in E$ has a given capacity $c_e > 0$. The users pursue individual interests, choosing the routes of traffic transmission to minimize the maximal traffic delay on the way from node s to node t. Each user defines his strategy $R_i \in Z_i$, which is the route used by player i for his traffic. Consequently, the vector $R = (R_1, \ldots, R_n)$ forms the pure strategy profile of all users. For a strategy profile R, again denote by $(R_{-i}, R_i') = (R_1, \ldots, R_{i-1}, R_i', R_{i+1}, \ldots, R_n)$ the strategy profile in which user i modified his strategy from R_i to R_i' whereas the other users keep their strategies invariable.

For each channel e, define the load $n_e(R)$ as the number of players involving this channel in a strategy profile R. The traffic delay on a given route depends on the loads of all channels on this route. Consider the linear latency function $f_e(k) = a_e k + b_e$, where a_e and b_e are nonnegative constants. For simplicity, we will study the case $f_e(k) = k$. Note that all further results can be easily extended to the general case.

Each user i seeks to minimize the total traffic delay over all channels on his route:

$$c_i(R) = \sum_{e \in R_i} f_e(n_e(R)) = \sum_{e \in R_i} n_e(R).$$

This function describes the individual cost of user i.

A Nash equilibrium is defined as a strategy profile in which none of the players benefits by a unilateral deviation given the same strategies of the other players.

Definition 18. A strategy profile R is called a Nash equilibrium if $c_i(R) \leq c_i(R_{-i}, R_i')$ for each user $i \in N$.

We emphasize that this game is a particular case of the congestion game in which the players choose some objects (channels) from their admissible sets $Z_i, i \in N$, and the payoff function of each player depends on the number of other players choosing the same object. This observation guarantees that the game in question always possesses a pure strategy equilibrium. Therefore, further consideration is confined to the class of pure strategies only.

Take the linear (total) cost of all players as the social cost, that is,

$$SC(R) = \sum_{i=1}^{n} c_i(R) = \sum_{i=1}^{n} \sum_{e \in R_i} n_e(R) = \sum_{e \in E} n_e^2(R).$$

Denote by OPT the minimal social cost. Evaluate the ratio of the social cost in the worst-case Nash equilibrium and the optimal cost. In other words, find the price of anarchy

$$PoA = \sup_{R\text{-equilibrium}} \frac{SC(R)}{OPT}.$$

Theorem 9. *For the asymmetric model with unsplittable traffic and linear delays, the price of anarchy is $5/2$.*

Proof. We begin with derivation of an upper estimate. Let R^* be a Nash equilibrium, and let R be an arbitrary strategy profile (possibly, the optimal one). To construct an upper estimate for the price of anarchy, compare the social cost in these strategy profiles. In the Nash equilibrium R^*, the cost of player i under switching to the strategy R_i does not decrease:

$$c_i(R^*) = \sum_{e \in R_i^*} n_e(R^*) \leq \sum_{e \in R_i} n_e(R_{-i}^*, R_i).$$

In the case of switching of player i, the number of players on each channel may increase by 1 only. Therefore,

$$c_i(R^*) \leq \sum_{e \in R_i} (n_e(R^*) + 1).$$

Summing up these inequalities over all i yields

$$SC(R^*) = \sum_{i=1}^{n} c_i(R^*) \leq \sum_{i=1}^{n} \sum_{e \in R_i} (n_e(R^*) + 1) = \sum_{e \in E} n_e(R)(n_e(R^*) + 1).$$

We need the following technical result.

Lemma 5. *Any nonnegative integers α, β satisfy the inequality*

$$\beta(\alpha + 1) \leq \frac{1}{3}\alpha^2 + \frac{5}{3}\beta^2.$$

Proof. Fix β and consider the function $f(\alpha) = \alpha^2 + 5\beta^2 - 3\beta(\alpha + 1)$. This is a parabola whose vertex lies at the point $\alpha = 3/2\beta$. The minimal value is

$$f\left(\frac{3}{2}\beta\right) = \frac{1}{4}\beta(11\beta - 12).$$

For $\beta \geq 2$, this value is positive. Hence, the lemma holds for $\beta \geq 2$. In the cases $\beta = 0, 1$ the inequality can be verified directly. □

Using Lemma 5, we obtain the upper estimate

$$SC(R^*) \leq \frac{1}{3}\sum_{e \in E} n_e^2(R^*) + \frac{5}{3}\sum_{e \in E} n_e^2(R) = \frac{1}{3}SC(R^*) + \frac{5}{3}SC(R),$$

whence it follows that

$$SC(R^*) \leq \frac{5}{2}SC(R)$$

for any strategy profiles R. This immediately implies $PoA \leq 5/2$.

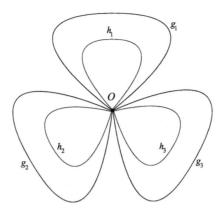

Figure 3.8 A network with three players and three channels $(h_1, h_2, h_3, g_1, g_2, g_3)$

For proving $PoA \geq 5/2$, we give an example of the network in which the price of anarchy is $5/2$. Consider a network with the topology illustrated by Fig. 3.8. Three players located at node 0 are sending their traffic through the channels of this network, $\{h_1, h_2, h_3, g_1, g_2, g_3\}$. Each player chooses between just two pure strategies. For player 1, these are the routes (h_1, g_1) or (h_2, h_3, g_2); for player 2, the routes (h_2, g_2) or (h_1, h_3, g_3); and for player 3, the routes (h_3, g_3) or (h_1, h_2, g_1). Evidently, the optimal distribution of the players consists in choosing their first admissible strategies (h_1, g_1), (h_2, g_2), and (h_3, g_3). The corresponding social cost is 2. The worst-case Nash equilibrium results from the second strategies (h_2, h_3, g_2), (h_1, h_3, g_3), and (h_1, h_2, g_1). Indeed, suppose that, for example, player 1 with an equilibrium cost of 5 switches to the first strategy (h_1, g_1). Then his cost still is 5.

Therefore, the price of anarchy in the described network is $5/2$. This concludes the proof of the theorem.   □

The symmetric model where all players have the same strategy set yields a smaller price of anarchy.

Theorem 10. *For the n-player symmetric model with unsplittable traffic and linear delays, the price of anarchy is $(5n - 2)/(2n + 1)$.*

Proof. Let R^* be a Nash equilibrium, and let R be the optimal strategy profile that minimizes the social cost. We will estimate the cost of player i in the equilibrium, that is, the value $c_i(R^*)$. As he deviates from the equilibrium by choosing another strategy R_j (this is possible, since the strategy sets of all players coincide), the cost rises accordingly:

$$c_i(R^*) = \sum_{e \in R_i^*} n_e(R^*) \le \sum_{e \in R_j} n_e(R_{-i}^*, R_j).$$

Moreover, $n_e(R_{-i}^*, R_j)$ differs from $n_e(R^*)$ by 1 for the channels where $e \in R_j - R_i^*$. Hence it appears that

$$c_i(R^*) \le \sum_{e \in R_j} n_e(R^*) + |R_j - R_i^*|,$$

where $|R|$ denotes the number of elements in R. Using the equality $A - B = A - A \cap B$, we have

$$c_i(R^*) \le \sum_{e \in R_j} n_e(R^*) + |R_j| - |R_j \cap R_i^*|.$$

Summation over all $j \in N$ gives the inequalities

$$nc_i(R^*) \le \sum_{j=1}^{n} \sum_{e \in R_j} n_e(R^*) + \sum_{j=1}^{n} (|R_j| - |R_j \cap R_i^*|)$$

$$\le \sum_{e \in E} n_e(R) n_e(R^*) + \sum_{e \in E} n_e(R) - \sum_{e \in R_i^*} n_e(R).$$

Now, summing up over all $i \in N$, we obtain

$$nSC(R^*) \le \sum_{i=1}^{n} \sum_{e \in E} n_e(R) n_e(R^*) + \sum_{i=1}^{n} \sum_{e \in E} n_e(R) - \sum_{i=1}^{n} \sum_{e \in R_i^*} n_e(R)$$

$$= n \sum_{e \in E} n_e(R) n_e(R^*) + n \sum_{e \in E} n_e(R) - \sum_{e \in E} n_e(R) n_e(R^*)$$

$$= (n - 1) \sum_{e \in E} n_e(R) n_e(R^*) + n \sum_{e \in E} n_e(R).$$

Write this inequality as

$$SC(R^*) \le \frac{n - 1}{n} \sum_{e \in E} \left(n_e(R) n_e(R^*) + n_e(R) \right) + \frac{1}{n} \sum_{e \in E} n_e(R),$$

and use Lemma 5:

$$SC(R^*) \leq \frac{n-1}{3n} \sum_{e \in E} n_e^2(R^*) + \frac{5(n-1)}{3n} \sum_{e \in E} n_e^2(R) + \frac{1}{n} \sum_{e \in E} n_e^2(R)$$

$$= \frac{n-1}{3n} SC(R^*) + \frac{5n-2}{3n} SC(R).$$

This immediately implies

$$SC(R^*) \leq \frac{5n-2}{2n+1} SC(R),$$

and the price of anarchy obeys the upper estimate $PoA \leq (5n-2)/(2n+1)$.

To obtain a lower estimate, it suffices to provide an example of the network with the price of anarchy $(5n-1)/(2n+1)$. We leave this exercise to the interested reader. □

Theorem 10 claims that the price of anarchy is smaller in the symmetric model than in its asymmetric counterpart. However, as n increases, the price of anarchy tends to 5/2.

3.6 THE MIXED PRICE OF ANARCHY IN THE MODEL WITH LINEAR SOCIAL COST AND UNSPLITTABLE TRAFFIC FOR AN ARBITRARY NETWORK

In the preceding sections, we have estimated the price of anarchy by considering only the pure strategy equilibria. To proceed, find the mixed price of anarchy for arbitrary networks with linear delays. Suppose the players can send their traffic of different volumes through the channels of a network $G = (V, E)$.

Well, consider an asymmetric optimal routing game $\Gamma = \langle N, G, Z, w, f \rangle$, in which the players $N = (1, 2, \ldots, n)$ send their traffic of volumes $\{w_1, w_2, \ldots, w_n\}$. For each user i, there is a given set Z_i of pure strategies, that is, a set of routes from s_i to t_i via the channels of the network G. The traffic delay on a route depends on the load of engaged channels. We understand the load of a channel as the total traffic volume transmitted through this channel. Let the latency function on channel e have the linear form $f_e(k) = a_e k + b_e$, where k denotes the channel load, and a_e and b_e are nonnegative constants. Then the total traffic delay on the complete route makes the sum of the traffic delays on each channel of a route.

The users pursue individual interests and choose routes for their traffic to minimize the delay during traffic transmission from s to t. Each user

$i \in N$ adopts a mixed strategy P_i, that is, player i sends his traffic w_i on a route $R_i \in Z_i$ with a probability $p_i(R_i), i = 1, \ldots, n,$

$$\sum_{R_i \in Z_i} p_i(R_i) = 1.$$

A set of mixed strategies forms a strategy profile $P = \{P_1, \ldots, P_n\}$ in this game.

Each user i seeks to minimize the expected delay of his traffic on all engaged routes:

$$c_i(P) = \sum_{R \in Z} \prod_{j=1}^{n} p_j(R_j) \sum_{e \in R_i} f_e(n_e(R)) = \sum_{R \in Z} \prod_{j=1}^{n} p_j(R_j) \sum_{e \in R_i} \left(a_e n_e(R) + b_e \right),$$

where $n_e(R)$ is the load of channel e in a given strategy profile R. The function $c_i(P)$ describes the individual cost of user i. On the other hand, the function

$$SC(P) = \sum_{i=1}^{n} w_i c_i(P) = \sum_{R \in Z} \prod_{j=1}^{n} p_j(R_j) \sum_{e \in E} n_e(R) f_e(n_e(R))$$

gives the social cost.

Let P^* be a Nash equilibrium. We underline that a Nash equilibrium exists due to the finiteness of the strategy set. Denote by R^* the optimal strategy profile yielding the minimal social cost. Obviously, it consists of the pure strategies of players, that is, $R^* = (R_1^*, \ldots, R_n^*)$. Then, for each user $i \in N$,

$$c_i(P^*) \leq c_i(P_{-i}^*, R_i^*).$$

Here (P_{-i}^*, R_i^*) means that player i chooses the pure strategy R_i^* in the strategy profile P^* instead of the mixed strategy P^*i. In the equilibrium, we have the condition

$$c_i(P^*) \leq c_i(P_{-i}^*, R_i^*) = \sum_{R \in Z} \prod_{j=1}^{n} p_j(R_j) \sum_{e \in R_i^*} f_e(n_e(R_{-i}, R_i^*)), i = 1, \ldots, n.$$

Note that, in any strategy profile (R_{-i}, R_i^*), only player i actually deviates, and hence the load of any channel on the route R_i^* may increase at most by w_i, that is, $f_e(n_e(R_{-i}, R_i^*)) \leq f_e(n_e(R) + w_i)$. It naturally follows that

$$c_i(P^*) \leq \sum_{R \in Z} \prod_{j=1}^{n} p_j(R_j) \sum_{e \in R_i^*} f_e(n_e(R) + w_i), \quad i = 1, \ldots, n.$$

Multiplying these inequalities by w_i and performing summation from 1 to n yield

$$SC(P^*) = \sum_{i=1}^{n} w_i c_i(P^*) \leq \sum_{R \in Z} \prod_{j=1}^{n} p_j(R_j) \sum_{i=1}^{n} \sum_{e \in R_i^*} w_i f_e(n_e(R) + w_i).$$

Using the linearity of the latency functions, we arrive at the inequalities

$$SC(P^*) \leq \sum_{R \in Z} \prod_{j=1}^{n} p_j(R_j) \sum_{i=1}^{n} \sum_{e \in R_i^*} w_i \left(a_e(n_e(R) + w_i) + b_e \right)$$

$$= \sum_{R \in Z} \prod_{j=1}^{n} p_j(R_j) \sum_{i=1}^{n} \left(\sum_{e \in R_i^*} a_e n_e(R) w_i + a_e w_i^2 \right) + \sum_{i=1}^{n} \sum_{e \in R_i^*} b_e w_i$$

$$\leq \sum_{R \in Z} \prod_{j=1}^{n} p_j(R_j) \sum_{e \in E} a_e \left(n_e(R) n_e(R^*) + n_e(R^*)^2 \right) + \sum_{e \in E} b_e n_e(R^*). \quad (3.6)$$

Further exposition requires the estimate from Lemma 6.

Lemma 6. *Any nonnegative numbers α and β satisfy the inequality*

$$\alpha\beta + \beta^2 \leq \frac{z}{2}\alpha^2 + \frac{z+3}{2}\beta^2, \quad (3.7)$$

where $z = (\sqrt{5} - 1)/2 \approx 0.618$ is the golden section of the interval $[0, 1]$.

Proof. Fix β and consider the function

$$f(\alpha) = \frac{z}{2}\alpha^2 + \frac{z+3}{2}\beta^2 - \alpha\beta - \beta^2 = \frac{z}{2}\alpha^2 + \frac{z+1}{2}\beta^2 - \alpha\beta.$$

This is a parabola with vertex $\alpha = \beta/z$ and the minimal value

$$f\left(\frac{\beta}{z}\right) = \beta^2(z + 1 - \frac{1}{z}).$$

For the golden section value of z, the expression in brackets actually vanishes. This directly gives inequality (3.7). $\qquad\square$

In combination with inequality (3.7), condition (3.6) implies

$$SC(P^*) \le \sum_{R \in Z} \prod_{j=1}^{n} p_j(R_j) \sum_{e \in E} a_e \left(\frac{z}{2} n_e(R)^2 + \frac{z+3}{2} n_e(R^*)^2 \right) + \sum_{e \in E} b_e n_e(R^*)$$

$$\le \frac{z}{2} \sum_{R \in Z} \prod_{j=1}^{n} p_j(R_j) \sum_{e \in E} \left(a_e n_e(R)^2 + b_e n_e(R) \right) + \frac{z+3}{2} \left(a_e n_e(R^*)^2 + b_e n_e(R^*) \right)$$

$$= \frac{z}{2} SC(P^*) + \frac{z+3}{2} SC(R^*). \tag{3.8}$$

Now, it is possible to estimate the price of anarchy for a pure strategy Nash equilibrium.

Theorem 11. *For the n-player asymmetric model with unsplittable traffic and linear delays, the mixed price of anarchy does not exceed* $z+2 = (\sqrt{5}+3)/2 \approx 2.618$.

Proof. It follows from (3.8) that

$$SC(P^*) \le \frac{z+3}{2-z} SC(R^*).$$

By the properties of the golden section, $\frac{z+3}{2-z} = z + 2$. Consequently, the ratio of the social cost in the Nash equilibrium and the optimal cost,

$$PoA = \frac{SC(P^*)}{SC(R^*)},$$

does not exceed $z + 2 \approx 2.618$. The proof of Theorem 11 is finished. □

Remark. As established earlier, the pure price of anarchy is $5/2 = 2.5$. Transition to the class of mixed strategies slightly increases the price of anarchy to 2.618. This seems quite natural, since the worst-case Nash equilibrium can be achieved in mixed strategies.

3.7 THE PRICE OF ANARCHY IN THE MODEL WITH MAXIMAL SOCIAL COST AND UNSPLITTABLE TRAFFIC FOR AN ARBITRARY NETWORK

In the case of linear social cost, the price of anarchy takes finite values (see the previous results). However, if we define the social cost as the maximal cost of a player, then the price of anarchy may have arbitrary large values. This phenomenon will be illustrated by an example of a network in Fig. 3.9.

Figure 3.9 A network with $k^2 - k + 1$ players. Player 1 follows the route $(v_0, v_1, \ldots, v_k)$. Node v_i contains $k - 1$ players who follow the route (v_i, v_{i+1}). The delay on the main channel is 1, whereas the delay on the other channels is k. The price of anarchy makes up k

The network consists of the basic nodes $\{v_0, v_1, \ldots, v_k\}$. The nodes v_i and v_{i+1} are connected through k routes; one of them (see the abscissa axis) has a length of 1, whereas the other routes a length of k. Player 1, who bears the maximal cost in this game, sends his traffic from node v_0 to node v_k. Note that he may employ the routes lying on the abscissa axis only. Each node v_i, $i = 0, \ldots, k-1$, contains $k - 1$ players transmitting their traffic from v_i to v_{i+1}. Evidently, the optimal social cost equal to k is achieved if player 1 sends his traffic via the route $v_0, v_1, \ldots, v_k$, whereas all other $k - 1$ players in the node v_i are distributed among the rest of the routes, a player per a specific route.

The readers can easily observe the following fact. In this model, the worst-case Nash equilibrium is when all $n = (k - 1)k + 1$ players send their traffic through the routes lying on the abscissa axis. However, then the cost of player 1 (*ergo*, the maximal social cost) constitutes $(k - 1)k + 1$. Hence, the price of anarchy in this model is

$$PoA = \frac{k^2 - k + 1}{k} = \sqrt{n} + O(1).$$

Now, construct an upper estimate for the price of anarchy in an arbitrary network with unsplittable traffic. Let R^* be a Nash equilibrium, and let R be the optimal strategy profile that yields the minimal social cost. In our case, the social costs are represented by the maximal cost of the players. Without loss of generality, assume in the equilibrium the maximal cost is achieved for player 1, i.e., $SC(R^*) = c_1(R^*)$. To estimate the price of anarchy, apply the same procedure as in the proof of Theorem 11, comparing the maximal cost $SC(R^*)$ in the equilibrium and the maximal cost in the strategy profile R, the value $SC(R) = \max_{i \in N} c_i(R)$.

Since R^* forms a Nash equilibrium, we have

$$c_1(R^*) \leq \sum_{e \in R_1} (n_e(R^*) + 1) \leq \sum_{e \in R_1} n_e(R^*) + |R_1| \leq \sum_{e \in R_1} n_e(R^*) + c_1(R).$$

The last inequality follows from clear considerations: if player 1 chooses channels from R_1, then his delay is surely greater than or equal to the number of channels in R_1.

Finally, let us estimate $\sum_{e \in R_1} n_e(R^*)$. Using the inequality $(\sum_{i=1}^{n} a_i)^2 \leq n \sum_{i=1}^{n} a_i^2$, we obtain

$$\left(\sum_{e \in R_1} n_e(R^*) \right)^2 \leq |R_1| \sum_{e \in R_1} n_e^2(R^*) \leq |R_1| \sum_{e \in E} n_e^2(R^*) = \sum_{i=1}^{n} c_i(R^*).$$

By the proof of Theorem 10,

$$\sum_{i=1}^{n} c_i(R^*) \leq \frac{5}{2} \sum_{i=1}^{n} c_i(R).$$

Consequently,

$$\left(\sum_{e \in R_1} n_e(R^*) \right)^2 \leq |R_1| \frac{5}{2} \sum_{i=1}^{n} c_i(R),$$

which gives

$$c_1(R^*) \leq c_1(R) + \sqrt{|R_1| \frac{5}{2} \sum_{i=1}^{n} c_i(R)}.$$

As $|R_1| \leq c_1(R)$ and $c_i(R) \leq SC(R)$, we arrive at the inequality

$$c_1(R^*) \leq SC(R)(1 + \sqrt{\frac{5}{2}n}).$$

This directly implies that the price of anarchy allows for the upper estimate $1 + \sqrt{5/2n}$. As a matter of fact, we have established the following result.

Theorem 12. *For the n-player asymmetric model with unsplittable traffic and the maximal cost of players as the social cost, the price of anarchy is $O(\sqrt{n})$.*

This theorem claims that the price of anarchy may have arbitrary large values.

3.8 THE WARDROP OPTIMAL ROUTING MODEL WITH SPLITTABLE TRAFFIC

The routing model studied in this section bases on the Wardrop model with splittable traffic suggested in 1952 (Wardrop, 1952). The optimality criterion is minimal traffic delay.

The optimal traffic routing problem is treated as a game $\Gamma = \langle n, G, w, Z, f \rangle$, where n users send their traffic through network channels. The network has the topology described by a graph $G = (V, E)$. For each user i, there exists a certain set Z_i of routes from s_i to t_i through channels G and a given volume of traffic w_i. Each channel $e \in E$ has some capacity $c_e > 0$. All users pursue individual interests and choose routes for their traffic to minimize the maximal delay during traffic transmission from s to t. Each user adopts a specific strategy $x_i = \{x_{iR_i} \geq 0\}_{R_i \in Z_i}$. The value x_{iR_i} determines the volume of the traffic sent by user i on route R_i, and $\sum_{R_i \in Z_i} x_{iR_i} = w_i$. Then $x = (x_1, \ldots, x_n)$ is a strategy profile of all users. For a strategy profile x, again denote by $(x_{-i}, x_i') = (x_1, \ldots, x_{i-1}, x_i', x_{i+1}, \ldots, x_n)$ a new strategy profile in which user i modified his strategy from x_i to x_i' whereas the other users keep their strategies invariable.

Define the load of each channel $e \in E$ (i.e., the total traffic sent through this channel) by

$$\delta_e(x) = \sum_{i=1}^{n} \sum_{R_i \in Z_i : e \in R_i} x_{iR_i}.$$

The traffic delay on a given route depends on the loads of the channels included in this route. For each user i and each route R_i chosen by him, we specify a continuous latency function $f_{iR_i}(x) = f_{iR_i}(\{\delta_e(x)\}_{e \in R_i})$ as a nondecreasing function in the loads of the channels on a route (ergo, in the variable x_{iR_i}).

Each user i seeks to minimize the maximal traffic delay over all channels on his route:

$$PC_i(x) = \max_{R_i \in Z_i : x_{iR_i} > 0} f_{iR_i}(x).$$

This function describes the individual cost of user i.

A Nash equilibrium is defined as a strategy profile in which none of the players benefits by a unilateral deviation given the same strategies of the other players. In terms of the current model, this is a strategy profile in which none of the players can reduce his individual cost by modifying his strategy.

Definition 19. A strategy profile x is called a Nash equilibrium if, for each user i and any strategy profile $x' = (x_{-i}, x_i')$, we have $PC_i(x) \leq PC_i(x')$.

Within the framework of network models, an important role is played by the concept of Wardrop equilibrium.

Definition 20. A strategy profile x is called a Wardrop equilibrium if, for each i and any $R_i, \rho_i \in Z_i$, the condition $x_{iR_i} > 0$ implies $f_{iR_i}(x) \leq f_{i\rho_i}(x)$.

This definition can be restated similarly to the definition of a Nash equilibrium.

Definition 21. A strategy profile x is a Wardrop equilibrium if the following condition holds for each i: the inequality $x_{iR_i} > 0$ implies $f_{iR_i}(x) = \min_{\rho_i \in Z_i} f_{i\rho_i}(x) = \lambda_i$ and the equality $x_{iR_i} = 0$ implies $f_{iR_i}(x) \geq \lambda_i$.

Such a definition yields an explicit system of equations and inequalities to calculate the Wardrop equilibria. Strictly speaking, the definitions of a Nash equilibrium and a Wardrop equilibrium are not equivalent. Their equivalence depends on the type of the latency functions chosen for the channels.

Theorem 13. *If a strategy profile x is a Wardrop equilibrium, then x is a Nash equilibrium.*

Proof. Let x be a strategy profile in which, for all i, the inequality $x_{iR_i} > 0$ implies $f_{iR_i}(x) = \min_{\rho_i \in Z_i} f_{i\rho_i}(x) = \lambda_i$ and the equality $x_{iR_i} = 0$ implies $f_{iR_i}(x) \geq \lambda_i$. Then, for all i and R_i, we have

$$\max_{\rho_i \in Z_i : x_{i\rho_i} > 0} f_{i\rho_i}(x) \leq f_{iR_i}(x).$$

Assume that user i modified his strategy from x_i to x_i'. Denote by $x' = (x_{-i}, x_i')$ a strategy profile in which the strategies on all routes $R_i \in Z_i$ of user i changed to $x_{iR_i}' = x_{iR_i} + \Delta_{R_i}$ so that $\sum_{R_i \in Z_i} \Delta_{R_i} = 0$. The other users $k \neq i$ use the same strategies as before, that is, $x_k' = x_k$.

If all $\Delta_{R_i} = 0$, then $PC_i(x) = PC_i(x')$. Suppose $x \neq x'$, that is, there exists a route R_i such that $\Delta_{R_i} > 0$. This route satisfies the condition $f_{iR_i}(x) \leq f_{iR_i}(x')$, since $f_{iR_i}(x)$ is a nondecreasing function in x_{iR_i}. Using $x_{iR_i}' > 0$, we get

$$f_{iR_i}(x') \leq \max_{\rho_i \in Z_i : x_{i\rho_i}' > 0} f_{i\rho_i}(x').$$

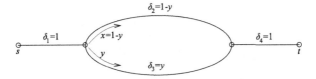

Figure 3.10 Nash equilibrium mismatches Wardrop equilibrium

In the final analysis,

$$\max_{\rho_i \in Z_i : x_{i\rho_i} > 0} f_{i\rho_i}(x) \leq \max_{\rho_i \in Z_i : x_{i\rho_i} > 0} f_{i\rho_i}(x'),$$

or $PC_i(x) \leq PC(x')$. Hence, by the arbitrary choice of i and x'_i, the strategy profile x is a Nash equilibrium. □

Any Nash equilibrium in the model considered also forms a Wardrop equilibrium under the following sufficient condition imposed on all latency functions. For a given user, it is always possible to redistribute a small part of his traffic from any route to other less loaded routes for him, so that the traffic delay on this route becomes strictly smaller.

Example 9. Consider a simple example explaining the difference between the definitions of a Nash equilibrium and a Wardrop equilibrium. The system sends traffic of volume 1 from node s to node t on two routes (see Fig. 3.10). Since the traffic volume is splittable we interpret players as a continuum set of packages. Each player's interest is to minimize maximal delay during traffic transmission from node s to node t. It is a time which is necessary to transmit the whole traffic volume using two routes.

Assume that the latency functions on route 1 (which includes the upper channel at Fig. 3.10) and on route 2 (which includes the lower channel at Fig. 3.10) have the form $f_1(x) = \max\{1, x, 1\} = 1$ and $f_2(y) = \min\{1, y, 1\} = y$, respectively, where $x = 1 - y$. Both functions are continuous and nondecreasing in x and y, respectively. The inequality $f_1(x) > f_2(y)$ holds for all admissible strategy profiles (x, y) such that $x + y = 1$. However, any reduction in x (the volume of traffic through channel 1) does not affect $f_1(x)$. In this model, a Nash equilibrium is any strategy profile $(x, 1 - x)$, where $0 \leq x \leq 1$. Still, the delays for both channels coincide only in the strategy profile $(0, 1)$.

Definition 22. Let x be a strategy profile. The social cost is the total delay of all players in this strategy profile, that is,

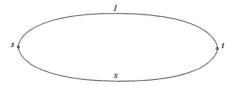

Figure 3.11 The Pigou model

$$SC(x) = \sum_{i=1}^{n} \sum_{R_i \in Z_i} x_{iR_i} f_{iR_i}(x).$$

Note that if x forms a Wardrop equilibrium, then by definition the delays on all routes R_i of each player i are equal to $\lambda_i(x)$. Therefore, the social cost in the equilibrium can be written as

$$SC(x) = \sum_{i=1}^{n} w_i \lambda_i(x).$$

Denote by $OPT = \min_x SC(x)$ the minimal social cost.

The price of anarchy [68,24,25] is a measure that compares the worst case performance Nash equilibrium to that of the optimal allocation.

Definition 23. The price of anarchy is the maximal value of the ratio $SC(x)/OPT$, where the social cost is calculated in the Wardrop equilibria only.

3.9 THE OPTIMAL ROUTING MODEL WITH PARALLEL CHANNELS. THE PIGOU MODEL. BRAESS'S PARADOX

We analyze the Wardrop model for a network with parallel channels.

Example 10 (The Pigou model (Pigou, 1920)). Consider a simple network with two parallel channels (see Fig. 3.11). One channel has a fixed capacity of 1, whereas the capacity of the other is proportional to traffic. Assume that very many users transmit their traffic from node s to node t so that the total load is 1. Each user seeks to minimize his cost. Then a Nash equilibrium is to employ the lower channel for each user: if the upper channel contains a certain number of players, then the lower channel always guarantees a smaller delay than the upper. Therefore, the cost of each player in the equilibrium is 1. Furthermore, the social cost equals 1 too.

Now, suppose that some share x of the users choose the upper channel whereas the other users (the share $1 - x$) employ the lower channel. Then the social cost makes up $x \cdot 1 + (1 - x) \cdot (1 - x) = x^2 - x + 1$. The minimal

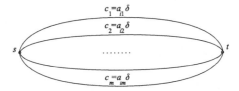

Figure 3.12 The Wardrop model with parallel channels and linear delays

social cost of $3/4$ corresponds to $x = 1/2$. Obviously, the price of anarchy in the Pigou model is $PoA = 4/3$.

Example 11. Consider the same two-channel network but let the delay in the lower channel be x^p, where p denotes a certain parameter. A Nash equilibrium also consists in sending the traffic of all users through the lower channel (the social cost is 1). Next, send some volume ϵ of traffic through the upper channel. The corresponding social cost $\epsilon \cdot 1 + (1 - \epsilon)^{p+1}$ takes arbitrary small values as $\epsilon \to 0$ and $p \to \infty$, and so, the price of anarchy may have arbitrary large values.

Example 12 (Braess's paradox). Recall that we have explored this phenomenon in the case of unsplittable traffic. Interestingly, Braess's paradox also arises in the models with splittable traffic. Consider a network composed of four nodes; see Fig. 3.12. There are two routes from node s to node t with identical delays $1 + x$. Assume the total traffic of all users is 1. Owing to the symmetry of this network, all users are divided into two equal-size groups with the same cost of $3/2$. This actually forms a Nash equilibrium.

Next, suppose that we have designed a new superspeed channel (CD) with zero delay. Then, for each user, the route $A \to C \to D \to B$ is always not worse than the route $A \to C \to B$ or $A \to D \to B$. Nevertheless, the cost of all players increases to 2 in the new equilibrium. This example shows that adding a new channel may raise the cost of individual players and also the social cost.

3.10 POTENTIAL IN THE MODEL WITH SPLITTABLE TRAFFIC FOR AN ARBITRARY NETWORK

Let $\Gamma = \langle n, G, w, Z, f \rangle$ be the Wardrop model in which n users send traffic through the channels of a network with the topology defined by a graph $G = (V, E)$. The value $W = \sum_{i=1}^{n} w_i$ gives the total volume of the data packets of all players. Denote by x_{iR_i} the strategy of player i, the part of traffic transmitted through the channel R_i. Note that $\sum\limits_{R_i \in Z_i} x_{iR_i} = w_i$, $x_{iR_i} \geq 0$. For each edge e, there is a given strictly increasing continuous function $f_e(\delta(x))$ taking nonnegative values on $[0, W]$, which describes the delay on this edge. Assume the delay of player i on the route R_i has the additive form

$$f_{iR_i}(\delta(x)) = \sum_{e \in R_i} f_e(\delta_e(x)),$$

that is, is the sum of delays on all channels of this route.

Consider a game with the payoff functions

$$PC_i(x) = \max_{R_i \in Z_i : x_{iR_i} > 0} f_{iR_i}(x) = \max_{R_i \in Z_i : x_{iR_i} > 0} \sum_{e \in R_i} f_e(\delta_e(x)).$$

Introduce the potential

$$P(x) = \sum_{e \in E} \int_0^{\delta_e(x)} f_e(t)\,dt.$$

Since $\int_0^{\delta} f_e(t)\,dt$ is a differentiable function with nondecreasing derivative, the potential has convexity.

Theorem 14. *A strategy profile x is a Wardrop equilibrium (hence, a Nash equilibrium) iff $P(x) = \min_y P(y)$.*

Proof. Let x be a Wardrop equilibrium, and let y be an arbitrary strategy profile. The convexity of the function $P(x)$ implies

$$P(y) - P(x) \geq \sum_{i=1}^{n} \sum_{R_i \in Z_i} \frac{\partial P(x)}{\partial x_{iR_i}}(y_{iR_i} - x_{iR_i}). \tag{3.9}$$

As easily observed,

$$\frac{\partial P(x)}{\partial x_{iR_i}} = \sum_{e \in R_i} f_e(\delta_e(x)).$$

By the Wardrop equilibrium condition, for any player i, we have

$$\lambda_i(x) = \sum_{e \in R_i} f_e(\delta_e(x)),\ x_{iR_i} > 0,$$

$$\lambda_i(x) \leq \sum_{e \in R_i} f_e(\delta_e(x)),\ x_{iR_i} = 0.$$

Expand the second sum in (3.9) into two sums as follows. When $y_{iR_i} - x_{iR_i}I \geq 0$, use the inequality $\frac{\partial P(x)}{\partial x_{iR_i}} \geq \lambda_i(x)$. For the second sum, we have $y_{iR_i} - x_{iR_i} < 0$, and therefore $x_{iR_i} > 0$. Then the equilibrium condition yields $\frac{\partial P(x)}{\partial x_{iR_i}} = \lambda_i(x)$.

As a result,

$$P(y) - P(x) \geq \sum_{i=1}^{n} \sum_{R_i \in Z_i} \lambda_i(x)(y_{iR_i} - x_{iR_i}) = \sum_{i=1}^{n} \lambda_i(x) \sum_{R_i \in Z_i} (y_{iR_i} - x_{iR_i}).$$

On the other hand, for any player i and any strategy profile, we have $\sum_{R_i \in Z_i} y_{iR_i} = \sum_{R_i \in Z_i} x_{iR_i} = w_i$. Then it follows that

$$P(y) \geq P(x) \ \forall y,$$

that is, x minimizes the potential $P(y)$.

Now, let the strategy profile x be the minimum point of the function $P(y)$. Hypothesize that x is not a Wardrop equilibrium. Then there exist player i and two routes R_i, $\rho_i \in Z_i$ such that $x_{R_i} > 0$ and

$$\sum_{e \in R_i} f_e(\delta_e(x)) > \sum_{e \in \rho_i} f_e(\delta_e(x)). \tag{3.10}$$

Take the strategy profile x and replace the traffic on the routes R_i and ρ_i, so that $y_{R_i} = x_{R_i} - \epsilon$ and $y_{\rho_i} = x_{R_i} + \epsilon$. This is always possible for a sufficiently small ϵ on the strength of $x_{R_i} > 0$. Then

$$P(x) - P(y) \geq \sum_{i=1}^{n} \sum_{R_i \in Z_i} \frac{\partial P(y)}{\partial x_{iR_i}} (y_{iR_i} - x_{iR_i})$$

$$= \epsilon \left(\sum_{e \in R_i} f_e(\delta_e(y)) - \sum_{e \in \rho_i} f_e(\delta_e(y)) \right) > 0$$

for a sufficiently small ϵ by inequality (3.10) and the continuity of the function $f_e(\delta_e(y))$. This contradicts the hypothesis that $P(x)$ is the minimal value of the potential. The proof of Theorem 14 is finished. $\square$

We emphasize that the potential is a continuous function defined on the compact set of all admissible strategy profiles x. Hence, this function always has a minimum, and a Nash equilibrium surely exists.

Generally, the researchers employ the linear latency functions $f_e(\delta) = a_e \delta + b_e$ and the latency functions of the form $f_e(\delta) = 1/(c_e - \delta)$ or $f_e(\delta) = \delta/(c_e - \delta)$, where c_e is the capacity of channel e.

3.11 SOCIAL COST IN THE MODEL WITH SPLITTABLE TRAFFIC FOR CONVEX LATENCY FUNCTIONS

Consider a network of an arbitrary topology in which the latency functions $f_e(\delta)$ are differentiable increasing convex functions. Then the social cost takes the form

$$SC(x) = \sum_{i=1}^{n} \sum_{R_i \in Z_i} x_{iR_i} \sum_{e \in R_i} f_e(\delta_e(x)) = \sum_{e \in E} \delta_e(x) f_e(\delta_e(x)),$$

also being a convex function. Note that

$$\frac{\partial SC(x)}{\partial x_{iR_i}} = \sum_{e \in R_i} \left(f_e(\delta_e(x)) + \delta_e(x) f_e'(\delta_e(x)) \right) = \sum_{e \in R_i} f_e^*(\delta_e(x)).$$

The expression $f_e^*(\delta_e(x))$ is called the marginal cost on channel e.

By repeating the argumentation of Theorem 14 for the function $SC(x)$ instead of potential we arrive at the following result.

Theorem 15. *A strategy profile x minimizes the social cost $SC(x) = \min_y SC(y)$ iff the inequality*

$$\sum_{e \in R_i} f_e^*(\delta_e(x)) \le \sum_{e \in \rho_i} f_e^*(\delta_e(x))$$

holds for any i and any routes $R_i, \rho_i \in Z_i$, where $x_{iR_i} > 0$.

For example, choose the linear latency functions $f_e(\delta) = a_e \delta + b_e$. Then the marginal cost is determined by $f_e^*(\delta) = 2a_e \delta + b_e$, and the minimum condition of the social cost in a strategy profile x takes the following form: for any player i and any routes $R_i, \rho_i \in Z_i$ where $x_{iR_i} > 0$,

$$\sum_{e \in R_i} \left(2a_e \delta_e(x) + b_e \right) \le \sum_{e \in \rho_i} \left(2a_e \delta(x) + b_e \right).$$

The last condition can be written as follows. For any player i, the inequality $x_{iR_i} > 0$ implies $\sum_{e \in R_i} \left(2a_e \delta_e(x) + b_e \right) = \lambda_i^*(x)$, whereas the equality $x_{iR_i} = 0$ leads to $\sum_{e \in R_i} \left(2a_e \delta_e(x) + b_e \right) \ge \lambda_i^*(x)$.

Comparing this result with the Wardrop equilibrium conditions for a strategy profile x, we establish the following fact.

Corollary 1. *If a strategy profile x is a Wardrop equilibrium in the model $\langle n, G, w, Z, f \rangle$ with linear latency function, then the strategy profile $x/2$ minimizes the social cost in the model $\langle n, G, w/2, Z, f \rangle$, where the traffic of all players is cut by half.*

3.12 THE PRICE OF ANARCHY IN THE MODEL WITH SPLITTABLE TRAFFIC FOR LINEAR LATENCY FUNCTIONS

Consider the game $\langle n, G, w, Z, f \rangle$ with linear latency functions $f_e(\delta) = a_e \delta + b_e$, where $a_e > 0, e \in E$. Let x^* be a strategy profile yielding the optimal social cost $SC(x^*) = \min_y SC(y)$.

Lemma 7. *The social cost in the Wardrop model with doubled traffic*

$$\langle n, G, 2w, Z, f \rangle$$

increases, at least, to the value

$$SC(x^*) + \sum_{i=1}^{n} \lambda_i^*(x^*) w_i.$$

Proof. Take an arbitrary strategy profile x in the model with double traffic. As easily verified,

$$(a_e \delta_e(x) + b_e) \delta_e(x) \geq (a_e \delta_e(x^*) + b_e) \delta_e(x^*) + (\delta_e(x) - \delta_e(x^*))(2 a_e \delta_e(x^*) + b_e).$$

This inequality is equivalent to $(\delta(x) - \delta(x^*))^2 \geq 0$. In the accepted notations, it takes the form

$$f_e(\delta_e(x)) \delta_e(x) \geq f_e(\delta_e(x^*)) \delta_e(x^*) + (\delta_e(x) - \delta_e(x^*)) f_e^*(\delta_e(x^*)).$$

Summation over all $e \in E$ gives the relationships

$$SC(x) = \sum_{e \in E} f_e(\delta_e(x)) \delta_e(x)$$
$$\geq \sum_{e \in E} f_e(\delta_e(x^*)) \delta_e(x^*) + \sum_{e \in E} (\delta_e(x) - \delta_e(x^*)) f_e^*(\delta_e(x^*)).$$

Consequently,

$$SC(x) \geq SC(x^*) + \sum_{i=1}^{n} \sum_{R_i \in Z_i} (x_{iR_i} - x_{iR_i}^*) \sum_{e \in R_i} f_e^*(\delta_e(x^*)).$$

Since x^* is the minimum point of $SC(x)$, we obtain $\sum_{e \in R_i} f_e^*(\delta_e(x^*)) = \lambda_i^*(x^*)$ under $x_{iR_i}^* > 0$ and $\sum_{e \in R_i} f_e^*(\delta_e(x^*)) \geq \lambda_i^*(x^*)$ under $x_{iR_i}^* = 0$ (see Theorem 15). Hence, it follows that

$$SC(x) \geq SC(x^*) + \sum_{i=1}^{n} \lambda_i^*(x^*) \sum_{R_i \in Z_i} (x_{iR_i} - x_{iR_i}^*).$$

By the earlier assumption, $\sum_{R_i \in Z_i}(x_{iR_i} - x^*_{iR_i}) = 2w_i - w_i = w_i$. Therefore,

$$SC(x) \geq SC(x^*) + \sum_{i=1}^{n} \lambda_i^*(x^*)w_i.$$

The proof of Lemma 7 is finished.   □

Theorem 16. *For the Wardrop model with linear latency functions, the price of anarchy is PoA = 4/3.*

Proof. Let x be a Wardrop equilibrium in the model

$$\langle n, G, w, Z, f \rangle.$$

Then, by the corollary of Theorem 15, the strategy profile $x/2$ yields the minimal social cost in the model

$$\langle n, G, w/2, Z, f \rangle.$$

By Lemma 7, if we double traffic in this model (getting back to the initial traffic w), then for any strategy profile y, the social cost can be estimated as follows:

$$SC(y) \geq SC(x/2) + \sum_{i=1}^{n} \lambda_i^*(x/2)\frac{w_i}{2} = SC(x/2) + \frac{1}{2}\sum_{i=1}^{n} \lambda_i(x)w_i.$$

As x forms a Wardrop equilibrium, we have $\sum_{i=1}^{n} \lambda_i(x)w_i = SC(x)$. Hence,

$$SC(y) \geq SC(x/2) + \frac{1}{2}SC(x).$$

Furthermore,

$$SC(x/2) = \sum_{e \in E} \delta_e(x/2)f_e(\delta_e(x/2)) = \sum_{e \in E} \frac{1}{2}\delta_e(x)\left(\frac{1}{2}a_e\delta_e(x) + b_e\right)$$

$$\geq \frac{1}{4}\sum_{e \in E}\left(a_e\delta_e^2(x) + b_e\delta_e(x)\right) = \frac{1}{4}SC(x).$$

These two inequalities lead to $SC(y) \geq \frac{3}{4}SC(x)$ for any strategy profile y (particularly, for the strategy profile yielding the minimal social cost). Consequently, we derive the following upper estimate for the price of anarchy:

$$PoA = \sup_{x\text{-equilibrium}} \frac{SC(x)}{OPT} \leq \frac{4}{3}.$$

The corresponding lower estimate has been established in the Pigou model; see Section 3.8. The proof of Theorem 16 is finished.   □

3.13 POTENTIAL IN THE WARDROP MODEL WITH PARALLEL CHANNELS FOR PLAYER-SPECIFIC LINEAR LATENCY FUNCTIONS

In the preceding sections, we have studied the models with the same latency function of all players on each channel, which depends on channel load only. However, in real games, channel delays may have different prices for different players. In this case, we speak about the network games with player-specific delays. Consider the Wardrop model $\langle n, G, w, Z, f \rangle$ with parallel channels (see Fig. 3.12) and linear latency functions of the form $f_{ie}(\delta) = a_{ie}\delta$. Here the coefficients a_{ie} are different for different players $i \in N$ and channels $e \in E$.

Let $x = \{x_{ie}, i \in N, e \in E\}$ be some strategy profile, $\sum_{e \in E} x_{ie} = w_i, i = 1, \ldots, n$. Introduce the function

$$P(x) = \sum_{i=1}^{n} \sum_{e \in E} x_{ie} \ln a_{ie} + \sum_{e \in E} \delta_e(x) \ln \delta_e(x).$$

Theorem 17. *A strategy profile x is a Wardrop equilibrium if and only if $P(x) = \min_y P(y)$.*

Proof. We begin with the necessity part. Let x be a Wardrop equilibrium. Find the derivative of the function P:

$$\frac{\partial P(x)}{\partial x_{ie}} = 1 + \ln a_{ie} + \ln \left(\sum_{k=1}^{n} x_{ke} \right) = 1 + \ln \left(a_{ie} \sum_{k=1}^{n} x_{ke} \right).$$

For all $i \in N$ and $e, l \in E$, the equilibrium conditions imply

$$x_{ie} > 0 \Rightarrow a_{ie} \sum_{k=1}^{n} x_{ke} \leq a_{il} \sum_{k=1}^{n} x_{kl}.$$

By the monotonicity of the function $\ln x$, this inequality yields

$$x_{ie} > 0 \Rightarrow \frac{\partial P(x)}{\partial x_{ie}} \leq \frac{\partial P(x)}{\partial x_{il}} \quad \forall i, e, l.$$

Further reasoning is similar to the proof of Theorem 14. The function $x \ln x$ and the linear function are convex. On the other hand, the sum of convex functions also represents a convex function. Consequently, the function $P(x)$ is convex and, besides, continuously differentiable. It follows from the convexity of $P(x)$ that

$$P(y) - P(x) \geq \sum_{i=1}^{n} \sum_{e \in E} \frac{\partial P(x)}{\partial x_{ie}}(x)(y_{ie} - x_{ie}).$$

Using the equilibrium conditions, we have

$$x_{ie} > 0 \Rightarrow \frac{\partial P(x)}{\partial x_{ie}} = \lambda_i \; \forall e \in E,$$
$$x_{ie} = 0 \Rightarrow \frac{\partial P(x)}{\partial x_{ie}} \geq \lambda_i \; \forall e \in E.$$

If the second condition $x_{ie} = 0$ holds, then $y_{ie} - x_{ie} \geq 0$, and thus $\frac{\partial P(x)}{\partial x_{ie}}(x)(y_{ie} - x_{ie}) \geq \lambda_i(y_{ie} - x_{ie})$. This leads to the relationships

$$P(y) - P(x) \geq \sum_{i=1}^{n} \sum_{e \in E} \lambda_i(y_{ie} - x_{ie}) = \sum_{i=1}^{n} \lambda_i \sum_{e \in E}(y_{ie} - x_{ie}) = 0.$$

Consequently, $P(y) \geq P(x)$ for all y; hence, x is the minimum point of the function $P(x)$.

Now, we prove the sufficiency part of Theorem 17. Let x be the minimum point of the function $P(y)$. Assume on the contrary that x is not a Wardrop equilibrium. Then, for some player k, there exist two channels p and q such that $x_{kp} > 0$ and $a_{kp}\delta_p(x) > a_{kq}\delta_q(x)$. In this case, it is possible to find a number $z : 0 < z < x_{kp}$ such that

$$a_{kp}(\delta_p(x) - z) \geq a_{kq}(\delta_q(x) + z).$$

Define a new strategy profile y such that all strategies of the players $i \neq k$ remain the same whereas the strategy of player k takes the form

$$y_{ke} = \begin{cases} x_{kp} - z & \text{if } e = p, \\ x_{kq} + z & \text{if } e = q, \\ x_{ke} & \text{otherwise.} \end{cases}$$

Consider the difference

$$P(x) - P(y) = \sum_{i=1}^{n}\sum_{e \in E}(x_{ie} - y_{ie})\ln a_{ie} + \sum_{e \in E}(\delta_e(x)\ln\delta_e(x) - \delta_e(y)\ln\delta_e(y)).$$

(3.11)

The nonzero terms in both sums of (3.11) correspond to player k and channels p, q only:

$$P(x) - P(y) = z(\ln a_{kp} - \ln a_{kq}) + \delta_p(x)\ln\delta_p(x) + \delta_q(x)\ln\delta_q(x)$$
$$- (\delta_p(x) - z)\ln(\delta_p(x) - z) - (\delta_q(y) + z)\ln(\delta_q(x) + z)$$
$$= \ln\left(a_{kp}^{z} \cdot \delta_p(x)^{\delta_p(x)} \cdot \delta_q(x)^{\delta_q(x)}\right)$$
$$- \ln\left(a_{kq}^{z} \cdot (\delta_p(x) - z)^{\delta_p(x)-z} \cdot (\delta_q(x) + z)^{\delta_q(x)+z}\right).$$

We further establish Lemma 8, which claims that the last expression is strictly positive. However, in this case, the resulting inequality $P(x) > P(y)$ obviously contradicts the condition that x is the minimum point of the function $P(y)$, and the conclusion follows. The proof of Theorem 17 is finished. $\square$

Lemma 8. *Let* a, b, u, v, *and* z *be nonnegative and* $u \geq z$. *If* $a(u-z) \geq b(v+z)$, *then*

$$a^{z} \cdot u^{u} \cdot v^{v} > b^{z} \cdot (u-z)^{u-z} \cdot (v+z)^{v+z}.$$

Proof. First, we show the inequality

$$\left(\frac{\alpha}{\alpha-1}\right)^{\alpha} > e > \left(1 + \frac{1}{\beta}\right)^{\beta}, \quad \alpha > 1, \beta > 0.$$

(3.12)

It suffices to notice that the function

$$f(\alpha) = \left(1 + \frac{1}{\alpha-1}\right)^{\alpha} = \exp\left(\alpha\ln(1 + \frac{1}{\alpha-1})\right),$$

being monotonically decreasing, tends to e as $\alpha \to \infty$. The monotonicity follows from the negativity of the derivative

$$f'(\alpha) = f(\alpha)\left(\ln(1 + \frac{1}{\alpha-1}) - \frac{1}{\alpha-1}\right) < 0 \quad \text{for all } \alpha > 1.$$

The right-hand inequality can be verified by analogy.

Now, let $\alpha = u/z$ and $\beta = v/z$. Then the condition $a(u - z) \geq b(v + z)$ implies $a(\alpha z - z) \geq b(\beta z + z)$, yielding $a(\alpha - 1) \geq b(\beta + 1)$. By inequality (3.12) we have

$$a\alpha^{\alpha}\beta^{\beta} > a(\alpha - 1)^{\alpha}(\beta + 1)^{\beta} \geq b(\alpha - 1)^{\alpha-1}(\beta + 1)^{\beta+1}.$$

Multiply the last inequality by $z^{\alpha+\beta}$,

$$a(z\alpha)^{\alpha}(z\beta)^{\beta} > b(z\alpha - z)^{\alpha-1}(z\beta + z)^{\beta+1},$$

and raise to the power of z to get

$$a^{z}(z\alpha)^{z\alpha}(z\beta)^{z\beta} > b^{z}(z\alpha - z)^{z\alpha-z}(z\beta + z)^{z\beta+z}.$$

The proof of Lemma 8 is finished. □

3.14 THE PRICE OF ANARCHY IN AN ARBITRARY NETWORK FOR PLAYER-SPECIFIC LINEAR LATENCY FUNCTIONS

Consider the Wardrop model $\langle n, G, w, Z, f \rangle$ for an arbitrary network with splittable traffic and linear latency functions of the form $f_{ie}(\delta) = a_{ie}\delta$. The coefficients a_{ie} are different for different players $i \in N$ and channels $e \in E$. An important characteristic consists in

$$\Delta = \max_{i,k \in N, e \in E} \left\{ \frac{a_{ie}}{a_{ke}} \right\},$$

that is, the maximal ratio of delays over all players and channels. As demonstrated earlier, the price of anarchy in an arbitrary network with linear identical delays of all players is 4/3. The price of anarchy may grow appreciably if the latency functions become player-specific. Still, it is bounded above by the value Δ.

The proof of this result relies on the following inequality.

Lemma 9. *For any $u, v \geq 0$ and $\Delta > 0$,*

$$uv \leq \frac{1}{2\Delta}u^2 + \frac{\Delta}{2}v^2.$$

Proof. The proof is immediate from the representation

$$\frac{1}{2\Delta}u^2 + \frac{\Delta}{2}v^2 - uv = \frac{\Delta}{2}\left(\frac{u}{\Delta} - v\right)^2 \geq 0.$$

□

Theorem 18. *For the Wardrop model with player-specific linear cost, the price of anarchy does not exceed* Δ.

Proof. Let x be a Wardrop equilibrium, and let x^* be the strategy profile yielding the minimal social cost. Consider the social cost in the equilibrium:

$$SC(x) = \sum_{i=1}^{n} \sum_{R_i \in Z_i} x_{iR_i} \sum_{e \in R_i} a_{ie} \delta_e(x).$$

By the definition of a Wardrop equilibrium, the delays on all used channels coincide, that is, $\sum_{e \in R_i} a_{ie} \delta_e(x) = \lambda_i$ if $x_{iR_i} > 0$. This implies

$$SC(x) = \sum_{i=1}^{n} \sum_{R_i \in Z_i} x_{iR_i} \sum_{e \in R_i} a_{ie} \delta_e(x) \leq \sum_{i=1}^{n} \sum_{R_i \in Z_i} x^*_{iR_i} \sum_{e \in R_i} a_{ie} \delta_e(x).$$

Write the last expression as

$$\sum_{i=1}^{n} \sum_{R_i \in Z_i} x^*_{iR_i} \sum_{e \in R_i} \frac{a_{ie}}{\delta_e(x^*)} \delta_e(x^*) \delta_e(x)$$

and take advantage of Lemma 9 in the following way:

$$SC(x) \leq \sum_{i=1}^{n} \sum_{R_i \in Z_i} x^*_{iR_i} \sum_{e \in R_i} \frac{a_{ie}}{\delta_e(x^*)} \left(\frac{\Delta}{2} \delta_e^2(x^*) + \frac{1}{2\Delta} \delta_e^2(x) \right)$$

$$= \frac{\Delta}{2} \sum_{i=1}^{n} \sum_{R_i \in Z_i} x^*_{iR_i} \sum_{e \in R_i} a_{ie} \delta_e(x^*) + \frac{1}{2\Delta} \sum_{e \in E} \sum_{i=1}^{n} \sum_{R_i \in Z_i : e \in R_i} \frac{x^*_{iR_i}}{\delta_e(x^*)} a_{ie} \delta_e^2(x)$$

$$= \frac{\Delta}{2} SC(x^*) + \frac{1}{2\Delta} \sum_{e \in E} \sum_{i=1}^{n} \sum_{R_i \in Z_i : e \in R_i} \frac{x^*_{iR_i}}{\delta_e(x^*)} \cdot a_{ie} \delta_e^2(x).$$

To estimate the second term in the last formula, make the following observation. If the equalities

$$x_1 + x_2 + \cdots + x_n = y_1 + y_2 + \cdots + y_n = 1$$

hold with nonnegative summands, then

$$\frac{a_1 x_1 + a_2 x_2 + \ldots + a_n x_n}{a_1 y_1 + a_2 y_2 + \ldots + a_n y_n} \leq \frac{\max\{a_i\}}{\min\{a_i\}}, \quad a_i > 0, i = 1, \ldots, n.$$

On the other hand, in the last expression, for any $e \in E$, we have

$$\sum_{i=1}^{n} \sum_{R_i \in Z_i : e \in R_i} \frac{x_{iR_i}^*}{\delta_e(x^*)} = \sum_{i=1}^{n} \sum_{R_i \in Z_i : e \in R_i} \frac{x_{iR_i}}{\delta_e(x)} = 1.$$

Hence,

$$SC(x) \leq \frac{\Delta}{2} SC(x^*) + \frac{1}{2\Delta} \Delta \sum_{e \in E} \sum_{i=1}^{n} \sum_{R_i \in Z_i : e \in R_i} \frac{x_{iR_i}}{\delta_e(x)} \cdot a_{ie} \delta_e^2(x).$$

After standard simplifications,

$$SC(x) \leq \frac{\Delta}{2} SC(x^*) + \frac{1}{2} \sum_{i=1}^{n} \sum_{R_i \in Z_i} x_{iR_i} \sum_{e \in R_i} a_{ie} \delta_e(x) = \frac{\Delta}{2} SC(x^*) + \frac{1}{2} SC(x).$$

As a result, the estimate

$$\frac{SC(x)}{SC(x^*)} \leq \Delta$$

applies to any equilibrium. The proof of Theorem 18 is finished.   □

Therefore, in an arbitrary network with player-specific linear delays, the price of anarchy is finite and depends on the ratio of the latency function coefficients of different players.

3.15 THE WARDROP MODEL WITH PARALLEL CHANNELS AND INCOMPLETE INFORMATION

In this section, we study the Bayesian setup of the Wardrop model with parallel channels, in which the players send heterogeneous traffic and each player knows only the type of his traffic [19]. A similar scheme of the problem with unsplittable traffic was presented in [34]. In what follows, we suggest a modification of this scheme for the network model with parallel channels and arbitrarily splittable traffic.

Consider a game $\Gamma = \langle n, m, f, T, p, w \rangle$ with n players (users), m parallel channels, and latency functions $f_{ie}(x) = a_{ie}x$ that depend on the capacities of the channels defined for each player. For each player i, there is a given set of traffic types T_i sent by him and also a given joint distribution $p(t_1, \ldots, t_n)$ of these types. For player i, the traffic of each type t has a volume $w_i(t)$. Within the framework of our model, each player i knows only the type t_i

of his traffic to be sent and has no information about the types of traffic sent by the other players. However, using the available joint distribution of traffic types, he can find the conditional distribution of the traffic types of the other players given his traffic type t_i, that is, $p(t_1, \ldots, t_{i-1}, t_{i+1}, \ldots, t_n | t_i = t) = \frac{p(t_1, \ldots, t, \ldots, t_n)}{p(i, t)}$, where $p(i, t) = \sum\limits_{(t_1, \ldots, t_n) \in T : t_i = t} p(t_1, \ldots, t_n)$ is the probability that player i sends traffic of type t.

In this game, strategy profiles have the form $x = \{x_i^{te}\}_{i \in [n], t \in T_i, e \in [m]}$, where x_i^{te} is the traffic of type t sent by player i through channel e. The components of a strategy profile must be nonnegative and satisfy the condition $\sum\limits_{e \in [m]} x_i^{te} = w_i(t)$. Denote by X the set of admissible strategy profiles x in the game Γ.

The expected load of channel e can be calculated by $\delta_e(x, p) = \sum\limits_{(t_1, \ldots, t_n) \in T} p(t_1, \ldots, t_n) \sum\limits_{i \in [n]} x_i^{t_i e}$, and the expected cost is $PC_i(x, p) = \max\limits_{e \in [m] : \exists t \in T_i : x_i^{te} > 0} f_{ie}(\delta_e(x, p))$.

Each player i knows the type of his traffic. The goal of each player i can be the optimal cost for each type of his traffic considered separately. In this case, we introduce the conditional expected cost function that depends on the conditional expected load of the network channels. For each channel e, this function has the form $\delta_e(x, (p | t_i = t)) = \delta_e^{-i}(x, (p | t_i = t)) + x_i^{te}$, where $\delta_e^{-i}(x, (p | t_i = t)) = \sum\limits_{(t_1, \ldots, t_n) \in T : t_i = t} p(t_1, \ldots, t_{i-1}, t_{i+1}, \ldots, t_n | t_i = t) \sum\limits_{i \in [n] \setminus \{i\}} x_i^{t_i e}$ is the conditional expected load of this channel by the traffic of all players except i.

Therefore, for player i sending traffic of type t, the conditional expected cost has the form $v_{(i,t)}(x, p) = \max\limits_{e \in [m] : x_i^{te} > 0} f_{ie}(\delta_e(x, (p | t_i = t)))$. In addition, define his Bayesian expected cost as $BPC_i(x, p) = \sum\limits_{t \in T_i} p(i, t) v_{(i,t)}(x, p)$. Note that each term in this sum is independent of the traffic types of all players except i.

Now, find the relationship between the expected and conditional expected loads of channel e:

$$\delta_e(x, p) = \sum_{(t_1, \ldots, t_n) \in T} p(t_1, \ldots, t_n) \sum_{i \in [n]} x_i^{t_i e}$$

$$= \sum_{t \in T_k} \sum_{(t_1, \ldots, t_n) \in T : t_k = t} p(t_1, \ldots, t_n) \sum_{i \in [n]} x_i^{t_i e}$$

$$= \sum_{t \in T_k} p(k, t) \sum_{(t_1, \ldots, t_n) \in T : t_k = t} p(t_1, \ldots, t_{k-1}, t_{k+1}, \ldots, t_n | t_k = t) \left(\sum_{i \in [n] \setminus \{k\}} x_i^{t_i e} + x_k^{te} \right).$$

For the time being, observe that

$$\sum_{(t_1,\ldots,t_n)\in T:t_k=t} p(t_1,\ldots,t_{k-1},t_{k+1},\ldots,t_n|t_k=t) = \sum_{(t_1,\ldots,t_n)\in T:t_k=t} \frac{p(t_1,\ldots,t,\ldots,t_n)}{p(k,t)}$$

$$= \sum_{(t_1,\ldots,t_n)\in T:t_k=t} \frac{p(t_1,\ldots,t_n)}{p(k,t)} = 1.$$

Then

$$\delta_e(x,p) =$$

$$= \sum_{t\in T_k} p(k,t) \left(\sum_{(t_1,\ldots,t_n)\in T:t_k=t} p(t_1,\ldots,t_{k-1},t_{k+1},\ldots,t_n|t_k=t) \sum_{i\in[n]\setminus\{k\}} x_i^{t_ie} + x_k^{te} \right)$$

$$= \sum_{t\in T_k} p(k,t)\delta_e(x,(p|t_k=t)).$$

Calculate the total expected load of the network as the sum of the loads $\delta_e(x,p)$:

$$\sum_{e\in[m]} \delta_e(x,p) = \sum_{e\in[m]} \sum_{(t_1,\ldots,t_n)\in T} p(t_1,\ldots,t_n) \sum_{i\in[n]} x_i^{t_ie}$$

$$= \sum_{(t_1,\ldots,t_n)\in T} p(t_1,\ldots,t_n) \sum_{i\in[n]} \sum_{e\in[m]} x_i^{t_ie}$$

$$= \sum_{(t_1,\ldots,t_n)\in T} p(t_1,\ldots,t_n) \sum_{i\in[n]} w_i(t_i) =: W.$$

In other words, this value is constant.

Another fruitful property of the load $\delta_e(x,p)$ consists in the form of its partial derivative:

$$\frac{\partial}{\partial x_k^{te}}\delta_e(x,p) = \frac{\partial}{\partial x_k^{te}} \left(\sum_{t\in T_k} p(k,t)\delta_e(x,(p|t_k=t)) \right)$$

$$= \frac{\partial}{\partial x_k^{te}} \left(\sum_{t\in T_k} p(k,t)\left(\delta_e^{-k}(x,(p|t_k=t)) + x_k^{te}\right) \right) = p(k,t).$$

3.16 EQUILIBRIA IN THE MODEL WITH INCOMPLETE INFORMATION

Definition 24. A strategy profile x in the game Γ is called a Wardrop equilibrium if, for each player $i\in[n]$ and any channels $e,q\in[m]$ such that $x_i^{te} > 0$, we have $f_{ie}(\delta_e(x,p)) \leq f_{iq}(\delta_q(x,p))$.

This definition is equivalent to that involving the inequality $PC_i(x, p) \leq PC(x', p)$, where x denotes a Wardrop equilibrium, and x' is the strategy profile obtained from x as the result of a unilateral deviation of some player. A Wardrop equilibrium is achieved when each player seeks to minimize his expected cost on all channels adopted by him with a nonzero probability at least for one of his traffic types.

Definition 25. A strategy profile x in the game Γ is called a Bayesian Wardrop equilibrium if, for each player $i \in [n]$, his traffic type $t \in T_i$, and channels $e, q \in [m]$ such that $x_i^{te} > 0$, we have $f_{ie}(\delta_e(x, (p|t_i = t))) \leq f_{iq}(\delta_q(x, (p|t_i = t)))$.

This definition is equivalent to that involving the inequality $BPC_i(x, p) \leq BPC(x', p)$, where x denotes a Bayesian Wardrop equilibrium, and x' is the strategy profile obtained from x as the result of a unilateral deviation of some player. A Bayesian Wardrop equilibrium is achieved when each player seeks to minimize his Bayesian expected cost by optimizing the transmission of his traffic of each type.

Proposition 1. *If x is a Bayesian Wardrop equilibrium in the game Γ, then $BPC_i(x, p) \leq PC_i(x, p)$.*

Proof. Let x be a Bayesian Wardrop equilibrium. In this case, for all $i \in [n]$, $t \in T_i$, and $e \in [m]$ such that $x_i^{te} > 0$, we obtain $a_{ie}\delta_e(x, (p|t_k = t)) = \lambda_i^t$; otherwise, $a_{ie}\delta_e(x, (p|t_k = t)) \geq \lambda_i^t$. Consequently,

$$BPC_i(x, p)$$
$$= \sum_{t \in T_i} p(i, t) \max_{e \in [m]: x_i^{te} > 0} a_{ie}\delta_e(x, (p|t_k = t)) = \sum_{t \in T_i} p(i, t)\lambda_i^t;$$

$$PC_i(x, p)$$
$$= \max_{e \in [m]: \exists \tau \in T_i: x_i^{\tau e} > 0} \delta_e(x, p)$$
$$= \max_{e \in [m]: \exists \tau \in T_i: x_i^{\tau e} > 0} \sum_{t \in T_i} p(i, t) a_{ie}\delta_e(x, (p|t_k = t))$$
$$= \max_{e \in [m]: \exists \tau \in T_i: x_i^{\tau e} > 0} \left(\sum_{t \in T_i: x_i^t > 0} p(i, t)\lambda_i^t + \sum_{t \in T_i: x_i^{te} = 0} p(i, t) \left(\lambda_i^t + \Delta_i^{te} \right) \right)$$
$$\geq \max_{e \in [m]: \exists \tau \in T_i: x_i^{\tau e} > 0} \left(\sum_{t \in T_i} p(i, t)\lambda_i^t \right) = BPC_i(x, p). \quad \square$$

Definition 26. A strategy profile x in the game Γ is normal if, for each player $i \in [n]$ and each channel $e \in [m]$, we have the following property: if $x_i^{te} > 0$ at least for one traffic type $t \in T_i$, then $x_i^{\tau e} > 0$ for all $\tau \in T_i$.

According to this definition, in a normal strategy profile a player uses the same collection of channels for all types of his traffic.

Definition 27. A Bayesian Wardrop equilibrium x in the game Γ is called normal if x forms a normal strategy profile in this game.

Theorem 19. *Any normal Bayesian Wardrop equilibrium in the game Γ is a particular case of a Wardrop equilibrium, but there may exist Wardrop equilibria that are not normal Bayesian ones.*

Proof. We show that a normal Bayesian Wardrop equilibrium represents a particular case of a Wardrop equilibrium. If x is a Bayesian Wardrop equilibrium, then the inequality $x_i^{te} > 0$ implies the inequality $a_{ie}\delta_e(x, (p|t_i = t)) \leq a_{iq}\delta_q(x, (p|t_i = t))$, where $e, q \in [m]$. On the other hand, if x is a normal Bayesian Wardrop equilibrium, then $x_i^{\tau e} > 0$ follows from $x_i^{te} > 0$ for all $\tau \in T_i$. Therefore, in a normal Bayesian Wardrop equilibrium, from $x_i^{te} > 0$ we have $a_{ie}\delta_e(x, (p|t_i = \tau)) \leq a_{iq}\delta_q(x, (p|t_i = \tau))$ for all $\tau \in T_i$, and hence $a_{ie}\delta_e(x, p) \leq a_{iq}\delta_q(x, p)$.

Now, let x be a certain Wardrop equilibrium and Bayesian Wardrop equilibrium in the game with $m = 2$ channels (fast and slow) and $n = 2$ players, each having $t = 2$ types of traffic (of large and small volumes). Choose the coefficients $a_{11} = a_{21} = 1$ and $a_{12} = a_{22} = 1000$. The players have the following sets of traffic types: $T_1 = \{1, 2\}$, $T_2 = \{3, 4\}$, with the volumes given by $w(1) = 1, w(2) = 1000, w(3) = 1, w(4) = 1000$. The joint distribution of the traffic types is such that $p(1, 4) + p(2, 3) = 1$. The Wardrop equilibrium strategy of each player consists in using different channels, the faster one for the traffic of large volume. Obviously, this strategy profile is not a normal Bayesian Wardrop equilibrium. $\square$

Theorem 20. *In the game Γ with $n = 2$ players, each having $t = 2$ types of traffic, and $m = 2$ channels, where the joint distribution of the traffic types satisfies $p(1, 4) + p(2, 3) = 1$, any Bayesian Wardrop equilibrium is a particular case of a Wardrop equilibrium.*

Proof. Let x be a Bayesian Wardrop equilibrium that is not normal (otherwise, this equilibrium clearly satisfies the definition of a Wardrop equilibrium). Thus, at least one of the players uses different collections of channels for different traffic types. Suppose this is player 1, who chooses channel 1 for traffic type 1 and channel 2 for traffic type 2. Hence, for player 1, we obtain the inequalities

$$a_{11}\delta_1(x, (p|t_1 = 1)) = a_{11}(w_1(1) + x_2^{41}) \leq a_{12}\delta_2(x, (p|t_1 = 1)) = a_{12}x_2^{42},$$
$$a_{11}\delta_1(x, (p|t_1 = 2)) = a_{11}x_2^{31} \geq a_{12}\delta_2(x, (p|t_1 = 2)) = a_{12}(w_1(2) + x_2^{32});$$

and for player 2, we obtain the inequalities

$$a_{21}\delta_1(x, (p|t_2 = 4)) = a_{21}(w_1(1) + x_2^{41}) \geq a_{22}\delta_2(x, (p|t_2 = 4)) = a_{22}x_2^{42},$$
$$a_{21}\delta_1(x, (p|t_2 = 3)) = a_{21}x_2^{31} \leq a_{22}\delta_2(x, (p|t_2 = 3)) = a_{22}(w_1(2) + x_2^{32}).$$

Note that all parts of these inequalities are positive. Denoting $A = a_{11}$, $B = a_{12}$, $C = a_{21}$, $D = a_{22}$, $a = w_1(1) + x_2^{41}$, $b = x_2^{42}$, $c = x_2^{31}$, $d = w_1(2) + x_2^{32}$ and using Lemma 10, we establish that these inequalities hold as equalities.   □

Lemma 10. *For any positive numbers A, B, C, D and a, b, c, d, the inequalities*

$$Aa \leq Bb, \qquad Ca \geq Db,$$
$$Ac \geq Bd, \qquad Cc \leq Dd$$

imply the equalities

$$Aa = Bb, \qquad Ca = Db,$$
$$Ac = Bd, \qquad Cc = Dd.$$

Proof. The first and second left inequalities yield $\frac{a}{b} \leq \frac{B}{A} \leq \frac{c}{d}$. The residual inequalities lead to $\frac{a}{b} \geq \frac{D}{C} \geq \frac{c}{d}$, and the conclusion follows.   □

Moreover, the next theorem states that a Bayesian Wardrop equilibrium is a Wardrop equilibrium even in the general setup of the game Γ.

Theorem 21. *Any Bayesian Wardrop equilibrium in the game Γ is a Wardrop equilibrium.*

Proof. Let x be a Bayesian Wardrop equilibrium. Then, for all $i \in [n]$, $t \in T_i$, and $e \in [m]$ such that $x_i^{te} > 0$, we have $a_{ie}\delta_e(x, (p|t_k = t)) = \lambda_i^t$; otherwise, $a_{ie}\delta_e(x, (p|t_k = t)) \geq \lambda_i^t$. Suppose x is not a Wardrop equilibrium. In this case, there exists at least one player i who can reduce his expected cost $PC_i(x, p)$

by a unilateral deviation from x, that is,

$$PC_i(x, p)$$

$$= \max_{e \in [m]: \exists \tau \in T_i: x_i^{\tau e} > 0} a_{ie} \delta_e(x, p) =$$

$$= \max_{e \in [m]: \exists \tau \in T_i: x_i^{\tau e} > 0} \sum_{t \in T_i} p(i, t) a_{ie} \delta_e(x, (p|t_k = t))$$

$$= \max_{e \in [m]: \exists \tau \in T_i: x_i^{\tau e} > 0} \left(\sum_{t \in T_i: x_i^{te} > 0} p(i, t) \lambda_i^t + \sum_{t \in T_i: x_i^{te} = 0} p(i, t) \left(\lambda_i^t + \Delta_i^{te} \right) \right).$$

Player i cannot decrease the load of the channels with the traffic delay exceeding λ_i^t, since he does not use these channels for traffic type t. Moving a certain part of traffic from channel e with delay λ_i^t to another channel q anyway increases the expected cost of the player due to a higher load of channel q. Indeed, one of the following situations takes place: (1) channel q has load λ_i^t initially (if used for traffic type t in the strategy profile x), or (2) the channel q receives a load higher than λ_i^t as the result of adding traffic of type t. In other words, player i cannot deviate with reducing his expected cost, and hence x is a Wardrop equilibrium. $\square$

3.17 POTENTIAL AND EXISTENCE OF WARDROP EQUILIBRIUM IN THE MODEL WITH INCOMPLETE INFORMATION

Consider the function

$$\Psi(x) = \sum_{i \in [n]} \sum_{t \in T_i} \sum_{e \in [m]} p(i, t) x_i^{te} \ln(a_{ie}) + \sum_{e \in [m]} \delta_e(x, p) \ln(\delta_e(x, p)),$$

which represents a probabilistic modification of the potential adopted in [33]. This function is convex as the sum of convex functions and has a minimum on a convex set X.

Theorem 22. *If the game Γ possesses a Wardrop equilibrium x, then $\Psi(x) = \min\limits_{y \text{ is strategy profile in } \Gamma} \Psi(y)$.*

Proof.

$$\frac{\partial \Psi(x)}{\partial x_i^{te}} = p(i, t) \ln(a_{ie}) + p(i, t) \ln(\delta_e(x, p)) + p(i, t)$$
$$= p(i, t)(\ln(a_{ie} \delta_e(x, p)) + 1).$$

In a Wardrop equilibrium, the inequality $x_i^{te} > 0$ implies $a_{ie}\delta_e(x, p) \leq a_{iq}\delta_q(x, p)$, and hence

$$p(i, t)(\ln(a_{ie}\delta_e(x, p)) + 1) \leq p(i, t)(\ln(a_{iq}\delta_q(x, p)) + 1).$$

Consequently,

$$\frac{\partial \Psi(x)}{\partial x_i^{te}} \leq \frac{\partial \Psi(x)}{\partial x_i^{tq}}.$$

Note that

$$\frac{\partial \Psi(x)}{\partial x_i^{te}} = \frac{\partial \Psi(x)}{\partial x_i^{tq}}$$

if $x_i^{te} > 0$ and $x_i^{tq} > 0$.

Using the Karush–Kuhn–Tucker conditions, it is possible to show that $\Psi(x) = \min_{y \text{ is a strategy profile in } \Gamma} \Psi(y)$. To this end, consider the Lagrange function

$$L(x, \lambda) = \Psi(x) - \sum_{i \in [n]} \sum_{t \in T_i} \lambda_i^t \left(\sum_{e \in [m]} x_i^{te} - w_i(t) \right)$$

and let $\lambda_i^t = \frac{\partial \Psi(x)}{\partial x_i^{te'}}$ with any $x_i^{te'} > 0$. Then $\frac{\partial}{\partial x_i^{te}} L(x, \lambda) = \frac{\partial}{\partial x_i^{te}} \Psi(x) - \lambda_i^t = 0$ for all $x_i^{te} > 0$ and $\frac{\partial}{\partial x_i^{tq}} L(x, \lambda) = \frac{\partial}{\partial x_i^{tq}} \Psi(x) - \lambda_i^t \geq 0$ for all $x_i^{tq} = 0$. $\qquad \square$

Theorem 23. *If a strategy profile x in the game Γ minimizes the function $\Psi(x)$, then x is a Wardrop equilibrium.*

Proof. By the Karush–Kuhn–Tucker conditions, x minimizes the function $\Psi(x)$ if and only if there exists a value λ such that, for $i \in [n]$, $t \in T_i$, $e \in [m]$, and

$$L(x, \lambda) = \Psi(x) - \sum_{i \in [n]} \sum_{t \in T_i} \lambda_i^t \left(\sum_{e \in [m]} x_i^{te} - w_i(t) \right),$$

we have the following:

$$\text{if } x_i^{te} > 0, \text{ then } \quad \frac{\partial}{\partial x_i^{te}} L(x, \lambda) = 0;$$

$$\text{if } x_i^{te} = 0, \text{ then } \quad \frac{\partial}{\partial x_i^{te}} L(x, \lambda) \geq 0.$$

Denoting $\alpha_i^t = e^{\left(\frac{\lambda_i^t}{p(i,t)} - 1 \right)}$, we obtain

$$a_{ie}\delta_e(x, p) = \alpha_i^t \text{ if } x_i^{te} > 0 \text{ and } a_{ie}\delta_e(x, p) \geq \alpha_i^t \text{ if } x_i^{te} = 0.$$

Since $a_{ie}\delta_e(x,p)$ is independent of the player's traffic type, α_i^t are the same for all traffic types of player i among which each pair shares at least one channel. Denote them as α_i. For the other traffic types τ, we have $\alpha_i^\tau \leq \alpha_i$.

On the other hand, traffic of type τ is sent through some channel q, where $x_i^{\tau q} > 0$. If $x_i^{tq} > 0$, then $a_{iq}\delta_q(x,p) = \alpha_i^\tau = \alpha_i^t = \alpha_i$. In the case $x_i^{tq} = 0$, $a_{iq}\delta_q(x,p) = \alpha_i^\tau \geq \alpha_i^t = \alpha_i$. Thus, $\alpha_i^\tau = \alpha_i^t = \alpha_i$.

Hence, for all $i \in [n]$ and $e \in [m]$ such that each player i uses channel e for sending at least one type of his traffic, we have $a_{ie}\delta_e(x,p) = \alpha_i$, where α_i are constants.   □

Note that the function $\Psi(x)$ has a minimum on the set X. This fact leads to the following result.

Theorem 24. *The game Γ always possesses a Wardrop equilibrium.*

Note that the game Γ may have several Wardrop equilibria and some of them can be Bayesian. This is illustrated by the following two examples.

Example 13. Here we describe a situation in which a Wardrop equilibrium is also Bayesian. Consider the game with $n = 2$ players, $m = 2$ channels, and $a_{11} = a_{21} = 1, a_{12} = a_{22} = 2$. The sets of traffic types of the players are defined as $T_1 = \{1, 2\}$ and $T_2 = \{3, 4\}$, where $w(1) = 1$, $w(2) = 25$, $w(3) = 1$, and $w(4) = 50$. The joint distribution of the traffic types is such that $p(1, 4) = p(2, 3) = 1/2$.

The strategies in a Wardrop equilibrium have the form

$$
\begin{aligned}
x_1^{11} &= 0, & x_1^{12} &= 1, \\
x_1^{21} &= 16\tfrac{1}{3}, & x_1^{22} &= 8\tfrac{2}{3}, \\
x_2^{31} &= 1, & x_2^{32} &= 0, \\
x_2^{41} &= 34, & x_2^{42} &= 16.
\end{aligned}
$$

For both channels, the conditional expected load coincides with the expected load $\Psi(x) \approx 124.939$.

Example 14. In this example, a Wardrop equilibrium is not Bayesian. Consider the game of the previous example. Another Wardrop equilibrium is the strategy profile

$$x_1^{11} = 1, \qquad x_1^{12} = 0,$$
$$x_1^{21} = 25, \qquad x_1^{22} = 0,$$
$$x_2^{31} = 1, \qquad x_2^{32} = 0,$$
$$x_2^{41} = 24\tfrac{1}{3}, \qquad x_2^{42} = 25\tfrac{2}{3}.$$

The expected load is the same for both channels, $\Psi(x) \approx 124.939$. However, the conditional expected load does not match a Bayesian Wardrop equilibrium. For example, for player 1,

$$a_{11}\delta_1(x, (p|t_1 = 1)) = x_1^{11} + x_2^{41} = 25\tfrac{1}{3},$$
$$a_{12}\delta_2(x, (p|t_1 = 1)) = x_1^{12} + x_2^{42} = 51\tfrac{1}{3},$$
$$a_{11}\delta_1(x, (p|t_1 = 2)) = x_1^{21} + x_2^{31} = 26,$$
$$a_{12}\delta_2(x, (p|t_1 = 2)) = x_1^{22} + x_2^{32} = 0.$$

CHAPTER 4

Load Balancing Game

Contents

The load balancing game [7,26] is also known as the scheduling problem for computing network nodes or processors in the form of a game equivalent to the KP-model with parallel different-capacity channels [54]. It is necessary to distribute several jobs of various volumes among processors of nonidentical speeds. The volume of a job is its completion time on a free unit-speed processor. Processor load is the total volume of jobs executed by a given processor. The ratio of processor load and speed defines its delay, that is, the job completion time by this processor. Within the game-theoretic approach to the load balancing problem, each player chooses a processor for his job striving to minimize job's delay. Players have egoistic behavior and reach a Nash equilibrium, viz., a job distribution such that none of them benefits from a unilateral change of the chosen processor. We further study pure strategy Nash equilibria only; as is well known [29], such an equilibrium always exists in the described class of games. The system cost (also called the social cost) is the maximal delay over all processors for an obtained job distribution. The price of anarchy (PoA) is defined as the maximal ratio of the social cost in the worst-case Nash equilibrium and the optimal social cost. In what follows, we derive upper estimates for the PoA in the cases of N and three processors [20]. It is shown that, under certain conditions, these estimates yield the exact PoA value. Moreover, we establish sufficient conditions for PoA increase under new processor inclusion into the system. In the case of three processors, we propose a computing algorithm of the exact PoA value based on solving a series of linear programming problems. If necessary, the algorithm can be extended to the case of an arbitrary number of processors.

Networking Games
https://doi.org/10.1016/B978-0-12-816551-5.00010-1

Copyright © 2019 Elsevier Inc.
All rights reserved.

4.1 A MODEL OF THE LOAD BALANCING GAME

Consider a system $S = S(N, v)$ composed of N processors operating with speeds $v_1, \ldots, v_N$. The system is used by a set of players $U = U(n, w)$: each of n players chooses an appropriate processor for his job execution. For player j, the volume of job is w_j, $j = 1, \ldots, n$. Denote by $W = \sum_{j=1}^{n} w_j$ the total volume of all jobs. Free processor i with speed v_i executes a job of volume w during the time w/v_i.

We study the following pure strategy game $\Gamma = \ <S(N, v), U(n, w), \lambda>$. Each player can choose any processor. The strategy of player j is processor l_j selected by him for his job execution. Then the strategy profile in the game Γ represents the vector $L = (l_1, \ldots, l_n)$. The load of processor i, that is, the total volume of all jobs assigned to the processor is defined by $\delta_i(L) = \sum_{j=1,\ldots,n: l_j = i} w_j$. The delay of processor i takes the form

$$\lambda_i(L) = \sum_{j=1,\ldots,n: l_j = i} w_j/v_i = \frac{\delta_i(L)}{v_i}.$$

In fact, this value is the same for all players selecting a given processor.

The social cost is described by the maximal delay over all processors:

$$SC(L) = \max_{i=1,\ldots,N} \lambda_i(L).$$

Denote by

$$OPT = OPT(S, U) = \min_{L \text{ is a profile in } \Gamma(S,U,\lambda)} SC(L)$$

the optimal cost (the social cost in the optimal case), where minimization runs over all admissible strategy profiles in the game $\Gamma(S, U, \lambda)$.

A strategy profile L such that none player benefits from a unilateral deviation (change of the processor chosen in L for his job execution) is a pure strategy Nash equilibrium. To provide a formal definition, let $L(j \rightarrow i) = (l_1, \ldots, l_{j-1}, i, l_{j+1}, \ldots, l_n)$ be the profile obtained from a profile L if player j replaces processor l_j chosen by him in the profile L for another processor i, whereas the remaining players use the same strategies as before (remain invariable).

Definition 28. A strategy profile L is said to be a pure strategy Nash equilibrium if each player chooses a processor with the minimum delay, that is, for each player $j = 1, \ldots, n$, we have the inequality $\lambda_{l_j}(L) \leq \lambda_i(L(j \to i))$ for all processors $i = 1, \ldots, N$.

Definition 29. The price of anarchy in the system S is the maximal ratio of the social cost in the worst-case Nash equilibrium and the social cost in the optimal case:

$$PoA(S) = \max_U \frac{\underset{L \text{ is a Nash equilibrium in } \Gamma(S,U,\lambda)}{\max} SC(L)}{OPT(S, U)}.$$

4.2 THE PRICE OF ANARCHY IN THE GENERAL CASE OF N PROCESSORS

We give the following obvious estimates for any game of the above type. They will be employed in further analysis.

- The equilibrium social cost is not higher than the social cost in the case where all jobs are executed by the fastest processor only:

$$SC(L) \leq \frac{W}{\underset{i=1,\ldots,N}{\max} v_i}. \tag{4.1}$$

- The optimal social cost is not smaller than the social cost in the case where the whole volume of jobs is distributed among processors proportionally to their speeds so that all processors have an identical delay:

$$OPT \geq \frac{W}{\sum\limits_{i=1}^{N} v_i}. \tag{4.2}$$

Estimates (4.1) and (4.2) directly yield the main upper estimate for the price of anarchy:

$$PoA(S) \leq \frac{\sum\limits_{i=1}^{N} v_i}{\underset{i=1,\ldots,N}{\max} v_i}. \tag{4.3}$$

According to the following theorem, this upper estimate coincides with the exact PoA value under certain conditions imposed on processor speeds.

Theorem 25. *For the system S composed of $N \geq 3$ processors with speeds $v_1 = 1 \leq v_2 \leq \cdots \leq v_{N-1} = r \leq v_N = s$ such that*

(1) $(s-r) \sum_{i=1}^{N} v_i \leq \frac{s}{v_{N-2}} \left(s^2 - r \sum_{i=1}^{N} v_i \right)$ and

(2) $(s-r) \sum_{i=1}^{N} v_i \leq \frac{s^2}{v_{N-2}}$,

the price of anarchy makes up $PoA(S) = \frac{\sum_{i=1}^{N} v_i}{s}$.

Proof. The upper estimate of the PoA defined by (4.3) holds for the system S. Now, we demonstrate that this estimate becomes the exact PoA value under conditions (1) and (2) of the theorem.

Consider an example of a system where $N+1$ players have jobs of volumes $w_1 = r \sum_i v_i$, $w_2 = s^2 - r \sum_i v_i$, and $w_{2+i} = s v_i$ for all $i = 1, \ldots, N-1$. Condition (1) guarantees the nonnegativity of w_2.

In the optimal case, the jobs are distributed among processors so that all processors have an identical delay s: the jobs of volumes w_1 and w_2 are assigned to processor N, and each job of volume w_{2+i} is assigned to processor i for all $i = 1, \ldots, N-1$.

In a Nash equilibrium, the job of volume w_1 moves to processor $N-1$, which shows the highest delay $\sum_{i=1}^{N} v_i$. The remaining jobs are assigned to processor N; its delay constitutes $\frac{(s-r) \sum_{i=1}^{N} v_i}{s}$. Player 1 benefits nothing from moving his job of volume w_1 to another processor, since its delay on processor N becomes the same as on processor $N-1$ of speed r, whereas its delay on any other processor k of speed $v_k \leq r$ is $\frac{r \sum_{i=1}^{N} v_i}{v_k} \geq \sum_{i=1}^{N} v_i$. Conditions (1) and (2) ensure that it is also nonbeneficial to move the jobs of volumes w_i, $i \geq 2$, from processor N to any other processor k of speed $v_k \leq r$.

In the example considered, the ratio of the equilibrium and optimal social cost makes up $\frac{\sum_{i=1}^{N} v_i}{s}$. Since this is the upper estimate of the PoA, this is in fact the maximal ratio. □

The exact PoA value allows us to derive sufficient conditions for PoA increase under new processor inclusion into the system, that is, in a situation resembling Braess's paradox [13,48,53,74]. The next theorem shows the speed of the new processor that causes this situation.

Theorem 26. *For the system S composed of $N \geq 2$ processors with speeds $v_1 = 1 \leq v_2 \leq \cdots \leq v_N = s$, the price of anarchy strictly increases as the result of adding a new processor of speed s' such that*

(1) *the new system with $N+1$ processors satisfies conditions (1) and (2) of Theorem 25 and*

(2) $s' < s \left(1 + \frac{s}{\sum\limits_{i=1}^{N-1} v_i} \right).$

Proof. For the system S, the price of anarchy obeys the estimate $PoA(S) \leq \frac{\sum\limits_{i=1}^{N} v_i}{s}$. Suppose the new system meets conditions (1) and (2) of Theorem 25. If $s' \leq s$, then, for the new system, the price of anarchy becomes equal to $\frac{\sum\limits_{i=1}^{N} v_i + s'}{s} > \frac{\sum\limits_{i=1}^{N} v_i}{s}$. On the other hand, in the case $s' > s$, for the new system, the price of anarchy is $\frac{\sum\limits_{i=1}^{N} v_i + s'}{s'} > \frac{\sum\limits_{i=1}^{N} v_i}{s}$ under $s' < s \left(1 + \frac{s}{\sum\limits_{i=1}^{N-1} v_i} \right).$ $\square$

According to the following result, for PoA evaluation, it suffices to consider only the games in which the optimal social cost is 1.

Theorem 27. *For the system S, the price of anarchy constitutes*

$$PoA(S) = \max_{U_1: OPT(S, U_1)=1} \quad \max_{L \text{ is a Nash equilibrium in } \Gamma(S, U_1, \lambda)} SC(L).$$

Proof. Let L be the worst-case equilibrium in the game $\Gamma(S, U, \lambda)$ with an arbitrary set of players $U(n, w)$. For each player j, the volume of his job is w_j, and the vector L_{OPT} gives the optimal strategy profile in this game. Let SC and OPT be the social cost in the profile L and the optimal social cost, respectively. The ratio of the worst-case equilibrium and optimal social cost is defined by $\frac{SC}{OPT}$. Since L represents an equilibrium, for any player j, we obtain $\frac{\sum\limits_{k=1,\ldots,n: l_k=l_j} w_k}{v_{l_j}} \leq \frac{\sum\limits_{k=1,\ldots,n: l_k=i} w_k + w_j}{v_i}$ for any processor i.

Now, explore the game with the same set of processors and players, where each player j has the job of volume $\frac{w_j}{OPT}$. The social costs in the profiles L and L_{OPT} are $\frac{SC}{OPT}$ and 1, respectively. Owing to the linear homogeneity of processor delays in their loads, the profiles L and L_{OPT} form the worst-case equilibrium and optimal profiles, respectively, in the new game. Particularly, the profile L is an equilibrium in the new game, since for any player j, the inequality $\frac{\sum\limits_{k=1,\ldots,n: l_k=l_j} w_k}{v_{l_j} OPT} \leq \frac{\sum\limits_{k=1,\ldots,n: l_k=i} w_k + w_j}{v_i OPT}$ holds for any processor i. Let L be any non-worst-case equilibrium in the new game. Then the game admits an equilibrium L' with a social cost $\frac{SC'}{OPT}$ such that the social cost in the profile L' exceeds that in the profile L, that is, $\frac{SC'}{OPT} > \frac{SC}{OPT}$. However, in the initial game the profile L' corresponds to the social cost $SC' > SC$, and the equilibrium L' is worse than its counterpart L. Similarly, L_{OPT} gives the optimal profile in the new game. Then the ratio of the worst-case equilibrium and optimal social cost in the new game also equals $\frac{SC}{OPT}$.

Consequently, any game $\Gamma(S, U, \lambda)$ corresponds to a game $\Gamma(S, U_1, \lambda)$ with normalized job volumes such that $OPT(S, U_1) = 1$. Moreover, the ratio of the worst-case equilibrium and optimal social cost is the same in both games. Hence, for PoA evaluation, it suffices to consider only the games with the unit optimal social cost. $\square$

4.3 THE PRICE OF ANARCHY IN THE CASE OF THREE PROCESSORS

As a matter of fact, the exact PoA value in the two-processor model with speeds $1 \leq s$ was found in [26]:

$$PoA(S) = \begin{cases} 1 + \frac{s}{s+2} & \text{if } 1 \leq s \leq \sqrt{2}, \\ s & \text{if } \sqrt{2} \leq s \leq \frac{1+\sqrt{5}}{2}, \\ 1 + \frac{1}{s} & \text{if } \frac{1+\sqrt{5}}{2} \leq s. \end{cases}$$

Consider the case of three processors in the system S. Without loss of generality, throughout this section, we believe that the processors have speeds $v_1 = 1 \leq v_2 = r \leq v_3 = s$, that is, processor 1 is the slowest one, processor 2 has medium speed, and processor 3 is the fastest one.

For three processors, the PoA estimate (4.3) acquires the following form:

$$PoA(S) \leq \frac{s+r+1}{s}. \tag{4.4}$$

Construct a system of inequalities to-be-satisfied in a Nash equilibrium. Let L be an arbitrary Nash equilibrium. Denote by a the total volume of jobs on processor 2 with speed r and by $b + c$ the volume of jobs on processor 3 with speed s, where c indicates the volume of the smallest job on this processor. Then $W - a - b - c$ gives the volume of jobs on the slowest processor 1 of speed 1. In an equilibrium, an attempt to move any job j from processor l_j to another processor increases its completion time. Obviously, this is the case where several jobs are moved from one processor to another, and the following system of inequalities holds in a Nash equilibrium:

$$\frac{a}{r} \leq \frac{b+c+a}{s}, \tag{4.5a}$$

$$\frac{a}{r} \leq W - b - c, \tag{4.5b}$$

$$\frac{b+c}{s} \leq \frac{a+c}{r}, \tag{4.5c}$$

$$\frac{b+c}{s} \leq W - a - b, \tag{4.5d}$$

$$W - a - b - c \leq \frac{W - b - c}{r}, \tag{4.5e}$$

$$W - a - b - c \leq \frac{W - a}{s}. \tag{4.5f}$$

Lemma 11. *For the system S composed of three processors with speeds $1 \leq r \leq s$, in any Nash equilibrium L the social cost does not exceed $\frac{W+c}{s+1-\frac{r}{s}}$, where c is the smallest job on the processor of speed s.*

Proof. Consider an arbitrary Nash equilibrium L. We have to show that on all processors the delay is not greater than $\frac{W+c}{s+1-\frac{r}{s}}$.

Take the delay on processor 2, which equals $\frac{a}{r}$. By inequality (4.5a) it is clear that $\frac{a}{r} \leq \frac{b+c}{s-r}$ and $b \geq \frac{s-r}{r}a - c$. Condition (4.5d) leads to $b + c \leq s(W - a - b)$, whence it appears that

$$\frac{a}{r}(s - r + rs) \leq s(W - b) \leq s\left(W - \frac{s-r}{r}a + c\right),$$

and then $\frac{a}{r}(s^2 + s - r) \leq (W + c)s.$

Next, take the delay on processor 3, that is, the value $\frac{b+c}{s}$. Inequality (4.5c) yields $\frac{a}{r} \geq \frac{b+c}{s} - \frac{c}{r}$, and using (4.5b), we establish that

$$b + c \leq W - \frac{a}{r} \leq W - \frac{b+c}{s} + \frac{c}{r},$$

$$\text{and so } \frac{b+c}{s} \leq \frac{W + \frac{c}{r}}{s+1} < \frac{W+c}{s+1-\frac{r}{s}}. \tag{4.6}$$

Finally, take the delay $W - a - b - c$ on the slowest processor. In combination with the obvious identity $a = W - b - c - (W - a - b - c)$, inequality (4.5f) leads to

$$b + c \geq (s - 1)(W - a - b - c), \qquad\qquad (4.7)$$

$$b \geq (s - 1)(W - a - b - c) - c. \qquad\qquad (4.8)$$

It follows from inequality (4.5c) that

$$\frac{b + c}{s} \leq \frac{W - b - c - (W - a - b - c) + c}{r} = \frac{W - b - (W - a - b - c)}{r}.$$

Applying inequalities (4.7) and (4.8) to the left- and right-hand sides, we obtain

$$\frac{s - 1}{s}(W - a - b - c) \leq \frac{W + c - s(W - a - b - c)}{r},$$

$$\text{and so } W - a - b - c \leq \frac{W + c}{s + r - \frac{r}{s}} \leq \frac{W + c}{s + 1 - \frac{r}{s}}. \qquad \square \quad (4.9)$$

Lemma 12. *For the system S composed of three processors with speeds $1 \leq r \leq s$, the social cost does not exceed $OPT \frac{s+r+2}{s+1-\frac{r}{s}}$ in any Nash equilibrium L such that the total volume of jobs on the processor of speed s is not higher than $s \cdot OPT$.*

Proof. Consider an arbitrary Nash equilibrium L. If $s \leq r^2 + r$, then estimates (4.1) and (4.2) lead to

$$SC(L) \leq \frac{W}{s} \leq OPT \cdot \frac{s + r + 1}{s} \leq OPT \cdot \frac{s + r + 2}{s + 1 - \frac{r}{s}}.$$

Now, let $s > r^2 + r$. Take the delay on processor 2, which equals $\frac{a}{r}$. By inequality (4.5a) we obtain

$$\frac{a}{r} \leq \frac{b + c}{s - r} \leq OPT \cdot \frac{s}{s - r} < OPT \cdot \frac{s + r + 2}{s + 1 - \frac{r}{s}}.$$

Processor 3 satisfies the condition

$$\frac{b + c}{s} \leq OPT < OPT \cdot \frac{s + r + 2}{s + 1 - \frac{r}{s}}.$$

Again, inequality (4.5f) in combination with the identity $a = W - b - c - (W - a - b - c)$ yields the following chain of inequalities for the slowest processor:

$$W - a - b - c \leq \frac{b+c}{s-1} \leq OPT \cdot \frac{s}{s-1} \leq OPT \cdot \frac{s}{s-r} < OPT \cdot \frac{s+r+2}{s+1-\frac{r}{s}}. \quad \square$$

Lemma 13. *For the system S composed of three processors with speeds $1 \leq r \leq s$, the social cost does not exceed $OPT \cdot \frac{s+r+2}{s+1-\frac{r}{s}}$ in any Nash equilibrium L such that the smallest job on the processor of speed s has the volume $c > r \cdot OPT$.*

Proof. Consider an arbitrary Nash equilibrium L. If on processor 3 each job has a volume greater than $r \cdot OPT$, then in the optimal profile, all these jobs also move to this processor. In other words, their total volume is not greater than $s \cdot OPT$, that is, the condition of Lemma 12 holds. $\quad \square$

Lemma 14. *For the system S composed of three processors with speeds $1 \leq r \leq s$, the social cost does not exceed $OPT \cdot \frac{s+r+2}{s+1-\frac{r}{s}}$ in any Nash equilibrium such that on the processor of speed s the smallest job has a volume $OPT < c \leq r \cdot OPT$ and the total volume of jobs on this processor is greater than $s \cdot OPT$.*

Proof. Consider an arbitrary Nash equilibrium L. For all values $c \leq r \cdot OPT$, using estimate (4.2), we have from (4.6) that

$$\frac{b+c}{s} \leq \frac{W + \frac{c}{r}}{s+1} \leq OPT \cdot \frac{s+r+2}{s+1-\frac{r}{s}}.$$

On the other hand, it appears from (4.6) that

$$W - a - b - c \leq \frac{W+c}{s+r-\frac{r}{s}} \leq OPT \cdot \frac{s+2r+2}{s+r-\frac{r}{s}} \leq OPT \cdot \frac{s+r+2}{s+1-\frac{r}{s}}.$$

If $a \leq r \cdot OPT$, then $\frac{a}{r} \leq OPT \leq OPT \cdot \frac{s+r+2}{s+1-\frac{r}{s}}$.

Now, let $a > r \cdot OPT$. Since $b + c > s \cdot OPT$ and the volume of each job on processor 3 is greater than OPT and does not exceed $r \cdot OPT$, in the optimal profile all these jobs are assigned to processors 2 and 3 only. Their total volume makes up $b+c$. Suppose the volume of each job on processor 2 in the Nash equilibrium L is also greater than OPT. In this case, in the optimal profile all these jobs are distributed between processors 2 and 3 only, and their total volume equals a. However, then we obtain $OPT \geq \frac{a+b+c}{s+r}$, which contradicts the inequalities $a > r \cdot OPT$ and $b + c > s \cdot OPT$. Consequently, in the Nash equilibrium L, processor 2 receives at least one job of volume not greater than OPT.

Then $\frac{a}{r} \leq \frac{b+c+OPT}{s}$, whence it follows that $\frac{b+c}{s} \geq \frac{a}{r} - \frac{OPT}{s}$ and $b \geq \frac{as}{r} - OPT - c$. Using estimate (4.2) and inequality (4.5d), we immediately derive

$$\frac{a}{r} - \frac{OPT}{s} \leq \frac{b+c}{s} \leq W - b - a \leq$$
$$\leq W - \frac{as}{r} + OPT + c - a \leq$$
$$\leq OPT \cdot (r + s + 1) - \frac{as}{r} + OPT + r \cdot OPT - a,$$

and $\dfrac{a}{r} \leq OPT \cdot \dfrac{s + 2r + 2 + \frac{1}{s}}{s + r + 1} \leq OPT \cdot \dfrac{s + r + 2}{s + 1 - \frac{r}{s}}.$ $\square$

The above lemmas lead to the generalized upper estimate of the PoA value in the three-processor model as follows.

Theorem 28. *For the system S composed of three processors with speeds $1 \leq r \leq s$, the price of anarchy can be estimated by*

$$PoA(S) \leq \begin{cases} \frac{s+r+1}{s} & \text{if } s \leq r^2 + r, \\ \frac{s+r+2}{s+1-\frac{r}{s}} & \text{otherwise.} \end{cases}$$

Proof. Consider an arbitrary Nash equilibrium L. Lemmas 12, 13, and 14 dictate that $SC(L) \leq OPT \cdot \frac{s+r+2}{s+1-\frac{r}{s}}$ in all cases where the volume of each job on processor 3 of speed s exceeds OPT. In the case where processor 3 receives at least one job of volume $c \leq OPT$, this estimate follows directly from Lemma 11.

In addition, we have estimate (4.4). Since $\frac{s+r+1}{s} \leq \frac{s+r+2}{s+1-\frac{r}{s}}$ for $s \leq r^2 + r$, the desired upper estimate holds. $\square$

To proceed, demonstrate that, for speeds s and r, there exist domains where the derived upper estimates give the exact PoA value. The following statement is a particular case of Theorem 25.

Theorem 29. *For the system S composed of three processors with speeds $1 \leq r \leq s$ such that $(s - r)(s + r + 1) \leq s(s^2 - r(s + r + 1))$ and $s \leq r^2 + r$, the price of anarchy constitutes $PoA(S) = \frac{s+r+1}{s}$.*

The next theorem determines the domains of s and r where $\frac{s+r+2}{s+1-\frac{r}{s}}$ is the exact PoA value.

Theorem 30. *For the system S composed of three processors with speeds $1 \leq r \leq s$ such that $s > r^2 + r$ and $s(s^2 - r(s + r + 1)) \geq 2(rs + s - r)$, the price of anarchy makes up $PoA(S) = \frac{s+r+2}{s+1-\frac{r}{s}}$.*

Proof. As the value $\frac{s+r+2}{s+1-\frac{r}{s}}$ is the upper estimate of the PoA, it suffices to show the following. For the system S, there exist games such that the ratio of the equilibrium and optimal social cost coincides with the given estimate.

Consider a game in which five players have the jobs of volumes

$$
\begin{aligned}
w_1 &= rs(s+r+2), \\
w_2 &= s^2 + s - r, \\
w_3 &= s - r - r^2 > 0 \text{ if } s > r + r^2, \\
w_4 &= r(s^2 + s - r) \geq w_2, \\
w_5 &= s^3 + s^2 + r^2 - rs^2 - sr^2 - 3sr - s + r \geq w_2 \\
&\quad \text{if } s(s^2 - r(s+r+1)) \geq 2(rs + s - r).
\end{aligned}
$$

In a Nash equilibrium, processor 2 receives the job of volume w_1, thereby becoming the processor with the largest delay $\lambda_2 = s(s+r+2)$. Processor 3 is assigned the jobs of volumes w_2, w_4, and w_5, which results in its delay $\lambda_3 = (s-r)(s+r+2) < \lambda_2$. The slowest processor 1 deals with the job of volume w_3 and therefore has the delay $\lambda_1 = s - r - r^2 < s^2 + (2s - r) - r - r^2 = \lambda_3$. In fact, this is the smallest load among all the processors.

Let us demonstrate that this profile is a Nash equilibrium. If the job of volume w_1 moves from the most loaded processor 2 to the less loaded processor 3, then its delay remains invariable. On the other hand, as this job moves to processor 1, the delay of the latter makes up $s - r - r^2 + s^2r + sr^2 + 2rs > \lambda_2$, and if the smallest job of volume w_2 moves from processor 3 to processor 1, then its delay is also the same.

In the optimal case, processor 2 executes the job of volume w_4; processor 3 executes the jobs of volumes w_1, w_3, and w_5; and processor 1 executes the job of volume w_2. All processors have the identical delay $s^2 + s - r$. Hence, the ratio of the equilibrium and optimal social cost is $\frac{s+r+2}{s+1-\frac{r}{s}}$. $\square$

In Fig. 4.1, the domain of s and r where the price of anarchy equals $\frac{s+r+1}{s}$ is bounded by the curves $s = r^2 + r$ (from the left) and $(s-r)(s+r+1) = s(s^2 - r(s+r+1))$ (from the right). The domain bounded by the curves $s = r^2 + r$ and $2(rs + s - r) = s(s^2 - r(s+r+1))$ from the right and below, respectively, corresponds to the price of anarchy $\frac{s+r+2}{s+1-\frac{r}{s}}$.

The following theorem gives sufficient conditions for PoA increase under new processor inclusion into the system.

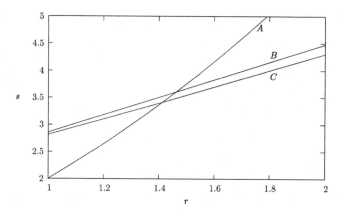

Figure 4.1 Estimation domains for $PoA(S)$: (A) curve $s = r^2 + r$, (B) curve $2(rs + s - r) = s(s^2 - r(s + r + 1))$, and (C) curve $(s - r)(s + r + 1) = s(s^2 - r(s + r + 1))$

Theorem 31. *For the system S composed of two processors with speeds $1 \le s$, the price of anarchy strictly increases as the result of adding a new processor of speed q that satisfies at least one of the following conditions:*

1) $1 \le q \le s$, $s \le q^2 + q$, and $(s - q)(s + q + 1) \le s(s^2 - q(s + q + 1))$;
2) $1 \le q \le s$, $s > q^2 + q$, $s(s^2 - q(s + q + 1)) \ge 2(qs + s - q)$, and $q > \frac{s+1}{s(s-1)}$;
3) $s < q < s^2 + s$ and $(q - s)(q + s + 1) \le q(q^2 - s(q + s + 1))$.

Proof. By estimate (4.3) the price of anarchy does not exceed $\frac{s+1}{s}$ in the system S containing two processors of speeds $1 < s$.

If $s \le q^2 + q$ and $(s - q)(s + q + 1) \le s(s^2 - q(s + q + 1))$, then by Theorem 29 the price of anarchy in the new system with three processors of speeds 1, q, and s constitutes $\frac{s+q+1}{s}$, that is, is higher than $\frac{s+1}{s}$.

Under $s > q^2 + q$ and $s(s^2 - r(s + q + 1)) \ge 2(qs + s - q)$, Theorem 30 claims that the price of anarchy in the new system equals $\frac{s+q+2}{s+1-\frac{q}{s}}$, thereby exceeding the value $\frac{s+1}{s}$ for $q > \frac{s+1}{s(s-1)}$.

Finally, in the case $s < q < s^2 + s$ and $(q - s)(q + s + 1) \le q(q^2 - s(q + s + 1))$, using Theorem 29, we obtain that the price of anarchy in the new system is $\frac{q+s+1}{q}$, which is greater than $\frac{s+1}{s}$ for $q < s^2 + s$. $\square$

4.4 A NUMERICAL METHOD TO CALCULATE THE PRICE OF ANARCHY

In the previous section, we have derived an analytical expression for the price of anarchy in the three-processor model with a rather high speed of the fastest processor. However, if the speeds of two fast processors are sufficiently close, the expression becomes cumbersome. In what follows, we suggest a computing method for the price of anarchy in the system of three processors. This method can be generalized to the systems composed of more processors. However, such a generalization increases the number of associated linear programming problems and the number of their variables and constraints.

Consider the following system of linear equations in the components of the vectors $a = (a_1, a_2, a_3)$, $b = (b_1, b_2, b_3)$, $c = (c_1, c_2, c_3)$:

$$\begin{cases} \dfrac{a_1+a_2+a_3}{v_i} \leq \dfrac{b_1+b_2+b_3+\min\limits_{k=1,2,3:a_k>0} a_k}{v_j}, \\[2ex] \dfrac{a_1+a_2+a_3}{v_i} \leq \dfrac{c_1+c_2+c_3+\min\limits_{k=1,2,3:a_k>0} a_k}{v_l}, \\[2ex] \dfrac{b_1+b_2+b_3}{v_j} \leq \dfrac{c_1+c_2+c_3+\min\limits_{k=1,2,3:b_k>0} b_k}{v_l} \quad \text{or} \quad \max\limits_{k=1,2,3} b_k = 0, \\[2ex] \dfrac{a_1+a_2+a_3}{v_i} \geq \dfrac{b_1+b_2+b_3}{v_j} \geq \dfrac{c_1+c_2+c_3}{v_l}, \\[2ex] a_k, b_k, c_k \geq 0, k = 1, 2, 3. \end{cases} \qquad (4.10)$$

This system describes a set of hyperplanes passing through the point $(0, 0, 0, 0, 0, 0, 0, 0, 0)$ in the 9D space, and the solution set is a domain in the space bounded by the hyperplanes. The system is feasible: for example, the triplet $a_1 = a_2 = a_3 = \alpha s_i$, $b_1 = b_2 = b_3 = \alpha s_j$, and $c_1 = c_2 = c_3 = \alpha s_l$ is a solution for all $\alpha > 0$. Furthermore, the solution set is unbounded, since α can be arbitrarily large.

Consider the system S composed of three processors with speeds $1 \leq r \leq s$ and n players. Let L be a Nash equilibrium in the system S such that processor i is slowest in this profile, processor j has a medium delay, and processor l is fastest. Suppose that, in the equilibrium L, processor i receives the total volume of jobs defined by $\sum\limits_{k=1,\ldots,n:l_k=i} w_k = a_1 + a_2 + a_3$ and the corresponding volumes for processors j and l are $\sum\limits_{k=1,\ldots,n:l_k=j} w_k = b_1 + b_2 + b_3$ and $\sum\limits_{k=1,\ldots,n:l_k=l} w_k = c_1 + c_2 + c_3$, respectively. The volume of jobs on each processor is somehow divided into three parts so that each component of the 3D vectors a, b, and c is either zero or positive and includes at least one job.

Lemma 15. *Let L be a Nash equilibrium in the game involving three processors i, j and l and n players such that*

$$\lambda_i(L) \geq \lambda_j(L) \geq \lambda_l(L),$$

$$\sum_{k=1,\ldots,n:l_k=i} w_k = a_1 + a_2 + a_3,$$

$$\sum_{k=1,\ldots,n:l_k=j} w_k = b_1 + b_2 + b_3,$$

$$\sum_{k=1,\ldots,n:l_k=l} w_k = c_1 + c_2 + c_3.$$

Here, for all $k = 1, 2, 3$, the component a_k is zero or the volume of at least one job on processor i, the component b_k is zero or the volume of at least one job on processor j, and the component c_k is zero or the volume of at least one job on processor l. Then the set of the vectors a, b, and c is a solution of system (4.10).

Proof. Suppose L forms a Nash equilibrium and $\lambda_i(L) \geq \lambda_j(L) \geq \lambda_l(L)$. In this case, the following inequalities hold:

$$
\begin{cases}
\dfrac{\sum\limits_{k=1,\ldots,n:l_k=i} w_k}{v_i} \leq \dfrac{\sum\limits_{k=1,\ldots,n:l_k=j} w_k + \min\limits_{k=1,\ldots,n:l_k=i,w_k>0} w_k}{v_j}, \\[4mm]
\dfrac{\sum\limits_{k=1,\ldots,n:l_k=i} w_k}{v_i} \leq \dfrac{\sum\limits_{k=1,\ldots,n:l_k=l} w_k + \min\limits_{k=1,\ldots,n:l_k=i,w_k>0} w_k}{v_l}, \\[4mm]
\dfrac{\sum\limits_{k=1,\ldots,n:l_k=j} w_k}{v_j} \leq \dfrac{\sum\limits_{k=1,\ldots,n:l_k=l} w_k + \min\limits_{k=1,\ldots,n:l_k=j,w_k>0} w_k}{v_l}, \quad \text{or} \quad \max\limits_{k=1,\ldots,n:l_k=i} w_k = 0, \\[4mm]
\dfrac{\sum\limits_{k=1,\ldots,n:l_k=i} w_k}{v_i} \geq \dfrac{\sum\limits_{k=1,\ldots,n:l_k=j} w_k}{v_j} \geq \dfrac{\sum\limits_{k=1,\ldots,n:l_k=l} w_k}{v_l}.
\end{cases}
$$

Since each nonzero value a_k $(k = 1, 2, 3)$ equals the volume of at least one job on processor i, we naturally have $\min\limits_{k:a_k>0} a_k \geq \min\limits_{k:l_k=i,w_k>0} w_k$. In a similar manner, $\min\limits_{k:a_k>0} a_k \geq \min\limits_{k:l_k=i,w_k>0} w_k$ and $\min\limits_{k:b_k>0} b_k \geq \min\limits_{k:l_k=j,w_k>0} w_k$. This means satisfaction of system (4.10).   □

Lemma 16. *Any solution of system (4.10) defines a Nash equilibrium L in the game involving the system S composed of three processors i, j, and l and the players whose jobs correspond to the nonzero components of the vectors a, b, and c and delays are sorted in the order $\lambda_i(L) \geq \lambda_j(L) \geq \lambda_l(L)$.*

Proof. Let the set of the vectors a, b, and c give a solution of system (4.10). Consider the game with three processors i, j, and l. Let each nonzero component of the vectors a, b, and c specify the job volume of a successive player. Consider a profile L such that the jobs of volumes $a_k > 0$, $b_k > 0$, and c_k are assigned to processors i, j, and l, respectively. As all inequalities (4.10) hold, the profile L gives the desired Nash equilibrium.   □

The following result is immediate.

Theorem 32. *Any Nash equilibrium L in the game involving the system S composed of three processors i, j, and l and n players corresponds to a Nash equilibrium L' in the game involving the same system S and at most nine players in which each processor receives no more than three jobs and the delays on all processors in L and L' coincide.*

Proof. Consider a Nash equilibrium L in the game with the system S of three processors and n players. Number the processors so that $\lambda_i(L) \geq \lambda_j(L) \geq \lambda_l(L)$. By Lemma 15, for any Nash equilibrium in the game involving the system S and any number of players, there exists a corresponding solution a, b, c of system (4.10). By Lemma 16 this solution determines a Nash equilibrium L' in the game with the system S such that the nonzero components of the vectors a, b, and c specify the job volumes on processors i, j, and l, respectively. By definition the element sum of the vector a is the load of processor i in a profile L. Hence the delays on processor i coincide in the equilibria L and L'. Similarly, for processors j and l, the delays in the equilibrium L coincide with the corresponding delays in the equilibrium L'.   □

This theorem claims that it is sufficient to consider only the games where each processor receives at most three jobs in an equilibrium and the equilibrium is the solution of system (4.10). In addition, the domain of the social cost coincides with the value domain of the games with an arbitrary number of players.

Let the components of the vectors a, b, and c be chosen as follows. In the optimal profile yielding the minimum social cost, processors i, j, and l receive the total volumes of jobs $a_1 + b_1 + c_1$, $a_2 + b_2 + c_2$, and $a_3 + b_3 + c_3$, respectively, and the highest delay can be on each of them. Furthermore, by Theorem 27 the volumes of jobs are assumed to be normalized so that in the optimal profile the maximal delay among all processors is 1. In our case, this means that

$$a_1 + b_1 + c_1 \leq v_i,$$
$$a_2 + b_2 + c_2 \leq v_j,$$
$$a_3 + b_3 + c_3 \leq v_l,$$

and at least one of these inequalities holds as an equality.

Lemma 17. *A solution of the linear programming problem*

$$LPP(v_i, v_j, v_l) : \begin{cases} a_1 + a_2 + a_3 \to \max \\[4pt] (r1) \quad \frac{a_1+a_2+a_3}{v_i} \leq \frac{b_1+b_2+b_3+\min\limits_{k:a_k>0} a_k}{v_j}, \\[8pt] (r2) \quad \frac{a_1+a_2+a_3}{v_i} \leq \frac{c_1+c_2+c_3+\min\limits_{k:a_k>0} a_k}{v_l}, \\[8pt] (r3) \quad \frac{b_1+b_2+b_3}{v_j} \leq \frac{c_1+c_2+c_3+\min\limits_{k:b_k>0} b_k}{v_l} \ or \ \max\limits_{k=1,2,3} b_k = 0, \\[8pt] (r4) \quad \frac{a_1+a_2+a_3}{v_i} \geq \frac{b_1+b_2+b_3}{v_j} \geq \frac{c_1+c_2+c_3}{v_l}, \\[6pt] (r5) \quad a_k, b_k, c_k \geq 0, k = 1, 2, 3, \\[4pt] (r6) \quad a_1 + b_1 + c_1 \leq v_i, \\[4pt] (r7) \quad a_2 + b_2 + c_2 \leq v_j, \\[4pt] (r8) \quad a_3 + b_3 + c_3 \leq v_l \end{cases} \tag{4.11}$$

with respect to the components of the vectors a, b, and c gives the maximal social cost in a Nash equilibrium among all games where in an equilibrium at most three jobs are assigned to each processor, i, j, and l indicate the numbers of the processors in the descending order of their delays, and the optimal social cost makes up 1.

Proof. By Lemma 16, any solution of inequalities $(r1)$–$(r5)$ in the problem $LPP(v_i, v_j, v_l)$ defines an equilibrium in the game with three processors where each processor receives at most three jobs and i, j, and l are the numbers of the processors in the descending order of their delays.

The goal function in this problem is bounded above only by the hyperplanes corresponding to inequalities $(r6)$–$(r8)$. Actually, inequalities $(r1)$–$(r5)$ admit arbitrarily large values of the goal function, for example, for the solution $a_1 = a_2 = a_3 = \alpha v_i$ with any value $\alpha > 0$, $b_1 = b_2 = b_3 = \alpha v_j$, and $c_1 = c_2 = c_3 = \alpha v_l$. Therefore, the maximum is reached on one of the boundaries related to the last three inequalities. Hence, one of them holds as equality, and the optimal cost in the game corresponding to the solution of the problem $LPP(v_i, v_j, v_l)$ is 1. □

Consequently, for exact PoA evaluation in the system S composed of three processors, it is necessary to solve a series of the linear programming problems $LPP(v_i, v_j, v_l)$ for all permutations $(1, r, s)$, and the maximal solution among them yields the value $PoA(S)$. In other words, we may establish the following fact.

Theorem 33. *For the system S composed of three processors, the price of anarchy constitutes*

$$PoA(S) = \max_{(v_i, v_j, v_l) \text{ are permutations } (1, r, s)} \left\{ \frac{a_1 + a_2 + a_3}{v_i} \mid a, b, c \text{ is a solution of } LPP(v_i, v_j, v_l) \right\},$$

where $LPP(v_i, v_j, v_l)$ is the linear programming problem (4.11).

Proof. By Lemma 17 the solution of problem (4.11) gives the maximal social cost in a Nash equilibrium, where i, j, and l are the numbers of the processors in the descending order of their delays, among all the games such that in an equilibrium each processor receives at most three jobs and the optimal cost is 1. The maximal solution among the problems for all admissible permutations $(1, r, s)$ as the values of (v_i, v_j, v_l) gives the maximal social cost in a Nash equilibrium among all the games where in an equilibrium at most three jobs are assigned to each processor and the optimal cost is 1.

By Theorem 32, for any equilibrium in the game involving the system S of three processors and an arbitrary number of players, it is possible to construct a corresponding equilibrium in the game with the same processors and a set of at most nine players, where each processor receives no more than three jobs, and the social cost coincides in both equilibria. Thus, for PoA evaluation, it suffices to consider only the games where each processor has at most three jobs in an equilibrium.

Using Theorem 27, we finally establish that, for PoA evaluation, it suffices to consider only the games where the social cost in the optimal profile is 1.   □

4.5 COMPUTING EXPERIMENTS

To estimate the price of anarchy in the three-processor model, we have developed a program for a visual comparison of the upper PoA estimates and its exact value constructed by solving a series of the linear programming problems. The parameters of the system S are adjusted in the program; by assumption the speed of processor 1 is 1, whereas an exact value and a certain range are specified for the speeds of processors 2 and 3, respectively. This approach allows us to study the PoA dynamics under a varying speed of one processor.

The graphs in Figs. 4.2 and 4.3 illustrate the PoA estimates under the speeds $r = 2$ and $r = 5$ of processor 2, respectively. The speed of processor 1

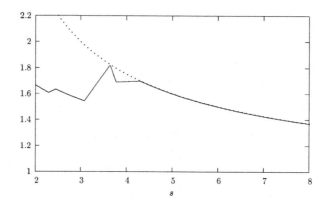

Figure 4.2 PoA estimate for system S with $r = 2$, $s \in [2, 8]$

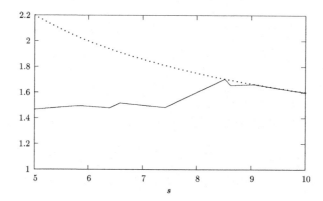

Figure 4.3 PoA estimate for system S with $r = 5$, $s \in [5, 10]$

is 1, and the speed of processor 3 (the parameter s) increases from r. The dotted line indicates the generalized upper estimate for the price of anarchy, and the solid line indicates its exact value.

CHAPTER 5

Cover Game

Contents

The cover problem of computing network nodes or processors represents another modification of the scheduling problem and is also considered in the form of a game equivalent to the KP-model with parallel different-capacity channels but with the following distinctive feature. Unlike the setup studied in the previous chapter (maximal delay minimization), here the system objective is to maximize the minimal delay among all processors. Again, it is necessary to distribute several jobs of various volumes among processors of nonidentical speeds. The volume of a job is its completion time on a free unit-speed processor. Processor load is the total volume of jobs executed by a given processor. The ratio of processor load and speed defines its delay, that is, the job completion time by this processor. The players also have egoistic behavior and reach a Nash equilibrium. Only pure strategies are considered in the cover game, which always exist for these problems. The system payoff (also called the social payoff) is the minimal delay over all processors for an obtained job distribution. The price of anarchy (PoA) is defined as the maximal ratio of the optimal social payoff and the social payoff in the worst-case Nash equilibrium.

The problem setup where a system seeks to maximize the minimal delay among all nodes originated from the concept of fair sharing and efficient utilization of network resources. Epstein et al. [27] were the first who analyzed the efficiency of equilibria in this model and also illustrated the motivation for such optimality criteria using several examples. The main idea is that all elements of the system must be loaded as much as possible with minimum possible downtime. For example, if each player pays the amount of his delay to the system for execution of his job, then (1) there must be no "privileged" players paying considerably smaller than the other owing to a successful choice of processor, and (2) there must be no processors with small profit or without any profit at all.

Networking Games
https://doi.org/10.1016/B978-0-12-816551-5.00011-3

Copyright © 2019 Elsevier Inc.
All rights reserved.

In what follows, we derive a lower estimate for the PoA in the cases of three or more processors [22] and find the exact PoA value for three heterogeneous processors. Moreover, in the case of two processors, we establish that the PoA remains invariable or increases under new processor inclusion into the system. In the case of three processors, we propose a computing algorithm of the exact PoA value based on solving a series of linear programming problems. If necessary, the algorithm can be extended to the case of an arbitrary number of processors.

5.1 A MODEL OF THE COVER GAME

Consider a system $S = S(N, v)$ composed of N processors operating with speeds $v_1 = 1 \leq \cdots \leq v_N = s$. Note that such a choice of processor speeds in the system does not violate generality: it is always possible to normalize the speeds using division by the speed of the slowest processor. The system is used by a set of players $U = U(n, w)$: each of n players chooses an appropriate processor for his job execution. For player j, the volume of job is $w_j, j = 1, \ldots, n$. Denote by $W = \sum_{j=1}^{n} w_j$ the total volume of all jobs. Free processor i with speed v_i executes a job of volume w during the time w/v_i.

We study the following pure strategy game $\Gamma = \langle S(N, v), U(n, w), \lambda \rangle$. Each player can choose any processor. The strategy of player j is processor l_j selected by him for his job execution. Then the strategy profile in the game Γ represents the vector $L = (l_1, \ldots, l_n)$. The load of processor i, that is, the total volume of all jobs assigned to the processor is defined by $\delta_i(L) = \sum_{j=1,\ldots,n:l_j=i} w_j$. The delay of processor i takes the form

$$\lambda_i(L) = \sum_{j=1,\ldots,n:l_j=i} w_j/v_i = \frac{\delta_i(L)}{v_i}.$$

In fact, this value is the same for all players selecting a given processor.

Suppose that the system objective is to minimize the delay of the least loaded processor, that is, to maximize its job completion time or delay. The social payoff is described by the minimal delay over all processors:

$$SC(L) = \min_{i=1,\ldots,N} \lambda_i(L).$$

Define the optimal payoff (the social payoff in the optimal case) as

$$OPT = OPT(S, U) = \max_{L \text{ is a profile in } \Gamma(S,U,\lambda)} SC(L),$$

where maximization runs over all admissible strategy profiles in the game $\Gamma(S, U, \lambda)$.

A strategy profile L such that none of the players benefits from a unilateral deviation (change of the processor chosen in L for his job execution) is a pure strategy Nash equilibrium. To provide a formal definition, let $L(j \to i) = (l_1, \ldots, l_{j-1}, i, l_{j+1}, \ldots, l_n)$ be the profile obtained from a profile L if player j replaces processor l_j chosen by him in the profile L for another processor i, whereas the remaining players use the same strategies as before (remain invariable).

Definition 30. A strategy profile L is said to be a pure strategy Nash equilibrium if and only if each player chooses a processor with the minimum delay, that is, for each player $j = 1, \ldots, n$, we have the inequality $\lambda_{l_j}(L) \le \lambda_i(L(j \to i))$ for all processors $i = 1, \ldots, N$.

Definition 31. The price of anarchy in the system S is the maximal ratio of the optimal social payoff and the social payoff in the worst-case Nash equilibrium:

$$PoA(S) = \max_U \frac{OPT(S, U)}{\min_{L \text{ is a Nash equilibrium in } \Gamma(S,U,\lambda)} SC(L)}.$$

5.2 THE PRICE OF ANARCHY IN THE GENERAL CASE OF N PROCESSORS

In this section, we present some assumptions and auxiliary results that will be fruitful for further analysis.

Consider $N \ge 2$ processors with speeds $v_1 = 1 \le \cdots \le v_N = s$. If the number of jobs n is smaller than the number of processors N, then obviously the system has zero payoff in any strategy profile. In this case, the ratio of the optimal social payoff and the social payoff in the worst-case Nash equilibrium is assumed to be 1. We further let $n \ge N$.

If $s \ge 2$, then the price of anarchy is infinite [27]. This can be easily demonstrated by studying an example of N jobs with the same volume s. Clearly, in the optimal strategy profile, each job is executed by a separate processor, and the social payoff equals 1. Note that the worst-case Nash equilibrium is the strategy profile in which two jobs are executed by the fastest processor with delay $\frac{2s}{s} = 2 \le s$ and there is a free processor in the system. In this case, the social payoff equals 0, whereas the price of anarchy becomes infinite. From this point onwards, we make the assumption $s < 2$. If the number of jobs n coincides with or exceeds the number of processors N, then all processors are naturally busy in the optimal case. Furthermore, then all processors remain busy in any equilibrium.

The optimal social payoff can be obviously estimated as

$$OPT \le \frac{W}{\sum\limits_{i=1}^{N} v_i}, \tag{5.1}$$

since the minimal delay on a processor is not greater than in the case of the same delay on all processors.

The following lemmas gives estimates for the equilibrium delays and volumes of some jobs on processors. For a complete exposition, we will also provide proofs for the lemmas imported from other publications.

Lemma 18. *(Tan et al. [79].) If the total number of jobs n is not smaller than the number of processors N, then, for any equilibrium, the loads of all processors exceed zero.*

Proof. Consider an arbitrary equilibrium L. Let some processor i have zero load. Then there exists a processor k that executes at least two jobs. As $v_1 = 1 \le \cdots \le v_N = s < 2$, we obtain $v_i > \frac{v_k}{2}$. Let w_k be the volume of the smallest job on processor k. If it moves to a free processor i, then its delay becomes $\frac{w_k}{v_i} < \frac{2w_k}{v_k} \le \lambda_k(L)$, thereby decreasing in comparison with the delay in the strategy profile L. □

For a strategy profile L, denote by n_k the number of jobs on processor k.

Lemma 19. *(Tan et al. [79].) If L is an equilibrium and $SC(L) = \lambda_i(L)$, then, for any processor k, the inequality $n_k > \frac{v_k}{v_i}$ implies the inequality $\lambda_k(L) \le \frac{n_k v_i}{n_k v_i - v_k} \lambda_i(L)$.*

Proof. Let w be the volume of the smallest job on processor k. Then $w \le \frac{v_k}{n_k} \lambda_k(L)$. Since L represents an equilibrium, we have $\lambda_k(L) \le \lambda_i(L) + \frac{w}{v_i} \le \lambda_i(L) + \frac{v_k}{n_k v_i}$, whence it follows that $\lambda_k(L) \le \frac{n_k v_i}{n_k v_i - v_k} \lambda_i(L)$. □

Lemma 20. *If L is an equilibrium and $SC(L) = \lambda_i(L)$, then, for any processor k, the inequalities $n_k \ge 2$ and $1 \le \frac{v_k}{v_i} < 2$ imply that the volume of any job w_j on processor k does not exceed $\frac{v_i v_k}{2v_i - v_k} \lambda_i(L)$. Furthermore, the total volume of the other jobs on processor k is also not greater than $\frac{v_i v_k}{2v_i - v_k} \lambda_i(L)$.*

Proof. Suppose processor k executes at least two jobs. Let w be the volume of the smallest job on processor k. Then the volume of the other jobs on processor k makes up $v_k \lambda_k(L) - w$. Since L is an equilibrium, $\lambda_k(L) = \frac{v_k \lambda_k(L)}{v_k} \le \lambda_i(L) + \frac{w}{v_i}$, which yields $v_k \lambda_k(L) - w \le v_k \lambda_i(L) + \left(\frac{v_k}{v_i} - 1\right) w \le v_k \lambda_i(L) + \left(\frac{v_k}{v_i} - 1\right) w_{j:l_j=k} \le v_k \lambda_i(L) + \left(\frac{v_k}{v_i} - 1\right)(v_k \lambda_k(L) - w)$. Then $w \le w_{j:l_j=k} \le v_k \lambda_k(L) - w \le \frac{v_i v_k}{2v_i - v_k} \lambda_i(L)$. $\qquad\square$

The next theorem establishes a lower estimate for the price of anarchy in the system with $N \ge 3$ processors. This estimate is defined by the speeds of three processors in the system, namely, the first and second ones (in fact, the slowest processors) and the last processor, which has the highest speed.

Theorem 34. *For the system S composed of $N \ge 3$ processors with speeds $v_1 = 1 \le v_2 = r \le v_3 \le \cdots \le v_N = s < 2$, the price of anarchy is not smaller than*

$$est(r, s) = \min \left\{ \frac{2 + s}{(1 + r)(2 - s)}, \frac{2}{r(2 - s)} \right\}. \tag{5.2}$$

Proof. To obtain this upper estimate for the price of anarchy, it suffices to give examples of systems S yielding the ratios of the optimal and worst-case equilibrium payoffs stated by the theorem. Suppose each processor i in the system S has a speed v_i for all $i = 1, \ldots, N$.

1. First, let $rs \le 2$. Then $est(r, s) = \frac{2+s}{(1+r)(2-s)}$. Consider a set of jobs $w_1 = w_2 = (1 + r)s$, $w_3^i = v_i(2 + s)$, where $i = 3 \ldots, N$, $w_4 = 2r - s$, and $w_5 = 2 - rs$. In a strategy profile L, the jobs of volumes w_1 and w_2 are assigned to processor N, each job of volume w_3^i, $i = 3 \ldots, N$, to processor $i - 1$, and the jobs of volumes w_4 and w_5 to processor 1. We demonstrate that this is an equilibrium and calculate the social payoff.

The loads on processors N and 1 are $2s(1 + r)$ and $(1 + r)(2 - s)$, respectively. For each of processors $i = 2, \ldots, N - 1$, the load makes up $v_{i+1}(2 + s)$. Since $\lambda_N(L) = 2(1 + r) > (1 + r)(2 - s) = \lambda_1(L)$ and $\lambda_i(L) = \frac{v_{i+1}(2+s)}{v_i} \ge (1 + r)(2 - s) = \lambda_1(L)$, $i = 2, \ldots, N - 1$, in view of $2 + s > 1 + r$, $v_{i+1} \ge v_i$, and $2 - s \le 1$, we find that processor 1 has the smallest delay coinciding with its load.

Denote by $\lambda_i^j(L) = \lambda_i(L) + \frac{w_j}{v_i}$ the delay on processor i in the case where job j deviates from the strategy profile L, moving to processor i from another processor. The job of volume w_1 or w_2 does not move to processor i, $i = 2, \ldots, N - 1$, due to the inequality $\lambda_N(L) = 2(1 + r) \le (2 + s) + (1 + r) \le \frac{v_{i+1}(2+s)+s(1+r)}{v_i} = \lambda_i^1(L) = \lambda_i^2(L)$. In addition, this job does not move to processor 1, since $\lambda_N(L) = 2(1 + r) = (1 + r)(2 - s) + s(1 + r) = \lambda_1^1(L) = \lambda_1^2(L)$.

Each of the jobs of volumes w_3^i, $i = 3, \ldots, N$, does not move to processor N because of $\lambda_{i-1}(L) = \frac{v_i(2+s)}{v_{i-1}} \leq 2(1+r) + \frac{v_i(2+s)}{s} = \lambda_N^{i3}(L)$, which is equivalent to the inequality $(s - v_{i-1})v_i(2+s) \leq 2sv_{i-1}(1+r)$; the latter follows from $s - v_{i-1} < 1$, $2 + s < 4$, and $2\frac{s}{v_i}v_{i-1}(1+r) \geq 4$. Besides, none of the jobs of volumes w_3^i, $i = 3, \ldots, N$, moves to processor $j > i - 1$, as follows from the conditions $\lambda_{i-1}(L) = \frac{v_i(2+s)}{v_{i-1}} < \frac{2v_i(2+s)}{v_j} \leq \frac{(v_i+v_j)(2+s)}{v_j} = \lambda_j^{i3}(L)$. Finally, the job of volume w_3^i does not move to the slower processor 1 or $j < i - 1$, and none of the jobs executed by processor 1 moves to another processor because this processor has the minimal delay. Therefore, the strategy profile under consideration is an equilibrium with the social payoff $(1+r)(2-s)$.

Consider a strategy profile in which each job of volume w_3^i, $i = 3, \ldots, N$, is assigned to processor i, the jobs of volumes w_1 and w_4 to processor 2, and the jobs of volumes w_2 and w_5 to processor 1. In this strategy profile, the social payoff is $2 + s$, and hence $OPT \geq 2 + s$.

2. Now, let $rs > 2$. Then $est(r,s) = \frac{2}{r(2-s)}$. Consider the set of jobs of volumes $w_1 = w_2 = rs$, $w_3^i = 2v_i$, $i = 3, \ldots, N$, and $w_4 = r(2-s)$. In a strategy profile L, the jobs of volumes w_1 and w_2 are assigned to processor N, each job of volume w_3^i, $i = 3, \ldots, N$, to processor $i - 1$, and the job of volume w_4 to processor 1. Let us show that this is an equilibrium and find the social payoff.

Since $\lambda_N(L) = 2r > r(2-s) = \lambda_1(L)$ and $\lambda_i(L) = \frac{2v_{i+1}}{v_i} \geq r(2-s) = \lambda_1(L)$, $i = 2, \ldots, N - 1$, owing to $\frac{2}{s} \geq 1$, $v_{i+1} \geq r$, and $2 - s < 1$, processor 1 has the minimal delay equal to $r(2-s)$. The job of volume w_1 or w_2 does not move to processor i, $i = 2, \ldots, N - 1$, due to the inequality $\lambda_N(L) = 2r = r + r \leq \frac{2v_{i+1}+rs}{v_i} = \lambda_i^1(L) = \lambda_i^2(L)$. In addition, this job does not move to processor 1, since $\lambda_N(L) = 2r = r(2-s) + rs = \lambda_1^1(L) = \lambda_1^2(L)$. Each of the jobs of volumes w_3^i, $i = 3, \ldots, N$, does not move to processor N because of $\lambda_{i-1}(L) = \frac{2v_i}{v_{i-1}} \leq 2r + \frac{2v_i}{v_i} = \lambda_N^{i3}(L)$, which holds by $\frac{2v_i(s-v_{i-1})}{s} \leq 2rv_i$. Besides, none of the jobs of volumes w_3^i, $i = 3, \ldots, N$, moves to processor $j > i - 1$, as follows from the conditions $\lambda_{i-1}(L) = \frac{2v_i}{v_{i-1}} \leq \frac{4v_i}{v_j} \leq \frac{2(v_i+v_j)}{v_j} = \lambda_j^{i3}(L)$. Finally, the job of volume w_3^i does not move to the slower processor 1 or $j < i - 1$, and none of the jobs executed by processor 1 moves to another processor with the same or greater delay. Therefore, the strategy profile under consideration is an equilibrium with the social payoff $r(2-s)$.

Consider a strategy profile in which each job of volume w_3^i, $i = 3, \ldots, N$, is assigned to processor i, the jobs of volumes w_1 and w_4 to processor 2, and the job of volumes w_2 to processor 1. In this strategy profile, the social payoff is 2, and hence $OPT \geq 2$.

In both cases under study, the ratio of the optimal and worst-case equilibrium payoffs takes the value $est(r, s)$, and consequently the price of anarchy is not smaller than this value.   ☐

In accordance with estimate (5.2), as the speed of the fastest processor increases and tends to 2, the lower estimate of the PoA has infinite growth. Thus, we may formulate the following corollary of Theorem 34.

Corollary 2. *For the system S composed of $N \geq 3$ processors with speeds $v_1 = 1 \leq v_2 = r \leq v_3 \leq \cdots \leq v_N = s < 2$, the price of anarchy goes to infinity as $s \to 2 - 0$.*

As shown by the next result, for PoA calculation it suffices to consider only the games in which the optimal social payoff is 1.

Theorem 35. *For the system S, the price of anarchy makes up*

$$PoA(S) = \max_{U_1 : OPT(S, U_1) = 1} \frac{1}{\min_{L \text{ is a Nash equilibrium in } \Gamma(S, U_1, \lambda)} SC(L)}.$$

Proof. For proving this theorem, we will demonstrate that in any game $\Gamma(S, U, \lambda)$ the volumes of jobs can be normalized so that the optimal payoff is 1 whereas the ratio of the optimal and worst-case equilibrium payoffs remains invariable.

Let L be the worst-case equilibrium in the game $\Gamma(S, U, \lambda)$ with an arbitrary set of players $U(n, w)$, where the volume of job of each player j is w_j, and L_{OPT} denotes the optimal strategy profile in this game. The social payoffs in the strategy profile L and in the optimal strategy profile are SC and OPT, respectively. The ratio of the optimal and worst-case equilibrium payoffs is $\frac{OPT}{SC}$. Since L represents an equilibrium, for any player j, we have

$$\frac{\sum\limits_{k=1,\dots,n : l_k = l_j} w_k}{v_{l_j}} \leq \frac{\sum\limits_{k=1,\dots,n : l_k = i} w_k + w_j}{v_i} \text{ for any processor } i.$$

Now, consider the game with the same set of processors and players in which the volume of job assigned to each player j is $\frac{w_j}{OPT}$. The social payoffs in the strategy profiles L and L_{OPT} are $\frac{SC}{OPT}$ and 1, respectively. Owing to the linear homogeneity of delays on processors with respect to their loads, the strategy profiles L and L_{OPT} form the worst-case equilibrium and the optimal strategy profile, respectively, in the new game. Particularly, L is an equilibrium in the new game, since for any player j, the inequal-

ity $\dfrac{\sum\limits_{k=1,\dots,n : l_k = l_j} w_k}{v_{l_j} OPT} \leq \dfrac{\sum\limits_{k=1,\dots,n : l_k = i} w_k + w_j}{v_i OPT}$ holds for any processor i. Let L be not the worst-case equilibrium in the new game. Then this game possesses an equilibrium L' with the social payoff $\frac{SC'}{OPT}$ such that $\frac{SC'}{OPT} < \frac{SC}{OPT}$ (i.e., the social payoff in L' is smaller than in L). Then in the original game the strategy profile L' yields the social payoff $SC' < SC$, and hence the equilibrium L' is worse than the equilibrium L. Similarly, L_{OPT} is the optimal strategy profile in the new game. As a result, in the new game the ratio of the optimal and worst-case equilibrium payoffs also constitutes $\frac{OPT}{SC}$.

Consequently, any game $\Gamma(S, U, \lambda)$ is associated with a game $\Gamma(S, U_1, \lambda)$ in which the volumes of jobs are normalized so that $OPT(S, U_1) = 1$. Yet, both games have the same ratio of the optimal and worst-case equilibrium payoffs. This means that, for PoA calculation, we may consider only the games in which the optimal payoff is 1. □

5.3 THE PRICE OF ANARCHY IN THE CASE OF THREE PROCESSORS

Note that, in the case of two processors with speeds $1 \leq s$, the exact PoA value was found in [79]:

$$\begin{cases} \frac{2+s}{(1+s)(2-s)} & \text{for } 1 \leq s \leq \sqrt{2}, \\ \frac{2}{s(2-s)} & \text{for } \sqrt{2} < s < 2. \end{cases}$$

For a particular case of three processors with speeds $1 = 1 \leq s$, the cited authors also calculated the price of anarchy

$$\frac{2+s}{2(2-s)} \text{ for } 1 \leq s < 2.$$

Now, analyze the case where the system S consists of three heterogeneous processors. Without loss of generality, in this section, we consider the systems S in which $v_1 = 1 \leq v_2 = r \leq v_3 = s$, that is, processor 1 is the slowest one, processor 2 has medium speed, and processor 3 is the fastest one.

Lemma 21. *For the system S composed of three processors with speeds $v_1 = 1 \leq v_2 = r \leq v_3 = s$, the inequality $OPT \leq \frac{W - w_k}{1+r}$ holds for any job of volume w_k.*

Proof. Suppose there exists a job of volume w_k assigned to processor i in the optimal strategy profile L and $OPT > \frac{W - w_k}{1+r}$. Then the optimal delays on all processors exceed $\frac{W - w_k}{1+r}$. In addition, it is clear that $\lambda_i(L) \geq \frac{w_k}{v_i}$, and hence $W = v_i \lambda_i(L) + v_j \lambda_j(L) + v_l \lambda_l(L) > w_k + (v_j + v_l) \frac{W - w_k}{1+r} \geq w_k + (1+r) \times \frac{W - w_k}{1+r} = W$. □

Lemma 22. *For the system S composed of three processors with speeds $v_1 = 1 \leq v_2 = r \leq v_3 = s$, let two jobs of volumes w_{k_1} and w_{k_2} be assigned to the same processor in the optimal strategy profile. Then $OPT \leq \frac{W - w_{k_1} - w_{k_2}}{1+r}$.*

Proof. Suppose $OPT > \frac{W - w_{k_1} - w_{k_2}}{1+r}$ and the jobs of volumes w_{k_1} and w_{k_2} are assigned to processor i in the optimal strategy profile. In this case, the optimal delays on all processors are greater than $\frac{W - w_{k_1} - w_{k_2}}{1+r}$, and $\lambda_i(L) \geq \frac{w_{k_1} + w_{k_2}}{v_i}$. As a result, $W = v_i \lambda_i(L) + v_j \lambda_j(L) + v_l \lambda_l(L) > w_{k_1} + w_{k_2} + (v_j + v_l)\frac{W - w_{k_1} - w_{k_2}}{1+r} \geq w_{k_1} + w_{k_2} + (1 + r)\frac{W - w_{k_1} - w_{k_2}}{1+r} = W$. $\square$

We will need a series of auxiliary lemmas to prove the forthcoming theorems.

Lemma 23. *For any real values $1 \leq r \leq s < 2$, we have $s \leq \min\{\frac{2+s}{(1+r)(2-s)}, \frac{2}{r(2-s)}\}$.*

Proof. The inequality $\frac{2}{r(2-s)} \geq \frac{2}{s(2-s)} \geq s$ holds, since $s^3 - 2s^2 + 2 = s(s-1)^2 + (2 - s) > 0$.

On the other hand, we have $\frac{2+s}{(1+r)(2-s)} \geq \frac{2+s}{(1+s)(2-s)} \geq s$ by $s^3 - s^2 - s + 2 > s^3 - 2s^2 + 2 = s(s-1)^2 + (2 - s) > 0$. $\square$

Lemma 24. *For any real values $1 \leq r \leq s < 2$, we have $\frac{3s}{1+r} \leq \min\{\frac{2+s}{(1+r)(2-s)}, \frac{2}{r(2-s)}\}$.*

Proof. First, observe that $3s \leq \frac{2+s}{2-s}$ since $3s^2 - 5s + 2 = (s - 1)(3s - 2) > 0$. Second, the inequality $\frac{3s}{1+r} \leq \frac{2}{r(2-s)}$ is valid because $6rs - 3rs^2 - 2 - 2r = r(6s - 3s^2 - 2) - 2 = r(1 - 3(s - 1)^2) - 2 \leq r - 2 < 0$. $\square$

Lemma 25. *For $v_i < v_j$, where $v_i, v_j \in \{1, r, s\}$ with real values r, s such that $1 \leq r \leq s < 2$, we have $\frac{2v_i^2 + v_i v_j}{2v_i - v_j} \leq \frac{2+s}{2-s}$.*

Proof. If $v_i < v_j$, then the expression $\frac{2v_i^2 + v_i v_j}{2v_i - v_j}$ is decreasing in v_i and increasing in v_j, since $4v_i^2 - 4v_i v_j - v_j^2 < 0$ and $v_i(2v_i - v_j) + 2v_i^2 + v_i v_j > 0$. $\square$

Lemma 26. *For any real values $1 \leq r \leq s < 2$, we have $\frac{2r^2 + rs}{(1+r)(2r-s)} < \frac{2}{r(2-s)}$.*

Proof. The desired inequality is equivalent to $f(r, s) = -r^2 s^2 - 2s(r^3 - r^2 - r - 1) + 4(r^3 - r^2 - r) < 0$. We will verify this condition by showing that $f_r'(r, s) = -2rs^2 + 2(2 - s)(3r^2 - 2r - 1) < 0$, which yields $f(r, s) \leq f(1, s) = -s^2 + 4s - 4 = -(2 - s)^2 < 0$.

For each fixed s, the function $f'_r(r, s)$ represents a parabola with ascending branches. Hence, the maximal value is achieved at one of the limits of the interval $r \in [1, s]$. At the left limit, we have $f'_r(1, s) = -2s^2 < 0$; at the right limit, $f'_r(s, s) = -8s^3 + 16s^2 - 6s - 4 = -8s(s - 1)^2 - 2(2 - s) < 0$.   □

Lemma 27. *For $v_i \neq v_j \neq v_l$, where $v_i, v_j, v_l \in \{1, r, s\}$ with real values r, s such that $1 \leq r \leq s < 2$, we have $f(v_i, v_j, v_l) = v_i + \frac{2v_iv_j}{2v_i-v_j} + \frac{3v_iv_l}{3v_i-v_l} \leq 1 + \frac{2s}{2-s} + \frac{3s}{3-s}$.*

Proof. Obviously, $f(v_i, v_j, v_l)$ is increasing in v_j and v_l; hence, $f(v_i, v_j, v_l) \leq v_i + \frac{2sv_i}{2v_i-s} + \frac{3sv_i}{3v_i-s} = g(v_i)$.

Now, let us how that $g(v_i)$ is decreasing in v_i. The derivative $g'_{v_i}(v_i) = 1 - \frac{2s^2}{(2v_i-s)^2} - \frac{3s^2}{(3v_i-s)^2}$ is increasing in v_i, thereby not exceeding $g'_{v_i}(s) = 1 - 2 - \frac{3}{4} < 0$.

Thus $g(v_i) \leq g(1) = 1 + \frac{2s}{2-s} + \frac{3s}{3-s}$.   □

Lemma 28. *For any real values $1 \leq r \leq s < 2$, we have $\frac{1+\frac{2s}{2-s}+\frac{3s}{3-s}}{1+r+s} \leq \min\{\frac{2+s}{(1+r)(2-s)}, \frac{2}{r(2-s)}\}$.*

Proof. At the beginning, we will obtain the inequality $1 + \frac{2s}{2-s} + \frac{3s}{3-s} \leq \frac{(1+r+s)(2+s)}{(1+r)(2-s)}$. The right-hand side is decreasing in r, and therefore it suffices to demonstrate that $1 + \frac{2s}{2-s} + \frac{3s}{3-s} \leq \frac{(1+2s)(2+s)}{(1+s)(2-s)}$. This is equivalent to $s \leq s^2$, which holds for $s \geq 1$.

Next, let us show that $1 + \frac{2s}{2-s} + \frac{3s}{3-s} \leq \frac{2(1+r+s)}{r(2-s)}$. The right-hand side is decreasing in r, and therefore it suffices to demonstrate that $1 + \frac{2s}{2-s} + \frac{3s}{3-s} \leq \frac{2(1+2s)}{s(2-s)}$. The last inequality is equivalent to $-4s^3 + 11s^2 - 4s - 6 = -s(2s - 3)^2 - (2 - s)(3 - s) < 0$.   □

Theorem 36. *For the system S composed of thee processors with speeds $v_1 = 1 \leq v_2 = r \leq v_3 = s < 2$, the price of anarchy does not exceed $est(r, s) = \min\{\frac{2+s}{(1+r)(2-s)}, \frac{2}{r(2-s)}\}$.*

Proof. To prove this result, we consider different cases with certain numbers of jobs assigned to each of the two most loaded processors. In each case, we will derive the required estimate for the price of anarchy. Let L be an equilibrium such that $SC(L) = \lambda_i(L)$, that is, processor i has the smallest delay. Let us analyze different cases of the equilibrium L.

1. Each of processors j and l executes one job. In the optimal strategy profile, these two jobs occupy at most two processors. Then this profile includes processor k carrying the equilibrium load of processor i only (in part or in full), that is, $OPT \leq \frac{v_i\lambda_i(L)}{v_k} \leq s\lambda_i(L)$. By Lemma 23, $s \leq est(r, s)$.

2. Processor j executes $n_j \geq 2$ jobs, and processor l executes $n_l = 1$ job. By Lemma 19, $\lambda_j(L) \leq \frac{2v_j}{2v_i - v_j}\lambda_i(L)$. At the same time, by Lemma 21, $OPT \leq$

$$\frac{v_i\lambda_i(L) + \frac{2v_jv_j}{2v_i - v_j}\lambda_i(L)}{1 + r} = \lambda_i(L)\frac{2v_i^2 + v_iv_j}{(1+r)(2v_i - v_j)}.$$

a) First, let $v_i \geq v_j$. Then $2v_i^2 + v_iv_j \leq 3v_i^2$, since this expression is increasing in v_j. In addition, $2v_i - v_j \geq v_i$, as this expression is also decreasing in v_j. As a result, $OPT \leq \lambda_i(L)\frac{3v_i}{1+r} \leq \lambda_i(L)\frac{3s}{1+r} \leq \lambda_i(L)est(r, s)$ by Lemma 24.

b) Now, let $v_i < v_j$. Then, by Lemma 25, $\frac{2v_i^2 + v_iv_j}{(1+r)(2v_i - v_j)} < \frac{2+s}{(1+r)(2-s)}$.

To proceed, consider two cases as follows. The first case corresponds to $v_i = r$ and $v_j = s$. Using Lemma 26, here we obtain $\frac{2r^2 + rs}{(1+r)(2r-s)} < \frac{2}{r(2-s)}$.

The second case corresponds to $v_i = 1$. By Lemma 20, $w_k \leq \frac{v_k}{2-v_k}\lambda_i(L) \leq \frac{s}{2-s}\lambda_i(L)$ and $v_j\lambda_j(L) - w_k \leq \frac{s}{2-s}\lambda_i(L)$ for any job of volume w_k from the ones assigned to processor j.

If all the jobs assigned to processor j in the strategy profile L also stay on this processor in the optimal strategy profile, then we have to consider two possible situations as follows: (1) the unique job on processor l in the equilibrium also stays there in the optimal strategy profile (hence the load of processor i may only decrease as the result of passing to the optimal strategy profile), and (2) the unique job leaves processor l (hence, in the optimal strategy profile, processor l has a load not exceeding $\lambda_i(L)$, which moves from processor i). In both situations, $OPT \leq \lambda_i(L)$.

If during transition to the optimal strategy profile the jobs of processor j move to processor l only, then we have to consider the same two situations. If the unique job on processor l in the equilibrium also stays there in the optimal strategy profile, then the load of processor i may only decrease as the result of passing to the optimal strategy profile. Consequently, $OPT \leq \lambda_i(L)$. Otherwise, the unique job leaves processor l, and then in the optimal strategy profile processor l has a load not exceeding $\lambda_i(L) + \frac{s}{2-s}\lambda_i(L)$, which moves from processors i and j. In this situation, $OPT \leq \lambda_i(L)\frac{1 + \frac{s}{2-s}}{v_l} \leq \lambda_i(L)\frac{1 + \frac{s}{2-s}}{r} = \lambda_i(L)\frac{2}{r(2-s)}$.

If during transition to the optimal strategy profile, some jobs of processor j move to processor i, then we have to consider the same two situations. If the unique job on processor l in the equilibrium also stays there in the optimal strategy profile, then the load of processor j becomes not higher than $\lambda_i(L) + \frac{s}{2-s}\lambda_i(L)$, which comprises the remaining jobs of processor j and the jobs from processor i. So, $OPT \leq \lambda_i(L)\frac{1 + \frac{s}{2-s}}{v_j} \leq \lambda_i(L)\frac{1 + \frac{s}{2-s}}{r} = \lambda_i(L)\frac{2}{r(2-s)}$. Otherwise, the unique job leaves processor l, and then in the optimal strategy profile, processor l has a load not exceeding $\lambda_i(L) + \frac{s}{2-s}\lambda_i(L)$, which moves from processors i and j.

3. Each of processors j and l executes two jobs, i.e., $n_j = n_l = 2$. In total, processors j and l have four jobs and there are three processors in the system S. Therefore, in the optimal strategy profile, at least two of these jobs (of volumes w_{k_1} and w_{k_2}) move to the same processor. By Lemma 22, $OPT \le \frac{W - w_{k_1} - w_{k_2}}{1+r} = \frac{v_i\lambda_i(L) + w_{k_3} + w_{k_4}}{1+r}$, where w_{k_3} and w_{k_4} are the volumes of the two other jobs assigned to processors j and l.

Consider processor $k \in \{j, l\}$. If $v_i \le v_k$, then by Lemma 20 the volume of any job on processor k does not exceed $\lambda_i(L)\frac{v_iv_k}{2v_i - v_k}$.

Now, let $v_i > v_k$. Recall that L forms an equilibrium, and hence $\lambda_k(L) \le \lambda_i(L) + \frac{w}{v_i}$, where w is the volume of the smallest job on processor k. Consequently, $w \ge v_i\lambda_k(L) - v_i\lambda_i(L)$. By Lemma 19, $\lambda_k(L) \le \lambda_i(L)\frac{2v_i}{2v_i - v_k} \le 2\lambda_i(L)$, since $2v_i - v_k \ge v_i$, which gives $w \le \lambda_i(L)$. The second (larger) job on processor k has a volume $v_k\lambda_k(L) - w \le v_k\lambda_k(L) = v_i\lambda_i(L) - (v_i - v_k)\lambda_k(L) \le v_i\lambda_i(L) - (v_i - v_k)\lambda_i(L) = v_k\lambda_i(L) \le r\lambda_i(L) \le \lambda_i(L)\frac{rs}{2r-s} \le \lambda_i(L)\frac{s}{2-s}$.

a) Let $v_i = s$; then $OPT \le \lambda_i(L)\frac{s+2r}{1+r} \le \lambda_l(L)\frac{3s}{1+r} \le \lambda_i(L)est(r, s)$ by Lemma 24.

b) Let $v_i = r$; then $OPT \le \lambda_i(L)\frac{r + 2\frac{rs}{2r-s}}{1+r} = \lambda_i(L)\frac{2r^2+rs}{(1+r)(2r-s)} \le \lambda_i(L)est(r, s)$ by Lemma 25.

c) Let $v_i = 1$; then $OPT \le \lambda_i(L)\frac{r + 2\frac{s}{2-s}}{1+r} = \lambda_i(L)\frac{2+s}{(1+r)(2-s)}$. On the other hand, as the system S consists of three processors, there exist two processors α and β executing at most one job of the four mentioned ones and, possibly, some load of processor i. In this case, OPT is not greater than the minimal load on these processors, that is, $OPT \le \min_{\alpha \ne \beta}\{\lambda_i(L)\frac{2}{v_\alpha(2-s)}, \lambda_i(L)\frac{2}{v_\beta(2-s)}\} \le \min\{\lambda_i(L)\frac{2}{1(2-s)}, \lambda_i(L)\frac{2}{r(2-s)}\} = \lambda_i(L)\frac{2}{r(2-s)}$.

4. Processors j and l has the following allocation of jobs: $n_j \ge 2$, $n_l \ge 3$. By Lemma 19, $\lambda_j(L) \le \lambda_i(L)\frac{2v_i}{2v_i - v_j}$ and $\lambda_l(L) \le \lambda_i(L)\frac{3v_i}{3v_i - v_l}$. Then, in accordance with estimate (5.1), $OPT \le \lambda_i(L)\frac{v_i + \frac{2v_iv_j}{2v_i - v_j} + \frac{3v_iv_l}{3v_i - v_l}}{1+r+s} \le \lambda_i(L)est(r, s)$ by Lemmas 27 and 28. $\square$

The next theorem is a particular case of Theorem 34 for the three-processor system.

Theorem 37. *For the system S composed of three processors with speeds $v_1 = 1 \le v_2 = r \le v_3 = s < 2$, the price of anarchy is not smaller than $est(r, s) = \min\{\frac{2+s}{(1+r)(2-s)}, \frac{2}{r(2-s)}\}$.*

Then Theorems 36 and 37 give the exact PoA value for the three-processor system.

Theorem 38. *For the system S composed of three processors with speeds* $v_1 = 1 \leq v_2 = r \leq v_3 = s < 2$, *the exact PoA value is*

$$
\begin{cases}
\frac{2+s}{(1+r)(2-s)} & \text{if } rs \leq 2, \\
\frac{2}{r(2-s)} & \text{if } rs > 2.
\end{cases}
$$

The exact PoA value allows us to analyze a possible growth of this characteristic as a new processor is included into the system (i.e., a situation resembling Braess's paradox in qualitative terms when the system of higher capacity demonstrates worse performance). According with the next result, the price of anarchy increases or remains invariable as a new processor is included into the system.

Theorem 39. *For the system S composed of two processors with speeds* $1 \leq s$, *the price of anarchy does not decrease as the result of adding a new processor of speed* $1 \leq q < 2$.

Proof. 1. Let a new processor of speed $q \leq s$ be included into the system. If $qs \leq s^2 < 2$, then the price of anarchy does not decrease, since $\frac{2+s}{(1+s)(2-s)} \leq \frac{2+s}{(1+q)(2-s)}$. In the case $s^2 > 2$ and $qs \leq 2$, the price of anarchy does not decrease because $\frac{2}{s(2-s)} \leq \frac{2+s}{(1+s)(2-s)} \leq \frac{2+s}{(1+q)(2-s)}$. Finally, under $s^2 > 2$ and $qs > 2$, the price of anarchy does not decrease owing to $\frac{2}{s(2-s)} \leq \frac{2}{q(2-s)}$.

2. Let a new processor of speed $s < q < 2$ be included into the system, that is, the new processor is faster than the other ones. If $qs \leq 2$, then $s^2 \leq 2$, and the price of anarchy does not decrease, since $\frac{2+s}{(1+s)(2-s)} \leq \frac{2+q}{(1+s)(2-q)}$. In the case $qs > 2$ and $s^2 \leq 2$, the price of anarchy does not decrease because $\frac{2+s}{(1+s)(2-s)} \leq \frac{2}{s(2-s)} \leq \frac{2}{s(2-q)}$. Finally, under $qs > 2$ and $s^2 > 2$, the price of anarchy does not decrease owing to $\frac{2}{s(2-s)} \leq \frac{2}{s(2-q)}$. $\square$

5.4 A NUMERICAL METHOD TO CALCULATE THE PRICE OF ANARCHY

In the previous section, we have derived an analytical expression for the price of anarchy in the three-processor model. In what follows, we suggest a computing method for the price of anarchy in the system of three processors, which is similar to the method developed earlier for the load balancing game (see Chapter 4). This method can be generalized to the systems composed of more processors. But such a generalization increases the number of associated linear programming problems and the number of their variables and constraints. Particularly, for the system S composed of N processors, it is necessary solve $N!$ linear programming problems with $(2^N - 1)^{N-1}$ subproblems, each containing N^2 variables.

Consider the following system of linear equations in the components of the vectors $a = (a_1, a_2, a_3)$, $b = (b_1, b_2, b_3)$, $c = (c_1, c_2, c_3)$:

$$
\begin{cases}
\dfrac{a_1+a_2+a_3}{v_i} \leq \dfrac{b_1+b_2+b_3+\min\limits_{k=1,2,3:a_k>0} a_k}{v_j}, \\[2ex]
\dfrac{a_1+a_2+a_3}{v_i} \leq \dfrac{c_1+c_2+c_3+\min\limits_{k=1,2,3:a_k>0} a_k}{v_l}, \\[2ex]
\dfrac{b_1+b_2+b_3}{v_j} \leq \dfrac{c_1+c_2+c_3+\min\limits_{k=1,2,3:b_k>0} b_k}{v_l}, \\[2ex]
\dfrac{a_1+a_2+a_3}{v_i} \geq \dfrac{b_1+b_2+b_3}{v_j} \geq \dfrac{c_1+c_2+c_3}{v_l}, \\[2ex]
\max\limits_{k=1,2,3} a_k > 0, \\[1ex]
\max\limits_{k=1,2,3} b_k > 0, \\[1ex]
a_k, b_k, c_k \geq 0, k = 1,2,3.
\end{cases}
\tag{5.3}
$$

This system describes a set of hyperplanes passing through the point $(0,0,0,0,0,0,0,0,0)$ in the 9D space, and the solution set is a domain in the space bounded by the hyperplanes. The system is feasible: for example, the triplet $a_1 = a_2 = a_3 = \alpha v_i$, $b_1 = b_2 = b_3 = \alpha v_j$, and $c_1 = c_2 = c_3 = \alpha v_l$ is a solution for all $\alpha > 0$. Furthermore, the solution set is unbounded, since α can be arbitrarily large.

Consider the system S composed of three processors with speeds $1 \leq r \leq s < 2$ and n players. Let L be a Nash equilibrium in the system S such that processor i is slowest in this profile, processor j has a medium delay, and processor l is fastest. Assume that, in the equilibrium L, processor i receives the total volume of jobs defined by $\sum\limits_{k=1,\dots,n:l_k=i} w_k = a_1 + a_2 + a_3$ and the corresponding volumes for processors j and l are $\sum\limits_{k=1,\dots,n:l_k=j} w_k = b_1 + b_2 + b_3$ and $\sum\limits_{k=1,\dots,n:l_k=l} w_k = c_1 + c_2 + c_3$, respectively. The volume of jobs on each processor is somehow divided into three parts so that each component of the 3D vectors a, b, and c is either zero or positive and includes at least one job.

Lemma 29. *Let L be a Nash equilibrium in the game involving three processors i, j, and l and n players such that*

$$\lambda_i(L) \geq \lambda_j(L) \geq \lambda_l(L),$$

$$\sum_{k=1,\dots,n:l_k=i} w_k = a_1 + a_2 + a_3,$$

$$\sum_{k=1,\dots,n:l_k=j} w_k = b_1 + b_2 + b_3,$$

$$\sum_{k=1,\dots,n:l_k=l} w_k = c_1 + c_2 + c_3.$$

Here, for all $k = 1, 2, 3$, the component a_k is zero or the volume of at least one job on processor i, the component b_k is zero or the volume of at least one job on processor j, and the component c_k is zero or the volume of at least one job on processor l. Then the set of the vectors a, b, and c is the solution of system (5.3).

Proof. Suppose L forms a Nash equilibrium and $\lambda_i(L) \geq \lambda_j(L) \geq \lambda_l(L)$. In this case, by Lemma 18 all $\lambda_k(L) > 0$, $k = i, j, l$. Then the following inequalities hold:

$$
\begin{cases}
\dfrac{\sum_{k=1,\dots,n:l_k=i} w_k}{v_i} \leq \dfrac{\sum_{k=1,\dots,n:l_k=j} w_k + \min\limits_{k=1,\dots,n:l_k=i, w_k>0} w_k}{v_j}, \\[2ex]
\dfrac{\sum_{k=1,\dots,n:l_k=i} w_k}{v_i} \leq \dfrac{\sum_{k=1,\dots,n:l_k=l} w_k + \min\limits_{k=1,\dots,n:l_k=i, w_k>0} w_k}{v_l}, \\[2ex]
\dfrac{\sum_{k=1,\dots,n:l_k=j} w_k}{v_j} \leq \dfrac{\sum_{k=1,\dots,n:l_k=l} w_k + \min\limits_{k=1,\dots,n:l_k=j, w_k>0} w_k}{v_l}, \\[2ex]
\dfrac{\sum_{k=1,\dots,n:l_k=i} w_k}{v_i} \geq \dfrac{\sum_{k=1,\dots,n:l_k=j} w_k}{v_j} \geq \dfrac{\sum_{k=1,\dots,n:l_k=l} w_k}{v_l}.
\end{cases}
$$

Since each nonzero value a_k ($k = 1, 2, 3$) equals the volume of at least one job on processor i, we naturally have $\min\limits_{k:a_k>0} a_k \geq \min\limits_{k:l_k=i, w_k>0} w_k$, which yields the first two inequalities of system (5.3). In a similar manner, $\min\limits_{k:b_k>0} b_k \geq \min\limits_{k:l_k=j, w_k>0} w_k$. This means satisfaction of system (5.3).   □

Lemma 30. *Any solution of system (5.3) defines a Nash equilibrium L in the game involving the system S composed of three processors i, j, and l and the players whose jobs correspond to the nonzero components of the vectors a, b, and c and delays are sorted in the order $\lambda_i(L) \geq \lambda_j(L) \geq \lambda_l(L)$.*

Proof. Let the set of the vectors a, b, and c give a solution of system (5.3). Consider the game with three processors i, j, and l. Let each nonzero component of the vectors a, b, and c specify the job volume of a successive player. Consider a profile L such that the jobs of volumes $a_k > 0$, $b_k > 0$, and c_k are assigned to processors i, j, and l, respectively. As all inequalities (5.3) hold, the profile L is the desired Nash equilibrium.   □

The following result is immediate.

Theorem 40. *Any Nash equilibrium L in the game involving the system S composed of three processors i, j, and l and n players corresponds to a Nash equilibrium L' in the game involving the same system S and at most nine players in which each processor receives no more than three jobs and the delays on all processors in L and L' coincide.*

Proof. Consider a Nash equilibrium L in the game with the system S of three processors and n players. Number the processors so that $\lambda_i(L) \geq \lambda_j(L) \geq \lambda_l(L)$. By Lemma 29, for any Nash equilibrium in the game involving the system S and any number of players, there exists a corresponding solution a, b, c of system (5.3). By Lemma 30 this solution determines a Nash equilibrium L' in the game with the system S such that the nonzero components of the vectors a, b, and c specify the job volumes on processors i, j, and l, respectively. By definition the element sum of the vector a is the load of processor i in the profile L. Hence the delays on processor i coincide in the equilibria L and L'. Similarly, for processors j and l, the delays in the equilibrium L coincide with the corresponding delays in the equilibrium L'.   □

This theorem claims that it is sufficient to consider only the games where each processor receives at most three jobs in an equilibrium and the equilibrium is the solution of system (5.3). In addition, the domain of the social payoff coincides with the value domain of the games with an arbitrary number of players.

Let the components of the vectors a, b, and c be chosen as follows. In the optimal profile yielding the maximal social payoff, processors i, j, and l receive the total volumes of jobs $a_1 + b_1 + c_1$, $a_2 + b_2 + c_2$, and $a_3 + b_3 + c_3$, respectively, and the smallest delay can be on each of them. Furthermore, by Theorem 35 the volumes of jobs are assumed to be normalized so that in the optimal profile the minimal delay among all processors is 1. In our case, this means that

$$a_1 + b_1 + c_1 \geq v_i,$$
$$a_2 + b_2 + c_2 \geq v_j,$$
$$a_3 + b_3 + c_3 \geq v_l,$$

and at least one of these inequalities holds as an equality.

Lemma 31. *A solution of the linear programming problem*

$$LPP(v_i, v_j, v_l): \begin{cases} c_1 + c_2 + c_3 \to \min \\ (r1) \quad \dfrac{a_1 + a_2 + a_3}{v_i} \leq \dfrac{b_1 + b_2 + b_3 + \min\limits_{k:a_k>0} a_k}{v_j}, \\ (r2) \quad \dfrac{a_1 + a_2 + a_3}{v_i} \leq \dfrac{c_1 + c_2 + c_3 + \min\limits_{k:a_k>0} a_k}{v_l}, \\ (r3) \quad \dfrac{b_1 + b_2 + b_3}{v_j} \leq \dfrac{c_1 + c_2 + c_3 + \min\limits_{k:b_k>0} b_k}{v_l}, \\ (r4) \quad \dfrac{a_1 + a_2 + a_3}{v_i} \geq \dfrac{b_1 + b_2 + b_3}{v_j} \geq \dfrac{c_1 + c_2 + c_3}{v_l}, \\ (r5) \quad \max\limits_{k=1,2,3} a_k > 0, \\ (r6) \quad \max\limits_{k=1,2,3} b_k > 0, \\ (r7) \quad a_k, b_k, c_k \geq 0, k = 1, 2, 3, \\ (r8) \quad a_1 + b_1 + c_1 \geq v_i, \\ (r9) \quad a_2 + b_2 + c_2 \geq v_j, \\ (r10) \quad a_3 + b_3 + c_3 \geq v_l, \end{cases} \tag{5.4}$$

with respect to the components of the vectors a, b, and c gives the minimal social payoff in a Nash equilibrium among all games where in an equilibrium at most three jobs are assigned to each processor, i, j, and l indicate the numbers of the processors in the descending order of their delays and the optimal social payoff makes up 1.

Proof. By Lemma 30 any solution of inequalities (r1)–(r7) in the problem $LPP(v_i, v_j, v_l)$ defines an equilibrium in the game with three processors where each processor receives at most tree jobs and $i, j,$ and l are the numbers of the processors in the descending order of their delays.

The goal function in this problem is bounded below only by the hyperplanes corresponding to inequalities (r8)–(r10). In fact, inequalities (r1)–(r7) admit arbitrarily small nonnegative values of the goal function, including the zero value. Therefore the minimum is reached on one of the boundaries related to the last three inequalities. Hence, one of them holds as equality, and the optimal payoff in the game corresponding to the solution of the problem $LPP(v_i, v_j, v_l)$ is 1. $\qquad\square$

Consequently, for exact PoA evaluation in the system S composed of three processors, it is necessary to solve a series of the linear programming problems $LPP(v_i, v_j, v_l)$ for all permutations $(1, r, s)$, and the minimal solution among them yields the value $\frac{1}{PoA(S)}$. In other words, we may establish the following fact.

Theorem 41. *For the system S composed of three processors, the inverse value of the price of anarchy PoA(S) is*

$$\frac{1}{PoA(S)} = \min_{(v_i, v_j, v_l) \text{ are permutations } (1, r, s)} \left\{ \frac{c_1 + c_2 + c_3}{v_l} \, | \, a, b, c \text{ is solution of } LPP(v_i, v_j, v_l) \right\},$$

where $LPP(v_i, v_j, v_l)$ is the linear programming problem (5.4).

Proof. By Lemma 31 the solution of problem (5.4) gives the minimal social payoff in a Nash equilibrium, where i, j, and l are the numbers of the processors in the descending order of their delays, among all the games such that in an equilibrium each processor receives at most three jobs and the optimal payoff is 1. The minimal solution among the problems for all admissible permutations $(1, r, s)$ as the values of (v_i, v_j, v_l) gives the minimal social payoff in a Nash equilibrium among all the games where in an equilibrium at most three jobs are assigned to each processor and the optimal payoff is 1.

By Theorem 40, for any equilibrium in the game involving the system S of three processors and an arbitrary number of players, it is possible to construct a corresponding equilibrium in the game with the same processors and a set of at most nine players, where each processor receives no more than three jobs and the social payoff coincides in both equilibria. Thus, for PoA evaluation, it suffices to consider only the games where each processor has at most three jobs in an equilibrium.

Using Theorem 35, we finally establish that, for PoA evaluation, it suffices to consider only the games where the social payoff in the optimal profile is 1. □

5.5 COMPUTING EXPERIMENTS

To estimate the price of anarchy in the three-processor model, we have developed a program for a visual comparison of the lower PoA estimates and its exact value constructed by solving a series of the linear programming problems. In addition, the program allows us to track the PoA variations in the system S with a greater number of processors that have not been theoretically estimated so far. The parameters of the system S are adjusted in the program; by assumption the speed of processor 1 is 1, whereas exact values are specified for the speeds of other processors and a range of values

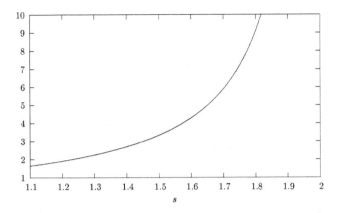

Figure 5.1 Price of anarchy for system S with $r = 1.1, s \in [r, 2)$

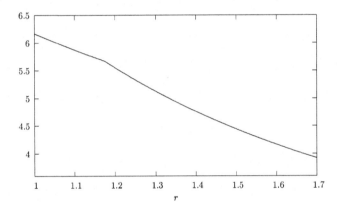

Figure 5.2 Price of anarchy for system S with $s = 1.7, r \in [1, s]$

for one of them. This approach allows us to study the PoA dynamics under varying speed of one processor.

The graphs in Figs. 5.1 and 5.2 illustrate the PoA estimates under different speeds of processors 2 and 3, respectively. In Fig. 5.1, the speed of processor 2 is $r = 1.1$, whereas the speed of processor 3 varies within the range $s \in [r, 2)$. In Fig. 5.2, the speed of the fastest processor is $s = 1.7$, whereas the speed of processor 2 varies within the range $r \in [1, s]$. Note that the theoretical estimates coincide with the calculated values of the price of anarchy.

As a matter of fact, the following example is more interesting. Consider the system S composed of four processors with speeds $v_1 = 1 \leq v_2 = q \leq v_3 = r \leq v_4 = s < 2$. The graphs in Figs. 5.3 and 5.4 show the PoA variations

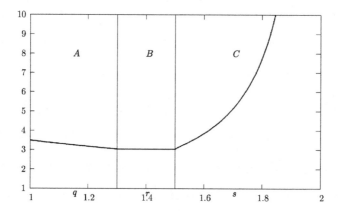

Figure 5.3 Price of anarchy for four-processor system S

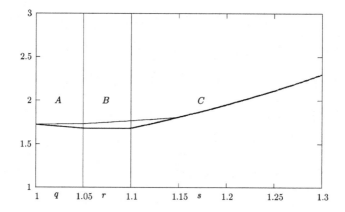

Figure 5.4 Price of anarchy for four-processor system S with low speeds

in comparison with the lower estimate (5.2), which is in fact the PoA value for the three of these four processors with speeds $1 \le r \le s < 2$. In Fig. 5.3, we present the PoA dynamics in several cases as follows. In the domain A, $r = 1.3$ and $s = 1.5$, whereas the value q varies within the range $[1, r]$. Next, in the domain B, $q = 1.3$ and $s = 1.5$, whereas the value r varies within the range $[q, s]$. Finally, in the domain C, $q = 1.3$ and $r = 1.5$, whereas the value s varies within the range $[r, 2)$. In all these cases, the price of anarchy for the four processors coincides with its lower estimate (5.2).

The graphs in Fig. 5.4 illustrate the PoA variations for the systems S with almost the same speeds of processors, that is, in the normalized form they are very close to 1. In this case, the PoA value (light line) exceeds its estimate (5.2) (heavy line). As the speeds grow, the graphs meet each other.

In the domain A, $r = 1.05$ and $s = 1.1$, whereas the value q varies within the range $[1, r]$. Next, in the domain B, $q = 1.05$ and $s = 1.1$, whereas the value r varies within the range $[q, s]$. Finally, in the domain C, $q = 1.05$ and $r = 1.1$, whereas the value s varies within the range $[r, 1.3]$.

CHAPTER 6

Networks and Graphs

Contents

As a matter of fact, communication networks and social networks represent graphs. Therefore, the methods of graph theory are the main analysis tool for such networks. There exist directed and undirected graphs. An undirected graph $G = (V, E)$ consists of a node set V and an edge set E. Edges are unordered pairs of nodes, further denoted by ij or (i, j); the relationship $ij \in E$ means that nodes $i \in V$ and $j \in V$ are connected by an edge in a graph G.

For a graph G, a sequence of different nodes $\{i_1, \ldots, i_k\}$, $k \geq 2$, is a path from i_1 to i_k if $i_h i_{h+1} \in G$ for all $h = 1, \ldots, k - 1$. The length l of a path is the number of its edges, that is, $l = k - 1$. The distance between two nodes is the length of a minimal path between them.

A graph G is connected if, for any two nodes of its set V, there exists a path in G from one node to the other. A connected component is a maximal connected subset of a given graph; We denote by $V|G$ the set of all connected components in a graph G. The graph obtained from a given graph G by eliminating an edge (link) ij is denoted by $G - ij$. By analogy, the graph obtained from a given graph G by adding an edge (link) ij is denoted by $G + ij$.

Edges of a graph G may have certain weights. A weighted graph $G = (V, E, W)$ is defined by a node set V, an edge set E, and a weight matrix W, where an element w_{ij} specifies the weight of an edge ij.

Networking Games
https://doi.org/10.1016/B978-0-12-816551-5.00012-5

Copyright © 2019 Elsevier Inc.
All rights reserved.

6.1 CLASSICAL BETWEENNESS CENTRALITY FOR THE NODES AND EDGES OF A GRAPH

Betweenness centrality is a basic concept in network analysis. The first (most simple) measure of significance consists in the degree of a node, that is, the number of incident edges or the number of links for a node. This measure well describes the propagation of infectious diseases.

Another (more complicated) measure of significance is the so-called betweenness centrality suggested in the pioneering paper [30]. The betweenness centrality of a node gives the number of geodesics between all nodes that contain this node. The betweenness centrality of a node is an important measure that reflects the level of its participation in the dissemination of information between other nodes in a graph. Formally, the betweenness centrality of a node can be defined as

$$c_B(v) = \frac{1}{n_B} \sum_{s,t \in V} \frac{\sigma_{s,t}(v)}{\sigma_{s,t}}, \tag{6.1}$$

where $\sigma_{s,t}$ indicates the number of geodesics (shortest paths) between nodes s and t, and $\sigma_{s,t}(v)$ means the number of geodesics between nodes s and t containing node v. The normalization coefficient n_B has the form $n_B = (n-1)(n-2)$ if node v is neither initial s nor terminal t node, and $n_B = n(n-1)$ otherwise. In other words, $c_B(v)$ can be interpreted as the average share of paths containing a given node v under an equiprobable selection of nodes s and t.

For betweenness centrality evaluation, it is necessary to find all geodesics between all pairs of nodes in a given graph [10,31,32,67]; with the Floyd–Warshall algorithm, such calculations have a complexity of $O(n^3)$. For sparse graphs, the Johnson algorithm can be more efficient as its complexity makes up $O(n^2 \log n + nm)$, where m is the number of edges in a graph under consideration. For unweighted graphs, the best computational complexity of betweenness centrality evaluation algorithms reaches $O(mn)$; see [14].

Example 15 (A graph of five nodes). Consider a simple example of betweenness centrality evaluation for an unweighted graph with five nodes and five edges illustrated in Fig. 6.1.

Evaluate the betweenness centrality of node B: $c_B(B) = ((\sigma_{AC}(B)/\sigma_{AC}) + (\sigma_{AD}(B)/\sigma_{AD}) + (\sigma_{AE}(B)/\sigma_{AE}) + (\sigma_{CD}(B)/\sigma_{CD}) + (\sigma_{CE}(B)/\sigma_{CE}) + (\sigma_{DE}(B)/\sigma_{DE}))/6 = ((1/1) + (1/1) + (2/2) + (1/2) + 0 + 0)/6 = 3.5/6 \approx 0.583$.

Similarly, calculate the betweenness centrality of the other nodes: $c_B(A) = 0$, $c_B(B) = 7/12$, $c_B(C) = c_B(D) = 1/6$, and $c_B(E) = 1/12$.

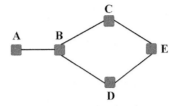

Figure 6.1 Unweighted graph with five nodes and five edges

Figure 6.2 Railway network of Finland

Example 16 (The railway network of Finland). The railway network of Finland is shown in Fig. 6.2. Its total length reaches 5794 km. The railway network of Finland connects almost all cities of the country with each other.

The undirected graph corresponding to the railway network of Finland contains 55 nodes and 66 edges and has the following characteristics: diam-

Table 6.1 Centrality measures for railway network of Finland

Node	Betweenness centrality c_B	Node	Degree
Pieksämäki	0.704	Pieksämäki	5
Kouvola	0.527	Kouvola	4
Tampere	0.413	Seinäjoki	4
Iisalmi	0.401	Oulu	3
Lahti	0.399	Tampere	4
Mikkeli	0.396	Vihanti	3
Ylivieska	0.375	Ylivieska	3
Kuopio	0.373	Kajaani	3
Seinäjoki	0.364	Kontiomäki	3
Toijala	0.353	Vuokatti	3

eter 16, average path length 5.95, the number of geodesics 2970, average degree 2.4.

The graph includes the edges between the following cities: Nurmes, Kontiomäki, Kajaani and Vuokatti; Savonlinna and Pieksämäki; Rauma and Kokemäki; Pietarsaari and Pännäinen; finally, Raahe and Vihanti.

Table 6.1 gives the centrality measures for the first ten cities calculated by formula (6.1). Clearly, the top three cities in terms of betweenness centrality are Pieksämäki, Kouvola, and Tampere.

Remark. The betweenness centrality of edges is defined by analogy using the formula

$$c_B(e) = \frac{1}{n_B} \sum_{s,t \in V} \frac{\sigma_{s,t}(e)}{\sigma_{s,t}},$$

where $\sigma_{s,t}$ indicates the number of geodesics (shortest paths) between nodes s and t, and $\sigma_{s,t}(e)$ means the number of geodesics between nodes s and t containing an edge e. Note that the pair of nodes s, t is chosen randomly.

6.2 THE PAGERANK METHOD

As a matter of fact, the PageRank method is a popular technique to calculate node centrality in a directed graph. The idea of PageRank was suggested by Brin and Page [17]. Nowadays, the Google search engine ranks the web pages according to their PageRank values.

There exist various interpretations of PageRank. Perhaps, the most widespread interpretation is associated with random walking. A random walk process follows hyperlinks, thereby forming a Markov chain. Denote by n the total number of web pages. The transition rate matrix P of dimensions $n \times n$ is defined in the following way. Let a node v_i have $k > 0$ outbound links. Then $p_{ij} = 1/k$ if v_j is an outbound link and $p_{ij} = 0$ otherwise.

PageRank is described by a stationary distribution of a Markov chain with the set of all web pages as its state space and the transition rate matrix of the form

$$\tilde{P} = \alpha P + (1 - \alpha)(1/n)E,$$

where $\alpha \in (0, 1)$, and E denotes the matrix of compatible dimensions with all unit entries. The transition rate matrix $\tilde{P}$ corresponds to a random walk search by the outbound hyperlinks with the probability α. Note that this search procedure may begin from an arbitrary web page with the probability $1 - \alpha$. In the Google search engine, the parameter α is adjusted to 0.85. The matrix $\tilde{P}$ is stochastic, nonperiodic, and irreducible. By the ergodic theorem of Markov chains, there exists a unique vector π such that $\pi \tilde{P} = \pi, \pi \underline{1} = 1$, where $\underline{1}$ means a column vector composed of unit elements. In the probabilistic sense, the vector π is the share of time a random walk process spends on a given web page. This limit vector defines the centrality values based on the PageRank method.

Actually, the PageRank method can be used to analyze weighted graphs. For a weighted graph with a weight matrix W, the transition rate matrix P is defined as $P = D^{-1}W$, where D denotes the diagonal matrix of powers. Then the transition rate matrix for ranking of weighted graph nodes takes the form

$$\tilde{P} = \alpha D^{-1} W + (1 - \alpha)(1/n)E.$$

Remark. The PageRank method is often employed to rank network nodes. However, we may also adopt it for edge centrality evaluation. For example, if π_i gives the rank of node i and p_{ij} is the transition rate from node i to j, then the centrality measure of the edge (i, j) can be defined as πp_{ij}.

Clearly, the interpretation of PageRank as an absorbing Markov chain is a simple and natural descriptive model of this procedure.

According to available information, Google uses the standard iterative process for calculating the PageRank values. Let the initial approximation be the uniform distribution, that is, the vector has the form $\pi^{(0)} = (1/n)\underline{1}^T$. Then, at iteration k, this vector is calculated as

$$\pi^{(k)} = \pi^{(k-1)} \tilde{P}, \ k \geq 1.$$

The iterative process stops as soon as a desired accuracy ϵ is achieved. The resulting number of iterations can be estimated by $\frac{\log \epsilon}{\log \alpha} nnz(P)$, where $nnz(P)$ denotes the number of nonzero elements in the matrix P [51]. Some researchers suggested different approaches to accelerate the iterative process for PageRank value calculation. See [47], [41], and [52] and [65]. Among other approximate calculation methods of PageRank values, we mention the Monte Carlo simulations owing to a series of advantages as follows:

- the web pages with the highest PageRank value are found with good accuracy even after the first iteration;
- there is a natural possibility to organize parallel computations;
- the current PageRank values can be updated subject to recent changes in the Web structure.

The Monte Carlo simulations to calculate PageRank values were presented in [5] and [16]. Note that the PageRank method can be applied to rank the nodes of any graph, not only web pages of the global network.

Example 17 (The graph of bordering countries in Europe and Asia). The next example considers the geographic location specifics of countries in Europe and Asia. In the graphs further, the nodes are countries, whereas an edge between two nodes indicates land borders between the corresponding countries. Such graphs are used during geography lessons at schools and colleges as a visual means to study the geographic location benefits of one countries with respect to the other. The graphs below include only the countries belonging to the principal component. For this reason, Iceland, Ireland, UK, and Malta are absent in the graph of European countries (see Fig. 6.3), whereas Japan, Taiwan, Cyprus, Bahrain, Philippines, Singapore, Sri-Lanka, and Maldives in the graph of Asian countries (see Fig. 6.4). Note that Russia and Turkey are included in both graphs.

The graph of European countries contains 41 nodes and 84 edges and has the following characteristics: diameter 8, average degree 4.098, average path length 3.38, and the number of geodesics 1640. The PageRank values calculated for this graph are given in Table 6.2.

The graph of Asian countries (see Fig. 6.4) contains 40 nodes and 81 edges and has the following characteristics: diameter 9, average degree 4.05, average path length 3.6, and the number of geodesics 1560.

The PageRank values calculated for this graph are given in Table 6.3.

Finally, we also calculate the PageRank values for the combined graph of Eurasian countries. This graph contains 79 nodes and 165 edges and has

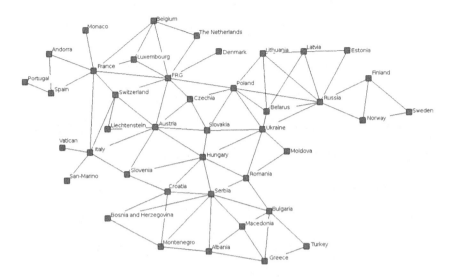

Figure 6.3 Graph of bordering countries in Europe

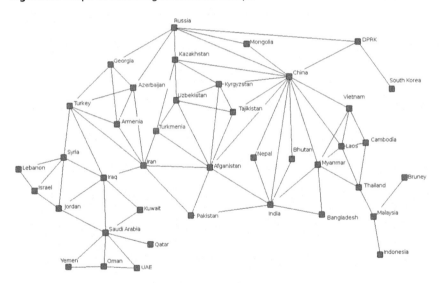

Figure 6.4 Graph of bordering countries in Asia

the following characteristics: diameter 10, average degree 4.177, average path length 4.315, and the number of geodesics 6162.

Table 6.4 presents the top 20 countries of Eurasia in terms of the PageRank value. Interestingly, the top 10 list consists mostly of European countries.

Table 6.2 PageRank values calculated for graph of European countries, $\alpha = 0.85$

Node	PageRank value $\alpha = 0.85$	Node	PageRank value $\alpha = 0.85$
France	0.052	Slovenia	0.022
Germany	0.052	Montenegro	0.022
Russia	0.043	Lithuania	0.022
Austria	0.043	Czech Republic	0.021
Serbia	0.041	Norway	0.020
Italy	0.039	Finland	0.020
Poland	0.035	Luxembourg	0.019
Ukraine	0.035	Bosnia and Herzegovina	0.017
Hungary	0.035	Andorra	0.016
Switzerland	0.029	Sweden	0.015
Bulgaria	0.028	The Netherlands	0.014
Romania	0.026	Turkey	0.013
Croatia	0.026	Liechtenstein	0.013
Belarus	0.026	Estonia	0.013
Slovakia	0.025	Moldova	0.012
Belgium	0.025	Portugal	0.010
Spain	0.025	Vatican	0.009

6.3 CENTRALITY MEASURE FOR WEIGHTED GRAPHS BASED ON KIRCHHOFF'S LAW

For node centrality evaluation in weighted graphs, an obvious analogy with electrical circuits can be used [4,6,15,40,81,82]. According to this approach, a graph is treated as an electrical circuit with a new grounded node, and a unit amount of current is induced at each node equiprobably. Then the average amount of current flowing through a given node defines its centrality measure, called the current flow centrality (CF-centrality). In the physical sense, this corresponds to the second law of thermodynamics, that is, the system is in a thermodynamical equilibrium, and the entropy of the equilibrium system is a centrality measure of a network. In this section, we calculate the centrality based on Kirchhoff's laws for electric circuits in the form of a system of linear equations. As shown further, this new measure can be expressed analytically for some classes of networks such as bipartite graphs and stars. In the general case, the problem is reduced to matrix inversion, and well-known numerical methods are applicable here. Finally, we adopt the new concept of centrality to model real social and commu-

Table 6.3   PageRank values calculated for graph of Asian countries, $\alpha = 0.85$

Node	PageRank value $\alpha = 0.85$	Node	PageRank value $\alpha = 0.85$
China	0.06	Georgia	0.024
Saudi Arabia	0.05	Armenia	0.023
Russia	0.039	Vietnam	0.023
Iran	0.037	Tajikistan	0.022
Iraq	0.037	Turkmenistan	0.022
India	0.036	Israel	0.021
Afghanistan	0.036	Cambodia	0.021
Turkey	0.034	Pakistan	0.017
Syria	0.032	Yemen	0.017
Malaysia	0.031	UAE	0.017
Laos	0.030	Lebanon	0.015
Azerbaijan	0.028	Kuwait	0.015
Kazakhstan	0.028	South Korea	0.015
Myanmar	0.028	Mongolia	0.013
Uzbekistan	0.028	Brunei	0.012
Thailand	0.028	Indonesia	0.012
Jordan	0.026	Bangladesh	0.012
Kyrgyzstan	0.026	Nepal	0.012
North Korea	0.027	Bhutan	0.012
Oman	0.024	Qatar	0.01

Table 6.4   PageRank values calculated for graph of Eurasian countries, $\alpha = 0.85$

Node	PageRank value $\alpha = 0.85$	Node	PageRank value $\alpha = 0.85$
Russia	0.039	Ukraine	0.018
China	0.029	Iran	0.018
France	0.027	Iraq	0.018
Germany	0.027	India	0.018
Saudi Arabia	0.025	Hungary	0.018
Austria	0.022	Afghanistan	0.018
Turkey	0.021	Syria	0.016
Serbia	0.021	Malaysia	0.016
Italy	0.02	Switzerland	0.016
Poland	0.019	Laos	0.015

nication networks, also comparing the results with the standard PageRank method and the method of geodesics.

Consider a weighted graph $G = (V, E, W)$ with a node set V, an edge set E, and a weight matrix W,

$$W(G) = \begin{pmatrix} 0 & w_{1,2} & \cdots & w_{1,n} \\ w_{2,1} & 0 & \cdots & w_{2,n} \\ \vdots & \vdots & \ddots & \vdots \\ w_{n,1} & w_{n,2} & \cdots & 0 \end{pmatrix}.$$

Here $w_{i,j} \geqslant 0$ is the weight of an edge between nodes i and j, and $n = |V|$ gives the number of nodes. Note that $w_{i,j} = 0$ if nodes i and j are not adjacent. For an undirected graph G, we assume that $w_{i,j} = w_{j,i}$.

Denote by $D(G)$ the matrix of the node degrees of a graph G of the form

$$D(G) = \begin{pmatrix} d_{v_1} & 0 & \cdots & 0 \\ 0 & d_{v_2} & \cdots & 0 \\ \vdots & \vdots & \ddots & \vdots \\ 0 & 0 & \cdots & d_{v_n} \end{pmatrix},$$

where $d_{v_i} = \sum_{j=1}^n w_{i,j}$ is the total weight of all incident edges for node v_i in the graph G.

Definition 32. The matrix $L(G)$ defined by

$$L(G) = D(G) - W(G) = \begin{pmatrix} d_{v_1} & -w_{1,2} & \cdots & -w_{1,n} \\ -w_{2,1} & d_{v_2} & \cdots & -w_{2,n} \\ \vdots & \vdots & \ddots & \vdots \\ -w_{n,1} & -w_{n,2} & \cdots & d_{v_n} \end{pmatrix} \qquad (6.2)$$

is called the Laplacian matrix of a weighted graph G.

Let the graph G' be obtained from the graph G by adding single node v_{n+1} connected to all other nodes of the graph G via the edges of a constant conductance δ. Then the Laplacian matrix for the modified graph G' takes the form

$$L(G') = D(G') - W(G') = \begin{pmatrix} d_{v_1} + \delta & -w_{1,2} & \cdots & -w_{1,n} & -\delta \\ -w_{2,1} & d_{v_2} + \delta & \cdots & -w_{2,n} & -\delta \\ \vdots & \vdots & \ddots & \vdots & \vdots \\ -w_{n,1} & -w_{n,2} & \cdots & d_{v_n} + \delta & -\delta \\ -\delta & -\delta & \cdots & -\delta & \delta n \end{pmatrix}. \qquad (6.3)$$

Suppose that a unit amount of current flows into some node $s \in V$ and that node v_{n+1} is grounded. Let φ_i^s characterize the electric potential in node v when an electric charge is concentrated in node s. By Kirchhoff's current law the vector of all potentials $\varphi^s(G') = [\varphi_{v_1}^s, \ldots, \varphi_{v_n}^s, \varphi_{v_{n+1}}^s]^T$ at the nodes of the graph G' satisfies the following system of equations:

$$\varphi^s(G') = L(G')^{-1} b_s', \tag{6.4}$$

where b_s' is the $(n+1)$-dimensional vector

$$b_s'(v) = \begin{cases} 1 & \text{for } v = s, \\ 0 & \text{otherwise.} \end{cases} \tag{6.5}$$

The Laplacian matrix (6.2) is singular, and the potentials can be determined up to a constant. Hence, without loss of generality, assume that the potential in node v_{n+1} is 0 (a grounded node).

Then it follows from (6.3) that

$$\tilde{\varphi}^s(G') = \tilde{L}(G')^{-1} b_s, \tag{6.6}$$

where $\tilde{\varphi}^s(G')$, $\tilde{L}(G')$, and b_s are obtained from (6.3) by eliminating the last row and column that correspond to node v_{n+1}. Note that the zero elements are eliminated in $\varphi^s(G')$ and b_s'.

As easily observed,

$$\tilde{\varphi}^s(G') = [D(G) - W(G) + \delta I]^{-1} b_s, \tag{6.7}$$

where I denotes the identity matrix of dimension n.

Thus, the vector $\tilde{\varphi}^s(G')$ can be considered as the vector of potentials at the nodes of the graph G, that is,

$$\tilde{\varphi}^s(G) = [L(G) + \delta I]^{-1} b_s.$$

Write expression (6.7) as

$$\tilde{\varphi}^s(G) = [(D(G) + \delta I) - W(G)]^{-1} b_s$$
$$= [I - (D(G) + \delta I)^{-1} D(G) D^{-1}(G) W(G)]^{-1} (D(G) + \delta I)^{-1} b_s.$$

The matrices $(D(G) + \delta I)^{-1}$ and $(D(G) + \delta I)^{-1} D(G)$ are diagonal with the diagonal elements $\frac{1}{d_i + \delta}$ and $\frac{d_i}{d_i + \delta}$, respectively, $i = 1, \ldots, n$; denote these matrices as D_1 and D_2, respectively. The matrix $D^{-1}(G)W(G)$ is stochastic; denote it by P. Then

$$\tilde{\varphi}^s(G) = [I - D_2 P]^{-1} D_1 b_s = \sum_{k=0}^{\infty} (D_2 P)^k D_1 b_s. \qquad (6.8)$$

By (6.8) the potential can be calculated recursively using the formulas

$$\tilde{\varphi}^s_{k+1}(G) = D_2 P \tilde{\varphi}^s_k(G) + D_1 b_s, \quad \tilde{\varphi}^s_0(G) = 0.$$

According to Ohm's law, for the edge $e = (v_i, v_j)$, the let-through current is $x^s_e = |\varphi^s_{v_i} - \varphi^s_{v_j}| \cdot w_{i,j}$. Given that the electric charge is concentrated at any node equiprobably, the average amount of current flowing through edge e describes the current flow centrality (CF-centrality) of this edge, that is,

$$CE_\delta(e) = \frac{1}{n} \sum_{s \in V} x^s_e.$$

Given that the electric charge is concentrated in node s, the average amount of current flowing through node v is

$$x^s(v) = \frac{1}{2}(b_s(v) + \sum_{e:v \in e} x^s_e), \qquad (6.9)$$

where $b_s(v) = \begin{cases} 1 & \text{for } v = s, \\ 0 & \text{otherwise.} \end{cases}$

Consequently, the current flow centrality of node i can be defined as

$$CE_\delta(v) = \frac{1}{n} \sum_{s \in V} x^s(v). \qquad (6.10)$$

The algorithm to evaluate the current flow centrality (6.10) for weighted graphs has the same computational complexity as the inversion algorithm for a matrix of dimension n, that is, $O(n^3)$.

Note that expression (6.10) can be calculated using Monte Carlo simulations (the law of large numbers). Approximate calculation methods play an important role in the analysis of large-scale graphs. In a quite easy and natural way, Monte Carlo simulations yield a rapid estimate of current flow centrality. For example, we may choose some subset of graph nodes

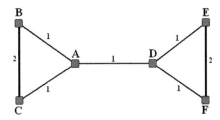

Figure 6.5 A weighted network of six nodes

Table 6.5 Centrality measures for weighted graph of six nodes

Nodes	A	B	C	D	E	F
Classical betweenness centrality	0.65	0	0	0. 65	0	0
PageRank-based centrality	1/6	1/6	1/6	1/6	1/6	1/6
Current flow centrality with $\delta = 1$	0.27	0.19	0.19	0.27	0.19	0.19

$V_1 \subset V$, independently and equiprobably, as the initial nodes for further approximate calculation of current flow centrality for all nodes of the graph, that is,

$$CE_B(i) \approx \frac{1}{|V_1|} \sum_{s \in V_1} x^s(i). \tag{6.11}$$

Thus, using merely a subset of graph nodes as initial nodes, it is possible to find the nodes with the largest current flow centrality values by Monte Carlo simulations.

Example 18 (A weighted network of six nodes). We begin with a simple example of a six-node network, which elucidates the advantages of current flow centrality (see Fig. 6.5). To this end, we calculate the basic centrality measures for this weighted graph. The results of calculations are given in Table 6.5. Clearly, the classical betweenness centrality allows us to assess only nodes A and D, yielding values 0 for the other nodes (though they are also important). Next, the PageRank method ranks all nodes equally, that is, assigns the same values to them; hence, this method is inapplicable to this special case. Finally, the current flow centrality measures node centrality in a quite expected way. In particular, it yields high values for nodes A and D.

Example 19 (An unweighted network of eleven nodes). Now, consider an example of an unweighted network of eleven nodes to illustrate the weak properties of the centrality based on geodesics (see Fig. 6.6).

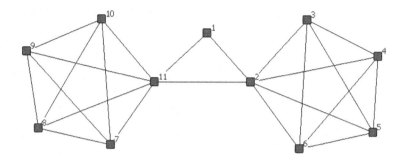

Figure 6.6 An unweighted network of eleven nodes

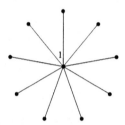

Figure 6.7 A star of *n* nodes

The graph of this network contains two sets of nodes connected by three nodes 1, 2, and 11. Nodes 2 and 11 have higher values of betweenness centrality, as all geodesics between the two sets contain these nodes. Hence, node 1 has zero centrality based on geodesics. Actually, node 1 plays an important role in information dissemination. Information can be transmitted not only directly from one node to another, but also via an additional node.

Next, compute the current flow centrality $CE_\delta(v)$ for the nodes of this network with $\delta = 0.5$. This method ranks nodes 2 and 11 as higher ones with centrality value 0.291 and node 1 as the third with centrality value 0.147. The other nodes have centrality value 0.127.

Finally, calculate CE_δ for the edges of this graph. The centrality value of edge $(2, 11)$ is 0.137, whereas the centrality values of edges $(1, 2)$ and $(1, 11)$ are 0.101. The other edges have the centrality value 0.0647.

Example 20 (A special case of graph G (star)). Consider the following special case (see Fig. 6.7). A graph G is a star with n nodes in which an edge has weight k, whereas the other edges have unit weight.

Let node 1 be the center of this star, and let node 2 be incident to the edge with weight k. Then the Laplacian matrix is

$$\tilde{L} = L + \delta I = D(G) - W(G) + \delta I$$

$$= \begin{pmatrix} n-2+k+\delta & -k & -1 & \cdots & -1 \\ -k & k+\delta & 0 & \cdots & 0 \\ -1 & 0 & 1+\delta & \cdots & 0 \\ \vdots & \vdots & \vdots & \ddots & \vdots \\ -1 & 0 & 0 & \cdots & 1+\delta \end{pmatrix}.$$

Its inverse has the form

$$\tilde{L}^{-1} = (L + \delta I)^{-1} = \frac{1}{\delta(1+\delta)X}$$

$$\times \begin{pmatrix} (k+\delta)(1+\delta)^2 & k(1+\delta)^2 & (k+\delta)(1+\delta) & \cdots & (k+\delta)(1+\delta) \\ k(1+\delta)^2 & (k+(n-1)\delta + k\delta + \delta^2)(1+\delta) & k(1+\delta) & \cdots & k(1+\delta) \\ (k+\delta)(1+\delta) & k(1+\delta) & k+\delta+\delta X & \cdots & k+\delta \\ \vdots & \vdots & \vdots & \ddots & \vdots \\ (k+\delta)(1+\delta) & k(1+\delta) & k+\delta & \cdots & k+\delta+\delta X \end{pmatrix},$$

where $X = nk + (n-1)\delta + 2k\delta + \delta^2$.

For $s = 1$, we obtain the current distribution

$$x^s(s) = \frac{1}{2}\left(1 + \frac{k(1+\delta) + (n-2)(k+\delta)}{nk + (n-1)\delta + 2k\delta + \delta^2}\right),$$

$$x^s(2) = \frac{1}{2}\frac{k(1+\delta)}{nk + (n-1)\delta + 2k\delta + \delta^2},$$

$$x^s(i) = \frac{1}{2}\frac{k+\delta}{nk + (n-1)\delta + 2k\delta + \delta^2}, \quad i = 3, \ldots, n.$$

For $s = 2$,

$$x^s(1) = \frac{1}{2}\frac{k(\delta + 2n - 3)}{nk + (n-1)\delta + 2k\delta + \delta^2},$$

$$x^s(s) = \frac{1}{2}\left(1 + \frac{k(\delta + n - 1)}{nk + (n-1)\delta + 2k\delta + \delta^2}\right),$$

$$x^s(i) = \frac{1}{2}\frac{k}{nk + (n-1)\delta + 2k\delta + \delta^2}, \quad i = 3, \ldots, n.$$

Finally, for $s = i$, where $i = 3, \ldots, n$,

$$x^s(1) = \frac{1}{2}\frac{\delta^2 + \delta(3k + 2n - 5) + k(2n - 3)}{(nk + (n-1)\delta + 2k\delta + \delta^2)(1+\delta)},$$

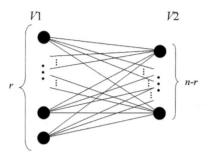

Figure 6.8 A bipartite unweighted graph

$$x^s(2) = \frac{1}{2} \frac{k}{nk + (n-1)\delta + 2k\delta + \delta^2},$$

$$x^s(s) = \frac{1}{2}(1 + \frac{1}{1+\delta} - \frac{k+\delta}{(nk + (n-1)\delta + 2k\delta + \delta^2)(1+\delta)}),$$

$$x^s(i) = \frac{1}{2} \frac{k+\delta}{(nk + (n-1)\delta + 2k\delta + \delta^2)(1+\delta)}, \quad i = 3, \ldots, n.$$

As a result, the current flow centrality is calculated by the formulas

$$CE_\delta(1) = \frac{1}{2n}(1 + \frac{2k(\delta + n - 1)}{X} + \frac{2(n-2)(\delta^2 + \delta(2k + n - 2) + k(n-1))}{(1+\delta)X}),$$

$$CE_\delta(2) = \frac{1}{2n}(1 + \frac{2k(\delta + n - 1)}{X}),$$

$$CE_\delta(i) = \frac{1}{2n}(1 + \frac{1}{1+\delta} + \frac{(k+\delta)(n-4)}{(1+\delta)X} + \frac{2k+\delta}{X}), \quad i = 3, \ldots, n.$$

Example 21 (A bipartite unweighted graph G). Consider a special case of a complete bipartite graph G with n nodes divided into two sets V_1 and V_2 (see Fig. 6.8) so that a node from V_1 is connected only to a node from V_2, and vice versa. Denote this graph by $K_{|V_1|,|V_2|}$. Here all edges have unit weights. Note that the current flow centrality of the star (the case $K_{1,n-1}$) has been analytically constructed in the previous example.

(Bipartite graph $K_{2,n-2}$). Let $V_1 = \{v_1, v_2\}$ and $v' \in V_2$. Then the Laplacian matrix is

$$D(G) - W(G) + \delta I$$

$$= \begin{pmatrix} n-2+\delta & 0 & -1 & -1 & \cdots & -1 \\ 0 & n-2+\delta & -1 & -1 & \cdots & -1 \\ -1 & -1 & 2+\delta & 0 & \cdots & 0 \\ -1 & -1 & 0 & 2+\delta & \cdots & 0 \\ \vdots & \vdots & \vdots & \vdots & \ddots & \vdots \\ -1 & -1 & 0 & 0 & \cdots & 2+\delta \end{pmatrix}.$$

Its inverse has the form

$$(D(G) - W(G) + \delta I)^{-1}$$

$$= \frac{1}{\delta(n+\delta)} \begin{pmatrix} \frac{n-2+n\delta+\delta^2}{n+\delta-2} & \frac{n-2}{n+\delta-2} & 1 & 1 & \cdots & 1 \\ \frac{n-2}{n+\delta-2} & \frac{n-2+n\delta+\delta^2}{n+\delta-2} & 1 & 1 & \cdots & 1 \\ 1 & 1 & \frac{2+n\delta+\delta^2}{2+\delta} & \frac{2}{2+\delta} & \cdots & \frac{2}{2+\delta} \\ 1 & 1 & \frac{2}{2+\delta} & \frac{2+n\delta+\delta^2}{2+\delta} & \cdots & \frac{2}{2+\delta} \\ \vdots & \vdots & \vdots & \vdots & \ddots & \vdots \\ 1 & 1 & \frac{2}{2+\delta} & \frac{2}{2+\delta} & \cdots & \frac{2+n\delta+\delta^2}{2+\delta} \end{pmatrix}.$$

For $s = v_1$, the amounts of current are distributed so that

$$x^s(v_1) = \frac{1}{2}\left(1 + \frac{(\delta + n - 1)(n - 2)}{(n+\delta)(n+\delta - 2)}\right),$$

$$x^s(v_2) = \frac{(n - 2)}{2(n+\delta - 2)(\delta + n)},$$

$$x^s(v') = \frac{1}{2(n+\delta - 2)}.$$

Since nodes v_1 and v_2 are located symmetrically, for $s = v_2$, we obtain

$$x^s(v_1) = \frac{(n - 2)}{2(n+\delta - 2)(\delta + n)},$$

$$x^s(v_2) = \frac{1}{2}\left(1 + \frac{(\delta + n - 1)(n - 2)}{(n+\delta)(n+\delta - 2)}\right),$$

$$x^s(v') = \frac{1}{2(n+\delta - 2)}.$$

For $s = v'$,

$$x^s(v_1) = x^s(v_2) = \frac{\delta + 2n - 4}{2(2 + \delta)(\delta + n)},$$

$$x^s(s) = \frac{1}{2}\left(1 + \frac{2(\delta + n - 1)}{(2+\delta)(\delta+n)}\right),$$

$$x^s(\nu') = \frac{1}{(2+\delta)(\delta+n)},$$

which yields

$$CE_\delta(\nu_1) = CE_\delta(\nu_2) = \frac{1}{2n}\left(1 + \frac{n-2}{n+\delta-2} + \frac{(n-2)(\delta+2n-4)}{(2+\delta)(\delta+n)}\right),$$

$$CE_\delta(\nu') = \frac{1}{2n}\left(1 + \frac{2}{n+\delta-2} + \frac{2(\delta+2n-4)}{(2+\delta)(\delta+n)}\right).$$

(Bipartite graph $K_{3,n-3}$). Let $V_1 = \{\nu_1, \nu_2, \nu_3\}$ and $\nu' \in V_2$. In this case, the Laplacian matrix is

$$D(G) - W(G) + \delta I$$

$$= \begin{pmatrix}
n-3+\delta & 0 & 0 & -1 & -1 & \cdots & -1 \\
0 & n-3+\delta & 0 & -1 & -1 & \cdots & -1 \\
0 & 0 & n-3+\delta & -1 & -1 & \cdots & -1 \\
-1 & -1 & -1 & 3+\delta & 0 & \cdots & 0 \\
-1 & -1 & -1 & 0 & 3+\delta & \cdots & 0 \\
\vdots & \vdots & \vdots & \vdots & \vdots & \ddots & \vdots \\
-1 & -1 & -1 & 0 & 0 & \cdots & 3+\delta
\end{pmatrix}.$$

Its inverse has the form

$$(D(G) - W(G) + \delta I)^{-1} = \frac{1}{\delta(n+\delta)}$$

$$\times \begin{pmatrix}
\frac{n-3+n\delta+\delta^2}{n+\delta-3} & \frac{n-3}{n+\delta-3} & \frac{n-3}{n+\delta-3} & 1 & 1 & \cdots & 1 \\
\frac{n-3}{n+\delta-3} & \frac{n-3+n\delta+\delta^2}{n+\delta-3} & \frac{n-3}{n+\delta-3} & 1 & 1 & \cdots & 1 \\
\frac{n-3}{n+\delta-3} & \frac{n-3}{n+\delta-3} & \frac{n-3+n\delta+\delta^2}{n+\delta-3} & 1 & 1 & \cdots & 1 \\
1 & 1 & 1 & \frac{3+n\delta+\delta^2}{3+\delta} & \frac{3}{3+\delta} & \cdots & \frac{3}{3+\delta} \\
1 & 1 & 1 & \frac{3}{3+\delta} & \frac{3+n\delta+\delta^2}{3+\delta} & \cdots & \frac{3}{3+\delta} \\
\vdots & \vdots & \vdots & \vdots & \vdots & \ddots & \vdots \\
1 & 1 & 1 & \frac{3}{3+\delta} & \frac{3}{3+\delta} & \cdots & \frac{3+n\delta+\delta^2}{3+\delta}
\end{pmatrix}.$$

By analogy with the case $K_{2,n-2}$, for $K_{3,n-3}$, it follows that

$$CE_\delta(\nu_1) = CE_\delta(\nu_2) = CE_\delta(\nu_3)$$

$$= \frac{1}{2n}\left(1 + \frac{(n-3)(\delta+n+1)}{(n+\delta-3)(\delta+n)} + \frac{(n-3)(\delta+2n-5)}{(3+\delta)(\delta+n)}\right),$$

$$CE_\delta(v') = \frac{1}{2n}\left(1 + \frac{3(\delta+n+1)}{(n+\delta-3)(\delta+n)} + \frac{3(\delta+2n-5)}{(3+\delta)(\delta+n)}\right).$$

(Bipartite graph $K_{r,n-r}$). Let $v \in V_1$ and $v' \in V_2$, where $r = |V1|$ and $n - r = |V2|$. Using the same considerations as before, calculate the following current flow centrality values for the nodes of the complete bipartite graph $K_{r,n-r}$:

$$CE_\delta(v) = \frac{1}{2n}\left(1 + \frac{(n-r)(\delta+n-2+r)}{(n+\delta-r)(\delta+n)} + \frac{(n-r)(\delta+2n-2-r)}{(r+\delta)(\delta+n)}\right),$$

$$CE_\delta(v') = \frac{1}{2n}\left(1 + \frac{r(\delta+n-2+r)}{(n+\delta-r)(\delta+n)} + \frac{r(\delta+2n-2-r)}{(r+\delta)(\delta+n)}\right).$$

6.4 CENTRALITY MEASURE FOR WEIGHTED GRAPHS AS A SOLUTION OF COOPERATIVE GAME

For node centrality evaluation, it is possible to use cooperative game theory methods. In what follows, we study a game with partial cooperation described by an undirected communication graph.

Assume that graph nodes are identified with players whereas graph edges with pairwise relations between them. Two players may interact directly only if they have a relation. The notion of a relation can be interpreted as an information transfer or resource distribution, a cooperation or friendship, a transport connection, or even a mutual influence and subordination. The nodes can be individuals, organizations, countries, or web pages.

This setup leads to a communication (network) game defined by a triplet consisting of a finite set of players, a characteristic function, and a graph of relations between players. A useful solution of the communication game is the Myerson value [3,63], which has component efficiency and pairwise stability. The efficiency means that, for each component of the graph, the common payoff is equal to the value of this component. The stability means that if a connection between two players is eliminated, then both players have equal deviations in the payoff allocation. Jackson and Wolinsky [42–44] proposed the model of networking game in which the utility depends of the structure of the network. They apply the Myerson value to analyze the betweenness of the nodes in the network. Despite the fact that other allocation rules were proposed (see, for instance, [11,12,18,

42,76–78]), the Myerson vector is widely used as an allocation rule in many cooperative games.

Despite the seeming simplicity of its form, the Myerson value is not easy to calculate. In this section, we consider a transferable utility game with a special characteristic function and propose a rather simple allocation procedure using a generation function, proving that the resulting imputation coincides with the Myerson value.

We begin with basic definitions. Let $N = \{1, 2, \ldots, n\}$ be a finite set of players. Denote by 2^N the set of all subsets of N. A cooperative game of n players is a pair $< N; v >$, where $N = \{1, 2, \ldots, n\}$ is the set of players, and $v : 2^N \to R$ is a map associating each coalition $S \in 2^N$ with some value $v(S)$ such that $v(\emptyset) = 0$. This function v is called the characteristic function of the cooperative game $< N; v >$; for details, we refer to the book [55].

An undirected graph $g = (N, E)$ consists of a node set N and an edge set E. As mentioned earlier, graph nodes are identified with players, and an edge ij means that players i and j may interact directly only if $ij \in g$.

A graph g on the set N is connected if, for any two nodes i and j, there exists a path in g connecting i and j. A coalition S is connected if any two nodes in S are connected by a path that consists of nodes from S only. A connected component is a maximal connected subset. We denote by $N|g$ the set of all connected components in a graph g.

First, consider unweighted networks in the form of a tree and define a centrality measure for them based on the Myerson value. Then, proceed with a similar analysis for general networks.

6.4.1 The Myerson value

Let $< N, v >$ be a cooperative game with partial cooperation presented by a graph g, a set of players N, and a characteristic function v. An allocation rule Y describes how the value associated with a network is distributed to the individual players. For each player i, $Y_i(v, g)$ is the value allocated to player i in a graph g under a characteristic function v. The Myerson value is the unique allocation rule $Y(v, g) = (Y_1(v, g), \ldots, Y_n(v, g))$ determined by the following axioms.

Axiom 1. If S is a connected component of g, then the members of the coalition S allocate to themselves the total value $v(S)$ available to them, that is, for all $S \in N|g$,

$$\sum_{i \in S} Y_i(v, g) = v(S).$$

Axiom 2. For all g and $ij \in g$, both players i and j obtain equal payoffs as the result of adding or eliminating link ij, that is,

$$Y_i(v, g) - Y_i(v, g - ij) = Y_j(v, g) - Y_j(v, g - ij).$$

For any coalition S, let us define the characteristic function

$$v_g(S) = \sum_{K \in S|g} v(K).$$

Then the Myerson value can be calculated using the formula

$$Y_i(v, g) = \sum_{S \subset N \setminus \{i\}} (v_g(S \cup i) - v_g(S)) \frac{s!(n-s-1)!}{n!},$$

where $s = |S|$ and $n = |N|$.

6.4.2 Characteristic function

Consider a game in which the graph g is a tree consisting of n nodes whereas the characteristic function is determined by the Jackson-Wolinsky scheme [44]: each direct connection—a path of length 1—gives an impact r, $0 \le r \le 1$, to a coalition S. Moreover, the players also obtain a smaller impact from indirect connections as follows. Each path of length 2 gives the impact r^2 to a coalition S; each path of length 3 gives the impact r^3, and so on. Therefore, for any coalition S, we have

$$v(S) = a_1 r + a_2 r^2 + \cdots + a_k r^k + \cdots + a_L r^L = \sum_{k=1}^{L} a_k r^k,$$

where L is the maximal distance between two nodes in this coalition, and a_k denotes the number of paths of length k in this coalition.
Note that

$$v(i) = 0 \ \forall i \in N.$$

Example 22 (A tree of six nodes). For the tree in Fig. 6.9, we find $L = 4$ and $a_1 = 5$, $a_2 = 5$, $a_3 = 3$, $a_4 = 2$. Consequently, the value of the grand-coalition is

$$v(N) = 5r + 5r^2 + 3r^3 + 2r^4.$$

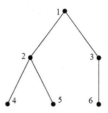

Figure 6.9 A tree with root 1

For the coalition $S = \{1, 2, 4, 5\}$, we obtain $L = 2$, $a_1 = 3$, and $a_2 = 3$, which yields

$$v(S) = 3r + 3r^2.$$

6.4.3 Allocation principle

Here we propose an allocation procedure of the general gain $v(N)$ to each player i [59].

Stage 1. Two directly connected players obtain r. Individually, they receive nothing, and so each of them expects to receive at least $r/2$. If player i has several direct connections, then he receives the value $r/2$ owing to each of them. Hence, the payoff of such player i should be multiplied by the number of paths of length 1 containing node i.

Stage 2. Three connected players obtain r^2, and thus each of them receives $r^2/3$ owing to the paths of length 2 containing his node.

Arguing in the same way, we construct the allocation rule

$$Y_i(v, g) = \frac{a_1^i}{2}r + \frac{a_2^i}{3}r^2 + \cdots + \frac{a_L^i}{L+1}r^L = \sum_{k=1}^{L} \frac{a_k^i}{k+1}r^k, \tag{6.12}$$

where a_k^i is the number of all paths of length k containing node i.

Example 23 (A tree of six nodes). Let us calculate the payoff of player 2 in the previous example. Mark all the paths containing node 2. The paths of length 1 are $\{1, 2\}$, $\{2, 4\}$, and $\{2, 5\}$, and hence $a_1^2 = 3$. Next, the paths of length 2 are $\{1, 2, 4\}$, $\{1, 2, 5\}$, $\{4, 2, 5\}$, and $\{2, 1, 3\}$, which yields $a_2^2 = 4$. The paths of length 3 are $\{3, 1, 2, 4\}$, $\{3, 1, 2, 5\}$, and $\{2, 1, 3, 6\}$, so that $a_3^2 = 3$. Finally, the paths of length 4 are $\{4, 2, 1, 3, 6\}$ and $\{5, 2, 1, 3, 6\}$, and the result is $a_4^2 = 2$. Consequently,

$$Y_2 = \frac{3}{2}r + \frac{4}{3}r^2 + \frac{3}{4}r^3 + \frac{2}{5}r^4.$$

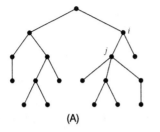 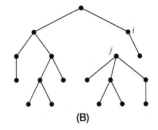

(A)   (B)

Figure 6.10 Trees g and $g - ij$

Now, we show that the suggested allocation rule satisfies Axioms 1 and Axiom 2, thereby coinciding with the Myerson value.

Axiom 1 holds by the definitions of the characteristic function and the allocation rule. The allocation rule also satisfies Axiom 2. Indeed, eliminate the link between nodes i and j to obtain the tree $g - ij$, which consists of the two subtrees illustrated in Fig. 6.10.

The number of paths of length k not containing link ij remains the same for both players after this elimination. On the other hand, the number of paths of length k passing through link ij decreases equally for players i and j. As the allocation rule depends only on the number of paths, the resulting changes in the payoffs are the same for both players.

Hence, it follows that

$$Y_i(v, g) - Y_i(v, g - ij) = Y_j(v, g) - Y_j(v, g - ij).$$

6.4.4 Generating function for the number of paths

For large N, a direct application of formula (6.12) to calculate the Myerson value causes difficulty. We will simplify computations using the generating function approach as follows.

Consider a tree $g_p = (N, E)$ with the root in node p. Introduce the generating function

$$\varphi_p(x) = \sum_{k=1}^{L} \alpha_k^p x^k,$$

where α_k^p is the number of paths that consist of k nodes (length $k - 1$) and contain node p.

For calculating this function, we develop a modified version of Jamison's algorithm [45], who suggested the generating function for the number of subtrees containing k nodes of a tree g.

Let us calculate the generating function recursively. First, set

$$\varphi_q(x) = x$$

at the final nodes q of the tree g_p.

Denote by l the number of players on the maximal length path $\{p, \ldots, q\}$. Consider the nodes q for which the path $\{p, \ldots, q\}$ contains $l-1$ players. If it is not the root p, then let

$$\varphi_q(x) = x\left(1 + \sum_{i=1}^{d} \varphi_{q_i}(x)\right)$$

with summation over all descendants q_i, $i = 1, \ldots, d$, of node q. Continue the process until $l = 2$.

For $l = 2$, the generating function is determined for all descendants of node p. Now, let

$$\varphi_p(x) = x\left(1 + \sum_{i=1}^{d} \varphi_{q_i}(x) + \sum_{i \neq j} \varphi_{q_i}(x)\varphi_{q_j}(x)\right) \tag{6.13}$$

with summation over all descendants q_i, $i = 1, \ldots, d$, of node p.

The proof employs the following considerations. Let $q_1, \ldots, q_d$ be the descendants of node $q \neq p$. Then any path from node q to node s in the tree g_q passes through one of the nodes q_i, and the difference in the path lengths is 1.

On the other hand, if $q = p$, then, in addition to the paths containing k nodes with origin in node p, we have to consider the paths with k nodes that pass through node p and can be composed from the paths containing $k_1 < k$ nodes in the tree g_{q_i} and from the paths containing $k - k_1$ nodes in the tree g_{q_j}, where $i \neq j$. The number of such compound paths is determined by the product in the second sum of expression (6.13).

Example 24 (A tree of six nodes). Consider the tree of the previous example. For the first player, we obtain

$\varphi_4(x) = \varphi_5(x) = \varphi_6(x) = x,$

$\varphi_2(x) = x(1 + \varphi_4(x) + \varphi_5(x)) = x(1 + 2x),$

$\varphi_3(x) = x(1 + \varphi_6(x)) = x(1 + x),$

$\varphi_1(x) = x(1 + \varphi_2(x) + \varphi_3(x) + \varphi_2(x)\varphi_3(x)) = x + 2x^2 + 4x^3 + 3x^4 + 2x^5.$

As a result, $a_1^1 = \alpha_2^1 = 2$, $a_2^1 = \alpha_3^1 = 4$, $a_3^1 = \alpha_4^1 = 3$, and $a_4^1 = \alpha_5^1 = 2$.

6.4.5 General case

Consider a general case where the cooperative game is determined on a weighted graph $g = <N, E>$.

Characteristic function (payoff of coalition S) can be defined by the same way as for the trees. Usually the definition of game-theoretic centrality measure is based on discounting paths. However, we do not consider in general case the shortest paths but rather *simple paths*.

Let us elaborate a bit more on the construction of the characteristic function. Each edge (or direct connection) gives to coalition S the value r, where $0 \leq r \leq 1$. Moreover, players obtain a value from indirect connections. Namely, each *simple* path of length 2 belonging to coalition S gives to this coalition the value r^2, a simple path of length 3 gives to the coalition the value r^3, etc. Set

$$v(i) = 0, \ \forall i \in N.$$

Thus, for any coalition S, we can define the characteristic function as follows:

$$v(S) = a_1(g, S)r + a_2(g, S)r^2 + \ldots = \sum_{k=1}^{\infty} a_k(g, S)r^k, \tag{6.14}$$

where $a_k(g, S)$ is the number of simple paths of length k in this coalition. Note that we write as infinity the limit of summation only for convenience. Clearly, the length of a simple path is bounded by $n - 1$. The following theorem provides a convenient way to calculate the Myerson value corresponding to the characteristic function (6.14).

Theorem 42. *Let the characteristic function of a coalition $S \in 2^N$ be defined by Eq. (6.14). Then the Myerson value of a node i is given by*

$$Y_i(v, g) = \frac{a_1^{(i)}(g, S)}{2}r + \frac{a_2^{(i)}(g, S)}{3}r^2 + \ldots = \sum_{k=1}^{\infty} \frac{a_k^{(i)}(g, S)}{k+1}r^k, \tag{6.15}$$

where $a_k^{(i)}$ is the number of simple paths of length k containing node i.

Proof. We shall prove the theorem by checking directly the Myerson value axioms, i.e., **Axiom 1** and **Axiom 2**.

First, we note the following:

$$(k+1)a_k(g, S) = \sum_{i \in S} a_k^{(i)}(g, S).$$

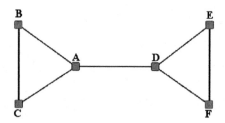

Figure 6.11 A network of six nodes

Since every simple path contains k+1 different nodes, every simple path of the length k is counted k+1 times in the sum $\sum_{i \in S} a_k^{(i)}(g, S)$.

Thus, **Axiom 1** is satisfied:

$$\sum_{i \in S} Y_i(v, g) = \sum_{i \in S} \sum_{k=1}^{\infty} \frac{a_k^{(i)}(g, S)}{k+1} r^k = \sum_{i \in S} a_k(g, S) r^k = v(S).$$

For $ij \in g$, let $a_k^{(ij)}(g, S)$ denote the number of paths of length k traversing the edge ij. Then

$$a_k^{(i)}(g, S) - a_k^{(i)}(g - ij, S) = a_k^{(ij)}(g, S) = a_k^{(j)}(g, S) - a_k^{(j)}(g - ij, S)$$

Thus, **Axiom 2** is satisfied as well.   □

Example 25 (The Myerson value for a network of six nodes). Consider an unweighted network of six nodes, $N = \{A, B, C, D, E, F\}$, presented in Fig. 6.11. For this network, we find $L = 5$ and $a_1 = 7$, $a_2 = 10$, $a_3 = 8$, $a_4 = 8$, $a_5 = 4$. Consequently, the value of the grand-coalition is

$$v(N) = 7r + 10r^2 + 8r^3 + 8r^4 + 4r^5.$$

Let us calculate the payoff of player B using the formula (6.15). Mark all the paths containing node B. The paths of length 1 are $\{A, B\}$, and $\{B, C\}$, hence $a_1^B = 2$. Next, the paths of length 2 are $\{A, B, C\}$, $\{A, C, B\}$, $\{B, A, C\}$, and $\{B, A, D\}$, which yields $a_2^B = 4$. The paths of length 3 are $\{C, B, A, D\}$, $\{B, C, A, D\}$, $\{B, A, D, E\}$, and $\{B, A, D, F\}$, so $a_3^B = 4$. The paths of length 4 are $\{C, B, A, D, E\}$, $\{C, B, A, D, F\}$, $\{B, C, A, D, E\}$, $\{B, C, A, D, F\}$, $\{B, A, D, E, F\}$, and $\{B, A, D, F, E\}$, so $a_4^B = 6$.

Finally, the paths of length 5 are $\{B, C, A, D, E, F\}$, $\{B, C, A, D, F, E\}$, $\{C, B, A, D, E\}$, $\{C, B, A, D, E, F\}$, and $\{B, C, A, D, F, E\}$, and the result is

Figure 6.12 A chain of n nodes

$a_5^B = 2$. Consequently,

$$Y_B = Y_C = Y_E = Y_F = \frac{2}{2}r + \frac{4}{3}r^2 + \frac{4}{4}r^3 + \frac{6}{5}r^4 + \frac{4}{6}r^5.$$

Now we calculate the payoff of player A using the formula (6.15). Mark all the paths containing node A. The paths of length 1 are $\{A, B\}$, $\{A, C\}$, and $\{A, D\}$, hence $a_1^A = 3$. Next, the paths of length 2 are $\{A, B, C\}$, $\{A, C, B\}$, $\{B, A, C\}$, $\{B, A, D\}$, $\{C, A, D\}$, $\{A, D, E\}$, and $\{A, D, F\}$ which yields $a_2^A = 7$. The paths of length 3 are $\{C, B, A, D\}$, $\{B, C, A, D\}$, $\{B, A, D, E\}$, $\{B, A, D, F\}$, $\{C, A, D, E\}$, $\{C, A, D, F\}$, $\{A, D, E, F\}$, and $\{A, D, F, E\}$, so $a_3^A = 8$. The paths of length 4 are $\{C, B, A, D, E\}$, $\{C, B, A, D, F\}$, $\{B, C, A, D, E\}$, $\{B, C, A, D, F\}$, $\{B, A, D, E, F\}$, $\{B, A, D, F, E\}$, $\{C, A, D, E, F\}$, and $\{C, A, D, F, E\}$, so $a_4^A = 8$. Finally, the paths of length 5 are $\{B, C, A, D, E, F\}$, $\{B, C, A, D, F, E\}$, $\{C, B, A, D, E, F\}$, and $\{C, B, A, D, F, E\}$, and the result is $a_5^A = 4$. Consequently,

$$Y_A = Y_D = \frac{3}{2}r + \frac{7}{3}r^2 + \frac{8}{4}r^3 + \frac{8}{5}r^4 + \frac{4}{6}r^5.$$

6.4.6 The Myerson value for a linear graph and star

First, consider a linear graph g (chain) of n nodes.

Let a graph g be a chain of n nodes, as illustrated in Fig. 6.12. The maximal distance between two nodes is $L = n - 1$. The characteristic function of the grand-coalition has the form

$$v(N) = \sum_{i=1}^{n-1}(n - i) \cdot r^i.$$

For any chain, the number of any-length paths that contain nodes 1 and n obviously is $a_k^1 = a_k^n = 1$; besides, for any player, the number of maximal-length paths is $a_{n-1}^i = 1$.

In addition, we can easily establish that, for players $i = \overline{2, n-1}$,

$$a_k^i = \begin{cases} k + 1 & \text{if} \quad 1 \le k \le i - 1, \\ i & \text{if} \quad i \le k \le n - i, \\ n - k & \text{if} \quad n - i + 1 \le k \le n - 2. \end{cases}$$

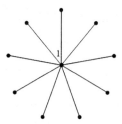

Figure 6.13 A star with center 1

Consequently, the payoffs of players 1 and n are

$$Y_1(v,g) = Y_n(v,g) = \frac{1}{2} \cdot r + \frac{1}{3} \cdot r^2 + \cdots + \frac{1}{k+1} \cdot r^k + \cdots + \frac{1}{n} \cdot r^{n-1} = \sum_{k=1}^{n-1} \frac{1}{k+1} r^k,$$

whereas the payoff of player i, $i \neq 1, n$, makes up

$$Y_i(v,g) = \sum_{k=1}^{i-1} r^k + \sum_{k=i}^{n-i} \frac{i}{k+1} \cdot r^k + \sum_{k=n-i+1}^{n-2} \frac{n-k}{k+1} \cdot r^k + \frac{1}{n} \cdot r^{n-1}.$$

Let the graph g be a star consisting of n nodes, with node 1 being its center (see Fig. 6.13). We calculate the Myerson value directly by definition.

The maximal distance between two nodes in a star is $L = 2$. The characteristic function has the form

$$v(N) = |N-1| \cdot r + C_{|N-1|}^2 \cdot r^2,$$
$$\forall S \not\ni 1, \quad v(S \cup 1) = |S| \cdot r + C_{|S|}^2 \cdot r^2,$$
$$v(S) = 0.$$

The payoff of player 1 is

$$Y_1(v,g) = \sum_{S \subset N \setminus \{i\}} \frac{s!(n-s-1)!}{n!} \left(v(g|_{S \cup 1}) - v(g|_S) \right)$$
$$= \sum_{S \subset N \setminus \{i\}} \frac{s!(n-s-1)!}{n!} v(g|_{S \cup 1}).$$

The value of any coalition containing player 1 depends on the number of its members. On the other hand, the number of coalitions containing s players except for player 1 is C_{n-1}^s. This gives

$$Y_1\left(v,\,g\right)=\sum_{s=1}^{n-1}\frac{s!\cdot(n-s-1)!\cdot C_{n-1}^s}{n!}\cdot\left(r\cdot s+r^2\cdot C_s^2\right)$$

$$=\frac{1}{n}\cdot\sum_{i=1}^{n-1}\left(r\cdot s+r^2\cdot C_s^2\right)=\frac{1}{n}\cdot\sum_{i=1}^{n-1}\left(r\cdot s+r^2\cdot\frac{s\cdot(s-1)}{2}\right)$$

$$=\frac{1}{n}\cdot\left(r\cdot\frac{(n-1)\cdot n}{2}+r^2\cdot\frac{(n-2)\cdot(n-1)\cdot n}{6}\right)=\frac{n-1}{2}\cdot\left(r+r^2\cdot\frac{n-2}{3}\right).$$

For the other players $i=2,\,3,\ldots,n,$

$$Y_i\left(v,\,g\right)=\frac{1}{n-1}\cdot(v(N)-v(1))$$

$$=\frac{1}{n-1}\cdot\left((n-1)\cdot r+\frac{(n-1)\,(n-2)}{2}\cdot r^2-\frac{(n-1)}{2}\cdot r-\frac{(n-1)\,(n-2)}{6}\cdot r^2\right)$$

$$=\frac{1}{2}\cdot r+\frac{n-2}{3}\cdot r^2.$$

Compare these results with the payoffs calculated by formula (6.12):

$$Y_1=\frac{a_1^1}{2}\cdot r+\frac{a_2^1}{3}\cdot r^2=\frac{n-1}{2}\cdot r+\frac{C_{n-1}^2}{3}\cdot r^2$$

$$=\frac{n-1}{2}\cdot r+\frac{(n-1)\cdot(n-2)}{3\cdot 2}\cdot r^2=\frac{n-1}{2}\cdot\left(r+r^2\cdot\frac{n-2}{3}\right),$$

$$Y_i=\frac{a_1^i}{2}\cdot r+\frac{a_2^i}{3}\cdot r^2=\frac{1}{2}\cdot r+\frac{C_{n-2}^1}{3}\cdot r^2=\frac{1}{2}\cdot r+\frac{n-2}{3}\cdot r^2.$$

Clearly, the calculations using the definition of the Myerson value and formula (6.12) yielded the same payoffs, which was to be proved.

6.4.7 Transportation networks

Fig. 6.14 presents the scheme of freight traffic by the Transsiberian Railway. Transsib is a railway network in Russia that connects neighbor countries on the East, namely, South and North Koreas, China and Mongolia with neighbor countries on the West, thereby maintaining economic ties between Asia-Pacific, Europe, and Central Asia. Using the generating function method, calculate the Myerson value for the graph corresponding to this scheme (see Fig. 6.14) with the parameters $r=0.9$, $r=0.5$, and $r=0.2$.

The resulting Myerson values for the top 10 nodes of the graph are given in Table 6.6. We see that Moscow is the largest transportation hub, as it has the maximal Myerson value for all the three values of the parameter r. According to the table, Novosibirsk, Yekaterinburg, and Omsk are also

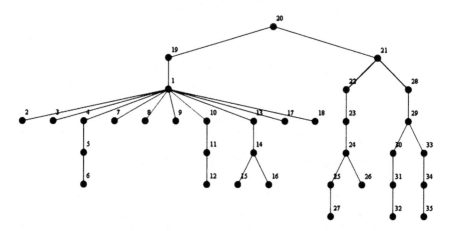

Figure 6.14 Graph corresponding to the Transsiberian Railway

Table 6.6 Myerson value-based ranking of Transsib hubs

$r = 0.9$			$r = 0.5$		
1	Moscow	52.156	1	Moscow	10.162
21	Novosibirsk	26.260	19	Yekaterinburg	2.601
19	Yekaterinburg	24.887	13	Kiev	2.474
20	Omsk	23.035	21	Novosibirsk	0.411
28	Irkutsk	16.341	10	Brest	2.228
29	Ulan-Ude	16.106	4	St. Petersburg	2.228
13	Kiev	14.471	20	Omsk	1.918
22	Almaty	13.687	29	Ulan-Ude	1.916
10	Brest	11.952	14	Choir	1.823
4	St. Petersburg	11.952	28	Irkutsk	1.57

$r = 0.2$		
1	Moscow	1.998
13	Kiev	0.412
21	Novosibirsk	0.411
29	Ulan-Ude	0.405
19	Yekaterinburg	0.401
10	Brest	0.394
4	St. Petersburg	0.394
14	Choir	0.385
24	Tashkent	0.379
20	Omsk	0.292

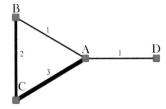

Figure 6.15 A weighted graph

large hubs, though this is not clear from the scheme. Really, these cities have a priority depending on the number of direct links, yet being inferior to Kiev if we also take into account the number of indirect links.

6.4.8 The Myerson value as centrality measure for weighted networks

The approach described in the previous subsections can be applied to weighted networks too. Consider a weighted graph in which the edges have integer weights. Transform each edge of weight m into m parallel edges of weight 1, thereby obtaining a multigraph. The simple path between two nodes in a multigraph is defined in the same way as in an unweighted graph. Note that the number of simple paths increases due to multiedges. If nodes i_1 and i_2 are connected by m edges while nodes i_2 and i_3 by n edges, then obviously nodes i_1 and i_3 are connected by $m \cdot n$ paths. Using the same considerations for the nodes of this multigraph, we naturally define a centrality measure for the original weighted network.

Example 26 (A weighted network of four nodes). Consider a simple example of a weighted graph (see Fig. 6.15) with the following weight matrix:

$$
\begin{array}{c c}
& \begin{array}{cccc} A & B & C & D \end{array} \\
\begin{array}{c} A \\ B \\ C \\ D \end{array} &
\left(\begin{array}{cccc}
0 & 1 & 3 & 1 \\
1 & 0 & 2 & 0 \\
3 & 2 & 0 & 0 \\
1 & 0 & 0 & 0
\end{array} \right).
\end{array}
$$

First, calculate the centrality measure based on geodesics; see Table 6.7. It is intuitively clear that node C has a greater centrality value than node B, since C is connected to A with a higher weight than B. However, we see that node C (and D) has a value zero because there are no shortest paths passing through this node. The node B has a positive centrality value, since

Table 6.7 Centrality measures for weighted graph of four nodes

Nodes	A	B	C	D
Classical betweenness centrality	2/3	1/3	0	0
Myerson value-based centrality ($r = 0.2$)	0.553	0.313	0.540	0.153

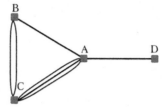

Figure 6.16 Multigraph

the nodes A and C have two connected geodesics AC and ABC, one of which passes through B. Also the nodes C and D have two connected geodesics CAD and $CBAD$ one of which passes through B. So,

$$\sigma_B(B) = \frac{1}{3}(\frac{1}{2} + \frac{1}{2}) = \frac{1}{3}.$$

The node A has a maximal betweenness centrality. The nodes B and D have only one shortest path BAD passing through A. The nodes C and D have two connected shortest paths CAD and $CBAD$ both passing through A. So,

$$\sigma_B(A) = \frac{1}{3}(1+1) = \frac{2}{3}.$$

Now, transform this graph into a multigraph (Fig. 6.16) and calculate the Myerson value.

For this network, we find $L = 3$ and $a_1 = 7$, $a_2 = 15$, $a_3 = 8$. Consequently, the value of the grand-coalition is

$$v(N) = 7r + 15r^2 + 8r^3.$$

Our analysis begins with node A. Here are all simple paths containing node A.

The paths of length 1: $\{A, B\}$, three paths $\{A, C\}, \{A, D\}$, and hence $a_1^A = 5$.

The paths of length 2: $\{B, A, D\}$, two paths $\{A, B, C\}$, three paths $\{C, A, D\}$, three paths $\{B, A, C\}$, six paths $\{A, C, B\}$, and hence $a_2^A = 12$.

The paths of length 3: two paths $\{C, B, A, D\}$ and six paths $\{B, C, A, D\}$, and hence $a_3^A = 8$.

Consequently,

$$Y_A = \frac{5}{2}r + \frac{15}{3}r^2 + \frac{8}{4}r^3 = \frac{5}{2}r + 5r^2 + 2r^3.$$

In a similar fashion, for other players, we find

$$Y_B(G) = \frac{3}{2}r + \frac{1}{3}r^2,$$

$$Y_C(G) = \frac{5}{2}r + r^2,$$

$$Y_D(G) = \frac{1}{2}r + \frac{4}{3}r^2.$$

The centrality values based on the Myerson value with $r = 0.2$ are combined in Table 6.7. This table illustrates the difference in the centrality values of nodes B and C. In contrast to the betweenness centrality approach the Myerson value of the node C is greater than the Myerson value of B.

This algorithm to evaluate the Myerson value-based centrality is difficult due to a nontrivial calculation of the number of simple paths between two nodes in a graph. Recall that we have suggested the generating function approach to find simple paths in an unweighted tree. Let us modify it for the case of weighted trees. The fundamental difference is that, while ascending to the root, we have to copy all the subtrees constructed at each node according to the multiplicity of parallel edges coming from this node.

More precisely put, consider a tree $g_p = (N, E)$ with weighted edges and the root in node p. Introduce the generating function

$$\varphi_p(x) = \sum_{k=1}^{L} \alpha_k^p x^k,$$

where α_k^p is the number of paths containing k nodes (i.e., of length $k - 1$) in the multigraph that pass through node p.

For the final nodes, let

$$\varphi_q(x) = x.$$

For the other nodes of the multigraph except for the root, let

$$\varphi_q(x) = x(1 + \sum_i w(q, q_i)\varphi_{q_i}(x)),$$

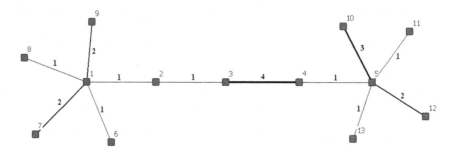

Figure 6.17 Two weighted stars

where q_i denotes the number of all descendants of node q, and $w(q, q_i)$ is the weight of the edge (q, q_i). For the root p, let

$$\varphi_p(x) = x\left(1 + \sum_{i=1}^{d} w(p, q_i)\varphi_{q_i}(x) + \sum_{i \neq j} w(p, q_i)\varphi_{q_i}(x) \cdot w(p, q_j)\varphi_{q_j}(x)\right).$$

$$(6.16)$$

Example 27 (A graph of 13 nodes). Now, we utilize this generating function approach to calculate the centrality measure of node 4 in a weighted tree shown in Fig. 6.17. The weights of the graph edges are given in the figure. Suppose node 4 is the root of this tree.

For the final nodes of the tree, let
$$\varphi_6(x) = \varphi_7(x) = \varphi_8(x) = \varphi_9(x) = \varphi_{10}(x) = \varphi_{11}(x) = \varphi_{12}(x) = \varphi_{13}(x) = x.$$
For the other nodes, calculate
$$\varphi_1(x) = x(1 + \varphi_6(x) + 2 \cdot \varphi_7(x) + \varphi_8(x) + 2 \cdot \varphi_9(x)) = x(1 + 6x);$$
$$\varphi_5(x) = x(1 + 3 \cdot \varphi_{10}(x) + \varphi_{11}(x) + 2 \cdot \varphi_{12}(x) + \varphi_{13}(x)) = x(1 + 7x);$$
$$\varphi_2(x) = x(1 + \varphi_1(x)) = x(1 + x + 6x^2);$$
$$\varphi_3(x) = x(1 + \varphi_2(x)) = x(1 + x + x^2 + 6x^3).$$
For root 4, formula (6.16) yields
$$\varphi_4(x) = x(1 + 4 \cdot \varphi_3(x) + \varphi_5(x) + 4 \cdot \varphi_3(x) \cdot \varphi_5(x)) = x + 5x^2 + 15x^3 + 36x^4 + 56x^5 + 52x^6 + 168x^7.$$
Therefore, $a_1^4 = \alpha_2^4 = 5$, $a_2^4 = \alpha_3^4 = 15$, $a_3^4 = \alpha_4^4 = 36$, $a_4^4 = \alpha_5^4 = 56$, $a_5^4 = \alpha_6^4 = 52$, $a_6^4 = \alpha_7^4 = 168$.
In the final analysis, using formula (6.13), we find

$$Y_4 = \frac{5}{2}r + 5r^2 + 9r^3 + \frac{56}{5}r^4 + \frac{26}{3}r^5 + \frac{168}{7}r^6.$$

CHAPTER 7

Social Networks

Contents

Social networks represent a new phenomenon of our life. They are operated using web resources and intended for social interactions. The growing popularity of social networks in the Web dates back to 1995 when American portal *Classmates.com* was launched. This project facilitated the soon appearance of online social networks (*SixDegrees*, *LiveJournal*, *LinkedIn*, *MySpace*, *Facebook*, *Twitter*, *YouTube*, and others) in the early 2000s. In Russia, the most popular networks are *VKontakte* and *Odnoklassniki*. The analysis methods of social networks are crucial to identify modern trends in different fields of science and to improve communication and exchange of scientific information between different research organizations.

Social networks are visualized using social graphs. Therefore, graph theory provides main analysis tools for social networks. In particular, by calculating centrality measures for nodes and edges we may detect active participants (members) of a social network.

Prior to structural analysis of a social network, we have to construct its graph.

7.1 GRAPH CONSTRUCTION FOR SOCIAL NETWORK

In this section, we show how to construct the graph of a social network using *Twitter* as an example. This is a popular online news and social networking service based on short messages called tweets. Tweets were originally restricted to 140 characters, but on 7 November 2017, the limit was doubled to 280 characters for all languages except Japanese, Korean, and Chinese. As its attributes, each tweet has the author, text content, and author's residence. A retweet is a tweet is which one author refers to another. In a message, such a reference has the form

Networking Games
https://doi.org/10.1016/B978-0-12-816551-5.00013-7
Copyright © 2019 Elsevier Inc.
All rights reserved.

"@nameofAnotherAuthor."

An example of a tweet is

"Attended the lecture together with @VictorPetrov."

After a brief description of *Twitter*, let us construct a graph of this social network. Graph nodes are authors. Edges correspond to retweets. If there exists a retweet of user j by user i and vice versa, then we may draw an edge between nodes i and j.

Authors communicate with each other, thereby forming different communities. A community is a certain group of users with common interests (e.g., political, professional, etc.). Additional information for a structural analysis of a social network graph can be extracted from the messages of network members. We adopt the vector space model to define the weights of a link (edge) in a given graph. Let each author $i \in N$ be associated with the so-called bag of words. This is a document d_i containing all words mentioned in the text of all his tweets.

Form a large bag of words from all documents of a community under study, that is, $D = \cup_{i=1}^{n} d_i$. Suppose it consists of K words.

For each word $k \in d_i$ (also called term), calculate the frequency of occurrence in a document d_i and denote it by w_{ik}. This is the weight of word k in a document d_i. Then each document $d_i, i \in N$, is characterized by a K-dimensional vector $d_i = (w_{i1}, w_{i2}, \ldots, w_{iK})$ in the space R^K. In this case, the weight of a link between two authors i and j (i.e., between documents d_i and d_j) can be defined as the cosine measure of the vectors d_i and d_j, that is,

$$\cos(d_i, d_j) = \frac{(d_i, d_j)}{|d_i||d_j|}.$$

If the cosine measure is 0 or close to 0, then there exists no link at all, or the link is weak. Conversely, if this measure is close to 1, then the link between the corresponding authors is strong.

Note that messages often contain words of little information, such as prepositions, copulas, etc. Then the weight of word k in a document d_i is measured using the term frequency-inverse document frequency

$$w'_{ik} = w_{ik} + \log \frac{n}{|\{d_i \in D : k \in d_i\}|},$$

where the first summand denotes the frequency of occurrence for word k in the document d_i (as before), whereas the second summand characterizes how often this word is mentioned in all other documents from D. With this definition of weights, the links between two documents are measured by analogy to the previous case.

As the result of such calculations, we obtain a weighted graph that reflects a community within the social network under study. A community consists of users, some being very active and the other not. Much information passes through certain users, whereas the others are not remarkable in this sense. Moreover, users have some reputation. All these characteristics should be calculated by appropriate algorithms in order to process large data arrays. It is desirable to have algorithms of moderate complexity and good approximation, for example, with Monte Carlo simulations.

7.2 CENTRALITY MEASURES FOR SOCIAL NETWORKS

Consider a weighted graph constructed for a segment of *VKontakte*, a popular Russian social network. The graph describes an online society dedicated to game theory. This society has 483 participants (members). The weight of an edge is the number of friends in common for corresponding members. By assumption, the probability of friendly relations between two members depends on the total number of friends. This approach is standard in social network analysis.

Fig. 7.1 shows the principal component of the game theory society, which consists of 275 nodes. Using the representation in Fig. 7.1, it is difficult to identify most significant nodes in the sense of connectivity in the graph structure. Therefore, let us modify the graph by removing the nodes with the weights less than 3. The resulting graph is illustrated in Fig. 7.2. The thickness of edges depends on their weights, that is, the number of friends in common.

The current flow centrality values CE_δ calculated for *VKontakte* are given in Table 7.1. Note that $\delta = 0.3$. It seems interesting to compare the current flow centrality values with the results yielded by the PageRank method. This table contains the top-10 nodes in terms of each centrality measure considered.

According to Table 7.1, both methods rank the two main nodes 1 and 8 in the same way. Node 52 connects the component $\{3, 4, 6, 7, 17, 20\}$ with the other nodes of the graph; see Fig. 7.2. Thus, we may expect that node 52 has a high centrality. Similarly, node 7 should be assigned a high rank. The ranking procedure based on the current flow centrality confirms this intuitive hypothesis, as the nodes in question receive ranks 3 and 7, respectively (Table 7.2). Also note that nodes 4, 20, 6, 17, and 3 have ranks

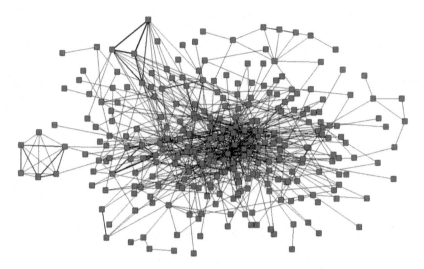

Figure 7.1 Principal component of game theory society in *VKontakte*: the number of nodes 275; the number of edges 805; average path length 3.36

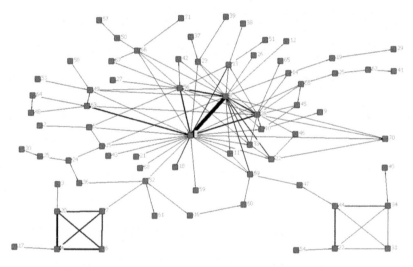

Figure 7.2 Principal component of game theory society in *VKontakte* after removing edges with weights less than 3: the number of nodes 71; the number of edges 116; average path length 3.75

22, 24, 36, 68, and 69, respectively. However, PageRank places nodes 52 and 7 merely to positions 22 and 12, respectively. Furthermore, this method yields ranks 6, 8, and 10 for nodes 4, 20, and 6, respectively, placing them even higher than node 52. This result was not suggested by intuition.

Table 7.1 Centrality measures for *VKontakte* nodes

Nodes	Current flow centrality ($\delta = 0.3$)	Nodes	PageRank-based centrality ($\alpha = 0.85$)
1	0.417	1	0.136
8	0.314	8	0.119
52	0.146	56	0.043
69	0.145	28	0.037
28	0.13	44	0.028
56	0.127	4	0.027
7	0.1	32	0.025
15	0.093	20	0.024
66	0.092	63	0.023
63	0.09	6	0.021

Table 7.2 Results of Monte Carlo simulations

Nodes	Current flow centrality ($\delta = 0.3$)	Nodes	Monte Carlo simulations 10% nodes
1	0.417	1	0.504
8	0.314	8	0.413
52	0.146	52	0.247
69	0.145	23	0.231
28	0.13	28	0.226
56	0.127	20	0.2
7	0.1	7	0.198
15	0.093	24	0.187
66	0.092	63	0.179
63	0.09	10	0.179

In Table 7.2, we present the results of Monte Carlo simulations (see Eq. (6.13)) with a 10% sample of the graph nodes. As before, nodes 1 and 8 are the leaders; the results of simulation experiments also include six nodes from the top-10 list. The Monte Carlo method also properly calculates the ranks of two key nodes 52 and 7.

7.3 MODELING PROFESSIONAL LINKS BY COAUTHORED PUBLICATIONS

This subsection illustrates how the professional links can be revealed by coauthored publications. We apply the described methods to rank the nodes

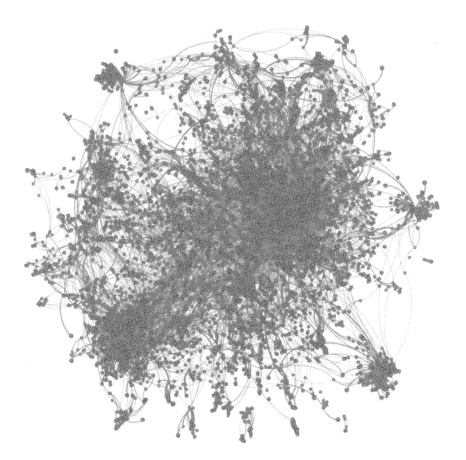

Figure 7.3 *Math-Net.ru* publications graph

of the graph associated with *Math-Net.ru*, a Web portal of mathematical publications [85]. At the moment of our study, the total number of registered authors on the portal was 78 839.

A subgraph of *Math-Net.ru* publications is shown in Fig. 7.3. We consider only one connected component with 7606 mathematicians and 10 747 publications coauthored by them. The nodes of this graph describe the authors, whereas the link weights describe the number of coauthored publications. Note that the publications with more than six coauthors were ignored.

For simplicity, all links with the weights smaller than 7 were deleted; see the principal component of the resulting graph in Fig. 7.4.

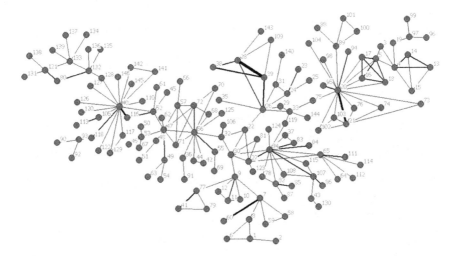

Figure 7.4 Principal component of *Math-Net.ru* publications graph

Table 7.3 Ranking results for *Math-Net.ru* graph nodes

Node	Current flow centrality (CE_δ)	Node	PageRank-based centrality
40	0.157	40	0.044
34	0.149	34	0.032
20	0.136	20	0.032
47	0.125	56	0.027
56	0.125	47	0.020
26	0.108	39	0.018
30	0.090	28	0.018
9	0.081	21	0.016
33	0.080	65	0.016
32	0.079	26	0.015
22	0.079	107	0.014

Clearly, nodes 40, 34, 56, and 20 are the centers of "local" stars and hence must have a high centrality. Note that also node 32 must have a high centrality, since it connects two separate components to form the graph.

Table 7.3 presents the ranking results for the first 11 nodes of the graph using current flow centrality (formula (6.10) with the parameter $\delta = 1$) and the PageRank method with the parameter $\alpha = 0.85$.

As expected, nodes 40, 34, 56, and 20 have high centrality in all ranking methods considered. But the PageRank method assigned a low rank (34) to node 32.

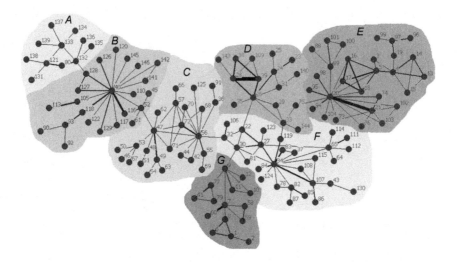

Figure 7.5 Community structure of *Math-Net.ru* graph

7.4 COMMUNITY DETECTION IN NETWORKS

An important problem is to detect communities in social networks. A common detection procedure involves hierarchical trees (dendrograms). The basic idea of this approach lies in the following. As a rule, the edges connecting different communities have a high centrality, and therefore they should be removed from a graph in the first place [38]. For edge centrality evaluation, it is possible to choose any of the measures described in Chapter 6. After removal of several edges, centrality values vary considerably and hence should be recalculated.

We give a brief description of the hierarchical clustering algorithm.

Step 1. Find the centrality values of all edges in a graph.

Step 2. Remove the edge with maximum centrality value from the graph.

Step 3. Recalculate the centrality values of all edges in the modified graph and get back to Step 2.

Terminating this process at some iteration, we partition the graph into communities (clusters): a separate community consists of the nodes of each connected component. Using current flow centrality, the *Math-Net.ru* publications graph was partitioned into seven clusters, as illustrated in Fig. 7.5.

After removal of each edge, the procedure to check the number of connected components in the graph is computationally intensive. We suggest an alternative approach with the following actions:

1. form the list of removed edges in the order of removal;
2. place each node in a separate community;
3. go over the list of removed edges backward and unite the communities that include the nodes of a successive edge.

This approach allows us to form the list of removed edges only once (which is a very computationally intensive procedure due to centrality recalculation), later experimenting with the number of communities.

In network clustering based on game-theoretic methods, communities are represented by coalitions of players. Then community detection can be treated as a stable partition of a player set into coalitions so that each player benefits nothing from changing his coalition.

We can propose the following algorithm for network partitioning based on the Myerson value: Start with a partition of the network $N = \{1, \ldots, n\}$, where each node forms her own coalition. Consider a coalition S_l and a player $i \in S_l$. In the cooperative game with partial cooperation presented by the graph $g|S_l$ we find the Myerson value for player i, $Y_i(g|S_l)$. This is the reward of player i in coalition S_l. Suppose that player i decides to join the coalition S_k. In the new cooperative game with partial cooperation presented by the graph $g|S_k \cup i$ we find the Myerson value $Y_i(g|S_k \cup i)$. So, if for the player $i \in S_l$: $Y_i(g|S_l) \geq Y_i(g|S_k \cup i)$ then player i has no incentive to join to new coalition S_k, otherwise the player changes the coalition.

The partition $N = \{S_1, \ldots, S_K\}$ is the Nash stable or internally stable if for any player there is no benefit to move from his coalition. Notice that our definition of the characteristic function implies that for any coalition it is always beneficial to accept a new player (of course, for the player himself it might not be profitable to join that coalition). Thus, it is important that in the above algorithm we consider the internal and not external stability. If one makes moves according to the external stability, then the result will always be the grand coalition.

We would like to note that the above approach also works in the case of multi-graphs, where several edges (links) are possible between two nodes. In such a case, if two paths contain different links between the same pair of nodes, we consider these paths as different.

Example 28. Consider the network

$$N = \{A, B, C, D, E, F\}$$

presented in Fig. 7.6 (upper graph). First, we transform this weighted graph to the multi-graph as shown in Fig. 7.6 (lower graph). A natural partition

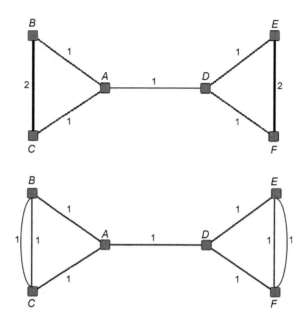

Figure 7.6 A network of six nodes

here consists in $\{S_1 = (A, B, C), S_2 = (D, E, F)\}$. Establish conditions under which this structure is the stable partition.

Suppose that the characteristic function is defined by (6.14). To calculate the imputations, we use the allocation rule from previous chapter. In the coalition S_1, node A participates in 2 simple paths of length 1 $\{\{A, B\}, \{A, C\}\}$ and in 5 simple paths of length 2 $\{\{A, B, C\}, \{A, B, C\}, \{A, C, B\}, \{A, C, B\}, \{B, A, C\}\}$ (note that since the network example is a multi-graph we count twice the paths $\{A, B, C\}$ and $\{A, C, B\}$). Thus, we have

$$Y_A(g|S_1) = \frac{2}{2}r + \frac{5}{3}r^2.$$

In the coalition $S_2 \cup A$, node A participates in 1 simple path of length 1 $\{A, D\}$, in 2 simple paths of length 2 $\{\{A, D, E\}, \{A, D, F\}\}$ and in 4 simple paths of length 3 $\{\{A, D, E, F\}, \{A, D, E, F\}, \{A, D, F, E\}, \{A, D, F, E\}\}$ (again these paths are counted twice for the multi-graph). Thus,

$$Y_A(g|S_2 \cup A) = \frac{1}{2}r + \frac{2}{3}r^2 + \frac{4}{4}r^3.$$

We see that for player A it is not profitable to move from S_1 to $S_2 \cup A$, if

$$\frac{1}{2}r + r^2 - r^3 > 0,$$

which is valid for all r in the interval $(0, 1]$. Therefore, in this partition node A has no incentive to change the coalition under any choice of r. So, the partition $\{S_1 = (A, B, C), S_2 = (D, E, F)\}$ is the Nash stable for any r.

7.5 HEDONIC GAMES

It is possible to apply game-theoretic methods to network partitioning problem within the framework of hedonic games [9]. This approach is based on specification of a preference relation.

Suppose that the set of players $N = \{1, \ldots, n\}$ is divided into K coalitions, that is, $\Pi = \{S_1, \ldots, S_K\}$. Let $S_\Pi(i)$ denote a coalition $S_k \in \Pi$ such that $i \in S_k$. The preferences of player i are represented by a complete, reflexive, and transitive binary relation $\succeq_i$ over the set $\{S \subset N : i \in S\}$. The preferences are additively separable if there exists a value function $v_i : N \to \mathbb{R}$ such that $v_i(i) = 0$ and

$$S_1 \succeq_i S_2 \Leftrightarrow \sum_{j \in S_1} v_i(j) \geq \sum_{j \in S_2} v_i(j).$$

The preferences $\{v_i, i \in N\}$ are symmetric if $v_i(j) = v_j(i) = v_{ij} = v_{ji}$ for all $i, j \in N$. The symmetry property defines a very important class of hedonic games.

As in the previous section, a network partition Π is *Nash stable* if $S_\Pi(i) \succeq_i S_k \cup \{i\}$ for all $i \in N$ and $S_k \in \Pi \cup \{\emptyset\}$. In the Nash-stable partition, none of the players benefits from leaving his coalition.

A potential of a coalition partition $\Pi = \{S_1, \ldots, S_K\}$ is

$$P(\Pi) = \sum_{k=1}^{K} P(S_k) = \sum_{k=1}^{K} \sum_{i,j \in S_k} v_{ij}.$$

Our method for detecting a stable community structure is based on the following best-reply dynamics.

Start from an arbitrary partition of the network $N = \{S_1, \ldots, S_K\}$. Choose any player i and any coalition S_k different from $S_\Pi(i)$. If $S_k \cup \{i\} \succeq_i S_\Pi(i)$, then assign node i to the coalition S_k; otherwise, keep the partition unchanged and choose another pair of candidates (node and coalition).

Since the game has potential $P(\Pi)$, the algorithm converges in a finite number of steps.

Theorem 43. *If the players' preferences are additively separable and symmetric ($v_{ii} = 0$, $v_{ij} = v_{ji}$ for all $i, j \in N$), then the coalition partition Π yielding a local maximum of the potential $P(\Pi)$ is Nash stable.*

One natural way to define a symmetric value function v with a parameter $\alpha \in [0, 1]$ is as follows:

$$v_{ij} = \begin{cases} 1 - \alpha, & (i,j) \in E, \\ -\alpha, & (i,j) \notin E, \\ 0, & i = j. \end{cases} \tag{7.1}$$

For any subgraph $(S, E|S)$, $S \subseteq N$, denote by $n(S)$ the number of nodes in S and by $m(S)$ the number of edges in S. Then, for the value function (7.1), the potential takes the form

$$P(\Pi) = \sum_{k=1}^{K} \left(m(S_k) - \frac{n(S_k)(n(S_k) - 1)\alpha}{2} \right). \tag{7.2}$$

We can characterize the limiting cases $\alpha \to 0$ and $\alpha \to 1$.

Consider a special case of network partition into cliques. A clique is a fully connected subgraph of a graph G. First, find the maximal clique S_1 in a graph G (a maximal clique is a clique that is not contained in another clique). Eliminate all nodes that belong to the clique S_1 from G and consider the new graph G'. Then find the maximal clique S_2 in the graph G' and continue this procedure until obtaining a partition $\{S_1, \ldots, S_K\}$ of the network G into cliques. Call this procedure the sequential network decomposition into maximal cliques.

Theorem 44. *If $\alpha = 0$, then the grand coalition partition $\Pi_N = \{N\}$ yields the maximum of the potential P. As $\alpha \to 1$, the local maximum of this potential corresponds to a network decomposition into disjoint maximal cliques if such a decomposition exists.*

Proof. It is immediate to check that, for $\alpha = 0$, the grand coalition partition $\Pi_N = \{N\}$ gives the maximum of the potential P, and $P(\Pi_N) = m(N)$. For the values α close to 1, the partition into maximal cliques $\Pi = \{S_1, \ldots, S_K\}$ gives the maximum of the potential P. Indeed, suppose player i from the clique $S_{\Pi}(i)$ of size m_1 moves to a clique S_j of size $m_2 < m_1$. Player $i \in S_{\Pi}(i)$

and S_j are connected by at most m_2 links. The impact on $P(\Pi)$ of this movement is not greater than

$$m_2(1 - \alpha) - (m_1 - 1)(1 - \alpha) \leq 0,$$

which is nonbeneficial for player i. Now, suppose player i from the clique $S_\Pi(i)$ moves to a clique S_j of size $m_2 \geq m_1$. Note that the clique S_j was obtained using the sequential decomposition procedure before the clique $S_\Pi(i)$. Player $i \in S_\Pi(i)$ is connected with the clique S_j by at most $m_2 - 1$ links. Otherwise, the clique S_j would be increased by adding node i, which obviously contradicts the fact that S_j is the maximal clique in the decomposition procedure.

If player i benefits by moving from the coalition $S_\Pi(i)$ to the clique S_j, then for the new partition, the potential would increase in comparison with the partition Π at most by

$$m_2 - 1 - m_2\alpha - (m_1 - 1)(1 - \alpha) = m_2 - m_1 - \alpha(m_2 - m_1 + 1).$$

For α close to 1, this increment is negative, so player i benefits nothing from joining the coalition S_j.   □

The grand coalition and the maximal clique decomposition are two extreme stable partitions into communities. By varying the parameter α we can easily tune the resolution of the community detection algorithm.

Example 29. Consider the network shown in Fig. 7.6 under the assumption that all edges have weight 1. In this case, there are only two Nash-stable partitions, that is, $\Pi = N$ for small values $\alpha \leq 1/9$ and $\Pi = \{\{A, B, C\}, \{D, E, F\}\}$ for $\alpha > 1/9$.

Example 30. Consider a graph $G = G_1 \cup G_2 \cup G_3 \cup G_4$ that consists of $n = 26$ nodes and $m = 78$ (see Fig. 7.7). This graph includes four cliques, namely, $(G_1, 8, 28)$, with eight nodes connected by 28 edges, and $(G_2, 5, 10)$, $(G_3, 6, 15)$, and $(G_4, 7, 21)$. The subgraph G_1 is connected with G_2 by 1 edge, G_2 with G_3 by 2 edges, and G_3 with G_4 by 1 edge.

First, calculate the potential P for different values of the parameter $\alpha \in [0, 1]$. It is easy to find $P(G) = 78 - 325\alpha$, $P(\{G_1, G_2 \cup G_3 \cup G_4\}) = 77 - 181\alpha$, $P(\{G_1, G_2 \cup G_3, G_4\}) = 76 - 104\alpha$, and $P(\{G_1, G_2, G_3, G_4\}) = 74 - 74\alpha$.

Other coalition partitions yield smaller potentials: $P(\{G_1 \cup G_2, G_3 \cup G_4\}) = 76 - 156\alpha < 76 - 104\alpha$, $P(\{G_1 \cup G_2 \cup G_3, G_4\}) = 77 - 192\alpha <$

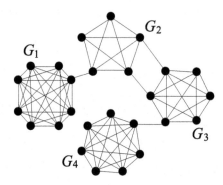

Figure 7.7 A network with four cliques

Table 7.4 Nash-stable coalition partitions in Example 30

α	Coalition partition	Potential
$[0, 1/144]$	$G_1 \cup G_2 \cup G_3 \cup G_4$	$78 - 325\alpha$
$[1/144, 1/77]$	$G_1, G_2 \cup G_3 \cup G_4$	$77 - 181\alpha$
$[1/77, 1/15]$	$G_1, G_2 \cup G_3, G_4$	$76 - 104\alpha$
$[1/15, 1]$	G_1, G_2, G_3, G_4	$74 - 74\alpha$

$77 - 181\alpha$, $P(\{G_1, G_2, G_3 \cup G_4\}) = 75 - 116\alpha < 76 - 104\alpha$, and $P(\{G_1 \cup G_2, G_3, G_4\}) = 75 - 114\alpha < 76 - 104\alpha$.

By solving a sequence of linear inequalities we find the maximum value of the potential for all $\alpha \in [0, 1]$. The results are presented in Table 7.4.

Example 31. Consider a popular example of the social network from Zachary karate club (see Fig. 7.8). In his study [84], Zachary observed 34 members of a karate club over a period of two years. A disagreement between the club's administrator and instructor caused the appearance of two new clubs associated with the instructor (node 1) and administrator (node 34) of sizes 16 and 18, respectively. The relations in a club are indicated by edges in Fig. 7.8.

The authors [38] divided this network into two groups (communities) of nearly equal size using the hierarchical clustering tree. It was demonstrated that the resulting partition almost perfectly matches the actual division of the club members after the break–up. Only one node, node 3, was classified incorrectly.

Now, let us apply the hedonic game approach to the karate club network. Start from the final partition $N = \{L, R\}$ obtained in [38], where

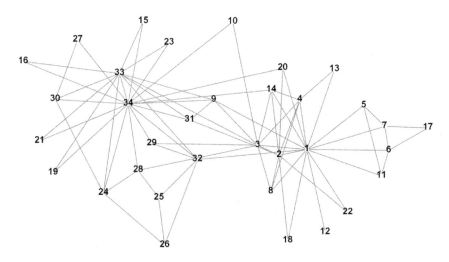

Figure 7.8 Zachary karate club network

$$R = \{1, 2, 4, 5, 6, 7, 8, 11, 12, 13, 14, 17, 18, 20, 22\}, L = N \setminus R.$$

Calculate the potential for the grand-coalition, $P(N) = 78 - 561\alpha$, and also for the final partition, $P(L, R) = 68 - 276\alpha$. By solving the equation $P(N) = P(L, R)$, obtain the cutoff point $\alpha = 2/57$. So, if $\alpha < 2/57$, then $P(N)$ is larger than $P(L, R)$; hence, the partition $\{L, R\}$ is not Nash-stable. For $\alpha = 2/57$, the potential increases if node 3 moves from L to R. For the new partition, $P(L_1, R_1) = 68 - 273\alpha$, where

$$R_1 = R \cup \{3\}, \quad L_1 = L \setminus \{3\}.$$

A direct comparison with the potential of the grand coalition gives the cutoff point $\alpha = 5/144$. For $\alpha = 5/144$, the potential increases if node 10 moves to R_1.

Now, $P(L_2, R_2) = 68 - 272\alpha$, where

$$R_2 = R_1 \cup \{10\}, \quad L_2 = L_1 \setminus \{10\},$$

and the new cutoff point is $\alpha = 10/289$.

Finally, for $1/16 \geq \alpha \geq 10/289$, the Nash-stable partition is

$$R_2 = \{1, 2, 3, 4, 5, 6, 7, 8, 10, 11, 12, 13, 14, 17, 18, 20, 22\} \cup \{N \setminus R_2\}.$$

Note that, in this new partition, node 3 belongs to the "right" coalition.

Another natural approach to define a symmetric preference relation is, roughly speaking, to compare the network under investigation with the configuration random graph model.

The paper [66] introduced the concept of modularity, which consists in the following. Suppose it is necessary to form a network with n nodes and m edges (links). A configuration random graph is constructed as follows. From each node i, random half-arcs d_i come to other nodes, where d_i is the degree of node i. Then the expected number of links between nodes i and j makes up $d_i d_j / (2m)$, where $m = 1/2 \sum d_i$ is the total number of links in the network. However, the real number of links between nodes i and j is A_{ij}. Then the difference between the real and expected numbers characterizes modularity. A partition that maximizes this difference mostly matches the real network.

Therefore, we may define a preference relation (value function) as

$$v_{ij} = \beta_{ij} \left(A_{ij} - \gamma \frac{d_i d_j}{2m} \right), \tag{7.3}$$

where A_{ij} is a number of links between nodes i and j, d_i and d_j denote the degrees of nodes i and j, respectively, $m = \frac{1}{2} \sum_{l \in N} d_l$ gives the total number of links in the network, and $\beta_{ij} = \beta_{ji}$ and γ represent some parameters.

Note that, if $\beta_{ij} = \beta$ for $i, j \in N$ and $\gamma = 1$, then the potential coincides with the network modularity [66].

Thus, we obtain the following game-theoretic interpretation of the modularity value function. The coalition partition $\Pi = \{S_1, \ldots, S_K\}$ that maximizes the potential

$$P(\Pi) = \sum_{k=1}^{K} \sum_{i,j \in S_k, i \neq j} \left(A_{ij} - \frac{d_i d_j}{2m} \right) \tag{7.4}$$

gives the Nash-stable partition of the network in the hedonic game with the value function defined by (7.3), where $\gamma = 1$ and $\beta_{ij} = \beta$.

Example 32. For the network presented in Fig. 7.6, we calculate $P(N) = 3/2$, $P(\{B, C\} \cup \{A, D\} \cup \{E, F\}) = P(\{A, B, C, D\} \cup \{E, F\}) = 7/2$, and $P(\{A, B, C\} \cup \{D, E, F\}) = 5$. Thus, using the modularity value function with $\gamma = 1$ and $\beta_{ij} = \beta$, we construct the unique Nash-stable partition $\Pi = \{\{A, B, C\}, \{D, E, F\}\}$.

Example 33 (Zachary karate club). According to numerical calculations, the partition $S_{17} \cup \{N \setminus S_{17}\}$ gives the maximum of the modularity-based potential function. In other words, this partition is Nash stable.

7.6 A SEARCH ALGORITHM FOR NASH STABLE PARTITION

In this section, we describe an algorithm to find a stable partition under a given potential of form (7.2) or (7.4) with a fixed value of the parameter α or γ, respectively. A stable partition is a partition that yields a local maximum of the potential.

Take an arbitrary starting partition Π_0 as the input of the algorithm. At each iteration, examine a current partition Π and a partition $\Pi'i$ that is obtained by moving player $i \in S_{\Pi(i)}$ to a coalition $S_k \in \Pi$. Between them, choose a partition Π' such that $P(\Pi') - P(\Pi) \to$ max. If $P(\Pi') - P(\Pi) > 0$, then the new current partition is Π'; otherwise, the current partition Π is the desired stable partition.

First, consider potential (7.2). Suppose that, in the current partition Π, player i moves from the coalition $S_{\Pi(i)}$ to a coalition S_k. In the coalition S_k, player i acquires $d_i(S_k \cup i)$ links of the weight $1 - \alpha$ minus $m(S_k) + 1 - d_i(S_k \cup i)$ links of the weight α. At the same time, in the old coalition, player i loses $d_i(S_{\Pi(i)})$ links of the weight $1 - \alpha$ minus $m(S_{\Pi(i)}) - d_i(S_{\Pi(i)})$ links of the weight α.

Therefore, the variation of the potential is

$$P(\Pi') - P(\Pi) = \quad d_i(S_k \cup i) - d_i(S_{\Pi(i)}) + \alpha(m(S_{\Pi(i)}) - m(S_k) - 1).$$

If player i has individual behavior, then the variation takes the form

$$P(\Pi') - P(\Pi) = \quad -d_i(S_{\Pi(i)}) + \alpha(m(S_{\Pi(i)}) - 1).$$

Now, find the variation of potential (7.4). Assume that, in the current partition Π, player i moves from the coalition $S_{\Pi(i)}$ to a coalition S_k. In the coalition S_k, potential increases by $d_i(S_k \cup i)$ links minus $\frac{\gamma d_i}{2m} \sum_{j \in S_k} d_j$ links. At the same time, in the old coalition, player i loses $d_i(S_{\Pi(i)})$ links, and the potential decreases by this value minus $\frac{\gamma d_i}{2m} \sum_{j \in S_{\Pi(i)} \setminus i} d_j$.

Hence,

$$P(\Pi') - P(\Pi) = -d_i(S_\Pi(i)) + d_i(S_k \cup i) +$$

$$\frac{\gamma d_i}{2m} \left(\sum_{j \in S_\Pi(i)} d_j - \sum_{j \in S_k} d_j \right) - \frac{\gamma d_i^2}{2m}.$$

As an example, consider the graph illustrated in Fig. 7.9. It consists of two complete subgraphs, $G_1 = \{A, B, C, D, E\}$ and $G_2 = \{J, K, L, M, N\}$.

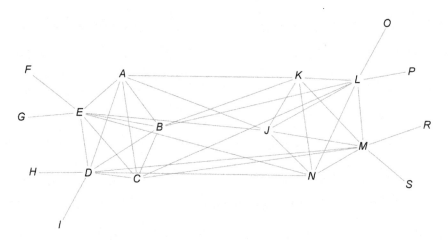

Figure 7.9 An example of graph

Besides, the graph contains 10 edges between G_1 and G_2, that is, the pairs (u, w) such that $u \in G_1$ and $w \in G_2$. Finally, there are four nodes adjacent to nodes from G_1 and also four nodes adjacent to G_2.

A most natural partition of this graph into two clusters is $\Pi = S_L \cup S_R = \{A, B, \ldots, H, I\} \cup \{J, K, \ldots, R, S\}$. The first cluster is represented by the nodes in the left part of the figure, whereas the second by its right part.

For potential (7.4), we have

$$P(S_L \cup S_R) = 28 - \gamma \cdot 31\tfrac{13}{19}.$$

Moving node J to the other cluster gives

$$P(\{S_L \setminus J\} \cup \{S_R \cup J\}) = 26 - \gamma \cdot 32\tfrac{12}{19}.$$

It is important that $P(S_L \cup S_R) > P(\{S_L \setminus J\} \cup \{S_R \cup J\})$ for any values $0 < \gamma < 1$. The other partitions into clusters that can be obtained from $S_L \cup S_R$ by moving only one node yield smaller values of the potential. In other words, the local maximum of the potential is achieved on $S_L \cup S_R$, and hence we have constructed a Nash-stable partition.

Now, calculate the potential using formula (7.2):

$$P(S_L \cup S_R) = 28 - 72\alpha.$$

If node J moves to the other cluster, then

$$P(\{S_L \setminus J\} \cup \{S_R \cup J\}) = 26 - 73\alpha.$$

Again, we may easily establish the inequality $P(S_L \cup S_R) > P(\Pi')$ for all partitions Π' obtained from $S_L \cup S_R$ by moving only one node and also for any values α. So, $S_L \cup S_R$ is a Nash stable partition in the game with potential (7.2).

However, there exist other partitions. Consider

$$\Pi^* = \{A, B, C, D, E, J, K, L, M, N\} \cup \{F\} \cup \{G\} \cup \{H\} \cup \{I\} \cup \{O\} \cup \{P\}$$
$$\cup \{R\} \cup \{S\}.$$

Using formula (7.2), we calculate the potential $P(\Pi^*) = 30 - 45\alpha$, that is, $P(\Pi^*) > P(S_L \cup S_R)$. Note that our stable partition algorithm has produced exactly this partition.

The modularity-based approach gives $P(\Pi^*) = 30 - \gamma \cdot 42\frac{12}{19}$. The inequality $P(\Pi^*) > P(S_L \cup S_R)$ holds for $\gamma < \frac{19}{108}$. However, under these values γ, the partition Π^* is not Nash-stable, and the stable partition algorithm unites all nodes into one cluster $\Pi = \{A, B, \ldots, R, S\}$.

CHAPTER 8

Games on Transportation Networks

Contents

Transportation problems have always been attracting the attention of researchers and engineers owing to their importance for real life. A competition on this market generates numerous game-theoretical models. Such problems arise in passenger and freight traffic analysis (railways, airlines), arrangement of transportation hubs, and so on. Traffic control is a pressing problem of this class, mostly for large cities and megalopolises. However, in recent time, even small cities and towns have encountered this problem. A growing number of vehicles, both in the segments of private and public transport, has overloaded road infrastructure and caused hours-long traffic jamming, inconvenience for pedestrians, an increased number of traffic accidents, and so on.

There exist different methods for resolving traffic jamming and associated transportation problems. Meanwhile, it is not easy to construct an adequate mathematical model of a transportation system for further optimization due to several peculiarities of such systems. In this context, we should mention:

1. the variability of traffic flows (i.e., flow characteristics can be assessed merely with some probability);

2. the irregularity of traffic flows (i.e., flow characteristics depend on the time of day, day of the week, etc.);

3. the incomplete regulation of traffic flows (i.e., even under the availability of exhaustive data on traffic flows and a technical feasibility to inform

Networking Games
https://doi.org/10.1016/B978-0-12-816551-5.00014-9
Copyright © 2019 Elsevier Inc.
All rights reserved.
171

drivers about appropriate actions in a current traffic situation, any messages are merely nonbinding recommendations);

4. the multiplicity of performance criteria (trip delay, average speed, the forecasted number of traffic accidents, etc.); most of them are interconnected, and a single criterion is insufficient for analysis;

5. the inherent complexity of measuring basic characteristics (e.g., traffic intensity).

In transportation modeling, we have also to take into account the existing passenger traffic flows on different routes. The volumes of passenger traffic on different routes partially affect public transport scheduling (the intensity and direction of bus service). Therefore, it is difficult to design an analytical model that incorporates all specifics of a transportation systems, including a conflict of interests between system participants. This conflict naturally leads to game-theoretic methods for solving transportation problems.

8.1 TRANSPORTATION NETWORK AND CORRESPONDENCE MATRIX

A typical example of an urban transportation network is shown in Fig. 8.1. In the general case, a transportation model can be represented by a graph with nodes acting as stops and edges as transport passageways (see Fig. 8.2).

In transportation problems, an important role is played by the correspondence matrix, which characterizes the intensity of passenger traffic between different stops. We will adopt the Poisson flow model, thereby treating passenger traffic intensity as the intensity of a Poisson process. Note that calculation of the correspondence matrix is not a trivial problem [36,37].

Choose a certain route of a transport vehicle (a city bus), that is, a sequence of K stops connected by edges. The correspondence matrix for this route, $\Lambda = (\lambda_{ij})$, $i, j = 1, 2, \ldots, K$, defines the passenger traffic intensity from node i to node j.

Suppose there are direct passenger traffic flows on this route. Denote by $x_1^r, x_2^r, \ldots, x_K^r$ the numbers of incoming passengers at stops $i = 1, \ldots, K$, respectively, in experiment r, where $r = 1, \ldots, N$. By analogy, the values $y_1^r, y_2^r, \ldots, y_K^r$ will characterize the number of outgoing passengers at stops $j = 1, \ldots, K$, respectively, in experiment r, where $r = 1, \ldots, N$. Obviously, $x_K^r = y_1^r = 0$ for any experiment r. The values x_i^r and y_j^r are observable in the model. Denote by λ_{ij}^r the number of passengers incoming at stop i and out-

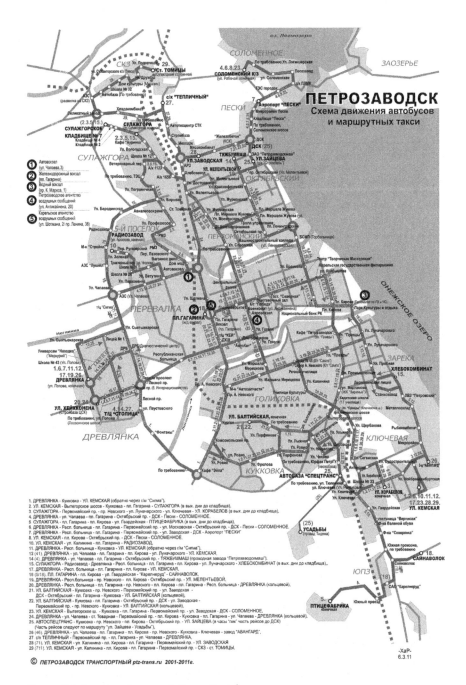

Figure 8.1 An urban transportation network

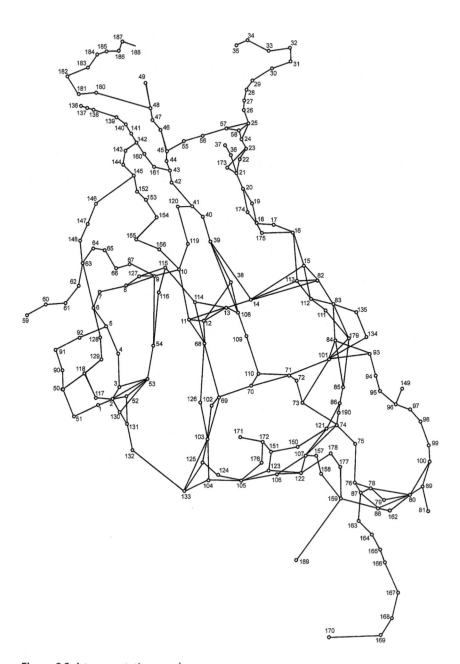

Figure 8.2 A transportation graph

Table 8.1 Information on incoming passengers

$y_{11}^r=0$	y_{12}^r	y_{13}^r	...	y_{1K-1}^r	y_{1K}^r	x_1^r
0	$y_{22}^r=0$	y_{23}^r	...	y_{2K-2}^r	y_{2K}^r	x_2^r
...	...	...	...			
0	0	0	...	$y_{K-1,K-1}^r=0$	$y_{K-1,K}^r$	x_{K-1}^r
0	0	0	...	0	0	$x_K^r=0$
$y_1^r=0$	y_2^r	y_3^r	...	y_{K-1}^r	y_K^r	

Table 8.2 Probability distribution of passengers

$p_{11}=0$	p_{12}	p_{13}	...	p_{1K-1}	p_{1K}	1
0	$p_{22}=0$	p_{23}	...	p_{2K-1}	p_{2K}	1
...	...	...	...	...	...	...
0	0	0	...	$p_{K-1,K-1}=0$	$p_{K-1,K}$	1

going at stop j. These are unobservable values that have to be estimated. For convenience, information on passenger traffic can be presented in tabular form, Table 8.1.

Table 8.1 demonstrates the results of experiment r. All elements in the last column are the sums of elements from the corresponding row; similarly, the last row contains the sums of elements from the corresponding column. The value λ_{ij}^r gives the (unobservable) number of passengers who get into the bus at stop i and get out at stop j in experiment r, that is,

$$y_j^r = \sum_{i=1}^{j-1} y_{ij}^r.$$

In each experiment, we observe the elements of the last column and row only. For all i and j, suppose that the passenger traffic flows y_{ij}^r are independent (for different r) random variables that obey the same distribution. Their average value is the intensity of passenger traffic over an appropriate route. Denote by p_{ij} the share of passengers who get into the bus at stop i and get out at stop j. We construct Table 8.2 from these values as follows.

In Table 8.2 the sum of elements in each row is 1. In fact, each row represents the polynomial distribution of the probabilities of getting out at different stops (columns of this row) for the passengers who get into the bus at the stop with the same index as this row.

Consider experiment r and multiply row i from Table 8.2 by x_i^r. Then the resulting row corresponds to row i from Table 8.1, since $x_i^r p_{ij}$ is the expected value of the random variable y_{ij}^r. Note that the random vari-

Table 8.3 Information on incoming passengers

Stop no.	Experiment no.														
	1	2	3	4	5	6	7	8	9	10	11	12	13	14	15
1	4	6	5	4	4	5	5	4	5	6	4	4	5	6	4
2	3	2	2	3	3	2	2	3	2	2	3	3	3	2	2
3	1	2	2	1	2	2	1	1	2	1	2	1	1	1	1
4	3	2	2	2	2	2	2	2	2	3	2	3	2	2	2

ables in the same column of Table 8.1 are mutually independent. Hence, their deviations from the expected value are random and independent and compensate each other in case of summation. Therefore, in a rough approximation, we have the equality

$$Y_j^r \approx \sum_{i=1}^{j-1} x_i^r p_{ij}.$$

For a large number of experiments N, the resulting equations are linearly independent because the coefficients in different equations represent mutually independent random variables. Consequently, these equations can be solved in the unknown probabilities p_{ij} $(i < j, j = 1, \ldots, K)$ using the least-squares method or the minimization method for the sum of absolute deviations.

After obtaining the estimates p_{ij}, we calculate the passenger traffic intensities between nodes i and j by the formula

$$\lambda_{ij} = \frac{1}{N} \sum_{r=1}^{N} x_i^r p_{ij}, \quad i, j = 1, 2, \ldots, K.$$

8.2 TRAFFIC INTENSITY CALCULATION: AN EXAMPLE

In this section, we illustrate the traffic intensity calculation method using a real example. Consider a city bus route that contains five stops. Let us analyze direct passenger traffic flows on this route. According to the model, p_{12} describes the passenger traffic flow between stops 1 and 2, p_{13} between stops 1 and 3, and so on. For evaluating the characteristics of passenger traffic flows, we have conducted 100 numerical experiments. The results of the first 15 experiments are combined in Tables 8.3 and 8.4.

To find the unknown variables p_{ij} $(i < j, j = 1, \ldots, K)$, we employ the least-squares method. It is necessary to minimize the sum of squared devi-

Table 8.4 Information on outcoming passengers

Stop no.	Experiment no.														
	1	2	3	4	5	6	7	8	9	10	11	12	13	14	15
2	3	3	3	3	2	3	2	3	3	2	3	3	3	3	4
3	3	5	4	4	3	4	4	4	3	5	3	3	3	4	2
4	3	3	3	1	4	3	2	1	3	2	4	2	3	3	2
5	2	1	1	2	2	1	2	2	2	3	1	3	2	1	1

ations

$$s = \sum_{r=1}^{N} \sum_{j=2}^{K} \left(y_j^r - \sum_{i=1}^{j-1} x_i^r p_{ij} \right)^2$$

subject to the constraints

$$\sum_{j=i+1}^{K} p_{ij} = 1, \ i = 1, \ldots, K-1,$$

and

$$p_{ij} \geq 0 \ \forall i, j.$$

For $N = 100$ and $K = 5$,

$$s = \sum_{r=1}^{100} \sum_{j=2}^{5} \left(y_j^r - \sum_{i=1}^{j-1} x_i^r p_{ij} \right)^2 = \sum_{r=1}^{100} \left[\left(y_2^r - x_1^r p_{12} \right)^2 \right.$$
$$+ \left(y_3^r - x_1^r p_{13} - x_2^r p_{23} \right)^2 + \left(y_4^r - x_1^r p_{14} - x_2^r p_{24} - x_3^r p_{34} \right)^2$$
$$\left. + \left(y_5^r - x_1^r p_{15} - x_2^r p_{25} - x_3^r p_{35} - x_4^r p_{45} \right)^2 \right] \to \min$$

subject to the constraints $p_{12} + p_{13} + p_{14} + p_{15} = 1$, $p_{23} + p_{24} + p_{25} = 1$, $p_{34} + p_{35} = 1$, and $p_{ij} \geq 0$ for all i and j.

The Lagrange method of multipliers yields the following estimates of the probabilities p_{ij}: $p_{12} = 0.48$, $p_{13} = 0.52$, $p_{14} = 0$, $p_{15} = 0$, $p_{23} = 0.67$, $p_{24} = 0.33$, $p_{25} = 0$, $p_{34} = 1$, $p_{35} = 0$, and $p_{45} = 1$.

Then we can calculate the passenger traffic intensities. Their approximate values are as follows: $\lambda_{12} = 2.27$, $\lambda_{13} = 2.45$, $\lambda_{14} = 0$, $\lambda_{15} = 0$, $\lambda_{23} = 1.54$, $\lambda_{24} = 0.76$, $\lambda_{15} = 0$, $\lambda_{34} = 1.4$, $\lambda_{35} = 0$, and $\lambda_{45} = 2.6$.

The unknown probabilities p_{ij} can be evaluated using the minimization method for the sum of absolute deviations. For $N = 100$ experiments and

$K = 5$ stops, the sum of absolute deviations s_1 has the form

$$s_1 = \sum_{r=1}^{100} \sum_{j=2}^{5} \left| y_j^r - \sum_{i=1}^{j-1} x_i^r p_{ij} \right| = \sum_{r=1}^{100} \left[|y_2^r - x_1^r p_{12}| \right.$$

$$+ \left| y_3^r - x_1^r p_{13} - x_2^r p_{23} \right| + \left| y_4^r - x_1^r p_{14} - x_2^r p_{24} - x_3^r p_{34} \right|$$

$$\left. + \left| y_5^r - x_1^r p_{15} - x_2^r p_{25} - x_3^r p_{35} - x_4^r p_{45} \right| \right] \to \min$$

subject to the constraints $p_{12} + p_{13} + p_{14} + p_{15} = 1$, $p_{23} + p_{24} + p_{25} = 1$, $p_{34} + p_{35} = 1$, and $p_{ij} \geq 0$ for all i and j.

Introduce the new variables

$$Z_j^r = \begin{cases} y_j^r - \sum_{i=1}^{j-1} x_i^r p_{ij} & \text{if } y_j^r - \sum_{i=1}^{j-1} x_i^r p_{ij} \geq 0, \\ 0 & \text{if } y_j^r - \sum_{i=1}^{j-1} x_i^r p_{ij} < 0 \end{cases}$$

and

$$W_j^r = \begin{cases} \sum_{i=1}^{j-1} x_i^r p_{ij} - y_j^r & \text{if } y_j^r - \sum_{i=1}^{j-1} x_i^r p_{ij} \leq 0, \\ 0 & \text{if } y_j^r - \sum_{i=1}^{j-1} x_i^r p_{ij} > 0. \end{cases}$$

Clearly,

$$y_j^r - \sum_{i=1}^{j-1} x_i^r p_{ij} = Z_j^r - W_j^r$$

and

$$\left| y_j^r - \sum_{i=1}^{j-1} x_i^r p_{ij} \right| = Z_j^r + W_j^r.$$

Then the problem is to minimize the function

$$S_1 = \sum_{r=1}^{100} \sum_{j=2}^{5} (Z_j^r + W_j^r)$$

subject to the constraints $p_{ij} \geq 0$ for all i and j; $\sum_{j=i+1}^{4} p_{ij} = 1$ for all i; $y_j^r = \sum_{i=1}^{j-1} x_i^r p_{ij} + Z_j^r - W_j^r$, $Z_j^r \geq 0$, and $W_j^r \geq 0$ for $j = 2, \ldots, 5$ and $r = 1, \ldots, 100$. The unknown variables are the values p_{ij}, Z_j^r, and W_j^r, where $i < j \leq 5$, $i = 1, \ldots, 4$, and $r = 1, \ldots, 100$. This setup is advantageous as the minimization problem here represents a linear programming problem; hence, powerful software packages can be used for an efficient solution.

The function S_1 achieves its minimum under the following parameter values: $p_{12} = 0.5$, $p_{13} = 0.49$, $p_{14} = 0.01$, $p_{15} = 0$, $p_{23} = 0.68$, $p_{24} = 0.32$, $p_{25} = 0$, $p_{34} = 1$, $p_{35} = 0$, and $p_{45} = 1$.

Now, we calculate the approximate values of the passenger traffic intensities as follows: $\lambda_{12} = 2.29$, $\lambda_{13} = 2.31$, $\lambda_{14} = 0.05$, $\lambda_{15} = 0$, $\lambda_{23} = 1.56$, $\lambda_{24} = 0.74$, $\lambda_{15} = 0$, $\lambda_{34} = 1.4$, $\lambda_{35} = 0$, and $\lambda_{45} = 2.6$.

A direct comparison with the results obtained by the least-squares method indicates slight differences. In view of the accumulated information, we may draw some conclusions on the volumes of passenger traffic. The largest passenger traffic flows exist between stops 1 and 2, between stops 1 and 3, and between stops 4 and 5.

Thus, using passenger traffic information acquired by different methods, it is possible to plan new routes and optimize the existing ones by adjusting bus schedules. In the forthcoming section, we consider the issues of incoming flow control. Here a key aspect is to compare competition with complete regulation.

8.3 A MODEL OF PUBLIC TRANSPORT SYSTEM

An aspect of public transport modeling consists in calculation of passenger service characteristics such as the required number of vehicles, their capacity, and schedule (routes and traffic intervals or intensities). Our consideration begins with the model composed of two carriers.

8.3.1 The system with two carriers

Let λ be the intensity of passenger traffic on a certain route. Suppose two carriers (players) deliver passengers on the route; their strategies are service rates μ_1 and μ_2. Denote by p a given fare for transportation. The transportation cost of both carriers is proportional to the volumes of passenger traffic with coefficients c_1 and c_2, respectively.

Under chosen service rates, the first carrier delivers $\lambda\mu_1/(\mu_1 + \mu_2)$ passengers per unit time, and its income makes up

$$H_1(\mu_1, \mu_2) = p\lambda\frac{\mu_1}{\mu_1 + \mu_2} - c_1\mu_1. \tag{8.1}$$

Similarly, the income of the second carrier is

$$H_2(\mu_1, \mu_2) = p\lambda\frac{\mu_2}{\mu_1 + \mu_2} - c_2\mu_2. \tag{8.2}$$

The payoff functions (8.1) and (8.2) are concave, and hence this game always possesses a Nash equilibrium by Theorem 1. The first-order optimality conditions $\partial H_i / \partial \mu_i = 0$, $i = 1, 2$, yield

$$\lambda p \mu_2 = c_1 (\mu_1 + \mu_2)^2, \quad \lambda p \mu_1 = c_2 (\mu_1 + \mu_2)^2,$$

and the Nash equilibrium has the form

$$\mu_1^* = p \lambda \frac{c_2}{(c_1 + c_2)^2}, \quad \mu_2^* = p \lambda \frac{c_1}{(c_1 + c_2)^2}.$$

8.3.2 The system with K carriers

In the general case, a transportation network is described by a graph with N stops served by K carriers. Denote by L_k the number of routes used by carrier k ($k = 1, \ldots, K$) and by λ_{ij} the intensity of a Poisson flow of the passengers that come to stop i with a view of moving to stop j. Assume that $\lambda_{ij} \geq 0$, $\lambda_{ii} = 0$, $i, j = 1, \ldots, N$. As before, p is the fare for public transportation; in addition, for carrier k, let c_{kl} specify the cost of a single trip on route l, where $l = 1, \ldots, L_k$, $k = 1, \ldots, K$.

We will write $\delta_k^l(ij) = 1$ if it is possible to move between stops i and j on route l using the service of carrier k and $\delta_k^l(ij) = 0$ otherwise ($i, j = 1, \ldots, N$, $l = 1, \ldots, L_k$, $k = 1, \ldots, K$).

Define the strategies of the players as μ_{kl}, which is the intensity of bus traffic (service rate) of carrier k on route l ($l = 1, \ldots, L_k$, $k = 1, \ldots, K$). Obviously, $\mu_{kl} \geq 0$ for $l = 1, \ldots, L_k$, $k = 1, \ldots, K$. Denote by μ the strategy profile.

The passenger flow of the intensity λ_{ij} can be served by several carriers operating on different routes. Therefore, the total service rate of the carriers on these routes must exceed λ_{ij}, that is,

$$\sum_{k=1}^{K} \sum_{l=1}^{L_m} \delta_k^l(ij) \mu_{kl} \geq \lambda_{ij} \ \forall i, j. \tag{8.3}$$

At each stop, the passengers get into a first bus with enough empty places that can move them to a desired stop. The other passengers wait for the next bus with enough empty places. As the Poisson flows of passengers are independent for different routes, the probability that the passengers will be delivered by a certain bus is proportional to the service rate of a given carrier on a given route. Therefore, the passenger traffic flow is distributed among the carriers proportionally to their service rates on a given route, that is, the average number of passengers delivered by carrier k on route l per unit time has the form

$$\sum_{i=1}^{N}\sum_{j=1}^{N}\lambda_{ij}\cdot\frac{\delta_{k}^{l}(ij)\mu_{kl}}{\sum_{m=1}^{K}\sum_{r=1}^{L_m}\delta_{m}^{r}(ij)\mu_{mr}}, \quad l=1,\ldots L_k, k=1,\ldots K.$$

The profit of carrier k is its income (the fares of all passengers) minus the transportation cost per unit time, that is,

$$H_k(\mu)=\sum_{i=1}^{N}\sum_{j=1}^{N}p\cdot\sum_{l=1}^{L_k}\lambda_{ij}\cdot\frac{\delta_{k}^{l}(ij)\mu_{kl}}{\sum_{m=1}^{K}\sum_{r=1}^{L_m}\delta_{m}^{r}(ij)\mu_{mr}}-\sum_{l=1}^{L_k}\alpha_{kl}\mu_{kl}, \quad k=1,\ldots,K. \tag{8.4}$$

In addition, the transportation cost must not exceed the maximum possible income from service, that is,

$$p\sum_{i=1}^{N}\sum_{j=1}^{N}\lambda_{ij}\delta_{k}^{l}(ij)\geq\sum_{l=1}^{L_k}c_{kl}\mu_{kl}, k=1,\ldots,K. \tag{8.5}$$

In this transportation game, the payoff functions (8.4) are concave, whereas the strategy sets defined by conditions (8.3) and (8.5) are convex compact sets. By Theorem 1 the game always possesses a Nash equilibrium. All Nash equilibria can be calculated using the first-order optimality conditions [49]; see the example above.

8.4 OPTIMAL DISTRIBUTION AND THE WARDROP EQUILIBRIUM PRINCIPLE

In 1952, Wardrop suggested the principle of equilibrium flows in the following statement: any transportation system reaches an equilibrium state after some period of time [83]. According to the Wardrop principle, the trip time along all existing routes is the same for all road users and smaller than the trip time of any road user deviating from his route. The average trip time achieves minimum in the equilibrium. It is possible to show that a Wardrop equilibrium represents a Nash equilibrium in a game with transport vehicles as players and routes as their strategies. Note that this game is a congestion game with a potential. Hence, equilibrium calculation comes to potential minimization. We will further illustrate this by an example of a

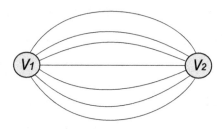

Figure 8.3 A transportation network of parallel channel

transportation network composed of n parallel routes, further called channels (see Fig. 8.3).

Assume that the incoming flow of players is described by a Poisson process X of intensity x and that the delay on channel i has a polynomial form often used in transportation models. More specifically, let the empirical latency function for the traffic flow of intensity x be given by

$$f_i(x) = t_i\left(1 + \alpha_i\left(\frac{x}{c_i}\right)^{\beta_i}\right), \quad i = 1, 2, \ldots, n,$$

where t_i indicates the trip time in the unoccupied channel i, c_i specifies the capacity of channel i, and the constants α_i, β_i are determined by road parameters (width, the number of traffic control devices, e.g., light signals, etc.). Note that these constants can be adjusted using statistical data. Generally, β takes values from 1 to 4. The empirical relationship under study is known as the BPR (Bureau of Public Road) latency function.

Without loss of generality, we believe that all channels are renumbered so that

$$t_1 \leq t_2 \leq \cdots \leq t_n.$$

In other words, the first channel is the fastest, whereas the last one is the slowest.

The players producing the traffic X seek to distribute themselves among the channels for minimizing their trip times. We consider two approaches. Within the first approach, the flow is distributed so that the total cost of all players (the social cost or system cost) achieves minimum; this solution will be called optimal. The second approach involves the Wardrop principle: find an equilibrium in which none of the players benefits from a unilateral deviation from his channel.

In both cases, the incoming flow X is decomposed into n subflows running through corresponding channels. Let x_i, $i = 1, \ldots, n$, be the values of the subflows. It is intuitively clear that $x_i \geq 0$ and

$$\sum_{i=1}^{n} x_i = X. \tag{8.6}$$

If some channel has no traffic, then $x_i = 0$. Denote by $x = (x_1, \ldots, x_n)$ the subflow profile.

We begin our analysis with the first problem, which is to find an optimal distribution of the flow X minimizing the social cost

$$SC(x) = \sum_{i=1}^{n} x_i f_i(x) = \sum_{i=1}^{n} x_i t_i \left(1 + \alpha_i \left(\frac{x_i}{c_i} \right)^{\beta_i} \right)$$

subject to condition (8.6).

Then we will consider the second problem, which is to calculate the Wardrop equilibrium. The associated transportation game with the BPR latency function represents a potential game. Using this fact, the problem can be solved by minimizing the potential

$$P(x) = \sum_{i=1}^{n} \int_{0}^{x_i} t_i \left(1 + \alpha_i \left(\frac{u}{c_i} \right)^{\beta_i} \right) du.$$

Now, we get back to the solution of the first problem.

8.4.1 Cooperative solution

Consider the optimization problem

$$SC(x) = \sum_{i=1}^{n} x_i t_i \left(1 + \alpha_i \left(\frac{x_i}{c_i} \right)^{\beta_i} \right) \rightarrow \min \tag{8.7}$$

subject to the constraint

$$\sum_{i=1}^{n} x_i = X,$$

$$x_i \geq 0, \quad i = 1, \ldots, n.$$

The solution gives the optimal distribution of the flow among the channels.

Lemma 32. *An optimal subflow profile x^* is a solution of problem (8.7) if there exists a nonnegative value λ (the Lagrange multiplier) such that*

$$t_i \left(1 + \alpha_i(\beta_i + 1)\left(\frac{x_i}{c_i}\right)^{\beta_i} \right) \begin{cases} = \lambda & \text{if } x_i > 0, \\ \geq \lambda & \text{if } x_i = 0, \end{cases}$$

$$\forall i \in \{1, n\}.$$

Proof. The idea is to employ the Karush–Kuhn–Tucker theorem. Owing to the convexity of the goal function (8.7) and admissible solution domain, the Karush–Kuhn–Tucker conditions become necessary and sufficient conditions of optimality. Construct the Lagrange function

$$L(x, \lambda) = \sum_{i=1}^{n} t_i \left(1 + \alpha_i \left(\frac{x_i}{c_i}\right)^{\beta_i} \right) x_i$$

$$+ \lambda(X - \sum_{i=1}^{n} x_i) + \sum_{i=1}^{n} \lambda_i(-x_i).$$

The first-order optimality conditions with respect to x_i yield the equations

$$t_i \left(1 + \alpha_i \left(\frac{x_i}{c_i}\right)^{\beta_i} \right) + \alpha_i \beta_i t_i \left(\frac{x_i}{c_i}\right)^{\beta_i} - \lambda_i = \lambda, \quad i = 1, \ldots, n.$$

The complementary slackness condition has the form

$$\lambda_i x_i = 0, \quad i = 1, \ldots, n.$$

These equalities hold if at least one of the multipliers is zero. Therefore, if $x_i > 0$ for some i, then $\lambda_i = 0$, and hence

$$t_i \left(1 + \alpha_i \left(\frac{x_i}{c_i}\right)^{\beta_i} \right) + \alpha_i \beta_i t_i \left(\frac{x_i}{c_i}\right)^{\beta_i} = \lambda.$$

In the case $x_i = 0$, the inequality $\lambda_i \geq 0$ is immediate, and

$$\lambda = t_i - \lambda_i.$$

This concludes the proof of Lemma 32. □

Recall that the channels are renumbered so that

$$t_1 \leq t_2 \leq \cdots \leq t_n. \tag{8.8}$$

Introduce the notation

$$g_i(x) = t_i \left(1 + \alpha_i(\beta_i + 1) \left(\frac{x}{c_i} \right)^{\beta_i} \right), \quad i = 1, \ldots, n.$$

The next result follows directly from Lemma 32. The optimal flow is distributed among the first k channels if, for some λ such that

$$t_1 \leq t_2 \leq \cdots \leq t_k < \lambda \leq t_{k+1} \leq \cdots \leq t_n, \tag{8.9}$$

we have

$$g_1(x_1) = g_2(x_2) = \cdots = g_k(x_k)$$
$$= \lambda \leq g_{k+1}(0) = t_{k+1}. \tag{8.10}$$

In fact, conditions (8.10) determine the optimal distribution flows x_i, $i = 1, \ldots, k$ ($k = 1, \ldots, n-1$).

The parameter λ depends on the flow X. More precisely, $\lambda(X)$ is a continuous nondecreasing function of X. The number of optimal distribution channels increases from k to $k+1$ as the function $\lambda(X)$ crosses the point t_{k+1}.

The functions $g_i(x)$, $i = 1, \ldots, n$, increase on the interval $[0; +\infty)$. Hence, there exists the inverse function $g^{-1}(y)$, which increases on $[0; +\infty)$. Denote by x_{ij} the solution of the equation

$$g_i(x) = t_j, \quad j = i+1, \ldots, n.$$

Using the monotonicity of the functions $g_i(x)$ and conditions (8.8), we arrive at the inequality

$$x_{i,i+1} \leq x_{i,i+2} \leq \cdots \leq x_{in} \ \forall i. \tag{8.11}$$

Let

$$V_k = \sum_{i=1}^{k} x_{i,k+1}, \quad k = 1, \ldots, n-1, V_0 = 0.$$

It appears from (8.11) that

$$V_1 \leq V_2 \leq \cdots \leq V_{n-1}.$$

Note that $V_1 = x_{12}$ is obtained from the equation

$$g_1(x) = t_2.$$

If the incoming flow is such that

$$X \le V_1,$$

then $g_1(X) \le t_2$, and the whole flow runs through channel 1. In the case $g_1(X) > t_2$, the flow is decomposed into two subflows, and some part of the flow corresponds to channel 2.

Let us demonstrate that, as the flow X exceeds the value V_k, the number of optimal distribution channels varies from k to $k+1$.

Suppose the optimal flow is distributed among k channels. The optimal distribution satisfies conditions (8.9)–(8.10). Expression (8.5) and the monotonicity of the functions $g_i^{-1}(y)$ give

$$x_i = g_i^{-1}(\lambda) \le g_i^{-1}(t_{k+1}) = x_{i,k+1}, \quad i = 1, \ldots, k.$$

Consequently,

$$X = \sum_{i=1}^{k} x_i = \sum_{i=1}^{k} g_i^{-1}(\lambda) \le \sum_{i=1}^{k} x_{i,k+1},$$

which leads to the inequality $X \le V_k$. On the other hand, assuming that the optimal flow runs through $k+1$ channels, we obtain the following result. Conditions (8.9)–(8.10)

$$g_1(x_1) = g_2(x_2) = \cdots = g_k(x_{k+1}) = \lambda > t_{k+1}$$

imply

$$X = \sum_{i=1}^{k+1} x_i = \sum_{i=1}^{k+1} g_i^{-1}(\lambda) > \sum_{i=1}^{k+1} x_{i,k+1} > V_k.$$

Summarizing the outcomes, we may formulate the following theorem.

Theorem 45. *For the optimal flow to be distributed among the first k channels, a necessary and sufficient condition is*

$$V_{k-1} < X \le V_k = \sum_{i=1}^{k} x_{i,k+1}, \quad k = 1, 2, \ldots, n.$$

Moreover, the optimal distribution x_{opt} is the solution of the combined equations

$$\begin{aligned} x_1 + x_2 + \cdots + x_k &= X, \\ g_1(x_1) = g_2(x_2) = \cdots &= g_k(x_k). \end{aligned} \tag{8.12}$$

8.4.2 Wardrop equilibrium

Now, consider the competitive equilibrium setup. As mentioned earlier, the equilibrium can be calculated by solving the minimization problem with the goal function

$$P(x) = \sum_{i=1}^{n} \int_{0}^{x_i} t_i \left(1 + \alpha_i \left(\frac{u}{c_i} \right)^{\beta_i} \right) du$$

and the constraints

$$\sum_{i=1}^{n} x_i = X,$$

$$x_i \geq 0, \quad i = 1, \ldots, n.$$

In the same way as before, we take advantage of the Karush–Kuhn–Tucker theorem. Construct the Lagrange function

$$L(x, \lambda) = P(x) + \lambda(X - \sum_{i=1}^{n} x_i) + \sum_{i=1}^{n} \lambda_i(-x_i)$$

and apply the first-order optimality conditions with respect to x_i to get

$$t_i \left(1 + \alpha_i \left(\frac{x_i}{c_i} \right)^{\beta_i} \right) - \lambda_i = \lambda, \quad i = 1, \ldots, n.$$

Using the same considerations as in the previous subsection, except that the functions $g_i(x)$, $i = 1, \ldots, n$, are replaced by the latency functions

$$f_i(x) = t_i \left(1 + \alpha_i \left(\frac{x}{c_i} \right)^{\beta_i} \right), \quad i = 1, \ldots, n,$$

we finally establish the following result.

Theorem 46. *For the equilibrium flow to be distributed among the first k channels, a necessary and sufficient condition is*

$$V'_{k-1} < X \leq V'_{k}, \quad k = 1, 2, \ldots, n.$$

Here $V'_k = \sum_{i=1}^{k} x'_{i,k+1}$, $k = 1, 2, \ldots, n$, and x'_{ij} satisfy the combined equations

$$f_i(x) = t_j, \quad j = i+1, \ldots, n.$$

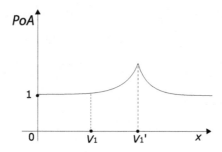

Figure 8.4 The price of anarchy

Moreover, the equilibrium distribution x_{eq} is the solution of the combined equations

$$\begin{cases} x_1 + x_2 + \cdots + x_k = X, \\ f_1(x_1) = f_2(x_2) = \cdots = f_k(x_k). \end{cases} \tag{8.13}$$

8.4.3 The price of anarchy

Let us compare the social cost $SC(x_{eq})$ in the equilibrium with the optimal social cost $SC(x_{opt})$. Their ratio $PoA = SC(x_{eq})/SC(x_{opt})$ is said to be the price of anarchy.

In this subsection, we analyze the case of networks with two parallel channels and linear latency functions; the general case was considered in [73]. The price of anarchy depending on the incoming flow X is shown in Fig. 8.4.

The maximum of this function is achieved at $X = V_1' = (t_2 - t_1)c_1/(\alpha_1 t_1)$. For this value, in the optimal distribution x_{opt} the flow uses both channels, whereas in the equilibrium distribution x_{eq} the flow runs through channel 1 only. By Theorem 46,

$$SC(x_{eq}) = V_1' t_2.$$

According to Theorem 45, the optimal subflows $x_{opt} = (x_1^{opt}, x_2^{opt})$ satisfy the conditions

$$x_1^{opt} + x_2^{opt} = V_1', \quad t_1\left(1 + 2\frac{\alpha_1}{c_1}x_1^{opt}\right) = t_2\left(1 + 2\frac{\alpha_2}{c_2}x_2^{opt}\right).$$

Hence, it follows that

$$x_1^{opt} = \frac{t_2 - t_1 + 2k_2 V_1'}{2(k_1 + k_2)},$$

where $k_1 = \alpha_1 t_1/c_1$ and $k_2 = \alpha_2 t_2/c_2$. The optimal social cost makes up

$$SC(x_{\mathrm{opt}}) = x_1^{\mathrm{opt}} t_1 \left(1 + \alpha_1 \frac{x_1^{\mathrm{opt}}}{c_1}\right) + x_2^{\mathrm{opt}} t_2 \left(1 + \alpha_2 \frac{x_2^{\mathrm{opt}}}{c_2}\right)$$

$$= (t_2 - t_1) \frac{4k_2 t_2 + k_1 t_1 + 3k_1 t_2}{4k_1(k_1 + k_2)}.$$

As a result,

$$PoA = \frac{SC(x_{\mathrm{eq}})}{SC(x_{\mathrm{opt}})} = 1 + \frac{k_1(t_2 - t_1)}{4k_2 t_2 + k_1 t_1 + 3k_1 t_2}.$$

For any parameter values, PoA is bounded by the value 4/3.

CHAPTER 9

Models of Transportation Market

Contents

In this chapter we consider the competition model on a transportation network. That is a market where the customers are distributed in the nodes of a transportation graph. The nodes of the graph represent the hubs (bus stops, airports, railway stations, etc.) while its edges correspond to the transportation links (railways, car, air lines, etc.). The customers in a node are the passengers who use this kind of transportation. The demand is determined by the passenger traffic. There are n companies (players) delivering a service in the market. Each player has some units of a resource. He distributes the resource among links of the graph. The game has three stages as follows. The players simultaneously distribute their resources among the links of the graph. Then the players simultaneously announce the prices for their resources. After that the customers choose a preferable service and the players obtain the payoffs depending on their transportation networks and prices. For the service market over the transportation graph we will construct a Nash equilibrium in the allocation game and also in the pricing game. We demonstrate how it can be used for modeling of air transportation market.

9.1 ALLOCATION MODEL OVER A GRAPH

Consider a market where the customers are distributed in the nodes of a transportation graph $G(V, E)$. Assume that this graph is undirected and possibly disconnected; see Fig. 9.1.

A product or service is delivered only if there exists a link between customers, that is, an edge $e_j \in E$ in the graph $G(V, E)$. The number of customers in a node $v_j \in V$ is called its capacity. The demand depends on the capacity of nodes connected by the edge e_j, that is, on the number of

Networking Games
https://doi.org/10.1016/B978-0-12-816551-5.00015-0

Copyright © 2019 Elsevier Inc.
All rights reserved.

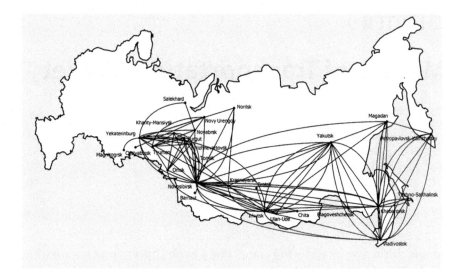

Figure 9.1 Russian air transportation market

customers in these nodes:

$$d(e_j) = d(v_1, v_2), \qquad e_j = (v_1, v_2).$$

Transportation networks are an example of such markets. Then the nodes of a graph $G(V, E)$ represent the hubs (bus stops, airports, railway stations, etc.), whereas its edges correspond to the transportation links (railways, car, air lines, etc.). The customers in a node v_j are the passengers who use this kind of transportation. The demand is determined by the passenger traffic. This model can be applied to describe telecommunication and computer networks.

There are n companies (players) delivering a service in the market. Let player i have m_i units of a resource. He distributes the resource among links of the graph $G(V, E)$. Our analysis will be confined to the case where each player distributes all m_i units of resource and may distribute only one unit of resource on each link.

By distributing the resource to a link e_j, a player connects the corresponding nodes, and then the customers may use the resource of player i. Therefore, each of the players forms his own transportation network E^i, which is a subset of the links in the graph $G(V, E)$. The problem of network formation is very popular in the literature on networking games

[43,69]. We touch it in connection with the pricing problem in the transportation market.

A competition occurs in the market only if a link e_j is included into several transportation networks simultaneously, that is,

$$\exists i, j \in N, \ i \neq j: \ E^i \cap E^j \neq \varnothing.$$

The demand on a link e_j is distributed among the players. Each of them delivers the service to a share M_{ij} of the customers on this link. The players announce their prices for the service on e_j, thereby competing with each other. For the demand $d(e_j)$, the share M_{ij} of the customers who prefer the service of player i depends on the price p_{ij} and the prices of other players on this link:

$$M_{ij} = M_{ij}(p_{ij}, \{p_{rj}\}_{r \in N_j \setminus \{i\}}), \tag{9.1}$$

where N_j is the set of competing players on e_j.

The number of customers who prefer the service of player i on a link e_j is

$$S_{ij}(\{p_{rj}\}_{r \in N_j}) = M_{ij}(p_{ij}, \{p_{rj}\}_{r \in N_j \setminus \{i\}}) d(e_j).$$

Denote by x_{ij} the distribution of player i on a link e_j, that is,

$$x_{ij} = \begin{cases} 1 & \text{if } e_j \in E^i, \\ 0 & \text{otherwise.} \end{cases}$$

Then the number of players on a link e_j is

$$|N_j| = \sum_{i=1}^{n} x_{ij}.$$

Player i with m_i units of the resource over the graph $G(V, E)$ attracts the number of customers

$$S_i = \sum_{j=1}^{|E|} M_{ij}(p_{ij}, \{p_{rj}\}_{r \in N_j \setminus \{i\}}) d(e_j) x_{ij}.$$

The income of player i on a link e_j depends on the price for the service and his share in the customer demand:

$$h_{ij}(\{p_{rj}\}_{r \in N_j}) = p_{ij} M_{ij}(p_{ij}, \{p_{rj}\}_{r \in N_j \setminus \{i\}}) d(e_j).$$

Supplying a unit of the resource on a link e_j, player i bears expenses c_{ij}. Assume that the cost of the resource is proportional to the number of customers using it. Then the payoff of player i over the graph $G(V, E)$ has the form

$$H_i(\{p_r\}_{r\in N}, \{x_r\}_{r\in N}) = \sum_{j=1}^{|E|}\left(h_{ij}(p_{ij}, \{p_{rj}\}_{r\in N_j\setminus\{i\}}) - c_{ij}S_{ij}(p_{ij}, \{p_{rj}\}_{r\in N_j\setminus\{i\}})\right)x_{ij},$$

(9.2)

where p_r is the price vector of player r in his network E^r, and x_r is a vector defining the allocation of m_r units of the resource by this player over the graph $G(V, E)$ $(r \in N)$.

First, the players form their transportation networks, and then they announce the prices for the service. Each player seeks to maximize his payoff.

As a result, we arrive at the following noncooperative n-player game Γ_G on the graph G with perfect information. The strategy of player i is a pair of vectors (x_i, p_i), $i \in N$. Player i chooses an allocation x_i of m_i units of the resource, that is, a vector of the form

$$\forall j\; x_{ij} \in \{0, 1\}, \quad \sum_{r=1}^{|E|} x_{ir} = m_i.$$

Then player i announces the prices in his network E^i:

$$\forall j\; p_{ij} \in [0, \infty), \quad e_j \in E^i.$$

The player's payoff is given by (9.2).

The game has three stages as follows.

1. The players simultaneously distribute their resources using allocations $\{x_i\}_{i\in N}$.

2. The players simultaneously announce the prices for their resources $\{p_i\}_{i\in N}$.

3. The customers choose a preferable service, and the players obtain the payoffs $\{H_i\}_{i\in N}$ depending on their transportation networks and prices.

For the service market over the graph $G(V, E)$, we will construct a Nash equilibrium in the allocation game and also in the pricing game.

In the allocation game, it is required to find a Nash equilibrium $\{x_i^*\}_{i \in N}$, that is, allocations x_i^* satisfying the condition

$$H_i\big(\{\tilde{p}_r(x_i, \{x_r^*\}_{r \in N \setminus \{i\}})\}_{r \in N}, x_i, \{x_r^*\}_{r \in N \setminus \{i\}}\big)$$
$$\leq H_i\big(\{\tilde{p}_r(x_i^*, \{x_r^*\}_{r \in N \setminus \{i\}})\}_{r \in N}, x_i^*, \{x_r^*\}_{r \in N \setminus \{i\}}\big)$$

for all x_i, $i \in N$, where $\{\tilde{p}_r(\{x_i\}_{i \in N})\}_{r \in N}$ is an equilibrium in the pricing game for a fixed resource distribution on the graph $G(V, E)$.

In the pricing game, it is required to find a Nash equilibrium $\{p_i^*\}_{i \in N}$, that is, prices p_i^* satisfying the condition

$$H_i\big(p_i, \{p_r^*\}_{r \in N \setminus \{i\}}, \{\tilde{x}_r\}_{r \in N}\big) \leq H_i\big(p_i^*, \{p_r^*\}_{r \in N \setminus \{i\}}, \{\tilde{x}_r\}_{r \in N}\big)$$

for all p_i, $i \in N$, where $\{\tilde{x}_r\}_{r \in N}$ are fixed transportation networks of the players over the graph $G(V, E)$.

9.2 PRICING GAME OVER A GRAPH

We suppose that the players have distributed their resources over the network and solve the pricing problem. We will describe the customer demand on the market $G(V, E)$ using the multinomial logit model. Consider briefly the main idea of this approach. The customers located in the nodes of the graph $G(V, E)$ obtain some utility from the resource of player i on a link e_j, that is,

$$u_{ij} = v_{ij} + \epsilon_{ij}.$$

Suppose some components of u_{ij} are unobservable, which means that the utility of resources has a random character. The observable factors affecting the utility are included in v_{ij}, whereas the unobservable ones are included in ϵ_{ij}.

Let the deterministic component v_{ij} of the utility consist of the characteristics of the resource supplied by player i and also of the factors that are the same for all customers using this resource. As examples of such factors, we mention per capita income, route length, etc.

Incorporate into v_{ij} the price p_{ij} paid by a customer for the resource. Let v_{ij} be a linear function of p_{ij}. Clearly, for a customer, the utility of the resource decreases as the price goes up.

Accept the hypothesis that the random components ϵ_{ij} are independent and obey the Weibull distribution. Then the probability that a customer chooses the resource of player i on a link e_j can be written as

$$M_{ij} = \frac{e^{a_1 p_{ij} + (a, v_i)}}{\sum\limits_{s \in N_j} e^{a_1 p_{sj} + (a, v_s)} + e^\rho}, \quad e_j \in E^i, \tag{9.3}$$

where v_i is a vector of characteristics (observable factors) for the service of player i except the price, N_j indicates the set of customers forming the demand on the link e_j, $a_1 < 0$, and a gives a constant vector of weights for the observable factors in the customer's utility function [60].

A customer may refuse of the resource on a link e_j if the players overprice their services. The model contains the term e^ρ in the denominator of (9.3), which describes the customers who prefer not to use any service at all on the link e_j.

Obviously, the probability M_{ij} takes the same value for all customers of demand on a link e_j, since the deterministic component of the utility does not include any customer characteristics.

Note that in the pricing game the profit of player i—the payoff function h_{ij}—depends only on the price p_{ij} announced by this player for his resource on a link e_j and also on the prices of the competing players on this link. Hence, it is possible to consider separate pricing problems associated with each link used by two or more players in the graph $G(V, E)$. If a single player allocates his resource to a link e_j, then the pricing problem is reduced to a simple optimization problem.

Thus, we have to find a Nash equilibrium $\{p_{ij}^*\}_{i \in N_j}$ in the pricing game Γ_G^j, that is, the prices p_{ij}^* that satisfy the condition

$$h_{ij}\left(p_{ij}, \{p_{rj}^*\}_{r \in N_j \setminus \{i\}}\right) - c_{ij} M_{ij}\left(p_{ij}, \{p_{rj}^*\}_{r \in N_j \setminus \{i\}}\right) d(e_j)$$
$$\leq h_{ij}\left(p_{ij}^*, \{p_{rj}^*\}_{r \in N_j \setminus \{i\}}\right) - c_{ij} M_{ij}\left(p_{ij}^*, \{p_{rj}^*\}_{r \in N_j \setminus \{i\}}\right) d(e_j) \quad (9.4)$$

for all p_{ij}, $i \in N_j$.

The pricing problem with such payoff functions represents a convex game. By Theorem 1 there exists a unique equilibrium $\{p_{ij}^*\}_{i \in N_j}$ in the game $\Gamma_{g,p}^j$.

The desired equilibrium $\{p_{ij}^*\}_{i \in N_j}$ can be constructed as a limiting strategy profile for a best-reply sequence of the players. To find the best reply of player i, calculate the maximum value of his payoff function in p_{ij}.

The function M_{ij} satisfies the equation

$$\frac{\partial M_{ij}}{\partial p_{ij}} = a_1 M_{ij}(1 - M_{ij}).$$

(9.5)

Differentiation of the payoff function (9.2) yields the following condition to calculate the best reply of player i:

$$M_{ij}d(e_j) + a_1 p_{ij}M_{ij}(1 - M_{ij})d(e_j) - a_1 c_{ij}M_{ij}(1 - M_{ij})d(e_j) = 0.$$

After simplifications, we get

$$(1 - M_{ij})(c_{ij} - p_{ij}) = \frac{1}{a_1}.$$

(9.6)

A successive solution of Eq. (9.6) for different players gives the equilibrium $\{p_{ij}^*\}_{i \in N_j}$. Eq. (9.6) may have no nonnegative solutions $p_{ij} \geq 0$. In this case, for player i, the income from supplying his resource to the customers does not cover its cost.

The form of Eq. (9.6) makes it clear that the customer demand on a link e_j does not affect the equilibrium prices. However, the higher the demand, the greater the equilibrium payoffs of the players.

Another approach to the description of the distribution of passenger demand in the market is presented in the paper [58].

9.3 ALLOCATION GAME OVER A GRAPH

In this section, we analyze an equilibrium in the allocation game Γ_G. Here the strategy of each player i is to allocate his resources over the transportation network by choosing links of the graph $G(V, E)$ for which $x_{ij} = 1$. Deviating from a chosen resource allocation, a player modifies the set of competing market participants on the links of the graph $G(V, E)$.

After the first stage of the game, the payoff of each player is given by the equilibrium in the pricing game. Imagine that a new player appears on a link e_j. What happens with equilibrium prices and payoffs in the pricing game?

Denote by γ a new player in the game and consider the new set of players $\tilde{N}_j = N_j \cup \{\gamma\}$ on the link e_j.

Find the price vector variation in the pricing problem for the original game $\Gamma_G^j = \langle N_j, \{p_{ij}\}_{i \in N_j}, H_{ij} \rangle$ and also for the game $\tilde{\Gamma}_G^j = \langle \tilde{N}_j, \{\tilde{p}_{ij}\}_{i \in \tilde{N}_j}, H_{ij} \rangle$

with $n_j + 1$ players, where $H_{ij} = h_{ij} - c_{ij} M_{ij} d(e_j)$. Let $\{p^*_{ij}\}_{i \in N_j}$ be an equilibrium in the original game, and let $\{\tilde{p}^*_{ij}\}_{i \in \tilde{N}_j}$ be an equilibrium in the extended game with additional player. Suppose a new player enters the market only in the case of profit-making.

Theorem 47. *In the pricing game with additional player $\tilde{\Gamma}^j_G$, the equilibrium prices are decreasing for all players except the new one, that is, $p^*_{ij} > \tilde{p}^*_{ij}$ for all $i \in N_j$.*

Proof. First, differentiate the payoff function of player i on the link e_j:

$$\frac{\partial H_{ij}}{\partial p_{ij}} = M_{ij} d(e_j) \big(1 + a_1 (p_{ij} - c_{ij})(1 - M_{ij})\big) = 0.$$

After certain transformations, we have

$$\sum_{r \in N_j} e^{a_1 p_{rj} + (a, v_r)} + e^\rho + a_1 (p_{ij} - c_{ij}) \left(\sum_{r \in N_j \setminus \{i\}} e^{a_1 p_{rj} + (a, v_r)} + e^\rho \right) = 0.$$

Hence, the price p_{ij} depends on the prices for the resources of other players on the link e_j in the following way:

$$e^\rho + \sum_{r \in N_j \setminus \{i\}} e^{a_1 p_{rj} + (a, v_r)} = \frac{-e^{a_1 p_{ij} + (a, v_i)}}{a_1 (p_{ij} - c_{ij}) + 1}. \tag{9.7}$$

Consider the function $g(x) = \dfrac{-e^{a_1 x + b}}{a_1 (x - c_{ij}) + 1}$ with constant b.
The derivative of this function has the form

$$g'(x) = \frac{-a_1^2 e^{a_1 x + b} (x - c_{ij})}{\big(a_1 (x - c_{ij}) + 1\big)^2},$$

taking negative values for $x > c_{ij}$. So, the function $g(x)$ is decreasing for $x > c_{ij}$.

Consequently, the right-hand side of the optimality equation (9.7) is a decreasing function in the price p_{ij} of player i. In the left-hand side of the equation, we have an expression that depends on the prices of other players. If we introduce a new player to the link e_j, then the left-hand side of the equation increases. Therefore, the root of the right-hand side of the equation decreases. We will demonstrate this property for the case $|N_j| = 1$.

Let $|N_j| = 1$. Then the equilibrium p^*_{1j} obeys the equation

$$e^\rho = \frac{-e^{\alpha p^*_{1j} + (a, v_1)}}{\alpha (p^*_{1j} - c_{1j}) + 1}.$$

In the game with additional player, the equilibrium price $\tilde{p}_{1j}^*$ of the first player satisfies the equation

$$e^\rho + e^{\alpha \tilde{p}_{2j}^* + (a, v_2)} = \frac{-e^{\alpha \tilde{p}_{1j}^* + (a, v_1)}}{\alpha(\tilde{p}_{1j}^* - c_{1j}) + 1}.$$

The monotonicity of the function $g(x)$ implies $p_{1j}^* > \tilde{p}_{1j}^*$.   □

Corollary 3. *In the pricing game with additional player $\tilde{\Gamma}_G^j$, the optimal payoffs are decreasing for all players except the new one, that is, for all $i \in N_j$,*

$$h_{ij}^p(\{p_{ij}^*\}_{i \in N_j}) > h_{ij}^p(\{\tilde{p}_{ij}^*\}_{i \in \tilde{N}_j}).$$

Proof. As shown in the proof of Theorem 47, the equilibrium satisfies the relationship

$$e^\rho + \sum_{r \in N_j \setminus \{i\}} e^{a_1 p_{rj} + (a, v_r)} = \frac{-e^{a_1 p_{ij} + (a, v_i)}}{a_1(p_{ij} - c_{ij}) + 1}. \tag{9.8}$$

Substituting it into the payoff function of player i in the game Γ_G^j gives

$$h_{ij}^p(\{p_{ij}\}_{i \in N_j}) = (p_{ij}^* - c_{ij}) \frac{e^{a_1 p_{ij}^* + (a, v_i)}}{e^\rho + \sum_{r \in N_j \setminus \{i\}} e^{a_1 p_{rj} + (a, v_r)} + e^{a_1 p_{ij}^* + (a, v_i)}} d(e_j).$$

Using the left-hand side of expression (9.8), we obtain

$$h_{ij}^p(\{p_{ij}^*\}_{i \in N_j}) = \left(p_{ij}^* - c_{ij} + \frac{1}{a_1}\right) d(e_j).$$

A similar relationship is the case for the extended game $\tilde{\Gamma}_G^j$.

By Theorem 47, $p_{ij}^* > \tilde{p}_{ij}^*$ for all $i \in N_j$. Since at the equilibrium point the payoff function is linear in the equilibrium price p_{ij}^*, we finally obtain the desired inequality $h_{ij}^p(\{p_{ij}^*\}_{i \in N_j}) > h_{ij}^p(\{\tilde{p}_{ij}^*\}_{i \in \tilde{N}_j})$.   □

Concluding this section, let us return to the allocation game Γ_G. At the first stage, the players distribute their resources among the links. After resource allocation, the pricing game takes place on each link, and the players receive some payoffs. By the corollary of Theorem 47 these payoffs are decreasing functions in the number of players choosing the same link. If the strategy sets of the players satisfy the conditions of Theorem 7 (see Chapter 2), then there exists a pure strategy equilibrium in the allocation game. Particularly, such an equilibrium exists if the players can deliver the service on all links of the graph E or, for example, if they have the same resources, that is, $m_1 = \cdots = m_n$.

Theorem 48. *Assume the strategy sets of the players in the allocation game Γ_G satisfy the conditions of Theorem 7. Then this game possesses a pure strategy equilibrium.*

9.4 MODELING OF AIR TRANSPORTATION MARKET

In this and forthcoming sections, we consider competition in an air transportation market. The players are the airlines operating in this market, which seek to increase the profit from passenger carriage. Each airline delivers its air transportation service over its transportation network, which consists of airports and air routes between them.

A flight performed by each airline has certain characteristics affecting the choice of an appropriate airline for the passengers. For example, these are departure and arrival times, flight time, aircraft type, departure and destination airports (for megalopolises), etc.

Two airports can be connected by the flights of several airlines. In this case, the airlines compete with each other to attract as much passengers as possible for profit maximization. Although the choice of a passenger is conditioned by many factors, we consider the price-based competition of the airlines.

For each flight performed, an airline obtains income from selling passenger tickets. The airline's income grows with the number of passengers. The total income of an airline is the sum of its income on all flights in the transportation network.

While performing flights, an airline bears certain expenses (the cost of passenger transportation). This cost includes aviation fuel, airport charges, aircraft repair and maintenance, crew wages, insurance, leasing, and so on.

The profit of a player is the difference between the sales income and transportation cost in its transportation network.

Each route can be described by a potential demand, that is, the maximum expected passenger traffic flow on this route. The potential passenger traffic flow also affects the level of competition. A low demand for air transportation restricts the entry of new players, whereas a high demand increases competition.

Table 9.1 Summary statistics for Russian market

Factor	Mean	σ	Median	Min	Max
Price (RUB)	9831	4111	9425	1500	21 630
Flight time (hours)	3.34	2.33	2.4	0.4	15.3
Frequency (flights per week)	2.8	2.04	1	1	14
Distance (km)	1774	1263	1486	215	7314
Annual income (RUB)	27 053	10 390	22 224	14 167	50 991
Population	499 430	394 948	327 423	44 334	1 498 921

Table 9.2 Summary statistics for Chinese market

Factor	Mean	σ	Median	Min	Max
Price (CNY)	1366	537	1300	540	2910
Flight time (hours)	2.23	1	2.08	0.75	5.72
Frequency (flights per week)	6.4	1.44	7	1	7
Distance (km)	1298	657	1233	351	3388
Annual income (CNY)	29 501	6903	28 731	18 400	40 742
Population (thousands)	10 968.7	7347.4	9325.05	2141.3	29 190

9.4.1 Modeling of passenger demand

Let us illustrate this model using the air transportation markets of Russia and China. Our analysis of the Russian market was focused on the airlines operating in the Far Eastern, Siberian, and Ural federal districts. The transportation network of each airline was limited to the flights between the airports in these federal districts. Modeling was based on the market data for year 2014.

An air transportation market is represented by a graph $G(V, E)$. Here V corresponds to a finite set of airports, and E corresponds to a finite set of routes between airports. The set E consists of the routes served at least by one airline. Note that the undirected graph model allows us to consider possible routes between airports in an given market.

There are n airlines operating in a given market. Each airline has its own transportation network E^i. Some of the airlines do not compete, as they operate in different federal districts. At the same time, the market includes airlines presented at two or three federal districts. The summary statistics for the markets are given in Tables 9.1 and 9.2.

The Russian market contains 27 airports with 95 routes in the graph $G(V, E)$ and is illustrated in Fig. 9.1. There exist 239 direct flights and

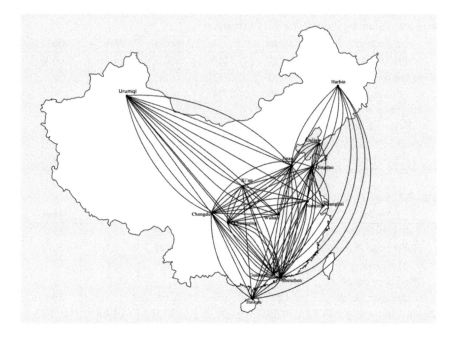

Figure 9.2 Chinese air transportation market

74 transfer flights (with connections). The number of airlines is 11 and the maximum number of competitive airlines on a single route is 5.

The Chinese market (see Fig. 9.2) has 14 airports with 61 routes in the graph $G(V, E)$. There exist 351 direct flights and 14 transfer flights. The number of airlines is 5, and the maximum number of competitive airlines on a single route is 3.

First, we have to estimate the market size for each flight e_j of a given air transportation network. The passenger traffic flow of an airline coincides with its share in the potential demand $d(e_j)$. According to an existing approach, the market size is considered to be proportional to some sociodemographic indicator P_j, that is,

$$d(e_j) = \alpha P_j, \quad \alpha > 0.$$

For example, the paper [8] assessed the market size in the auto industry as the number of households. It is possible to estimate the potential passenger demand in an air transportation market using the size of urban population, as suggested in [Hsiao 2008, http://www.nextor.org/pubs/]. Following this approach, we adjusted the coefficient of proportionality to 0.5 because the market under consideration is not intensive. Thus,

$$d(e_j) = \frac{\sqrt{P(v_1)P(v_2)}}{2},$$

where $P(v_1)$ denotes the size of urban population for a departure airport, and $P(v_2)$ is the size of urban population for a destination airport.

By assumption, on each route e_j of an air transportation graph $G(V, E)$ the passengers choose between n_j flights of airlines and the $(n_j + 1)$th alternative (another means of transportation or even refusal of trip). The number of passengers who prefer the $(n_j + 1)$th alternative can be estimated as the difference between the potential passenger traffic flow and the total passenger traffic flow over all airlines delivering their services on a route e_j.

9.4.2 Logit model of passenger traffic distribution

Consider the characteristics of a separate flight that corresponds to a link e_j in the transportation network E^i of airline i. In the general case, a transportation network of an airline includes transfer flights (with connections). The number of connections is an important characteristic of a flight, and such flights also belong to the set of alternatives considered by a passenger equally with direct flights. So, transfer flights correspond to a link e_j too.

In the course of modeling, we identified the following factors that affect the passenger demand on a link e_j ($e_j \in E^i$).

1. p_{ij}, the price of player i on the link e_j. Our model covers the prices of economy class only. The price for a transfer flight has no relationship to the prices for direct flights on a given route. This hypothesis well agrees with the reality, as there exist routes in which the prices for direct and transfer flights vary unessentially. We consider outward and homeward flights independently, and the prices for such flights may differ in the model. Our motivation is that there exist other factors affecting the share of an airline in the passenger traffic flow, which can be not the same for outward and homeward flights. A price increase reduces the utility u_{ij}.

2. t_{ij}, the flight time on a link e_j. As we deal with aggregated data for each flight, in the set of factors the temporal characteristic is present in the form of flight time only. A series of researchers also analyze the departure time from an airport, the mean flight delay of an airline, etc. For a route with connections, the flight time is the times for all direct flights on it plus the waiting times at transfer airports. The flight time has a negative impact on demand.

3. $dist_{ij}$, the distance between airports on a link e_j. If competition on a given link e_j is between direct flights only, then this factor describes the passenger flow distribution between air traffic service and other means of transportation (or refusal of trip). For a route with connections, the distance is defined as the total distance of all direct flights in it. Therefore the factor of distance in the passenger's utility partially compensates the dependence in the shares of direct and transfer flights in the total passenger flow.

    In this study, we assumed that the distance positively affects the demand. For greater distances, passengers give preference to air service rather than to automobiles or railway transportation; the shares of airlines in the total demand grow accordingly. At the same time, for very large distances, the total passenger flow decreases due to weaker economical and geographical relations of the cities; but the other means of transportation become uncompetitive or prohibitive for a passenger. To take these specifics into account, we incorporated the logarithmic distance into the utility function u_{ij} with a positive coefficient.

4. γ_{ij}, a dummy variable for a link e_j defined by

    $$\gamma_{ij} = \begin{cases} 1 & \text{if } e_j \text{ is a direct flight,} \\ 0 & \text{if } e_j \text{ is a transfer flight.} \end{cases}$$

    The variable γ_{ij} describes the difference in the preference for a direct flight against a transfer flight. All other factors held equal, passengers prefer direct flights, and γ_{ij} should be included in the utility function with a positive coefficient.

5. $income_{ij}$, the per capita income for departure and destination airports on a link e_j. This factor is evaluated as the geometrical mean of the per capita incomes in the regions of the departure and destination airports. The per capita income is also included in the set of factors as an indicator of the purchasing power of population. The greater its value, the higher the passenger flow for air service.

6. $load_{ij}$, the load of a flight e_j for airline i. By assumption, $load_{ij} = 1$ if the load exceeds 80% and 0 otherwise. This parameter was used to analyze the Chinese market only.

    The utility v_{ij} of a flight e_j may depend on other factors affecting the shares of airlines in the total passenger traffic distribution. The multinomial logit model allows us to extend the set of factors if necessary for a sample selected for utility parameter estimation.

Table 9.3 Parameter estimates

	a_1	a_2	a_3	a_4	a_5	a_6	Constant
Russia	−0.000656	−0.288	0.628	0.000141	3.83		−28.305
China	−0.00196	−1.138	0.135	3.845	−6.571	1.142	3.845

Table 9.4 Airlines in the market

Airline	Airports	Routes
Aurora (former *Vladivostok Avia*)	10	11
Yakutia	10	11
SAT Airlines	4	3
IrAero	13	14
S7 Airlines	11	14
Ural Airlines	9	9
Angara	5	4
Tomsk Avia	4	3
NordStar	11	10
RusLine	9	8
UTAir	12	21

Consequently, the observable factors in the passenger's utility from choosing airline i on a link $e_j \in E^i$ can be written as

$$v_{ij} = a_1 p_{ij} + a_2 t_{ij} + a_3 \gamma_{ij} + a_4 income_{ij} + a_5 \ln(dist_{ij}) + a_6 load_{ij} + const.$$

We may estimate the coefficients in this expression using regression analysis; see the results in Table 9.3. This can be done, for example, by the BLP method [8] based on the relationship

$$\ln M_{ij} - \ln M_{i_0 j} = v_{ij} - v_{i_0 j}.$$

As an alternative i_0, take the customer's refusal of air service.

The passenger traffic distribution in the air transportation market (calculation of the shares M_{ij}) was modeled using a sample of 313 observations. The data are aggregated as they describe the characteristics of flights only (the individual characteristics of passengers were not considered).

The air transportation market statistics were collected for a period from April to May, 2013. The sources of these data are the official web sites of the airlines (see Table 9.4) and also the database of the Main Center of the Uniform Air Traffic Control System of the Russian Federation (https://infogate.matfmc.ru/htme/dom.schedule.htme).

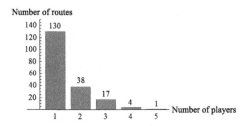

Figure 9.3 Competition in Russian market

The share of an airline in passenger traffic was calculated by the following scheme: the seat capacity × the annual number of flights × the percentage of booked seats. For separate flights in a transfer flight, the passenger traffic flow was divided as follows:

- for a flight with one connection, 0.6 for direct flights and 0.4 for flights with one connection;
- for a flight with two connections, 0.55 for direct flights, 0.35 for flights with one connection, and 0.1 for flights with two connections;
- for a flight with three connections, 0.4 for direct flights, 0.3 for flights with one connection, 0.2 for flights with two connections, and 0.1 for flights with three connections.

The percentage of booked seats and fuel consumption rate for different types of aircrafts were taken from reference books. Whenever the desired information was missed in the sources, we used the following values:

- for the percentage of booked seats, an available indicator for an airline with a similar aircraft fleet and a transportation network of comparable size;
- for fuel consumption rate, an available indicator for an aircraft with the same seat capacity.

For each departure airport, we considered the average price of aviation turbine fuel in the corresponding federal district. The fuel price statistics for largest airports in federal districts were collected from an information bulletin. The population size and per capita income data were provided by the Federal State Statistics Service of the Russian Federation.

The graph of the Russian air transportation market contains links served by a single airline. The maximal number of players on a link reaches 5. The competition in the Russian market is illustrated in Fig. 9.3.

The most intensive routes are the following.

- Irkutsk–Novosibirsk, served by 5 airlines (*S7 Airlines, IrAero, Angara, RusLine*, and *NordStar*);

Table 9.5 Airports in Russian market

Airport (city, IATA code)	Population	Airlines
Yuzhno-Sakhalinsk (UUS)	186 267	3
Petropavlovsk-Kamchatsky (PKC)	179 784	4
Vladivostok (VVO)	597 476	6
Magadan (GDX)	95 463	5
Khabarovsk (KHV)	585 556	7
Blagoveshchensk (BQS)	215 736	4
Yakutsk (YKS)	278 406	6
Chita (HTA)	327 423	3
Ulan-Ude (UUD)	411 646	4
Irkutsk (IKT)	597 846	8
Bratsk (BTK)	243 926	1
Krasnoyarsk (KJA)	997 316	6
Novosibirsk (OVB)	1 498 921	10
Norilsk (NSK)	177 273	3
Yekaterinburg (SVX)	1 377 738	4
Tomsk (TOF)	539 205	3
Barnaul (BAX)	621 669	1
Nizhnevartovsk (NJC)	258 780	4
Surgut (SGC)	316 624	3
Tyumen (TJM)	609 650	2
Khanty-Mansiysk (ICAO code: USHH)	327 423	1
Novy Urengoy (NUX)	177 273	3
Noyabrsk (NOJ)	109 236	1
Salekhard (SLY)	44 334	2
Chelyabinsk (CEK)	1 143 458	1
Magnitogorsk (MQF)	409 593	1
Omsk (OMS)	1 156 583	2

- Magadan–Khabarovsk, served by 4 airlines (*SAT Airlines*, *IrAero*, *Aurora*, and *Yakutia*);
- Yakutsk–Irkutsk, served by 4 airlines (*S7 Airlines*, *IrAero*, *Angara*, and *Yakutia*).

The market contains 27 different airports. Our study covered regional airports too. Some of them are hubs in the Russian air traffic system and have the status of international airports. Table 9.5 presents the list of airports used by the airlines.

Let us present some modeling results for this market. Consider the pricing game on the Irkutsk–Novosibirsk route, which is remarkable for the

Table 9.6 Flight characteristics for Irkutsk–Novosibirsk route

Airline	Flight time (hours)	Flights per week	Distance (km)	Connections
S7 Airlines	2.4	4	1462.6	0
IrAero	3.55	5	1520.918	1
Angara	2.1	3	1462.6	0
RusLine	2.4	3	1462.6	0
NordStar	5.2	3	1520.918	1

Table 9.7 Flight equilibrium for Irkutsk–Novosibirsk route

Airline	Price (RUB)	Income (million RUB)	Cost (million RUB)	Profit (million RUB)	Share in passenger traffic
S7 Airlines	3029.95	99.58	34.95	64.63	0.23
IrAero	2986.04	38.82	16.74	22.08	0.1
Angara	3347.28	39.16	16.9	22.26	0.2
RusLine	3115.01	24.3	9.2	15.1	0.21
NordStar	2854.08	20.48	8.73	11.75	0.07

maximum number of competing players. Here the equilibrium has the form shown in Table 9.7. The characteristics of this route for different airlines are given in Table 9.6.

Note that the airlines with direct flights from Irkutsk to Novosibirsk have the largest share in the passenger traffic owing to a small flight time and the convenience of flight. As a result, the airlines operating on this route with connections try to increase their competitiveness using price reduction.

The solution of the pricing game for all routes over the air transportation graph is presented in Fig. 9.4. The routes in the graph are ordered by the directions of flight.

Similar results were obtained for the Chinese air transportation market; see Fig. 9.5. Note that the behavior of the players in the market is close to the equilibrium behavior: the character and direction of price variations in the two graphs often agree with each other. The equilibrium prices are smaller than their real counterparts because the transportation cost in the model includes only fuel consumption, approximately 40% of the total transportation cost for Russian airlines.

Besides the pricing problem, we modeled the competitive allocation of resources in an air transportation network. According to the modeling results, some routes are not economically justified due to the remoteness and

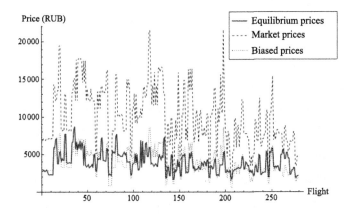

Figure 9.4 Equilibrium prices (Russian market)

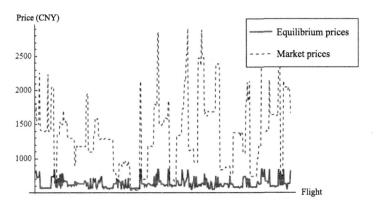

Figure 9.5 Equilibrium prices (Chinese market)

small population of some settlements. Here the principles of governmental support are often applied, which are not discussed in this book.

For each airline, transportation network development is an integral part of strategic management. Delivering air transportation service, the airlines compete with each other and also with alternative means of transportation for passenger traffic. To improve their performance, airlines can use game-theoretic methods.

CHAPTER 10

Games With Request Flows in Service Systems

Contents

This chapter is dedicated to optimal arrival time choice problems in service systems with loss. Players send their requests to a system for a successful service. The requests' arrival discipline is not defined or is unknown, and each player in a request flow seeks to choose an optimal arrival time for his request to maximize his individual payoff. A similar problem in which players choose arrival times for their requests in a system serving at most one request at each time was considered by Glazer and Hassin [39]. In this paper, the authors designed an optimal service system with one queue in the following setup: an optimality criterion is the minimum expected waiting time of a request in the queue, whereas a desired strategy is a probability distribution of the arrival times over a time interval of system operation. In this chapter, the models define the player's payoff as the probability of service for his request.

Networking Games
https://doi.org/10.1016/B978-0-12-816551-5.00016-2
Copyright © 2019 Elsevier Inc.
All rights reserved.

10.1 ARRIVAL TIME CHOICE IN A ONE-SERVER SYSTEM WITH SEQUENTIAL REQUESTS

In this section, we consider the optimal arrival time choice problem in a one-server system $?/M/1/0$ with a given "comfort" function [57]. Our model proceeds from the assumption that the requests sequentially arrive in the system (two or more requests may not come simultaneously). In other words, two or more players send their requests to the system at the same time with zero probability. Among such systems, we mention booking offices at railway stations and bus terminals, service windows in banks, gas stations, and so on (customers always form a queue). Another example describes different online booking services (transport, accommodation, and so on) with guarantee that the same reservation is not made by two customers simultaneously. A possible solution is to authorize at most one connection at each time (in our case, to place at most one order).

Another distinctive feature of our model consists in a comfort function. User's comfort in a service system depends on the time of day and may take positive or negative values (thereby expressing the user's gain or loss from the service of his request at time t). We suppose that a user necessarily sends his request to the system, despite the potential loss incurred by service (a negative value of his comfort function at the arrival time). An appropriate comfort function can be constructed in several ways, for example, using the user's degree of convenience to send requests at different times of day. The user's comfort function may depend on numerous factors (in particular, psychological ones, which are difficult to estimate numerically). It is possible to design this function based on statistical results of user polling. For example, consider an organization with a single shared-access workstation connected to the Internet. For each employee of this organization, it is convenient to use the workstation at the beginning and end of his working hours and also at the lunch time. Then the corresponding comfort function may have the graph illustrated in Fig. 10.1.

We further consider a service system $?/M/1/0$ with loss that operates in the following way.

- The requests come to the system sequentially; a simultaneous arrival of two or more requests is impossible.
- The requests' arrival discipline is not defined.
- The service time of a sequential request is a random variable that obeys the exponential distribution with parameter $1/\mu$, where $\mu > 0$.
- The system consists of one server and is able to serve at most one request at each time.

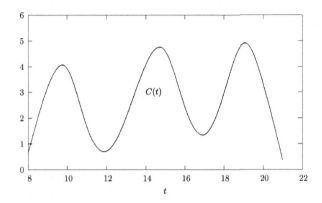

Figure 10.1 Comfort function of workstation use during working day: an example

- The system has no queue: if a current request is being served when a sequential request arrives in the system, then the latter is rejected.
- For each player, a given comfort function $C(t)$ describes his degree of convenience of sending his request to the system at time t.

For each player, it is required to find an equilibrium behavioral strategy, that is, a choice rule for an appropriate time t of sending his request to the system that maximizes his payoff over a time interval $[t_0, T]$, where t_0 and T are defined during solution of the problem. Let us construct a Nash equilibrium in the class of mixed strategies, that is, probability distributions of arrival times in the system in the interval $[t_0, T]$. Assume that these distributions have density functions; then the density functions uniquely define the desired strategies. Hence, from this point onward, under "the player's mixed strategy," we mean the density function of the arrival times of his requests in the system in the interval $[t_0, T]$.

10.1.1 Model of the system with two players

Suppose the service system is used by two players. They choose the arrival times of their requests, t and s, in the system. For a request that comes at time t, we have three possible cases:

1. $t < s$, that is, this request arrives in the system before the request of the other player;
2. $s < t$, that is, this request arrives in the system after the request of the other player, which is still being served at the time t;
3. $s < t$, that is, this request arrives in the system after the request of the other player, which has been served by the time t.

The request under consideration is served by the system in the first and third cases and rejected in the second case. If the request that arrives at time t is successfully served, then the first player obtains the profit $C(t)$.

Denote by $f(t)$ and $g(s)$ the strategies of the first and second players, respectively. The payoff functions of each player given the opponent's mixed strategy take the form

$$H_1(t, g) = C(t) \left(\int_{-\infty}^{t} g(s)(1 - e^{-\mu(t-s)}) ds + \int_{t}^{\infty} g(s) ds \right),$$

$$H_2(f, s) = C(s) \left(\int_{-\infty}^{s} f(t)(1 - e^{-\mu(s-t)}) dt + \int_{s}^{\infty} f(t) dt \right).$$

Since f and g are density functions,

$$H_1(t, g) = C(t) \left(1 - \int_{-\infty}^{t} g(s) e^{-\mu(t-s)} ds \right),$$

$$H_2(f, s) = C(s) \left(1 - \int_{-\infty}^{s} f(t) e^{-\mu(s-t)} dt \right).$$

Note that these payoff functions incorporate the comfort function as a factor. Hence, it can be calculated up to a constant multiplier.

Let us calculate a symmetric Nash equilibrium, that is, in which the desired strategies of both players coincide. In this case, it suffices to solve the maximization problem for the payoff function of the first player:

$$H(t, g) := H_1(t, g) = C(t) \left(1 - \int_{-\infty}^{t} g(s) e^{-\mu(t-s)} ds \right) \rightarrow \max.$$

More specifically, we have to find a time interval $[t_0, T]$ and a function $g(t)$ that describes the density function of the arrival times for the requests of the second player on this interval so that the payoff function is constant on it and takes the global maximum value. In mathematical terms, the problem is to find t_0, T and $g(t)$ such that

$\frac{\partial H(t, g)}{\partial t} = 0$ for all $t \in (t_0, T)$,

$\int_{t_0}^{T} g(t) dt = 1$, \hfill (10.1)

$g(t) \geq 0$ and $H(t, g) \leq H(t_0, g)$ for all $t \in (-\infty, \infty)$.

10.1.2 Nash equilibrium in the problem with two players

Consider problem (10.1). Making appropriate manipulations with $\frac{\partial H(t,g)}{\partial t} = 0$, we obtain the integral equation

$$\int_{-\infty}^{t} g(s)e^{\mu s}\,ds = \frac{C(t)g(t) - C'(t)}{\mu C(t) - C'(t)}e^{\mu t}. \tag{10.2}$$

Differentiation with respect to t and trivial transformations finally yield the following linear inhomogeneous differential equation for the desired function $g(t)$:

$$\begin{aligned}
&g'(t)\left(C^2(t)\mu - C(t)C'(t)\right) \\
&+ g(t)\left(C(t)C''(t) - 2(C'(t))^2 + C'(t)C(t)\mu\right) \\
&- \mu(C(t)C''(t) - 2(C'(t))^2 + C'(t)C(t)\mu) = 0.
\end{aligned} \tag{10.3}$$

The function $g(t)$ is defined on the time interval $[t_0, T]$ where the players send their requests to the system. Let $g(t) \equiv 0$ outside this interval.

Consider the case of a constant comfort function $C(t) \equiv C$. Then the equation takes the form $g'(t) = 0$, whence it follows that $g(t) \equiv const$ on the time interval $t \in (t_0, T)$. After substitution of this solution into the original integral equation, we get $g(t) \equiv 0$ on the interval $t \in (t_0, T)$. In other words, the solution of the problem with two players and a constant comfort function represents a pure strategy equilibrium in which one of the players sends his request at time t_0, whereas the other at time T. Therefore we further assume that the comfort function is not constant and $C'(t) \neq 0$ almost everywhere.

The general solution of the homogeneous differential equation has the form

$$g_{gen}(t) = Ke^{I(t)},$$

where

$$I(t) = \int_{t_0}^{t} \frac{\frac{C''(\tau)}{C'(\tau)} - 2\frac{C'(\tau)}{C(\tau)} + \mu}{1 - \mu\frac{C(\tau)}{C'(\tau)}}\,d\tau.$$

Clearly, a partial solution of the inhomogeneous differential equation is $g_{par}(t) = \mu$. Then the general solution of the inhomogeneous differential equation (10.3) can be written as

$$g(t) = Ke^{I(t)} + \mu,$$

where the constant K is calculated by substituting the solution of the differential equation into the original integral equation (10.2):

$$K = e^{\mu t_0} \left(\int_{t_0}^{t} e^{I(s) + \mu s} ds - \frac{C(t) e^{I(t) + \mu t}}{\mu C(t) - C'(t)} \right)^{-1}. \tag{10.4}$$

Since K is independent of t, letting $t = t_0$ in expression (10.4) gives

$$K = \frac{C'(t_0)}{C(t_0)} - \mu.$$

Finally, the desired density function has the form

$$g(t) = \left(\frac{C'(t_0)}{C(t_0)} - \mu \right) e^{I(t)} + \mu.$$

Recall that $g(t)$ is the density function of the arrival times for the player's requests in the system. Hence the limits of the time interval $[t_0, T]$ are chosen so that $g(t) \geq 0$ and $\int_{t_0}^{T} g(t) dt = 1$ for all $t \in [t_0, T]$.

The equilibrium payoff function is constant on $[t_0, T]$, that is, for all $t \in [t_0, T]$, we have $H(t, g) \equiv v = C(t_0)$. This equilibrium value gives the solution if $H(t, g) \leq C(t_0)$ for all $t \in (-\infty, \infty)$. The value of the payoff function for $t \in (-\infty, t_0]$ is $H(t, g) = C(t)$. In other words, the comfort function must satisfy the condition $C(t) \leq C(t_0)$ for all $t \in (-\infty, t_0]$.

For $t \in [T, \infty)$, the payoff function has the form

$$H(t, g) = C(t) \left(1 - e^{-\mu(t-T)} + K e^{-\mu t} \int_{t_0}^{T} e^{I(s) + \mu s} ds \right).$$

Since $H(t_0, g) = H(T, g)$, we obtain

$$C(t_0) = C(T) e^{-\mu T} K \int_{t_0}^{T} e^{I(s) + \mu s} ds,$$

$$\int_{t_0}^{T} e^{I(s) + \mu s} ds = e^{\mu T} \frac{C(t_0)}{K C(T)}.$$

Then, for $t \in [T, \infty)$, the payoff is given by

$$H(t, g) = C(t) \left(1 - e^{-\mu(t-T)} \left(1 - \frac{C(t_0)}{C(T)} \right) \right), \qquad (10.5)$$

and for $t \geq T$, the comfort function must satisfy the inequality

$$C(t_0) \geq C(t) \left(1 - e^{-\mu(t-T)} \left(1 - \frac{C(t_0)}{C(T)} \right) \right).$$

Consequently, we have established the following result.

Theorem 49. *The strategies*

$$g(t) = \left(\frac{C'(t_0)}{C(t_0)} - \mu \right) e^{\int_{t_0}^{t} \frac{\frac{C''(\tau)}{C'(\tau)} - 2\frac{C'(\tau)}{C(\tau)} + \mu}{1 - \mu \frac{C(\tau)}{C'(\tau)}} d\tau} + \mu$$

on a time interval $[t_0, T]$, where t_0 and T are such that

$$\int_{t_0}^{T} g(t)dt = 1 \ and \ g(t) \geq 0, \qquad (10.6)$$

$$C(t) \leq C(t_0) \ for \ all \ t \in (-\infty, t_0],$$

$$C(t_0) \geq C(t) \left(1 - e^{-\mu(t-T)} \left(1 - \frac{C(t_0)}{C(T)} \right) \right) \ for \ all \ t \in [T, \infty), \qquad (10.7)$$

yield a symmetric Nash equilibrium in the problem with two players and given comfort function $C(t)$. For each of the players, the equilibrium value of the payoff on the time interval $[t_0, T]$ is $H(t, g) \equiv C(t_0)$.

Example 34 (Solution for the exponential comfort function). Let the comfort function be $C(t) = -ae^{bt}$ for $t \geq t_0$ and $C(t) = -ae^{bt_0} = C(t_0)$ for $t \leq t_0$. Here we assume that $a > 0$ and $b > 0$. By Theorem 49 the equilibrium strategy has the form

$$g(t) = (b - \mu)e^{-b(t-t_0)} + \mu.$$

For a given left limit t_0, the right limit of the time interval $[t_0, T]$ is calculated using condition (10.6), that is,

$$\mu = \frac{be^{-b(T-t_0)}}{e^{-b(T-t_0)} - 1 + b(T - t_0)}.$$

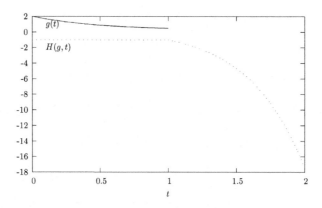

Figure 10.2 Solution for exponential comfort function

In this case, on the interval $[t_0, T]$ the equilibrium payoff function is given by $H(t, g) \equiv ae^{bt_0}$.

For $t \leq t_0$, the payoff function takes the value $C(t_0)$. This equilibrium yields the solution of the original problem if condition (10.7) holds: $-ae^{bt_0} \geq -ae^{bt}\left(1 - e^{-\mu(t-T)}(1 - e^{-b(t-t_0)})\right)$ for all $t \geq T$. This inequality is easily transformed into $1 - e^{-b(t-t_0)} \geq e^{-\mu(t-T)}\left(1 - e^{-b(t-t_0)}\right)$, which holds for all $t \geq T$ given $b > 0$ and $a > 0$.

The graph of $g(t)$ for $a = 1$, $b = 2$, $\mu = 0.238$, $t_0 = 0$, and $T = 1$ is illustrated in Fig. 10.2.

Example 35 (Solution for the parabolic comfort function). Let the comfort function be $C(t) = at(1 - t)$, where $a > 0$. According to Theorem 49, the equilibrium strategy has the form

$$g(t) = \frac{(1 - 2t - \mu t + \mu t^2)t_0(1 - t_0)}{t^2(1 - t)^2} + \mu. \tag{10.8}$$

The limits of the time interval $[t_0, T]$ must satisfy condition (10.6):

$$\mu = \frac{t_0(1 - t_0)}{T(1 - T)\left(T - t_0 + t_0(1 - t_0)\ln\frac{t_0(1-T)}{T(1-t_0)}\right)}. \tag{10.9}$$

In this case, on the interval $[t_0, T]$ the equilibrium payoff function is given by $H(t, g) \equiv at_0(1 - t_0)$.

For $t \leq t_0$, the payoff function takes the value $C(t)$. This equilibrium yields the solution of the original problem if condition (10.7) holds: for all

$t \geq T$,

$$at_0(1 - t_0) \geq at(1 - t)\left(1 - e^{-\mu(t-T)}\left(1 - \frac{t_0(1 - t_0)}{T(1 - T)}\right)\right).$$

Lemma 33. *There exists a pair composed of $t_0 \in (0, \frac{1}{2})$ and $T \in [\frac{1}{2}, 1)$ such that $g(T) = 0$, where $g(t)$ has form (10.8), and condition (10.9) holds.*

Proof. First, we show the existence of $T \in [\frac{1}{2}, 1)$ such that $g(T) = 0$, that is, $h_1(T) := (1 - 2T - \mu T + \mu T^2)t_0(1 - t_0) + \mu T^2(1 - T)^2 = 0$. Then

$$h_1\left(\frac{1}{2}\right) = -\frac{\mu}{4}t_0(1 - t_0) + \frac{\mu}{16} \geq -\frac{\mu}{4} \cdot \frac{1}{2}\left(1 - \frac{1}{2}\right) + \frac{\mu}{16} = 0$$

and

$$h_1(1) = -t_0(1 - t_0) < 0.$$

Hence there exists a value $T \in [\frac{1}{2}, 1)$ such that $g(T) = 0$. Now, we prove that, for this value T, it is possible to find a value $t_0 \in (0, \frac{1}{2})$ that satisfies condition (10.9):

$$h_2(t_0) := t_0(1 - t_0) - \mu T(1 - T)\left(T - t_0 + t_0(1 - t_0)\ln\frac{t_0(1 - T)}{T(1 - t_0)}\right) = 0,$$

$$h_2(0) = -\mu T(1 - T) < 0,$$

$$h_2\left(\frac{1}{2}\right) = \frac{1}{4} + \mu T(1 - T)\left(\frac{1}{4}\ln\frac{T}{1 - T} - T + \frac{1}{2}\right),$$

$$h_3(T) := \frac{1}{4}\ln\frac{T}{1 - T} - T + \frac{1}{2}, \quad h_3\left(\frac{1}{2}\right) = 0,$$

$$h_3'(T) = \frac{1}{4T(1 - T)} - 1 \geq \frac{1}{4} \cdot 4 - 1 = 0,$$

that is, $h_3(T) \geq 0$ for $T \in [\frac{1}{2}, 1)$. Then $h_2\left(\frac{1}{2}\right) \geq \frac{1}{4} > 0$. □

Lemma 34. *If the function $g(t)$ has form (10.8) and $g(T) = 0$, then, for all $t \in [t_0, T]$, it follows that $g(t) \geq g(T)$.*

Proof. Assume that $g(T) = 0$, that is,

$$\frac{1 - 2T - \mu T + \mu T^2}{T^2(1 - T)^2} = -\frac{\mu}{t_0(1 - t_0)}.$$

For some $t \in (t_0, T)$, let $g(t) < g(T)$, that is,

$$\frac{t_0(1 - t_0)(1 - 2t - \mu t + \mu t^2)}{t^2(1 - t)^2} < \frac{t_0(1 - t_0)(1 - 2T - \mu T + \mu T^2)}{T^2(1 - T)^2}.$$

Since $t_0(1 - t_0) > 0$, this inequality gives

$$\frac{(1 - 2t - \mu t + \mu t^2)}{t^2(1 - t)^2} < \frac{(1 - 2T - \mu T + \mu T^2)}{T^2(1 - T)^2} = -\frac{\mu}{t_0(1 - t_0)}. \tag{10.10}$$

Let $t \in [t_0, \frac{1}{2}]$. Then we obtain $t_0(1 - t_0)(1 - 2t) + \mu t(1 - t)(t(1 - t) - t_0(1 - t_0)) \geq 0$, which contradicts assumption (10.10). Let $t \in [\frac{1}{2}, T]$; in this case, $t(1 - t) \geq T(1 - T)$ and

$$(1 - 2t)T^2(1 - T)^2 - (1 - 2T)t^2(1 - t)^2$$
$$= (2T - 1)t^2(1 - t)^2 - (2t - 1)T^2(1 - T)^2$$
$$= \left(T^2 - (1 - T)^2\right)t^2(1 - t)^2 - \left(t^2 - (1 - t)^2\right)T^2(1 - T)^2$$
$$= T^2t^2\left((1 - t)^2 - (1 - T)^2\right)$$
$$\quad + (1 - t)^2(1 - T)^2\left(T^2 - t^2\right) \geq 0.$$

Consequently,

$$(1 - 2t - \mu t + \mu t^2)T^2(1 - T)^2 - (1 - 2T - \mu T + \mu T^2)t^2(1 - t)^2$$
$$= (1 - 2t)T^2(1 - T)^2 - (1 - 2T)t^2(1 - t)^2$$
$$\quad + \mu T(1 - T)t(1 - t)(t(1 - t) - T(1 - T)) \geq 0,$$

which contradicts assumption (10.10). $\qquad\square$

Lemma 35. *If the function $g(t)$ has form (10.8), $g(T) = 0$, and $T \in [\frac{1}{2}, 1)$, then the payoff function $H(t, g)$ (10.5) decreases on $t \in (T, \infty)$.*

Proof. Assume that $g(T) = 0$, that is,

$$t_0(1 - t_0)(1 - 2T) + \mu T(1 - T)(T(1 - T) - t_0(1 - t_0)) = 0.$$

For $t \geq T$,

$$H(t, g) = at(1 - t)\left(1 - e^{-\mu(t-T)}\left(1 - \frac{t_0(1 - t_0)}{T(1 - T)}\right)\right),$$

$$H'(t)/a = (1 - 2t)\left(1 - e^{-\mu(t-T)}\right)$$
$$\quad + \frac{e^{-\mu(t-T)}}{T(1-T)}\left(t_0(1 - t_0)(1 - 2t) + \mu t(1 - t)(T(1 - T) - t_0(1 - t_0))\right)$$
$$< (1 - 2t)\left(1 - e^{-\mu(t-T)}\right) +$$
$$\quad + \frac{e^{-\mu(t-T)}}{T(1-T)}\left(t_0(1 - t_0)(1 - 2T) + \mu T(1 - T)(T(1 - T) - t_0(1 - t_0))\right)$$
$$= (1 - 2t)\left(1 - e^{-\mu(t-T)}\right) < 0,$$

and the conclusion follows. $\qquad\square$

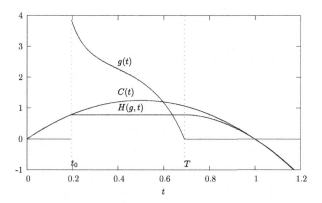

Figure 10.3 Solution for parabolic comfort function

Based on the above lemmas, we may formulate the following important result.

Theorem 50. *The strategies*

$$g(t) = \frac{(1 - 2t - \mu t + \mu t^2)t_0(1 - t_0)}{t^2(1 - t)^2} + \mu$$

on a time interval $[t_0, T]$, where $0 < t_0 < \frac{1}{2} \le T < 1$, such that $g(T) = 0$ and $\int_{t_0}^{T} g(t)\,dt = 1$, yield a symmetric Nash equilibrium in the problem with two players and the comfort function $C(t) = at(1 - t)$, where $a > 0$.

Proof. The nonnegativity of the density function $g(t)$ on $[t_0, T]$ follows from Lemma 34. In turn, Lemma 33 guarantees that $t_0 < \frac{1}{2}$, and hence the payoff function increases for $t < t_0$. By Lemma 35 the payoff function decreases for $t > t_0$. □

The graph of $g(t)$ for $a = 5$ and $\mu = 5$ is presented in Fig. 10.3. The equilibrium limits of the time interval are $t_0 \approx 0.195$ and $T \approx 0.691$.

10.1.3 Model of the system with three and more players

Suppose the service system is used by $n + 1$ players. They choose the arrival times of their requests $\tau_1, \ldots, \tau_n$, and t in the system. It is necessary to construct the payoff function of the player with the pure strategy t given all other players $i = 1, \ldots, n$ choose the same mixed strategies $g(\tau_i)$.

First, design the payoff function in the case of three players. The request from the player who chooses the arrival time t is not served if the request from one of the other two players has earlier arrived in the system and is still being served at time t. Let this be the player choosing the arrival time τ_1. For a successful service of his request, the request from the player choosing the arrival time τ_2 must have been arrived and served by time τ_1 or come after time τ_1. Then the probability that the request arriving at time t is served can be calculated as

$$
P_2(t,g) = 1 - 2 \int_{-\infty}^{t} g(\tau_1)e^{-\mu(t-\tau_1)}s
$$
$$
\times \left(\int_{-\infty}^{\tau_1} g(\tau_2)(1 - e^{-\mu(\tau_1-\tau_2)})d\tau_2 + \int_{\tau_1}^{+\infty} g(\tau_2)d\tau_2 \right) d\tau_1
$$
$$
= 1 - 2 \int_{-\infty}^{t} g(\tau_1)e^{-\mu(t-\tau_1)} \left(1 - \int_{-\infty}^{\tau_1} g(\tau_2)e^{-\mu(\tau_1-\tau_2)}d\tau_2 \right) d\tau_1.
$$

Similarly, in the case of $n+1$ players the corresponding probability is given by

$$
P_n(t,g) = 1 - n \int_{-\infty}^{t} g(\tau_1)e^{-\mu(t-\tau_1)} \left(1 - (n-1) \int_{-\infty}^{\tau_1} g(\tau_2)e^{-\mu(\tau_1-\tau_2)} \right.
$$
$$
\left. \times \left(1 - (n-2) \int_{-\infty}^{\tau_2} \ldots \right) d\tau_2 \right) d\tau_1.
$$

These probabilities can be recurrently represented:

$$
P_1(t,g) = 1 - \int_{-\infty}^{t} g(\tau_1)e^{-\mu(t-\tau_1)}d\tau_1,
$$
$$
P_2(t,g) = 1 - 2 \int_{-\infty}^{t} g(\tau_1)e^{-\mu(t-\tau_1)}P_1(\tau_1,g)d\tau_1,
$$
$$
\ldots,
$$
$$
P_n(t,g) = 1 - n \int_{-\infty}^{t} g(\tau_1)e^{-\mu(t-\tau_1)}P_{n-1}(\tau_1,g)d\tau_1,
$$

and the corresponding payoff functions are

$$
H(t,g^n) = C(t)P_n(t,g).
$$

Now, let us study this problem in an alternative setup. Which form must the comfort function have for yielding a desired Nash equilibrium? Our analysis begins with the uniform case and then switches to the exponential case as a more complicated one.

Example 36 (Comfort function in the case of uniform strategies of players). Suppose we are interested in a comfort function that yields the uniform density functions $g(t) = 1$ on the time interval $[0, 1]$ as the equilibrium strategies of the players.

Theorem 51. *For the equilibrium functions of the players to be the uniform density functions on the interval $[0, 1]$, the comfort function on this interval must have the form $C_n(t) = const/P_n(t, g)$, where*

$$P_n(t, g) = 1 + \frac{n!}{(-\mu)^n} \left(\sum_{i=0}^{n-1} \frac{(-\mu)^i}{i!} - e^{-\mu t} \sum_{i=0}^{n-1} \frac{(-\mu)^i(1-t)^i}{i!} \right).$$

Proof. We will use mathematical induction.

The base case: the probability of service for $n = 1$, that is, the system with two players, is

$$P_1(t, g) = 1 - \int_0^t e^{-\mu(t-\tau)} d\tau = 1 + \frac{e^{-\mu t}}{\mu} - \frac{1}{\mu}.$$

Hence the base case is true.

The inductive step: hypothesize that the formula is valid for $P_n(t, g)$ and prove it for $P_{n+1}(t, g)$:

$$P_{n+1}(t, g) = 1 - (n+1) \int_0^t e^{-\mu(t-\tau)} P_n(\tau, g) d\tau$$

$$= 1 - (n+1) e^{-\mu t} \frac{n!}{(-\mu)^n} \int_0^t \left(e^{\mu\tau} \sum_{i=0}^n \frac{(-\mu)^i}{i!} - \sum_{i=0}^{n-1} \frac{(-\mu)^i(1-\tau)^i}{i!} \right) d\tau$$

$$= 1 - e^{-\mu t} \frac{(n+1)!}{(-\mu)^n} \left(\frac{e^{\mu t}-1}{\mu} \sum_{i=0}^n \frac{(-\mu)^i}{i!} - \sum_{i=0}^{n-1} \frac{(-\mu)^i}{(i+1)!} + \sum_{i=0}^{n-1} \frac{(-\mu)^i(1-t)^{i+1}}{(i+1)!} \right)$$

$$= 1 - e^{-\mu t} \frac{(n+1)!}{(-\mu)^n} \left(\frac{e^{\mu t}-1}{\mu} \sum_{i=0}^n \frac{(-\mu)^i}{i!} - \sum_{i=1}^n \frac{(-\mu)^{i-1}}{i!} + \sum_{i=1}^n \frac{(-\mu)^{i-1}(1-t)^i}{(i)!} \right)$$

$$= 1 - e^{-\mu t} \frac{(n+1)!}{(-\mu)^n} \left(\frac{e^{\mu t}}{\mu} \sum_{i=0}^n \frac{(-\mu)^i}{i!} - \frac{1}{\mu} + \sum_{i=1}^n \frac{(-\mu)^{i-1}(1-t)^i}{i!} \right)$$

$$= 1 - e^{-\mu t} \frac{(n+1)!}{(-\mu)^n} \left(\frac{e^{\mu t}}{\mu} \sum_{i=0}^n \frac{(-\mu)^i}{i!} + \sum_{i=0}^n \frac{(-\mu)^{i-1}(1-t)^i}{i!} \right)$$

$$= 1 + \frac{(n+1)!}{(-\mu)^{n+1}} \left(\sum_{i=0}^n \frac{(-\mu)^i}{i!} - e^{-\mu t} \sum_{i=0}^n \frac{(-\mu)^i(1-t)^i}{i!} \right).$$

Since in the equilibrium the payoff function must be constant on the interval $[0, 1]$, then the comfort function on this interval must take the values $C_n(t) = const/P_n(t, g)$.   □

Consider the behavior of the service system under infinitely many players:

$$P_n(t, g) = 1 + \frac{n!}{(-\mu)^n} \left(e^{-\mu} - r_n(-\mu) - e^{-\mu t} + e^{-\mu t} r_n(-\mu(1 - t)) \right)$$
$$= 1 - \frac{n!}{(-\mu)^n} \left(r_n(-\mu) - e^{-\mu t} r_n(-\mu(1 - t)) \right),$$

where $r_n(x)$ denotes the remainder term in the Maclaurin expansion of e^x, which obeys the upper bound $|r_n(x)| \le \frac{x^{n+1}}{(n+1)!}$. Taking into account the inequalities

$$|r_n(-\mu) - e^{-\mu t} r_n(-\mu(1 - t))| \le |r_n(-\mu)| + |e^{-\mu t} r_n(-\mu(1 - t))|$$
$$\le \frac{\mu^{n+1}}{(n+1)!} + \frac{(\mu(1-t))^{n+1}}{(n+1)!} \le \frac{2\mu^{n+1}}{(n+1)!}$$

and the convergence $\left| \frac{n!}{(-\mu)^n} \frac{2\mu^{n+1}}{(n+1)!} \right| = \frac{2\mu}{n+1} \to 0$ as $n \to \infty$, we obtain $P_n(t, g) \to 1$ as $n \to \infty$. Thus, for infinitely many players, the probability of service tends to 1, whereas the comfort function on $[t_0, T]$ tends to $const$, that is, is independent of t.

Example 37 (Comfort function in the case of exponential strategies of players). Let the desired strategies of the players be $g(t) = \lambda e^{-\lambda t}$, where $t \ge 0$.

Theorem 52. *For the equilibrium functions of the players to be $g(t) = \lambda e^{-\lambda t}$, $t \ge 0$, the comfort function on this interval must have the form $C_n(t) = const/P_n(t, g)$, where*

$$P_n(t, g) = 1 + \sum_{i=1}^{n} \frac{n!}{(n-i)!} \frac{e^{-i\lambda t} - e^{-(n-i)\lambda t - \mu t}}{\prod_{j=1}^{i}(j - \mu/\lambda)}.$$

Proof. Again, we will use mathematical induction.

The base case: the probability of service for $n = 1$, that is, the system with two players, is

$$P_1(t, g) = 1 - \lambda \int_0^t e^{-\mu(t-\tau)-\lambda \tau} d\tau = 1 + \frac{e^{-\lambda t} - e^{-\mu t}}{1 - \mu/\lambda}.$$

Hence the base case is true.

The inductive step: hypothesize that the formula is valid for $P_n(t,g)$ and prove it for $P_{n+1}(t,g)$:

$$P_{n+1}(t,g) = 1 - (n+1)\lambda \int_0^t e^{-\mu(t-\tau)-\lambda\tau} P_n(\tau,g)d\tau$$

$$= 1 - (n+1)\lambda e^{-\mu t}\int_0^t e^{-(\lambda-\mu)\tau}\left(1 + \sum_{i=1}^n \frac{n!}{(n-i)!}\frac{e^{-i\lambda\tau}-e^{-(n-i)\lambda\tau-\mu\tau}}{\prod_{j=1}^i (j-\mu/\lambda)}\right)d\tau$$

$$= 1 - \frac{(n+1)(e^{-\mu t}-e^{-\lambda t})}{1-\mu/\lambda} - \sum_{i=1}^n \frac{(n+1)!(e^{-\mu t}-e^{-(i+1)\lambda t})}{(n-i)!\prod_{j=1}^{i+1}(j-\mu/\lambda)}$$

$$+ \sum_{i=1}^n \frac{(n+1)!(e^{-\mu t}-e^{-(n=i+1)\lambda t-\mu t})}{(n+1-i)!\prod_{j=1}^i (j-\mu/\lambda)}.$$

Changing the order of summation for

$$\sum_{i=0}^n \frac{(n+1)!e^{-\mu t}}{(n-i)!\prod_{j=1}^{i+1}(j-\mu/\lambda)} = \sum_{i=1}^{n+1}\frac{(n+1)!e^{-\mu t}}{(n+1-i)!\prod_{j=1}^i(j-\mu/\lambda)},$$

$$\sum_{i=0}^{n+1}\frac{(n+1)!e^{-(\lambda+i\lambda)t}}{(n-i)!\prod_{j=1}^{i+1}(j-\mu/\lambda)} = \sum_{i=1}^{n+1}\frac{(n+1)!e^{-i\lambda t}}{(n+1-i)!\prod_{j=1}^i(j-\mu/\lambda)},$$

we get

$$P_{n+1}(t,g) = 1 - \sum_{i=1}^{n+1}\frac{(n+1)!e^{-\mu t}}{(n+1-i)!\prod_{j=1}^i(j-\mu/\lambda)} + \sum_{i=1}^{n+1}\frac{(n+1)!e^{-i\lambda t}}{(n+1-i)!\prod_{j=1}^i(j-\mu/\lambda)}$$

$$- \sum_{i=1}^n \frac{(n+1)!e^{-\mu t}}{(n+1-i)!\prod_{j=1}^i(j-\mu/\lambda)} - \sum_{i=1}^n \frac{(n+1)!e^{-(n+1-i)\lambda t-\mu t}}{(n+1-i)!\prod_{j=1}^i(j-\mu/\lambda)}$$

$$= 1 - \frac{(n+1)!e^{-\mu t}}{(n+1-(n+1))!\prod_{j=1}^{n+1}(j-\mu/\lambda)} + \sum_{i=1}^{n+1}\frac{(n+1)!e^{-i\lambda t}}{(n+1-i)!\prod_{j=1}^i(j-\mu/\lambda)}$$

$$- \sum_{i=1}^n \frac{(n+1)!e^{-(n+1-i)\lambda t-\mu t}}{(n+1-i)!\prod_{j=1}^i(j-\mu/\lambda)}$$

$$= 1 + \sum_{i=1}^{n+1}\frac{(n+1)!e^{-i\lambda t}}{(n+1-i)!\prod_{j=1}^i(j-\mu/\lambda)} - \sum_{i=1}^{n+1}\frac{(n+1)!e^{-(n+1-i)\lambda t-\mu t}}{(n+1-i)!\prod_{j=1}^i(j-\mu/\lambda)}$$

$$= 1 + \sum_{i=1}^{n+1}\frac{(n+1)!\left(e^{-i\lambda t}-e^{-(n+1-i)\lambda t-\mu t}\right)}{(n+1-i)!\prod_{j=1}^i(j-\mu/\lambda)}.$$

Since in the equilibrium the payoff function must be constant for $t \geq 0$, the comfort function for $t \geq 0$ must take the values $C_n(t) = const/P_n(t,g)$.   □

Let μ be close to 0, that is, the average service time is very high. Then

$$\prod_{j=1}^{i}(j - \mu/\lambda) \approx i! \text{ and } e^{-\mu t} \approx 1,$$

$$P_n(t,g) \approx 1 + \sum_{i=1}^{n} \frac{n!}{(n-i)!} \frac{e^{-i\lambda t} - e^{-(n-i)\lambda t}}{i!}$$

$$= 1 + (1 + e^{-\lambda t})^n - 1 - (1 + e^{\lambda t})^n e^{-n\lambda t} + e^{-n\lambda t} = e^{-n\lambda t}.$$

Then the comfort function has the form $C_n(t) \approx const \cdot e^{n\lambda t}$. For large n, the probability of service $P_n(t,g)$ is close to 0, and the comfort function must take great values.

10.2 ARRIVAL TIME CHOICE IN A RANDOM-ACCESS TWO-SERVER SYSTEM WITH ARBITRARY REQUESTS

Consider the service system $?/M/m/0$. On a given time interval $[0, T]$, the requests arrive in the system and are included in the queue if there exist vacancies. The system has servers with identical functionality and, possibly, different performance. When a user request arrives in the system, it is randomly redirected to one of the servers and then served or lost.

For the model studied in this section, we assume that the requests may arrive in the system one after another or in groups at the same time simultaneously. Such a situation occurs, for example, if the service is highly demanded at certain times. In real applications, access protocols for different services (particularly, Internet services) are implemented with a sequential access of users to the system. Whenever two or more requests arrive in the system, they form a queue with random serial numbers assigned by a uniform random draw. The system has no buffer, and hence it serves several first requests in the queue depending on the number of free servers at a current time (and the other requests of the queue are lost). Therefore, if k requests simultaneously arrive in the system with m free servers, then, for each request, the probability of service is $\min\{1, \frac{m}{k}\}$.

An example of random access in the Internet is the round robin algorithm in a DNS system, which distributes a load among several servers with a certain Web service. Different users have different IP addresses while accessing a domain. In the elementary case, the IP addresses are assigned sequentially (first, second, etc.); in the general case, each address is assigned with a given probability. Besides load distribution for Web resources, such random-access models can be applied to optimize cloud computing, call centers, and so on.

In what follows, we analyze two request redistribution models. In the first model (further referred to as the model with the pure random-access scheme [23]), the system has no information about the server states, and each request can be redirected to a busy server even given a free server. For example, a real DNS system assigns a sequential IP address of a requested domain for a user without any information about its availability. In the second model, the access to servers is random only if both are free (the model with the rational random-access scheme [21]).

We will associate the following noncooperative game with each of these random-access models. As his pure strategy, each player chooses the time to send his request to the system or, as his mixed strategy, the distribution of such times. The payoff is the probability of service for the player's request. The symmetric Nash equilibrium acts in the same selfish way.

A similar model $?/M/1/0$ with one server was considered by Ravner and Haviv [70]. Formally speaking, it represents a particular case of the model with the pure random-access scheme in which the probability of redistribution to a server is 1. Later, the one-server model was extended to the case of several servers of identical performance [71]. The authors established the following qualitative properties of symmetric Nash equilibria in such models:

- the system possesses a unique symmetric Nash equilibrium;
- at the zero time, there is a strictly positive probability of request arrival in the system;
- on a time interval $(0, t_e)$, no requests arrive in the system;
- on the time interval $[t_e, T]$, there exists a strictly positive density function of request arrivals in the system.

The models examined further are probabilistic extensions of the Ravner–Haviv model with one server. As it will be demonstrated in the forthcoming subsections, these models also have the previously mentioned properties of symmetrical Nash equilibria. Our analysis is limited to the two-server systems only.

10.2.1 Two-server system. Noncooperative game

Consider a two-server system that receives user requests on a time interval $[0, T]$. Each server of the system may simultaneously perform only one request. The service times of the requests are independent random variables obeying the Poisson distribution with rates μ_1 and μ_2 for the first and second servers, respectively.

For this model, we consider two access schemes, namely, pure random and rational random. In the former case, a user request that arrives in the system is redirected with probability r to the first server and probability $\bar{r} = 1 - r$ to the second. It may happen that several users send their requests to the system at the same time. Then the system may redirect two or more requests to the same server. If the server is currently busy, then all requests arriving in it at this time are lost. Otherwise, the server chooses one of the currently arrived requests for further service by a uniform random draw.

The system with rational random access operates in the following way. If both servers are currently free, then a user request that arrives in the system is redirected with probability r to the first server and probability $\bar{r} = 1 - r$ to the second. If only one server is free, then the request is redirected to it. If both servers are busy, then the request is rejected. The system has no queues, and a rejected request is lost (not served). Note that, for $r \in \{0, 1\}$, the model under consideration is a queueing system with priorities. If several users send their requests to the system at the same time, then the system chooses one or two of them (depending on the number of free servers) by a uniform random draw.

The requests' arrival discipline is not defined in the system. It is actually formed by the users who maximize the probability of service for their requests.

Consider the optimal request discipline problem in the two-server system as a noncooperative game. Here the players are the system users sending their requests for service. Denote by $\mathbb{N}$ the player set. Each player chooses the time to send his request to the system, seeking to maximize the probability of service for his requests. The pure strategy of player i is the arrival time t_i of his request in the system. The mixed strategy of player i is the distribution function $F_i(t)$ of the arrival times in the system on the time interval $[0, T]$. Denote by $F = \{F_i(t), i \in \mathbb{N}\}$ the strategy profile in this game. At time t, the player's payoff is the probability of service for the request that arrives in the system at this time.

All players are identical and independent and have selfish behavior without cooperation. Therefore, as the optimality criterion, we choose the symmetric Nash equilibrium. In this case, the strategies of all players coincide, that is, $F_i(t) = F(t)$ for all i.

Definition 33. A distribution function $F(t)$ of the arrival times t in the system is a symmetric Nash equilibrium if there exists a constant C such that, at any time $t \in [0, T]$, the probability of service does not exceed C and is equal to C on the carrier of $F(t)$.

For each of the two access schemes, we will consider two cases. In the first case, the number of players is deterministic and known to each player. In the second case, each player knows that the number of opponents obeys the Poisson distribution with given parameter.

In the forthcoming subsections, we study in detail the properties of equilibria for both access schemes. Our analysis begins with the rational random-access model as a simpler one.

10.2.2 Game with rational random-access scheme

Consider a certain player trying to send his request to the system at time t given the requests of other players arrive in the system at this time with probability p. Denote by X_p the random number of his opponents sending their requests to the system, possibly preventing him from being served at time t. The number of players can be deterministic (i.e., each player has a fixed number N of opponents). In an alternative setup, N is a random variable. Then, for each value of (random or deterministic) N, the random variable $X_p = X_{N,p}$ obeys the binomial distribution $Bin(N, p)$. For convenience, we will omit the index N and accordingly specify the character of N.

Let p be the probability of request arrival at the zero time when the system is initially free. Then the probability of service at this time makes up

$$C(p) = E\left(\min\{1, \frac{2}{X_p + 1}\}\right). \tag{10.11}$$

For deterministic N, this probability is

$$P(X_p < 2) + \sum_{i=2}^{n}\left(\frac{2}{i+1}P(X_p = i)\right);$$

for random N, it is

$$P(X_p < 2) + \sum_{n=2}^{\infty} P(N = n)\sum_{i=2}^{N}\left(\frac{2}{i+1}P(X_p = i)\right).$$

Suppose the system receives no requests on a certain interval $(0, t)$ after the zero time. Hence, the probability of service at the time $t > 0$ is

$$1 - P(X_p \geq 2)e^{-(\mu_1+\mu_2)t} = P(X_p < 2) + P(X_p \geq 2)(1 - e^{-(\mu_1+\mu_2)t}).$$

Note that this probability increases in t.

Imagine the player sends his request to the system at the time $0+$, that is, infinitesimally close to the zero time from the right so that the following conditions hold: (a) each of the requests that arrived at the zero time is being served or has left the system, and (b) the system has not received new requests and also not completed the service of the currently processed requests. The corresponding probability constitutes

$$\lim_{t \to 0+} \left(P(X_p < 2) + P(X_p \geq 2)(1 - e^{-(\mu_1+\mu_2)t}) \right) = P(X_p < 2),$$

which is smaller than $C(p)$. Consequently, it is better to send the request to the system at the zero time than immediately after this time. We have the following result.

Lemma 36. *In the game with the rational random-access scheme, the player's payoff at the zero time exceeds his payoff at the time $0+$, that is, infinitesimally close to it from the right. The player's payoff at the time t increases in t if there are no request arrivals in the system on the interval $(0, t)$.*

Lemma 37. *In the game with the rational random-access scheme, the carrier of the equilibrium strategy contains an atom at the point $t = 0$. In other words, the equilibrium probability $p_e = F(0)$ of request arrivals at the initial (zero) time is strictly positive. There exists a subsequent time interval $(0, t_e)$ without request arrivals in the system.*

Proof. Indeed, the probability of request arrivals in the system at the zero time is positive. Assume on the contrary that none of the players sends his requests to the system at this time; then any player deviating from the equilibrium and sending his request to the system at the zero time receives service with probability 1.

By Lemma 36 the player's payoff increases for some period after the zero time, yet remaining smaller than at this time (even if we know that none of the players has sent the requests to the system during this period). This explains the existence of the time interval without request arrivals after the zero time. On this interval the payoff rises to the equilibrium value at the time t_e, until which there are no requests in the system.   □

Therefore the equilibrium strategy carrier contains the discontinuity interval $(0, t_e)$. This interval takes place as at the zero time (when the system is free) several requests may arrive simultaneously and the probability of winning vacancies for service in a tournament is higher at this time than the probability of service immediately after (when the system is more likely to be busy).

Suppose we know the equilibrium probability of request arrivals at the zero time, which is $0 < p_e \leq 1$. The probability of service at time $t > 0$ without request arrivals on the interval $(0, t)$ is an increasing function of t that tends to 1. At the time $t = 0+$, it is smaller than the probability of service at the zero time. Hence, there exists a time (perhaps, after the time T) when these probabilities coincide. For a given equilibrium probability of request arrival at the zero time, the solution of the equation

$$E\left(\min\{1, \frac{2}{X_{p_e} + 1}\}\right) = 1 - P(X_{p_e} \geq 2)e^{-(\mu_1 + \mu_2)t_e} \qquad (10.12)$$

yields the corresponding time $t_e > 0$ till which (since the zero time) there are no requests to the system.

For proving the next lemma, we will employ the framework of stochastic orders [75]. First, let us give the definitions from this source subject to our setup and formulate the theorems that are direct corollaries of the original general theorems. They will be repeatedly mentioned throughout our proof. Like in the cited book, by "increase" we actually mean "nondecrease," also adopting the term "strict increase" to avoid confusion. In addition, $[Z|A]$ denotes a random variable that has the conditional distribution of a random variable Z given A.

Definition 34. The random variable X_p stochastically increases in p in the usual stochastic order if and only if the probability $P(X_p \geq i)$ increases in p for all possible values $i \in (-\infty, +\infty)$.

Definition 35. The random variable X_p stochastically increases in p in the likelihood ratio order if and only if the ratio $\frac{P(X_p = i)}{P(X_q = i)}$ increases in $i \in (-\infty, +\infty)$ for all $0 \leq p \leq q \leq 1$.

Theorem 53 (Corollary of Theorem 1.C.1 [75]). *If the random variable X_p stochastically increases in p in the likelihood ratio order, then it also stochastically increases in p in the usual stochastic order.*

Theorem 54 (Corollary of Theorem 1.C.6 [75]). *If the random variable X_p stochastically increases in p in the likelihood ratio order, then the random variable $[X_p|X_p \geq i]$ also stochastically increases in p in the likelihood ratio order.*

Theorem 55 (Corollary of Theorem 1.C.8 [75]). *If the random variable X_p stochastically increases in p in the likelihood ratio order and ψ is an increasing function, then the random variable $\psi(X_p)$ also stochastically increases in p in the likelihood ratio order.*

Theorem 56 (Corollary of Theorem 1.C.9 [75]). *If for all $n = 1, 2, \ldots$, the random variables $X_{n,p}$ stochastically increase in p in the likelihood ratio order and their density functions are log-concave, then the random variable $\sum_n X_{n,p}$ also stochastically increases in p in the likelihood ratio order.*

Lemma 38. *For any real values $0 < p_e \leq 1$ and $\mu_1, \mu_2 > 0$, Eq. (10.12) defines a function $t_e(p_e)$ that strictly decreases in p_e.*

Proof. Transform Eq. (10.12) in the following way:

$$\frac{1 - E\left(\min\{1, \frac{2}{X_{p_e}+1}\}\right)}{P(X_{p_e} \geq 2)} = e^{-(\mu_1+\mu_2)t_e},$$

$$\frac{E\left(\max\{0, \frac{X_{p_e}-1}{X_{p_e}+1}\}\right)}{P(X_{p_e} \geq 2)} = e^{-(\mu_1+\mu_2)t_e},$$

which yields

$$E\left(\frac{X_{p_e} - 1}{X_{p_e} + 1}|X_{p_e} \geq 2\right) = e^{-(\mu_1+\mu_2)t_e}. \tag{10.13}$$

The right-hand side of Eq. (10.13) is independent of p_e and strictly increases in t_e. The left-hand side depends on p_e only, and we have to show its increase in p_e.

First, let N be deterministic. Check that, for any real values $0 \leq q < p \leq 1$, the ratio $\frac{P(X_p=i)}{P(X_q=i)}$ increases in the natural index i. The ratio $\frac{P(X_p=k+1)}{P(X_p=k)} = \frac{N-k}{k+1}\left(\frac{1}{1-p} - 1\right)$ increases in p. Then $\frac{P(X_q=k+1)}{P(X_q=k)} < \frac{P(X_p=k+1)}{P(X_p=k)}$ and $\frac{P(X_p=k)}{P(X_q=k)} < \frac{P(X_p=k+1)}{P(X_q=k+1)}$. By Definition 35 this means that the random variable X_{p_e} stochastically increases in p_e in the likelihood ratio.

Now, let N be random. By Theorem 56 the random variable $\sum_{n=1}^{\infty} P(N = n)X_{n,p_e}$ also stochastically increases in p_e in the likelihood ratio order, where X_{n,p_e} indicates X_{p_e} for each fixed value $N = n$, since the density function of the binomial distribution is log-concave [46]. Then the random variable X_{p_e} stochastically increases in p_e in the likelihood ratio order for random N.

By Theorem 54 the random variable $[X_{p_e}|X_{p_e} \geq 2]$ also stochastically increases in p_e in the likelihood ratio order. Using Theorem 55, we establish that the random variable $\left[\frac{X_{p_e}-1}{X_{p_e}+1}|X_{p_e} \geq 2\right]$ stochastically increases in p_e in the likelihood ratio.

By Theorem 53 the stochastic increase of a random variable in the likelihood ratio order implies its increase in the usual stochastic order and hence the increase of its expected value. Therefore $E\left(\frac{X_{p_e}-1}{X_{p_e}+1}|X_{p_e} \geq 2\right)$ increases in p_e. $\square$

Corollary 4. *The expected value* $E\left(\frac{1}{X_{p_e}+1}\right)$ *decreases in* p_e.

Proof. Based on the proof of Lemma 38, the random variable $\frac{1}{X_{p_e}+1}$ stochastically decreases in p_e in the usual stochastic order as a decreasing function of a random variable that stochastically increases in p_e. Consequently, its expected value also decreases in p_e. $\square$

As follows from Lemma 38, the higher the probability p_e of request arrivals in the system at the zero time, the smaller the left bound of the interval $[t_e, T]$ where the players again send their requests to the system with positive probability. Note that, for given p_e, the value t_e may even exceed T. In this case, for equilibrium search, we should increase the probability p_e. If $t_e(1) \geq T$, then the equilibrium strategy is pure, that is, sends the requests to the system at time $t = 0$ with probability 1. In the sequel, we will assume $t_e(1) < T$.

Lemma 39. *If* $t_e < T$, *then on the time interval* $[t_e, T]$, *there exists a strictly positive density function* $f(t) > 0$ *of the arrival times in the system. This interval has no atoms or discontinuities.*

Proof. Consider the interval $[t_e, T]$ on which the requests are again sent to the system. We will show that the equilibrium density function of the arrival times in the system is strictly positive on the whole interval. Assume on the contrary that there exists a subinterval $(s_1, s_2) \in [t_e, T]$ without request arrivals in the system. Denote by $p_{ij}(t)$ the probability of the system state (i, j) at time t, where $i, j \in \{0, 1\}$ are the states of the first and second servers, respectively (0 − free, 1 − busy). Then the probability of service at time s_1 makes up

$$p_{00}(s_1) + p_{01}(s_1) + p_{10}(s_1).$$

Recall that there are no arrivals on (s_1, s_2), and hence the payoff at time s_2 has the form

$$p_{00}(s_2) + p_{01}(s_2) + p_{10}(s_2)$$
$$= p_{00}(s_1) + p_{10}(s_1)(1 - e^{-\mu_1(s_2-s_1)}) + p_{01}(s_1)(1 - e^{-\mu_2(s_2-s_1)})$$
$$+ p_{11}(s_1)(1 - e^{-\mu_1(s_2-s_1)})(1 - e^{-\mu_2(s_2-s_1)})$$
$$+ p_{01}(s_1) + p_{11}(s_1)(1 - e^{-\mu_1(s_2-s_1)})$$
$$+ p_{10}(s_1) + p_{11}(s_1)(1 - e^{-\mu_2(s_2-s_1)}),$$

obviously exceeding the payoff at time s_1. This means that, after time t_e, the strategy carrier contains no such discontinuities.

Now, let us prove that, after time t_e, the strategy carrier has no atoms. Assume on the contrary that such an atom exists at a point $t \in [t_e, T]$ and the probability of request arrivals at time t is $p > 0$. Consider the time $s = t-$, that is, infinitesimally close to time t from the left so that with zero probability the served requests leave the system and new requests arrive in it. Take a certain player who tries to send his request to the system at time t, being aware of that the others send their requests at this time with probability p. Let the random variable X_p be the number of his opponents whose requests have arrived in the system at time t. Due to the strict positivity of the probability p, the expected value of this random variable must be positive too. The probability of service at time t constitutes

$$p_{00}(t)E\left(\min\{1, \tfrac{2}{X_p+1}\}\right) + (p_{01}(t) + p_{10}(t))E\left(\tfrac{1}{X_p+1}\right)$$
$$= p_{00}(s)E\left(\min\{1, \tfrac{2}{X_p+1}\}\right) + (p_{01}(s) + p_{10}(s))E\left(\tfrac{1}{X_p+1}\right),$$

which is smaller than the payoff at time s, that is, than

$$p_{00}(s) + p_{01}(s) + p_{10}(s).$$

In other words, if the distribution of request arrivals after time t_e contains an atom, then it is better to send the request to the system immediately after this time. In contrast to the zero time (when the system is initially free and a player merely has to win vacancies for service), here the servers may be busy, and the vacancy tournament reduces the probability of service.   □

10.2.3 Deterministic number of players in the rational random-access scheme game

Denote by $N+1$ the number of players sending their requests to the system. Each of them has N opponents, who may prevent from being served. Let $N > 1$; otherwise, the requests of all players are served regardless of arrival times. Assume that at time $t = 0$ each of N opponents sends his request to the system with probability p_e. The random variable X_{p_e} is the number of players who have sent their requests to a server at the zero time, which obeys the distribution $Bin(N, p_e)$. Both servers are initially free, and hence both requests are served if $X_{p_e} \geq 2$ and merely one of them otherwise. By (10.11) the probability of service at the zero time makes up

$$C(p_e) = (1 - p_e)^N + C_N^1 p_e (1 - p_e)^{N-1} + \sum_{i=2}^{N} C_N^i p_e^i (1 - p_e)^{N-i} \frac{2}{i+1}$$

$$= (1 - p_e)^N + \sum_{i=1}^{N} C_N^i p_e^i (1 - p_e)^{N-i} \frac{2}{i+1}$$

$$= (1 - p_e)^N + 2 \frac{1 - (1-p_e)^{N+1}}{p_e(N+1)} - 2(1 - p_e)^N = 2 \frac{1 - (1-p_e)^{N+1}}{p_e(N+1)} - (1 - p_e)^N.$$

$$(10.14)$$

Lt us find the probability of service at time $t_e > 0$ under the zero probabilities of request arrivals on the interval $(0, t_e)$. The desired probability is defined by

$$1 - P(X_{p_e} \geq 2) e^{-(\mu_1 + \mu_2)t_e}$$

$$= 1 - (1 - P(X_{p_e} = 0) - P(X_{p_e} = 1)) e^{-(\mu_1 + \mu_2)t_e}$$

$$= 1 - (1 - (1 - p_e)^N - N p_e (1 - p_e)^{N-1}) e^{-(\mu_1 + \mu_2)t_e}.$$

For a deterministic number of players, Eq. (10.12) then takes the form

$$\frac{2(1 - (1 - p_e)^{N+1})}{p_e(N + 1)} - (1 - p_e)^N$$

$$= 1 - (1 - (1 - p_e)^N - N p_e (1 - p_e)^{N-1}) e^{-(\mu_1 + \mu_2)t_e}. \quad (10.15)$$

By Lemma 38, if $t_e(1) \geq T$, then the equilibrium strategy is pure, that is, sends requests to the system at time $t = 0$ with probability 1. Otherwise, on the interval $[t_e, T]$, there exists a strictly positive density function of the arrival times in the system. We further suppose that $t_e(1) < T$.

It is necessary to find the equilibrium density function $f(t)$ of the arrival times in the system on the interval $[t_e, T]$. Define a Markov process with system states (i, j, k) at each time $t \in [t_e, T]$, where $i, j \in \{0, 1\}$ are the states of the first and second servers, respectively $(0 - \text{free}, 1 - \text{busy})$, and $k \in \{0, \ldots, N\}$ indicates the number of players who have sent their requests to the system before time t. This process is inhomogeneous in time, since the request rate in the system decreases in jumps as soon as a new request is received from a successive player. In particular, the request rate has the form $\lambda_k(t) = (N - k)\frac{f(t)}{1-F(t)}$. The Kolmogorov equations for the system state probabilities p_{ijk} are given by

$$p'_{000}(t) = -\lambda_0(t)p_{000}(t),$$
$$p'_{101}(t) = r\lambda_0(t)p_{000}(t) - (\lambda_1(t) + \mu_1)p_{101}(t),$$
$$p'_{011}(t) = \bar{r}\lambda_0(t)p_{000}(t) - (\lambda_1(t) + \mu_2)p_{011}(t),$$
$$p'_{00i}(t) = -\lambda_i(t)p_{00i}(t) + \mu_1 p_{10i}(t) + \mu_2 p_{01i}(t),$$
$$p'_{10i}(t) = r\lambda_{i-1}(t)p_{00i-1}(t) - (\lambda_i(t) + \mu_1)p_{10i}(t) + \mu_2 p_{11i}(t),$$
$$p'_{01i}(t) = \bar{r}\lambda_{i-1}(t)p_{00i-1}(t) - (\lambda_i(t) + \mu_2)p_{01i}(t) + \mu_1 p_{11i}(t),$$
$$p'_{11i}(t) = \lambda_{i-1}(t)(p_{01i-1}(t) + p_{10i-1}(t) + p_{11i-1}(t)) - (\lambda_i(t) + \mu_1 + \mu_2)p_{11i}(t),$$
$$i = 2, \ldots, N.$$

$$(10.16)$$

In the equilibrium the probability of service at any fixed time $t \in [t_e, T]$ is constant:

$$\sum_{i=0}^{N} p_{00i}(t) + \sum_{i=1}^{N} p_{01i}(t) + \sum_{i=1}^{N} p_{10i}(t) = 1 - \sum_{i=2}^{N} p_{11i}(t) = C(p_e).$$

Then the sum of the corresponding derivatives must be zero. Substituting the derivatives of the system state probabilities from the Kolmogorov equations (10.16) into these sums, we obtain the differential equation of the equilibrium density function:

$$\frac{f(t)}{1 - F(t)} = \frac{(\mu_1 + \mu_2)(1 - C(p_e))}{\sum_{i=0}^{N-1} (N - i)(p_{01i}(t) + p_{10i}(t))} \qquad (10.17)$$

for $t \in [t_e, T]$.

The carrier of the equilibrium distribution of the arrival times in the system belongs to the interval $[0, T]$, which means that $F(T) = 1$. This induces uncertainty in Eq. (10.17) at the point $t = T$ of the interval, where the arrival times in the system are described by a positive density function. We will transform Eq. (10.17) to obtain the equilibrium distribution to eliminate the factor $1 - F(t)$ from it.

Denote by T_i the times when the players $i \in \{1, \ldots, N\}$ send their requests to the system; they are independent and identically distributed with the function F. Let $A(t)$ be the number of request arrivals in the system before time t, and let $B_N(t) \in \{0, 1, 2\}$ be the number of busy servers at time t.

The denominator of the right-hand side in Eq. (10.17) can be rewritten as

$$N \sum_{i=0}^{N} (p_{01i}(t) + p_{10i}(t)) - \sum_{i=0}^{N} i(p_{01i}(t) + p_{10i}(t))$$
$$= NP(B_N(t) = 1) - E(A(t)\mathbb{1}_{B_N(t)=1}).$$

We transform the subtrahend as follows:

$$\phi(t) = E(A(t)\mathbb{1}_{B_N(t)=1}) = E \sum_{i=1}^{N} \mathbb{1}_{B_N(t)=1, T_i \le t}$$
$$= E \sum_{i=1}^{N} \mathbb{1}_{B_N(t)=1, T_1 \le t} = NE\mathbb{1}_{B_N(t)=1, T_1 \le t}$$
$$= NP(B_N(t) = 1, T_1 \le t).$$

As $t \to T$, the probability $P(B_N(t) = 1, T_1 \le t)$ tends to $P(B_N(t) = 1)$, and the denominator vanishes accordingly, which induces uncertainty for the density function in Eq. (10.17). Next, assuming that $t < T$, we find the density function expression and redefine this function at the point T as the limit:

$$\phi(t) = N(P(B_N(t) = 1) - P(B_N(t) = 1, T_1 > t)).$$

Then the denominator of the right-hand side in Eq. (10.17) takes the form

$$NP(B_N(t) = 0, T_1 > t) = NP(B_N(t) = 0 | T_1 > t)(1 - F(t)$$
$$= NP(B_{N-1}(t) = 0)(1 - F(t)),$$

where $B_{N-1}(t)$ is the number of busy servers at time t in the model with $N - 1$ players (as before, the arrival times of the requests sent by $N - 1$ players represent the independent identically distributed random variables with the function F). Note that here the request rates $\lambda_i(t)$ are the same as in the model with N players (up to constant factors $\frac{N-1}{N}$) as the distribution is not changed; however, the system state probabilities differ.

Then, for $t \in [t_e, T)$, the density function of the arrival times in the system can be described by the following expression that does not depend on $1 - F(t)$:

$$f(t) = \frac{(\mu_1 + \mu_2)(1 - C(p_e))}{NP(B_{N-1}(t) = 1)}. \tag{10.18}$$

The right-hand side of this formula is well defined at $t = T$. Using continuity, we may redefine the density function at the point $t = T$ as

$$f(T) = \frac{(\mu_1 + \mu_2)(1 - C(p_e))}{NP(B_{N-1}(T) = 1)}.$$

Consequently, expression (10.18) defines the density function of the request arrivals in the system on the whole interval $[t_e, T]$.

Using this expression, we may transform equations (10.16), eliminating the unknown density function $f(t)$ to obtain a system of differential equations for the state probabilities.

Let us define the initial conditions for the system, that is, the state probabilities at time t_e given no request arrivals on the interval $(0, t_e)$:

$$p_{00i}(t_e) = C_N^i p_e^i (1 - p_e)^{N-i} \left[\mathbb{1}_{i=0} + \mathbb{1}_{i=1} \left(r(1 - e^{-\mu_1 t_e}) + \bar{r}(1 - e^{-\mu_2 t_e}) \right) \right.$$
$$\left. + \mathbb{1}_{i>1} (1 - e^{-\mu_1 t_e})(1 - e^{-\mu_2 t_e}) \right],$$
$$i = 0, \ldots, N;$$
$$p_{10i}(t_e) = C_N^i p_e^i (1 - p_e)^{N-i} \left[\mathbb{1}_{i=1} r e^{-\mu_1 t_e} + \mathbb{1}_{i>1} e^{-\mu_1 t_e} (1 - e^{-\mu_2 t_e}) \right],$$
$$i = 1, \ldots, N;$$
$$p_{01i}(t_e) = C_N^i p_e^i (1 - p_e)^{N-i} \left[\mathbb{1}_{i=1} \bar{r} e^{-\mu_2 t_e} + \mathbb{1}_{i>1} (1 - e^{-\mu_1 t_e}) e^{-\mu_2 t_e} \right],$$
$$i = 1, \ldots, N;$$
$$p_{11i}(t_e) = C_N^i p_e^i (1 - p_e)^{N-i} \mathbb{1}_{i>1} e^{-\mu_1 t_e} e^{-\mu_2 t_e},$$
$$i = 2, \ldots, N.$$

$$(10.19)$$

Therefore, we have the Cauchy problem for differential equations (10.16) and initial conditions (10.19). The solution of this problem yields the state probabilities $p_{ijk}(t)$ that depend on the parameter p_e. Expression (10.18) with known state probabilities defines the equilibrium density function $f(t)$ on the interval $[t_e, T]$, which also depends on the parameter p_e. It is required that the density function of the arrival times takes its last positive value exactly at time T; to this effect, the parameter p_e is chosen so that

$$p_e + \int_{t_e}^T f(t) \, dt = 1. \tag{10.20}$$

Our analysis naturally gives the following result.

Theorem 57. *Any symmetric Nash equilibrium distribution of the arrival times in the two-server random-access system with loss described by the distribution function $F(t)$ on the interval $[0, T]$ has the following properties.*

1. *There exists a strictly positive probability $p_e = F(0) > 0$ of request arrival in the system at the zero time.*

2. *On the interval $(0, t_e)$, where*

$$t_e = \left(\ln \frac{1 - (1 - p_e)^N - Np_e(1 - p_e)^{N-1}}{1 - \frac{2(1-(1-p_e)^{N+1})}{p_e(N+1)} + (1 - p_e)^N} \right) / (\mu_1 + \mu_2),$$

the players send their requests to the system with zero probability.

3. *If for $p_e = 1$, Eq. (10.15) yields a solution $t_e > T$, then the equilibrium strategy is the pure strategy in which all players send their requests to the system at the zero time.*

4. *Otherwise, if $p_e < 1$, then on the interval $[t_e, T]$, there exists a continuous positive density function $f(t)$ of the arrival times in the system that is defined by formula (10.18).*

5. *The equilibrium probability of request arrival at the zero time is found from Eq. (10.20).*

6. *The value $C(p_e) = 2\frac{1-(1-p_e)^{N+1}}{p_e(N+1)} - (1 - p_e)^N$ gives the probability of service on the whole strategy carrier.*

Lemma 40. *The distribution function $F(t)$ representing the solution of (10.15) and (10.17) with the initial condition $F(0) = p$ increases in p at any point of the interval $[0, T]$.*

Proof. Consider two given probabilities $0 < p < q \le 1$ of request arrival at the zero time that define the initial conditions for constructing two distribution functions $F_p(t)$ and $F_q(t)$ as the solutions of (10.15) and (10.17). The corresponding probabilities of service $C(p)$ and $C(q)$ are constant on the whole distribution carrier. By Corollary 4 the function $C(\cdot)$ decreases. Then the probability of loss must be smaller for p than for q on the whole distribution carrier.

By Lemma 38 we have $t_q = t(q) < t_p = t(p)$ for the corresponding starting points of the intervals where the requests again arrive in the system. That is, the function $F_q(t)$ begins to increase from the value q at the time when $F_p(t)$ still remains the constant $p < q$. For $t \in [0, t_p]$, the lemma is true, since in this case $F_p(t) = p < q \le F_q(t)$.

Suppose there exists a certain time $s > t_p$ such that $F_p(t) < F_q(t)$ and $F_p(s) = F_q(s)$. Then $f_p(s) > f_q(s)$, as both functions do not decrease in t, and at the point s the function $F_p(t)$ must cross $F_q(t)$ upward. Hence, the slope of $F_p(t)$ exceeds that of $F_q(t)$, and therefore $\frac{f_p(s)}{1-F_p(s)} > \frac{f_q(s)}{1-F_q(s)}$. This means that the request rate at time s is higher for the probability p than for q, whereas the service rates are the same in both cases. Then the probability of loss at time s must be greater for p than for q, which obviously contradicts the fact that the probability of loss is smaller for p than for q on the whole distribution carrier. $\qquad\square$

Theorem 58. *The symmetric equilibrium distribution F of the arrival times that is defined by Theorem 57 exists and is unique.*

Proof. The uniqueness of the equilibrium follows from Lemma 40. The equilibrium condition (10.20) represents an equation whose left-hand side increases in p_e. For $p_e \approx 0$, the left-hand side equals the probability of request arrival on the interval $[t_e, T]$, which does not exceed 1. For $p_e = 1$, the left-hand side is not smaller than 1. Therefore there exists a unique solution p_e associated with the unique value t_e and density function $f(t)$ on $[t_e, T]$. $\qquad\square$

Computing experiments

To find the equilibria in the problem with $N > 1$, we adopt a numerical algorithm that integrates the dichotomy methods for the equations in one unknown with the Euler method for the combined first-order ordinary differential equations. First, the algorithm verifies the inequality $t_e(1) < T$ (otherwise, the equilibrium strategy represents the pure strategy in which all players send their requests to the system at the zero time). The next step is to choose a certain initial value p_e and find the corresponding time t_e as the solution of Eq. (10.15). Then at point t_e we calculate the initial values for systems (10.16) with N and $N-1$ players and also the value $f(t_e)$. For each successive point of division of the interval $[t_e, T]$, it is necessary to solve both systems by the Euler method, that is, $p_{ijk}(t+\delta) \approx p_{ijk}(t) + \delta p'_{ijk}(t)$, with calculation of $\lambda_i(t) = \frac{(N-i)f(t)}{1-F(t)}$ using relationship (10.17); then formula (10.18) yields the successive value of $f(t)$. Next, we calculate $F(T)$ and compare this value with 1. If the equality $F(T) = 1$ holds with a sufficiently small error ε, then the algorithm ends. If the above value exceeds 1, then p_e is reduced (otherwise, increased), and the algorithm continues to obtain the new value p_e.

Table 10.1 Equilibrium characteristics

N	r = 0.1			r = 0.9		
	p_e	t_e	$C(p_e)$	p_e	t_e	$C(p_e)$
2	0.236	0.999	0.981	0.397	0.099	0.947
5	0.275	0.085	0.836	0.319	0.082	0.794
10	0.255	0.067	0.632	0.267	0.065	0.613
100	0.169	0.011	0.117	0.169	0.011	0.117
200	0.161	0.006	0.061	0.162	0.006	0.061
300	0.159	0.004	0.042	0.159	0.004	0.042

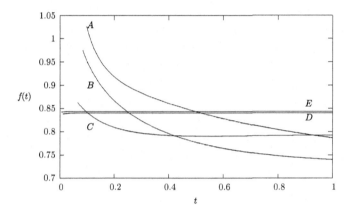

Figure 10.4 Equilibrium densities $f(t)$ for $T = 1, \mu_1 = 1, \mu_2 = 10, r = 0.1$, and (A) $N = 2$, (B) $N = 5$, (C) $N = 10$, (D) $N = 100$, (E) $N = 200$

Table 10.1 illustrates the resulting equilibria constructed by the algorithm under specific values of the system parameters. Here the system operates on the time interval [0, 1]. The first server has a considerably smaller performance than the second one, $\mu_1 = 1$ versus $\mu_2 = 10$. We compare the equilibria for different numbers of the players under high ($r = 0.1$) and low ($r = 0.9$) probabilities of request arrival to the fast server. The graphs in Figs. 10.4 and 10.5 are the corresponding equilibrium density functions of the arrival times in the system. In these examples, the distribution of the arrival times in the system tends to the uniform distribution as we increase the number of players, and the limiting distribution is the same for different probabilities of request arrival to the fast server. In the last three cases ($N = 100, 200, 300$), the equilibrium density function of the arrival times in the system is approximately 0.84 on the whole interval $[t_e, T]$. Finally, Fig. 10.6 shows how the equilibrium densities change their

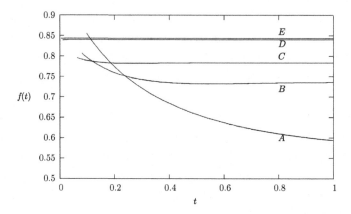

Figure 10.5 Equilibrium densities $f(t)$ for $T = 1, \mu_1 = 1, \mu_2 = 10, r = 0.9$, and (A) $N = 2$, (B) $N = 5$, (C) $N = 10$, (D) $N = 100$, (E) $N = 200$

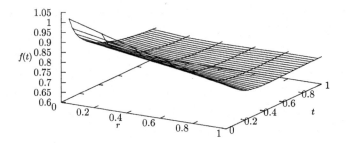

Figure 10.6 Equilibrium densities for $T = 1, \mu_1 = 1, \mu_2 = 10, N = 5$ under variation of r

graphs as we vary the parameter r (the probability that the player's request is redirected to the first server).

10.2.4 Poisson number of players in the rational random-access scheme game

Now, assume that none of the players knows the number of his opponents N. The only available information is that N represents a random variable obeying the Poisson distribution with parameter λ. At the zero time, each of the opponents sends his request to the system with probability p_e. Denote by X_{p_e} the random number of the players whose requests have arrived in the system at the zero time. Note that, for each value of the random variable N, the random variable X_{p_e} has the binomial distribution $Bin(N, p_e)$. Then the probability of service at the zero time (see (10.11)) is given by

$$C(p) = e^{-\lambda} \sum_{N=0}^{\infty} \frac{\lambda^N}{N!} \cdot \left((1-p_e)^N + C_N^1 p_e (1-p_e)^{N-1} \right.$$

$$\left. + \sum_{i=2}^{N} C_N^i p_e^i (1-p_e)^{N-i} \frac{2}{i+1} \right).$$

The parenthesized sum in the right-hand side of this expression is equal to the right-hand side of formula (10.14), so

$$C(p_e) = e^{-\lambda} \sum_{N=0}^{\infty} \frac{\lambda^N}{N!} \left(2 \frac{1-(1-p_e)^{N+1}}{p_e(N+1)} - (1-p_e)^N \right)$$

$$= 2 \frac{e^{-\lambda}}{p_e \lambda} \left(\sum_{N=0}^{\infty} \frac{\lambda^{N+1}}{(N+1)!} - \sum_{N=0}^{\infty} \frac{\lambda^{N+1}(1-p_e)^{N+1}}{(N+1)!} \right) - e^{-\lambda} e^{\lambda(1-p_e)} \qquad (10.21)$$

$$= 2 \frac{e^{-\lambda}}{p_e \lambda} \left(e^{\lambda} - e^{\lambda(1-p_e)} \right) - e^{-\lambda p_e} = 2 \frac{1-e^{-\lambda p_e}}{\lambda p_e} - e^{-\lambda p_e}.$$

Let us find the probability of service at time $t_e > 0$ given that on the interval $(0, t_e)$ the requests arrive in the system with zero probability. This probability is defined by

$$1 - P(X_{p_e} \geq 2)e^{-(\mu_1+\mu_2)t_e}$$

$$= 1 - (1 - P(X_{p_e} = 0) - P(X_{p_e} = 1))e^{-(\mu_1+\mu_2)t_e}$$

$$= 1 - (1 - e^{-\lambda} \sum_{N=0}^{\infty} \frac{\lambda^N}{N!}(1-p_e)^N - e^{-\lambda} \sum_{N=0}^{\infty} \frac{\lambda^N}{N!} N p (1-p_e)^{N-1})e^{-(\mu_1+\mu_2)t_e}$$

$$= 1 - (1 - e^{-\lambda p_e} - e^{-\lambda} \lambda p_e \sum_{N=1}^{\infty} \frac{\lambda^{N-1}}{(N-1)!}(1-p)^{N-1})e^{-(\mu_1+\mu_2)t_e}$$

$$= 1 - (1 - e^{-\lambda p_e} - e^{-\lambda} \lambda p_e \sum_{N=0}^{\infty} \frac{\lambda^N}{N!}(1-p_e)^N)e^{-(\mu_1+\mu_2)t_e}$$

$$= 1 - (1 - e^{-\lambda p_e} - e^{-\lambda} \lambda p_e e^{\lambda(1-p_e)})e^{-(\mu_1+\mu_2)t}$$

$$= 1 - (1 - e^{-\lambda p_e} - \lambda p_e e^{-\lambda p_e})e^{-(\mu_1+\mu_2)t_e}.$$

For the Poisson number of players, Eq. (10.12) takes the form

$$2 \frac{1-e^{-\lambda p_e}}{\lambda p_e} - e^{-\lambda p_e} = 1 - (1 - e^{-\lambda p_e} - \lambda p_e e^{-\lambda p_e})e^{-(\mu_1+\mu_2)t_e}. \qquad (10.22)$$

If $t_e(1) \geq T$, then the equilibrium strategy is pure, that is, sends the requests to the system at the time $t = 0$ with probability 1. We further assume that $t_e(1) < T$.

It is necessary to find the equilibrium density function $f(t)$ of the arrival times in the system on the interval $[t_e, T]$. Define a Markov process with system states (i, j) at each time $t \in [t_e, T]$, where $i, j \in \{0, 1\}$ are the states of the first and second servers, respectively (0 – free, 1 – busy). At each time t the request rate in the system is $\lambda f(t)$. The Kolmogorov equations for the system state probabilities p_{ij} are given by

$$
\begin{aligned}
p'_{00}(t) &= -\lambda f(t)p_{00}(t) + \mu_1 p_{10}(t) + \mu_2 p_{01i}(t),\\
p'_{10}(t) &= r\lambda f(t)p_{00}(t) - (\bar{r}\lambda f(t) + \mu_1)p_{10}(t) + \mu_2 p_{11}(t),\\
p'_{01}(t) &= \bar{r}\lambda f(t)p_{00}(t) - (r\lambda f(t) + \mu_2)p_{01}(t) + \mu_1 p_{11}(t),\\
p'_{11}(t) &= \lambda f(t)(p_{01}(t) + p_{10}(t)) - (\mu_1 + \mu_2)p_{11}(t).
\end{aligned}
\tag{10.23}
$$

In the equilibrium the probability of service at any fixed time $t \in [t_e, T]$ is constant and makes up $p_{00}(t) + p_{01}(t) + p_{10}(t) = 1 - p_{11}(t) = C(p_e)$. Then the sum of the corresponding derivatives must be zero. Substituting the derivatives of the system state probabilities from the Kolmogorov equations (10.23) into the above sums, we obtain the equilibrium density function

$$
f(t) = \frac{(\mu_1 + \mu_2)(1 - C(p_e))}{\lambda(p_{01}(t) + p_{10}(t))},
\tag{10.24}
$$

where $t \in [t_e, T]$.

Note that, for the one-server system, the equilibrium strategy on the interval $[t_e, T]$ is the uniform distribution. Now, we will show that in the general case this is not true.

Let us define the initial conditions for the system, that is, the state probabilities at time t_e given that there are no request arrivals on the interval $(0, t_e)$. For each state (i, j), the corresponding probability can be calculated by

$$
p_{ij}(t_e) = e^{-\lambda} \sum_{N=0}^{\infty} \frac{\lambda^N}{N!} \sum_{k=0}^{N} p_{ijk}^N(t_e),
$$

where $p_{ijk}^N(t_e)$ means the probability of state (i, j, k) at time t_e in the case of N players. Consequently,

$$
p_{00}(t_e) = e^{-\lambda} \sum_{N=0}^{\infty} \frac{\lambda^N}{N!}
$$

$$
\times \sum_{k=0}^{N} C_N^k p_e^k (1 - p_e)^{N-k} \left[\mathbb{1}_{k=0} + \mathbb{1}_{k=1} \left(r(1 - e^{-\mu_1 t_e}) + \bar{r}(1 - e^{-\mu_2 t_e}) \right) \right.
$$

$$
\left. + \mathbb{1}_{k>1}(1 - e^{-\mu_1 t_e})(1 - e^{-\mu_2 t_e}) \right].
$$

Transform the inner sum in the following way:

$$\sum_{k=0}^{N} C_N^k p_e^k (1 - p_e)^{N-k} \left[\mathbb{1}_{k=0} + \mathbb{1}_{k=1} \left(r(1 - e^{-\mu_1 t_e}) + \bar{r}(1 - e^{-\mu_2 t_e}) \right) \right.$$
$$\left. + \mathbb{1}_{k>1}(1 - e^{-\mu_1 t_e})(1 - e^{-\mu_2 t_e}) \right]$$
$$= (1 - p_e)^N + N p_e (1 - p_e)^{N-1} (r(1 - e^{-\mu_1 t_e}) + \bar{r}(1 - e^{-\mu_2 t_e}))$$
$$+ \left(1 - (1 - p_e)^N - N p_e (1 - p_e)^{N-1} \right) (1 - e^{-\mu_1 t_e})(1 - e^{-\mu_2 t_e}).$$

Then

$$p_{00}(t_e) = e^{-\lambda p_e} + \lambda p_e e^{-\lambda p_e} (r(1 - e^{-\mu_1 t_e}) + \bar{r}(1 - e^{-\mu_2 t_e}))$$
$$+ \left(1 - e^{-\lambda p_e} - \lambda p_e e^{-\lambda p_e} \right) (1 - e^{-\mu_1 t_e})(1 - e^{-\mu_2 t_e}).$$

Using the same transformation, we obtain the following expressions for all state probabilities at time t_e:

$$p_{00}(t_e) = e^{-\lambda p_e} + \lambda p e^{-\lambda p_e} (r(1 - e^{-\mu_1 t_e}) + \bar{r}(1 - e^{-\mu_2 t_e}))$$
$$+ \left(1 - e^{-\lambda p_e} - \lambda p_e e^{-\lambda p_e} \right) (1 - e^{-\mu_1 t_e})(1 - e^{-\mu_2 t_e}),$$
$$p_{10}(t_e) = \lambda p_e e^{-\lambda p_e} r e^{-\mu_1 t_e}$$
$$+ \left(1 - e^{-\lambda p_e} - \lambda p_e e^{-\lambda p_e} \right) e^{-\mu_1 t_e}(1 - e^{-\mu_2 t_e}), \qquad (10.25)$$
$$p_{01}(t_e) = \lambda p_e e^{-\lambda p_e} \bar{r} e^{-\mu_2 t_e}$$
$$+ \left(1 - e^{-\lambda p_e} - \lambda p_e e^{-\lambda p_e} \right) (1 - e^{-\mu_1 t_e}) e^{-\mu_2 t_e},$$
$$p_{11}(t_e) = \left(1 - e^{-\lambda p_e} - \lambda p_e e^{-\lambda p_e} \right) e^{-\mu_1 t_e} e^{-\mu_2 t_e}.$$

Therefore, we have the Cauchy problem with the combined differential equations (10.23) and the initial conditions (10.25). The solution of this problem yields the state probabilities $p_{ij}(t)$ that depend on the parameter p_e. Expression (10.24) with the known state probabilities defines the equilibrium density function $f(t)$ on the interval $[t_e, T]$, which also depends on the parameter p_e. It is required that the density function of the arrival times takes its last positive value exactly at time T; to this effect, the parameter p_e is chosen so that

$$p_e + \int_{t_e}^{T} f(t) \, dt = 1. \qquad (10.26)$$

Our analysis naturally gives the following result.

Theorem 59. *Any symmetric Nash equilibrium distribution of the arrival times in the two-server random-access system with loss described by the distribution function $F(t)$ on the interval $[0, T]$ has the following properties.*

1. *There exists a probability $p_e = F(0) > 0$ of request arrival in the system at the zero time.*
2. *The players send their requests to the system with zero probability on the interval $(0, t_e)$, where*

$$t_e = \left(\ln \frac{1 - e^{-\lambda p_e} - \lambda p_e e^{-\lambda p_e}}{1 - 2\frac{1-e^{-\lambda p_e}}{\lambda p_e} + e^{-\lambda p_e}} \right) / (\mu_1 + \mu_2).$$

3. *If for $p_e = 1$, Eq. (10.22) yields a solution $t_e > T$, then the equilibrium strategy is the pure strategy in which all players send their requests to the system at the zero time.*
4. *Otherwise, if $p_e < 1$, then on the interval $[t_e, T]$, there exists a continuous positive density function $f(t)$ of the arrival times in the system that is defined by formula (10.24).*
5. *The equilibrium probability of request arrival at the zero time is found from Eq. (10.26).*
6. *The value $C(p_e) = 2\frac{1-e^{-\lambda p_e}}{\lambda p_e} - e^{-\lambda p_e}$ gives the probability of service on the whole strategy carrier.*

Lemma 41. *The distribution function $F(t)$ representing the solution of (10.22) and (10.24) with the initial condition $F(0) = p$ increases in p at any point of the interval $[0, T]$.*

Proof. The proof is identical to that of Lemma 40 for the deterministic number of players. □

Then, just like in the case of the deterministic number of players, we obtain the following result.

Theorem 60. *The symmetric equilibrium distribution F of the arrival times that is defined by Theorem 59 exists and is unique.*

Computing experiments

To find the equilibria in the problem with $\lambda > 0$, we adopt a numerical algorithm that integrates the dichotomy methods for the equations in one unknown with the Euler method for the combined first-order ordinary differential equations. First, the algorithm verifies the inequality $t_e(1) < T$ (otherwise, the equilibrium strategy represents the pure strategy in which

Table 10.2 Equilibrium characteristics

λ	$r = 0.1$			$r = 0.9$		
	p_e	t_e	$C(p_e)$	p_e	t_e	$C(p_e)$
1	0.251	0.096	0.99	0.374	0.094	0.98
5	0.268	0.08	0.84	0.311	0.077	0.803
20	0.221	0.045	0.433	0.226	0.045	0.426
100	0.169	0.114	0.118	0.170	0.011	0.118
200	0.162	0.006	0.062	0.162	0.006	0.062
300	0.159	0.004	0.042	0.159	0.004	0.042

all players send their requests to the system at the zero time). The next step is to choose a certain initial value p_e and find the corresponding time t_e as the solution of Eq. (10.22). Then at point t_e we calculate the initial values for equations (10.23) and also the value $f(t_e)$. For each successive point of division of the interval $[t_e, T]$, it is necessary to solve both systems of equations by the Euler method, that is, $p_{ij}(t + \delta) \approx p_{ij}(t) + \delta p'_{ij}(t)$; formula (10.24) yields the successive value of $f(t)$. Next, we calculate $F(T)$ and compare this value with 1. If the equality $F(T) = 1$ holds with a sufficiently small error ε, then the algorithm ends. If the above value exceeds 1, then p_e is reduced (otherwise, increased), and the algorithm continues to obtain the new value p_e.

Table 10.2 illustrates the resulting equilibria constructed by the algorithm under specific values of the system parameters. Here the system operates on the time interval $[0, 1]$. The first server has a considerably smaller performance than the second one, $\mu_1 = 1$ versus $\mu_2 = 10$. We compare the equilibria for different numbers of the players under high ($r = 0.1$) and low ($r = 0.9$) probabilities of request arrival to the fast server. The graphs in Figs. 10.7 and 10.8 are the corresponding equilibrium density functions of the arrival times in the system. In these examples, like in the deterministic case, the distribution of the arrival times in the system tends to the uniform distribution as we increase λ, and the limiting distribution is the same for different probabilities of request arrival to the fast server. In the last three cases ($N = 100, 200, 300$), the equilibrium density function of the arrival times in the system is approximately 0.84 on the whole interval $[t_e, T]$. We finally acknowledge the identity of these results for the deterministic and Poisson numbers of players. Fig. 10.9 shows how the equilibrium densities change their graphs as we vary the parameter r (the probability that the player's request is redirected to the first server).

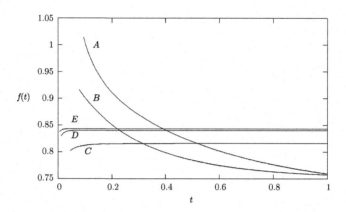

Figure 10.7 Equilibrium densities $f(t)$ for $T = 1, \mu_1 = 1, \mu_2 = 10, r = 0.1$, and (A) $\lambda = 1$, (B) $\lambda = 5$, (C) $\lambda = 20$, (D) $\lambda = 100$, (E) $\lambda = 200$

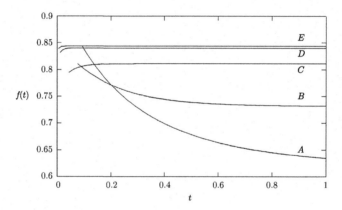

Figure 10.8 Equilibrium densities $f(t)$ for $T = 1, \mu_1 = 1, \mu_2 = 10, r = 0.9$, and (A) $\lambda = 1$, (B) $\lambda = 5$, (C) $\lambda = 20$, (D) $\lambda = 100$, (E) $\lambda = 200$

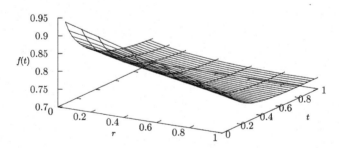

Figure 10.9 Equilibrium densities for $T = 1, \mu_1 = 1, \mu_2 = 10, \lambda = 5$ under variation of r

10.2.5 Game with pure random-access scheme

Consider a certain player trying to send his request to the system at time t given that the requests of other players arrive in the system at this time with probability p. Denote by X_p the random number of his opponents sending their requests to the system, possibly preventing him from being served at the time t. For each value of (random or deterministic) N, the random variable $X_p = X_{N,p}$ obeys the binomial distribution $Bin(N, p)$. For convenience, the index N will be omitted, and the character of N will be specified accordingly. Denote by X_{pr} the number of players from X_p that are redirected to the first server with probability r. For each value of X_p, the random variable X_{pr} has the binomial distribution $Bin(X_p, r)$. Then we obtain the probability

$$P(X_{pr} = j) = \sum_{i=j}^{N} C_N^i p^i (1-p)^{N-i} C_i^j r^j (1-r)^{i-j}$$

$$= \sum_{i=j}^{N} \frac{N!}{i!(N-i)!} \frac{i!}{j!(i-j)!} p^i (1-p)^{N-i} r^j (1-r)^{i-j}$$

$$= C_N^j \sum_{i=j}^{N} \frac{(N-j)!}{(N-i)!(i-j)!} p^i (1-p)^{N-i} r^j (1-r)^{i-j}$$

$$= C_N^j (pr)^j \sum_{k=0}^{N-j} \frac{(N-j)!}{(N-j-k)!k!} p^k (1-p)^{N-j-k} (1-r)^k$$

$$= C_N^j (pr)^j (1-p)^{N-j} \sum_{k=0}^{N-j} C_{N-j}^k \left(\frac{p(1-r)}{1-p} \right)^k$$

$$= C_N^j (pr)^j (1-p)^{N-j} \left(1 + \frac{p(1-r)}{1-p} \right)^{N-j} = C_N^j (pr)^j (1-pr)^{N-j}.$$

As a result, X_{pr} obeys the distribution $Bin(N, pr)$. In the same way, we may demonstrate that $X_{p\bar{r}}$, the number of players from X_p that are redirected to the second server with probability $\bar{r}$, has the distribution $Bin(N, p\bar{r})$ for each (deterministic or random) N.

Let p be the probability of request arrival at the zero time when the system is initially free. Then the probability of service at this time makes up

$$C(p) = E \left(\frac{r}{X_{pr} + 1} + \frac{\bar{r}}{X_{p\bar{r}} + 1} \right). \tag{10.27}$$

For deterministic N, this probability is

$$rP(X_{pr} = 0) + \bar{r}P(X_{p\bar{r}} = 0) + \sum_{i=1}^{N} \left(\frac{r}{i+1} P(X_{pr} = i) + \frac{\bar{r}}{i+1} P(X_{p\bar{r}} = i) \right),$$

and, for random N,

$$rP(X_{pr} = 0) + \bar{r}P(X_{p\bar{r}} = 0)$$

$$+ \sum_{n=1}^{\infty} P(N = n) \sum_{i=1}^{n} \left(\frac{r}{i+1} P(X_{pr} = i) + \frac{\bar{r}}{i+1} P(X_{p\bar{r}} = i) \right).$$

Assume that the system receives no requests on some interval $(0, t)$ after the zero time. Hence, the probability of service at time $t > 0$ is

$$1 - rP(X_{pr} \geq 1)e^{-\mu_1 t} - \bar{r}P(X_{p\bar{r}} \geq 1)e^{-\mu_2 t}$$
$$= r \left(P(X_{pr} = 0) + P(X_{pr} \geq 1)(1 - e^{-\mu_1 t}) \right)$$
$$+ \bar{r} \left(P(X_{p\bar{r}} = 0) + P(X_{p\bar{r}} \geq 1)(1 - e^{-\mu_2 t}) \right).$$

Note that this probability increases in t.

Imagine that the player sends his request to the system at the time $0+$, that is, infinitesimally close to the zero time from the right so that the following conditions hold: (a) each of the requests that arrived at the zero time is being served or has left the system, and (b) the system has not received new requests and also not completed the service of the currently processed requests. The corresponding probability constitutes

$$\lim_{t \to 0+} r \left(P(X_{pr} = 0) + P(X_{pr} \geq 0)(1 - e^{-\mu_1 t}) \right)$$

$$+ \bar{r} \left(P(X_{p\bar{r}} = 0) + P(X_{p\bar{r}} \geq 1)(1 - e^{-\mu_2 t}) \right)$$

$$= rP(X_{pr} = 0) + \bar{r}P(X_{p\bar{r}} = 0),$$

which is smaller than $C(p)$. Consequently, it is better to send the request to the system at the zero time than immediately after this time. We have the following result.

Lemma 42. *In the game with the pure random-access scheme, the player's payoff at the zero time exceeds his payoff at the time $0+$, that is, infinitesimally close to it from the right. The player's payoff at time t increases in t if there are no request arrivals in the system on the interval $(0, t)$.*

Lemma 43. *In the game with the pure random-access scheme, the carrier of the equilibrium strategy contains an atom at the point $t = 0$. In other words, the equilibrium probability $p_e = F(0)$ of request arrivals at the initial (zero) time is strictly positive. There exists a subsequent time interval $(0, t_e)$ without request arrivals in the system.*

Proof. In fact, the proof is the same as that for Lemma 37 using Lemma 42. □

Therefore, in the game with the pure random-access scheme, the equilibrium strategy carrier also has the discontinuity interval $(0, t_e)$.

Suppose we know the equilibrium probability of request arrivals at the zero time, which is $0 < p_e \leq 1$. The probability of service at time $t > 0$ without request arrivals on the interval $(0, t)$ is an increasing function of t that tends to 1. At the time $t = 0+$, it is smaller than the probability of service at the zero time. Hence, there exists a time (perhaps, after time T) when these probabilities coincide. For a given equilibrium probability of request arrival at the zero time, the solution of the equation

$$E\left(\frac{r}{X_{p_e r} + 1} + \frac{\bar{r}}{X_{p_e \bar{r}} + 1}\right) = 1 - rP(X_{p_e r} \geq 1)e^{-\mu_1 t_e} - \bar{r}P(X_{p_e \bar{r}} \geq 1)e^{-\mu_2 t_e}$$

(10.28)

yields the corresponding time $t_e > 0$ till which (since the zero time) there are no requests to the system.

Lemma 44. *For the case of two players ($N = 1$) and any real values $0 \leq r \leq 1$, $0 < p_e \leq 1$, and $\mu_1, \mu_2 > 0$, Eq. (10.28) defines a constant t_e that is independent of p_e. For any other number of players and any real values $0 \leq r \leq 1$, $0 < p_e \leq 1$, and $\mu_1, \mu_2 > 0$, Eq. (10.28) defines a function $t_e(p_e)$ that strictly decreases in p_e.*

Proof. In the case of two players, Eq. (10.28) takes the form

$$r^2 + \bar{r}^2 = 2(r^2 e^{-\mu_1 t_e} + \bar{r}^2 e^{-\mu_2 t_e}).$$

Let $N > 1$ or N be random. Transform Eq. (10.28) in the following way:

$$E\left(\frac{rX_{p_e r}}{X_{p_e r} + 1} + \frac{\bar{r}X_{p_e \bar{r}}}{X_{p_e \bar{r}} + 1}\right) = rP(X_{p_e r} \geq 1)e^{-\mu_1 t_e} + \bar{r}P(X_{p_e \bar{r}} \geq 1)e^{-\mu_2 t_e},$$

which gives

$$rP(X_{p_e r} \geq 1)E\left(\frac{X_{p_e r}}{X_{p_e r}+1}\Big|X_{p_e r} \geq 1\right)$$

$$+ \bar{r}P(X_{p_e \bar{r}} \geq 1)E\left(\frac{X_{p_e \bar{r}}}{X_{p_e \bar{r}}+1}\Big|X_{p_e \bar{r}} \geq 1\right)$$

$$= rP(X_{p_e r} \geq 1)e^{-\mu_1 t_e} + \bar{r}P(X_{p_e \bar{r}} \geq 1)e^{-\mu_2 t_e}. \quad (10.29)$$

Now, it is necessary to demonstrate that the factors containing p_e in Eq. (10.13) increase in p_e. Like for the rational random-access scheme, we will use the theory of stochastic orders for proving the increase of $P(X_{p_e r} \geq i)$ and $E\left(\frac{X_{p_e r}}{X_{p_e r}+1}\Big|X_{p_e r} \geq 1\right)$ in p_e. Obviously, the same holds for the corresponding factors with r replaced by $\bar{r}$.

First, let the number N be deterministic. Verify that, for any real numbers $0 \leq q < p \leq 1$, the ratio $\frac{P(X_{pr}=i)}{P(X_{qr}=i)}$ increases in natural index i. The ratio $\frac{P(X_{pr}=k+1)}{P(X_{pr}=k)} = \frac{N-k}{k+1}\left(\frac{1}{1-pr}-1\right)$ increases in p. Then we have $\frac{P(X_{qr}=k+1)}{P(X_{qr}=k)} < \frac{P(X_{pr}=k+1)}{P(X_{pr}=k)}$ and $\frac{P(X_{pr}=k)}{P(X_{qr}=k)} < \frac{P(X_{p}=k+1)}{P(X_{q}=k+1)}$. By Definition 35 this means that the random variable $X_{p_e r}$ stochastically increases in p_e in the likelihood ratio order.

Second, let the number N be random. By Theorem 56 the random variable $\sum_{n=1}^{\infty} P(N=n)X_{n,p_e r}$ also stochastically increases in p_e in the likelihood ratio order, where $X_{n,p_e r}$ denotes $X_{p_e r}$ for each fixed $N = n$ (the density function of the binomial distribution has logarithmic concavity). Consequently, for random N the random variable $X_{p_e r}$ stochastically increases in p_e in the likelihood ratio order.

By Theorem 53 the stochastic increase of a random variable in the likelihood ratio order implies its increase in the usual stochastic order, that is, $P(X_{p_e r} \geq i)$ increases in p_e for any natural index i.

By Theorem 54 the random variable $[X_{p_e r}|X_{p_e r} \geq 1]$ also stochastically increases in p_e in the likelihood ratio order. Then by Theorem 55 the random variable $\left[\frac{X_{p_e r}}{X_{p_e r}+1}\Big|X_{p_e r} \geq 1\right]$ stochastically increases in p_e in the likelihood ratio order too.

The stochastic increase of a random variable in the likelihood ratio order implies its increase in the usual stochastic order and hence the increase of its expected value. Therefore $E\left(\frac{X_{p_e r}}{X_{p_e r}+1}\Big|X_{p_e r} \geq 1\right)$ increases in p_e.

Now, consider two pairs (p_1, t_1) and (p_2, t_2) satisfying Eq. (10.29) and the inequality $p_1 < p_2$. Let $t_1 \leq t_2$. For $p_e = p_1$ and $t_e = t_1$, the left- and right-hand sides of (10.29) have the same value. If p_e and t_e grow from p_1 to p_2 and from t_1 to t_2, respectively, then the probabilities in the right- and left-hand sides have the same increase. The expected values in the left-hand side also grow, but the exponents in the right-hand size either decrease or remain invariable, which violates the equality. Hence, $t_1 > t_2$.   □

Corollary 5. *The expected values* $E\left(\frac{1}{X_{pe^r}+1}\right)$ *and* $E\left(\frac{1}{X_{pe^{\bar{r}}}+1}\right)$ *decrease in* p_e.

Proof. In accordance with the proof of Lemma 44, the random variable $\frac{1}{X_{pe^r}+1}$ stochastically decreases in p_e in the usual stochastic order as a decreasing function of a random variable that stochastically increases in p_e. Hence, its expected value also decreases in p_e.   □

As follows from Lemma 44, the higher the probability p_e of request arrivals in the system at the zero time, the smaller the left bound of the interval $[t_e, T]$ where the players again send their requests to the system with positive probability. Note that, for given p_e, the value t_e may even exceed T. In this case, for equilibrium search, we should increase the probability p_e. If $t_e(1) \geq T$, then the equilibrium strategy is pure, that is, sends the requests to the system at the time $t = 0$ with probability 1. We further assume that $t_e(1) < T$.

Lemma 45. *If* $t_e < T$, *then on the time interval* $[t_e, T]$, *there exists a strictly positive density function* $f(t) > 0$ *of the arrival times in the system. This interval has no atoms or discontinuities.*

Proof. Consider the interval $[t_e, T]$ on which the requests are again sent to the system. We will show that the equilibrium density function of the arrival times in the system is strictly positive on the whole interval. Assume on the contrary that there exists a subinterval $(s_1, s_2) \in [t_e, T]$ without request arrivals in the system. Denote by $p_{ij}(t)$ the probability of the system state (i, j) at time t, where $i, j \in \{0, 1\}$ are the states of the first and second servers, respectively (0 − free, 1 − busy). Then the probability of service at time s_1 makes up

$$p_{00}(s_1) + r p_{01}(s_1) + \bar{r} p_{10}(s_1).$$

Recall that there are no arrivals on (s_1, s_2), and hence the payoff at time s_2 has the form

$$p_{00}(s_2) + r p_{01}(s_2) + \bar{r} p_{10}(s_2)$$
$$= p_{00}(s_1) + p_{10}(s_1)(1 - e^{-\mu_1(s_2-s_1)}) + p_{01}(s_1)(1 - e^{-\mu_2(s_2-s_1)})$$
$$\quad + p_{11}(s_1)(1 - e^{-\mu_1(s_2-s_1)})(1 - e^{-\mu_2(s_2-s_1)})$$
$$\quad + r(p_{01}(s_1) + p_{11}(s_1)(1 - e^{-\mu_1(s_2-s_1)}))$$
$$\quad + \bar{r}(p_{10}(s_1) + p_{11}(s_1)(1 - e^{-\mu_2(s_2-s_1)})),$$

obviously exceeding the payoff at the time s_1. This means that, after time t_e, the strategy carrier contains no such discontinuities.

Now, let us prove that, after time t_e, the strategy carrier has no atoms. Assume on the contrary that such an atom exists at $t \in [t_e, T]$ and the probability of request arrivals at time t is $p > 0$. Consider the time $s = t-$, that is, infinitesimally close from the left to time t so that with zero probability the served requests leave the system and the new requests arrive in it. Take a player who tries to send his request to the system at time t, being aware of that the others send their requests at this time with probability p. Let the random variable X_p be the number of his opponents whose requests have arrived in the system at time t. In addition, denote by X_{pr} and $X_{p\bar{r}}$ the random numbers of players among X_p whose requests have been redirected to the first and second servers, respectively. Due to the strict positivity of the probability p, the expected values of these random variables must be positive too. The probability of service at time t equals

$$E\left(\frac{r(p_{00}(t)+p_{01}(t))}{X_{pr}+1} + \frac{\bar{r}(p_{00}(t)+p_{10}(t))}{X_{p\bar{r}}+1}\right)$$
$$= r(p_{00}(s) + p_{01}(s))E\frac{1}{X_{pr}+1} + \bar{r}(p_{00}(s) + p_{10}(s))E\frac{1}{X_{p\bar{r}}+1},$$

which is smaller than the payoff at time s, that is,

$$r(p_{00}(s) + p_{01}(s)) + \bar{r}(p_{00}(s) + p_{10}(s)).$$

In other words, if the distribution of request arrivals after time t_e contains an atom, then it is better to send the request to the system immediately after this time. In contrast to the zero time (when the system is initially free and a player merely has to win vacancies for service), here the servers may be busy, and the vacancy tournament reduces the probability of service.   □

10.2.6 Deterministic number of players in the pure random-access scheme game

Denote by $N + 1$ the number of players sending their requests to the system. Each of them has N opponents, who may prevent from being served. The random variable $X_{p_e r}$ is the number of players who have sent their requests to the first server with distribution $Bin(N, p_e r)$. Similarly, the random variable $X_{p_e \bar{r}}$ is the number of players who have sent their requests to the second server with distribution $Bin(N, p_e \bar{r})$. The probability of service at the zero time has form (10.27).

The first summand in (10.27) is

$$E\left(\frac{r}{X_{p_e r}+1}\right) = r\sum_{i=0}^{N} C_N^i (p_e r)^i (1-p_e r)^{N-i}\frac{1}{i+1}$$

$$= r\frac{(1-p_e r)^N}{N+1}\sum_{i=0}^{N} C_{N+1}^{i+1}\left(\frac{p_e r}{1-p_e r}\right)^i = r\frac{(1-p_e r)^{N+1}}{p_e r(N+1)}\sum_{i=1}^{N+1} C_{N+1}^i\left(\frac{p_e r}{1-p_e r}\right)^i$$

$$= r\frac{(1-p_e r)^{N+1}}{p_e r(N+1)}\left((1+\frac{p_e r}{1-p_e r})^{N+1}-1\right) = \frac{1-(1-p_e r)^{N+1}}{p_e(N+1)}.$$

In the same way, the second summand can be written as

$$E\left(\frac{\bar{r}}{X_{p_e \bar{r}}+1}\right) = \frac{1-(1-p_e\bar{r})^{N+1}}{p_e(N+1)}.$$

Then the payoff at the time $t = 0$ makes up

$$C(p) = \frac{2-(1-p_e r)^{N+1}-(1-p_e\bar{r})^{N+1}}{p_e(N+1)}. \tag{10.30}$$

Find the probability of service at time $t_e > 0$ under the zero probabilities of request arrivals on the interval $(0, t_e)$. The desired probability is defined by

$$1 - rP(X_{p_e r}\geq 1)e^{-\mu_1 t} - \bar{r}P(X_{p_e\bar{r}}\geq 1)e^{-\mu_2 t}$$
$$= 1 - r\left(1 - P(X_{p_e r}=0)\right)e^{-\mu_1 t} - \bar{r}\left(1 - P(X_{p_e\bar{r}}=0)\right)e^{-\mu_2 t}$$
$$= 1 - r\left(1 - (1-p_e r)^N\right)e^{-\mu_1 t} - \bar{r}\left(1 - (1-p_e\bar{r})^N\right)e^{-\mu_2 t}.$$

For a deterministic number of players, Eq. (10.28) then takes the form

$$\frac{2-(1-p_e r)^{N+1}-(1-p_e\bar{r})^{N+1}}{p_e(N+1)}$$
$$= 1 - r\left(1 - (1-p_e r)^N\right)e^{-\mu_1 t_e} - \bar{r}\left(1 - (1-p_e\bar{r})^N\right)e^{-\mu_2 t_e}. \tag{10.31}$$

By Lemma 44, if $t_e(1) \geq T$, then the equilibrium strategy is pure, that is, sends the requests to the system at the time $t = 0$ with probability 1. Otherwise, on the interval $[t_e, T]$, there exists a strictly positive density function of the arrival times in the system. We further suppose that $t_e(1) < T$.

It is necessary to find the equilibrium density function $f(t)$ of the arrival times in the system on the interval $[t_e, T]$. Define a Markov process with system states (i, j, k) at each time $t \in [t_e, T]$, where $i, j \in \{0, 1\}$ are the states of the first and second servers, respectively (0 − free, 1 − busy), and $k \in \{0, \ldots, N\}$ indicates the number of players who have sent their requests to the system before time t. This process is inhomogeneous in time, since the request rate in the system decreases in jumps as soon as a new request is received from a successive player. In particular, the request rate has the form $\lambda_k(t) = (N-k)\frac{f(t)}{1-F(t)}$. The Kolmogorov equations for the system state probabilities p_{ijk} are given by

$$p'_{000}(t) = -\lambda_0(t)p_{000}(t),$$
$$p'_{101}(t) = r\lambda_0(t)p_{000}(t) - (\lambda_1(t) + \mu_1)p_{101}(t),$$
$$p'_{011}(t) = \bar{r}\lambda_0(t)p_{000}(t) - (\lambda_1(t) + \mu_2)p_{011}(t),$$
$$p'_{00i}(t) = -\lambda_i(t)p_{00i}(t) + \mu_1 p_{10i}(t) + \mu_2 p_{01i}(t),$$
$$p'_{10i}(t) = r\lambda_{i-1}(t)(p_{00i-1}(t) + p_{10i-1}(t)) - (\lambda_i(t) + \mu_1)p_{10i}(t) + \mu_2 p_{11i}(t),$$
$$p'_{01i}(t) = \bar{r}\lambda_{i-1}(t)(p_{00i-1}(t) + p_{01i-1}(t)) - (\lambda_i(t) + \mu_2)p_{01i}(t) + \mu_1 p_{11i}(t),$$
$$p'_{11i}(t) = \lambda_{i-1}(t)(rp_{01i-1}(t) + \bar{r}p_{10i-1}(t) + p_{11i-1}(t)) - (\mu_1 + \mu_2 + \lambda_i(t))p_{11i}(t),$$
$$i = 2, \ldots, N.$$

$$(10.32)$$

In the equilibrium the probability of service at any fixed time $t \in [t_e, T]$ is constant:

$$\sum_{i=0}^{N} p_{00i}(t) + r\sum_{i=1}^{N} p_{01i}(t) + \bar{r}\sum_{i=1}^{N} p_{10i}(t) = C(p_e).$$

Then the sum of the corresponding derivatives must be zero. Substituting the derivatives of the system state probabilities from the Kolmogorov equations (10.32) into the above sums, we obtain the differential equation of the equilibrium density function:

$$\frac{f(t)}{1-F(t)} = \frac{r\mu_1\left(\sum_{i=1}^{N} p_{10i}(t) + \sum_{i=2}^{N} p_{11i}(t)\right) + \bar{r}\mu_2\left(\sum_{i=1}^{N} p_{01i}(t) + \sum_{i=2}^{N} p_{11i}(t)\right)}{\sum_{i=0}^{N-1}(N-i)(r^2(p_{00i}(t) + p_{01i}(t)) + \bar{r}^2(p_{00i}(t) + p_{10i}(t)))}$$

$$(10.33)$$

for $t \in [t_e, T]$.

The carrier of the equilibrium distribution of the arrival times in the system belongs to the interval $[0, T]$, which means that $F(T) = 1$. This induces uncertainty in Eq. (10.33) at the point $t = T$ of the interval where the arrival times in the system are described by the positive density function.

We will transform Eq. (10.33) to obtain the equilibrium distribution to eliminate the factor $1 - F(t)$ from it.

Denote by T_i the times when the players $i \in \{1, \dots, N\}$ send their requests to the system; they are independent and identically distributed with the function F. Let $A(t)$ be the number of request arrivals in the system before time t, and let $B_N^s(t) \in \{0, 1\}$ be the state of server s at time t ($0 -$ free, $1 -$ busy).

The denominator of the right-hand side in Eq. (10.33) can be rewritten as

$$N \sum_{i=0}^{N} (r^2(p_{00i}(t) + p_{01i}(t)) + \bar{r}^2(p_{00i}(t) + p_{10i}(t)))$$

$$- \sum_{i=0}^{N} i(r^2(p_{00i}(t) + p_{01i}(t)) + \bar{r}^2(p_{00i}(t) + p_{10i}(t)))$$

$$= N(r^2 P(B_N^1(t) = 0) + \bar{r}^2 P(B_N^2(t) = 0))$$

$$- (r^2 E(A(t)\mathbb{1}_{B_N^1(t)=0}) + \bar{r}^2 E(A(t)\mathbb{1}_{B_N^2(t)=0})).$$

We transform the subtrahend as follows:

$$\phi(t) = r^2 E(A(t)\mathbb{1}_{B_N^1(t)=0}) + \bar{r}^2 E(A(t)\mathbb{1}_{B_N^2(t)=0})$$

$$= r^2 E \sum_{i=1}^{N} \mathbb{1}_{B_N^1(t)=0, T_i \le t} + \bar{r}^2 E \sum_{i=1}^{N} \mathbb{1}_{B_N^2(t)=0, T_i \le t}$$

$$= r^2 E \sum_{i=1}^{N} \mathbb{1}_{B_N^1(t)=0, T_1 \le t} + \bar{r}^2 E \sum_{i=1}^{N} \mathbb{1}_{B_N^2(t)=0, T_1 \le t}$$

$$= N \left(r^2 E\mathbb{1}_{B_N^1(t)=0, T_1 \le t} + \bar{r}^2 E\mathbb{1}_{B_N^2(t)=0, T_1 \le t} \right)$$

$$= N \left(r^2 P(B_N^1(t) = 0, T_1 \le t) + \bar{r}^2 P(B_N^2(t) = 0, T_1 \le t) \right).$$

As $t \to T$, the probability $P(B_N^s(t) = 0, T_1 \le t)$ tends to $P(B_N^s(t) = 0)$, and the denominator vanishes accordingly, which induces uncertainty for the density function in Eq. (10.33). Next, assuming that $t < T$, we find the density function expression and redefine this function at the point T as the limit:

$$\phi(t) = N(r^2(P(B_N^1(t) = 0) - P(B_N^1(t) = 0, T_1 > t)$$

$$+ \bar{r}^2(P(B_N^2(t) = 0) - P(B_N^2(t) = 0, T_1 > t))).$$

Then the denominator of the right-hand side in Eq. (10.33) takes the form

$$N(r^2 P(B_N^1(t) = 0, T_1 > t) + \bar{r}^2 P(B_N^2(t) = 0, T_1 > t))$$

$$= N(r^2 P(B_N^1(t) = 0 | T_1 > t)(1 - F(t))$$

$$+ \bar{r}^2 P(B_N^2(t) = 0 | T_1 > t)(1 - F(t)))$$
$$= N(r^2 P(B_{N-1}^1(t) = 0)(1 - F(t)) + \bar{r}^2 P(B_{N-1}^2(t) = 0)(1 - F(t))),$$

where $B_{N-1}^s(t)$ is the state of server s at time t in the model with $N - 1$ players (as before, the arrival times of the requests sent by $N - 1$ players represent the independent identically distributed random variables with the function F). Note that here the request rates $\lambda_i(t)$ are the same as in the model with N players; however, the system state probabilities differ.

Then, for $t \in [t_e, T)$, the density function of the arrival times in the system can be described by the following expression that does not depend on $1 - F(t)$:

$$f(t) = \frac{r\mu_1 P(B_N^1(t) = 1) + \bar{r}\mu_2 P(B_N^2(t) = 1)}{N(r^2 P(B_{N-1}^1(t) = 0) + \bar{r}^2 P(B_{N-1}^2(t) = 0))}. \tag{10.34}$$

The right-hand side of this formula is well defined at $t = T$. Using continuity, we may redefine the density function at the point $t = T$ as

$$f(T) = \frac{r\mu_1 P(B_N^1(T) = 1) + \bar{r}\mu_2 P(B_N^2(T) = 1)}{N(r^2 P(B_{N-1}^1(T) = 0) + \bar{r}^2 P(B_{N-1}^2(T) = 0))}.$$

Consequently, expression (10.34) defines the density function of the request arrivals in the system on the whole interval $[t_e, T]$.

Using this expression, we may transform equations (10.32) by eliminating the unknown density function $f(t)$ to obtain a system of differential equations for the state probabilities.

Let us define the initial conditions for the system, that is, the state probabilities at time t_e given no request arrivals on the interval $(0, t_e)$:

$$p_{00i}(t_e) = C_N^i p_e^i (1 - p_e)^{N-i} \left[\mathbb{1}_{i=0} + \mathbb{1}_{i>0} \left(r^i(1 - e^{-\mu_1 t_e}) + \bar{r}^i(1 - e^{-\mu_2 t_e}) \right) \right.$$
$$\left. + \mathbb{1}_{i>1}(1 - r^i - \bar{r}^i)(1 - e^{-\mu_1 t_e})(1 - e^{-\mu_2 t_e}) \right],$$
$$i = 0, \ldots, N,$$
$$p_{10i}(t_e) = C_N^i p_e^i (1 - p_e)^{N-i} \left[r^i e^{-\mu_1 t_e} + \mathbb{1}_{i>1}(1 - r^i - \bar{r}^i)e^{-\mu_1 t_e}(1 - e^{-\mu_2 t_e}) \right],$$
$$i = 1, \ldots, N,$$
$$p_{01i}(t_e) = C_N^i p_e^i (1 - p_e)^{N-i} \left[\bar{r}^i e^{-\mu_2 t_e} + \mathbb{1}_{i>1}(1 - r^i - \bar{r}^i)(1 - e^{-\mu_1 t_e})e^{-\mu_2 t_e} \right],$$
$$i = 1, \ldots, N,$$
$$p_{11i}(t_e) = C_N^i p_e^i (1 - p_e)^{N-i}(1 - r^i - \bar{r}^i)e^{-\mu_1 t_e}e^{-\mu_2 t_e},$$
$$i = 2, \ldots, N.$$

$$\tag{10.35}$$

Therefore, we have the Cauchy problem for the differential equations (10.32) and the initial conditions (10.35). The solution of this problem yields the state probabilities $p_{ijk}(t)$ that depend on the parameter p_e. Expression (10.34) with the known state probabilities defines the equilibrium density function $f(t)$ on the interval $[t_e, T]$, which also depends on the parameter p_e. It is required that the density function of the arrival times takes its last positive value exactly at time T; to this effect, the parameter p_e is chosen so that

$$p_e + \int_{t_e}^{T} f(t)dt = 1. \tag{10.36}$$

Like for the rational random-access scheme, we have established the following:

Theorem 61. *Any symmetric Nash equilibrium distribution of the arrival times in the two-server random-access system with loss described by the distribution function $F(t)$ on the interval $[0, T]$ has the following properties.*

1. *There exists a probability $p_e = F(0) > 0$ of request arrival in the system at the zero time.*
2. *On the interval $(0, t_e)$, where t_e satisfies Eq. (10.31), the players send their requests to the system with zero probability.*
3. *If for $p_e = 1$, Eq. (10.31) yields a solution $t_e > T$, then the equilibrium strategy is the pure strategy in which all players send their requests to the system at the zero time.*
4. *Otherwise, if $p_e < 1$, then on the interval $[t_e, T]$, there exists a continuous positive density function $f(t)$ of the arrival times in the system that is defined by formula (10.34).*
5. *The equilibrium probability of request arrival at the zero time is found from Eq. (10.36).*
6. *The value $C(p_e) = \frac{2-(1-p_e r)^{N+1}-(1-p_e \bar{r})^{N+1}}{p_e(N+1)}$ gives the probability of service on the whole strategy carrier.*

Lemma 46. *The distribution function $F(t)$ representing the solution of (10.31) and (10.33) with the initial condition $F(0) = p$ increases in p at any point of the interval $[0, T]$.*

Proof. Consider two given probabilities $0 < p < q \le 1$ of request arrival at the zero time that define the initial conditions for constructing two distribution functions $F_p(t)$ and $F_q(t)$ as the solutions of (10.31) and (10.33). The corresponding probabilities of service $C(p)$ and $C(q)$ are constant on the whole distribution carrier. By Corollary 5 the function $C(\cdot)$ decreases. Then the probability of loss must be smaller for p than for q on the whole distribution carrier.

By Lemma 44 we have $t_q = t(q) < t_p = t(p)$ for the corresponding starting points of the intervals where the requests again arrive in the system. That is, the function $F_q(t)$ begins to increase from the value q at the time when $F_p(t)$ still remains the constant $p < q$. For $t \in [0, t_p]$, the lemma is true, since, in this case, $F_p(t) = p < q \leq F_q(t)$.

Assume that there exists a time $s > t_p$ such that $F_p(t) < F_q(t)$ and $F_p(s) = F_q(s)$. Then $f_p(s) > f_q(s)$, as both functions do not decrease in t, and at point s, the function $F_p(t)$ must cross $F_q(t)$ upward. Hence the slope of $F_p(t)$ exceeds that of $F_q(t)$, and therefore $\frac{f_p(s)}{1-F_p(s)} > \frac{f_q(s)}{1-F_q(s)}$. This means that the request rate at time s is higher for the probability p than for q, whereas the service rates are the same in both cases. Then the probability of loss at time s must be greater for p than for q, which obviously contradicts the fact that the probability of loss is smaller for p than for q on the whole distribution carrier. $\qquad\square$

Theorem 62. *The symmetric equilibrium distribution F of the arrival times that is defined by Theorem 61 exists and is unique.*

Proof. The uniqueness of the equilibrium follows from Lemma 46. The equilibrium condition (10.36) represents an equation whose left-hand side increases in p_e. For $p_e \approx 0$, the left-hand side equals the probability of request arrival on the interval $[t_e, T]$, which does not exceed 1. For $p_e = 1$, the left-hand side is not smaller than 1. Therefore, there exists a unique solution p_e that is associated with the unique value t_e and density function $f(t)$ on $[t_e, T]$. $\qquad\square$

Case of two players

Consider the system with two players only. In this case, $N = 1$ (each player has one opponent).

The equilibrium time t_e when the requests again arrive in the system is independent of the probability of request arrival p_e at the zero time and can be found from the equation

$$r^2 + \bar{r}^2 = 2(r^2 e^{-\mu_1 t_e} + \bar{r}^2 e^{-\mu_2 t_e}).$$

For the one-server system, the equilibrium strategy on the interval $[t_e, T]$ is the uniform distribution. Now, we show that in the general case this is not true.

According to (10.34), the density function of the arrival times in the system has the form

$$f(t) = \frac{r\mu_1 P(B_1^1(t)=1)+\bar{r}\mu_2 P(B_1^2(t)=1)}{N(r^2 P(B_0^1(t)=0)+\bar{r}^2 P(B_0^2(t)=0))}$$
$$= \frac{r\mu_1 p_{101}(t)+\bar{r}\mu_2 p_{011}(t)}{r^2+\bar{r}^2}. \tag{10.37}$$

Express the density through $C(p_e)$, the equilibrium probability of service, which is constant with respect to t:

$$f(t) = \frac{r\mu_1 p_{101}(t)+\bar{r}\mu_1 p_{011}(t)-\bar{r}\mu_1 p_{011}(t)+\bar{r}\mu_2 p_{011}(t)}{r^2+\bar{r}^2}$$
$$= \frac{\mu_1(1-C(p_e))+(\mu_2-\mu_1)\bar{r}p_{011}}{r^2+\bar{r}^2}. \tag{10.38}$$

Take the differential equation for p_{011} from system (10.32):

$$p'_{011}(t) = \lambda_0(t)\bar{r}p_{000}(t) - \mu_2 p_{011}(t). \tag{10.39}$$

By Eq. (10.33),

$$\frac{f(t)}{1-F(t)} = \frac{r\mu_1 p_{101}(t)+\bar{r}\mu_2 p_{011}(t)}{(r^2+\bar{r}^2)p_{000}(t)},$$

and by (10.37) we get $\lambda_0(t) = \frac{f(t)}{p_{000}(t)}$. Then Eq. (10.39) leads to

$$p'_{011}(t) = \bar{r}\frac{\mu_1(1-C(p_e))+(\mu_2-\mu_1)\bar{r}p_{011}}{r^2+\bar{r}^2} - \mu_2 p_{011}(t). \tag{10.40}$$

This equation is considered subject to the initial condition $p_{011}(t_e) = \bar{r}p_e e^{-\mu_2 t_e}$ and constraint (10.36).

The solution of the obtained problem has the form

$$p_e = \frac{1}{1 + \frac{\mu_1\mu_2(T-t_e)}{2A} + \frac{\mu_2-A}{A^2}\left(\frac{\mu_1}{2} - Ae^{-\mu_2 t_e}\right)(e^{-A(T-t_e)}-1)},$$

$$f(t) = \frac{\mu_1\mu_2 p_e}{2A} + \frac{(A-\mu_2)(B-A\bar{r}p_e e^{-\mu_2 t_e})e^{-A(t-t_e)}}{\bar{r}A}, \quad t \in [t_e, T],$$

where $A = \frac{r^2\mu_2+\bar{r}^2\mu_1}{r^2+\bar{r}^2}$ and $B = \frac{\bar{r}\mu_1 p_e}{2}$. The equilibrium payoff is

$$C(p_e) = 1 - \frac{p_e(r^2+\bar{r}^2)}{2}.$$

Now, let both servers have the same performance, that is, $\mu_1 = \mu_2 = \mu$. In this case, the equilibrium strategy coincides with its counterpart for the one-server system and does not depend on r: $t_e = \frac{\log 2}{\mu}$, $p_e = \frac{2}{2+\mu T - \log 2}$, $f(t) = \frac{\mu}{2+\mu T - \log 2}$, $t \in [t_e, T]$. The equilibrium payoff makes up $C(p_e) = \frac{1+\mu T - \log 2 + 2r\bar{r}}{2+\mu T - \log 2}$. For comparison, note that, for the one-server system, the equilibrium payoff is $\frac{1+\mu T - \log 2}{2+\mu T - \log 2}$; see [1] for details. We further call the expected number of served players the social utility of the system. In the equilibrium the social utility has the value $SU_{NE} = 2\,C(p_e)$. Accordingly, the socially optimal profile is a strategy profile that maximizes the social utility. The socially optimal profile is not necessarily symmetrical or equilibrium. In the case under consideration, the socially optimal profile is the pure strategy profile in which one player sends his request at the zero time and the other at time T. The optimal social utility constitutes $SU_{OPT} = 2 - (r^2 + \bar{r}^2)e^{-\mu T}$. The price of anarchy is the ratio of the equilibrium social utility and the optimal one. Here the price of anarchy is $PoA = \frac{(2-(r^2+\bar{r}^2)e^{-\mu T})(2+\mu T - \log 2)}{2(1+\mu T - \log 2 + 2r\bar{r})}$.

Computing experiments

To find the equilibria in the problem with $N > 1$, we adopt a numerical algorithm that integrates the dichotomy methods for the equations in one unknown with the Euler method for the combined first-order ordinary differential equations. First, the algorithm verifies the inequality $t_e(1) < T$ (otherwise, the equilibrium strategy represents the pure strategy in which all players send their requests to the system at the zero time). The next step is to choose an initial value p_e and find the corresponding time t_e as the solution of Eq. (10.31). Then, at point t_e, we calculate the initial values for systems (10.32) with N and $N - 1$ players and also the value $f(t_e)$. For each successive point of division of the interval $[t_e, T]$, it is necessary to solve both systems by the Euler method, that is, $p_{ijk}(t + \delta) \approx p_{ijk}(t) + \delta p'_{ijk}(t)$, with calculation of $\lambda_i(t) = \frac{(N-i)f(t)}{1-F(t)}$ using relationship (10.33); then formula (10.34) yields the successive value of $f(t)$. Next, we calculate $F(T)$ and compare this value with 1. If the equality $F(T) = 1$ holds with a sufficiently small error ε, then the algorithm ends. If the above value exceeds 1, then p_e is reduced (otherwise, increased), and the algorithm continues to obtain the new value p_e.

Table 10.3 illustrates the resulting equilibria constructed by the algorithm under specific values of the system parameters. Here the system operates on the time interval $[0, 1]$. The first server has a considerably smaller performance than the second one, $\mu_1 = 1$ versus $\mu_2 = 10$. We compare the equilibria for different numbers of the players under high ($r = 0.1$)

Table 10.3 Equilibrium characteristics

N	r = 0.1			r = 0.9		
	p_e	t_e	$C(p_e)$	p_e	t_e	$C(p_e)$
1	0.185	0.070	0.924	0.861	0.681	0.647
5	0.171	0.060	0.713	0.636	0.307	0.346
10	0.160	0.050	0.557	0.555	0.178	0.240
20	0.150	0.037	0.389	0.474	0.101	0.164
100	0.155	0.011	0.114	0.278	0.038	0.0069
200	0.160	0.006	0.061	0.223	0.024	0.044

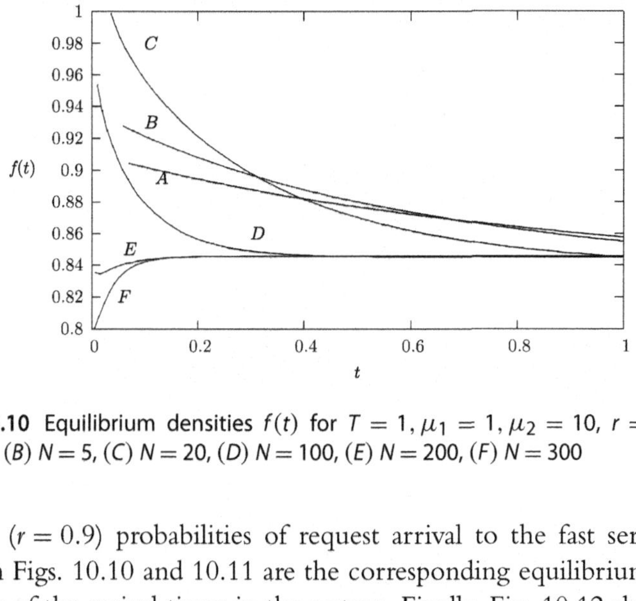

Figure 10.10 Equilibrium densities $f(t)$ for $T = 1, \mu_1 = 1, \mu_2 = 10$, $r = 0.1$, and (A) $N = 1$, (B) $N = 5$, (C) $N = 20$, (D) $N = 100$, (E) $N = 200$, (F) $N = 300$

and low ($r = 0.9$) probabilities of request arrival to the fast server. The graphs in Figs. 10.10 and 10.11 are the corresponding equilibrium density functions of the arrival times in the system. Finally, Fig. 10.12 shows how the equilibrium densities change their graphs as we vary the parameter r (the probability that the player's request is redirected to the first server).

10.2.7 Poisson number of players in the pure random-access scheme game

Now, assume that none of the players knows the number of his opponents N. The only available information is that N represents a random variable obeying the Poisson distribution with parameter λ. At the zero time, each of the opponents sends his request to the system with probability p_e. Denote by $X_{p_e r}$ the random number of the players whose requests have arrived in the first server at the zero time. Note that, for each value of the random variable N, the random variable $X_{p_e r}$ has the binomial dis-

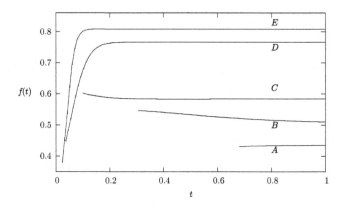

Figure 10.11 Equilibrium densities $f(t)$ for $T = 1, \mu_1 = 1, \mu_2 = 10, r = 0.9$, and (A) $N = 1$, (B) $N = 5$, (C) $N = 20$, (D) $N = 100$, (E) $N = 200$

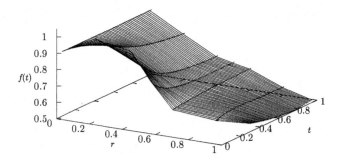

Figure 10.12 Equilibrium densities for $T = 1, \mu_1 = 1, \mu_2 = 10, N = 5$ under variation of r

tribution $Bin(N, p_e r)$. Similarly, denote by $X_{p_e \bar{r}}$ the random number of the players whose requests have arrived in the second server at the zero time, which has the binomial distribution $Bin(N, p_e \bar{r})$ for each value of N. Then the probability of service at the zero time (see (10.27)) is given by

$$C(p) = e^{-\lambda} \sum_{N=0}^{\infty} \frac{\lambda^N}{N!}$$

$$\times \left(r \sum_{i=0}^{N} C_N^i (p_e r)^i (1 - p_e r)^{N-i} \frac{1}{i+1} + \bar{r} \sum_{i=0}^{N} C_N^i (p_e \bar{r})^i (1 - p_e \bar{r})^{N-i} \frac{1}{i+1} \right).$$

The parenthesized sum is equal to the right-hand side of formula (10.30), and so

$$C(p) = e^{-\lambda} \sum_{N=0}^{\infty} \frac{\lambda^N}{N!} \frac{2 - (1-pr)^{N+1} - (1-p\bar{r})^{N+1}}{p(N+1)}$$

$$= \frac{e^{-\lambda}}{p\lambda} \left(2 \sum_{N=0}^{\infty} \frac{\lambda^{N+1}}{(N+1)!} - \sum_{N=0}^{\infty} \frac{\lambda^{N+1}(1-pr)^{N+1}}{(N+1)!} - \sum_{N=0}^{\infty} \frac{\lambda^{N+1}(1-p\bar{r})^{N+1}}{(N+1)!} \right)$$

$$= \frac{e^{-\lambda}}{p\lambda} \left(2e^{\lambda} - e^{\lambda(1-pr)} - e^{\lambda(1-p\bar{r})} \right) = \frac{2 - e^{-\lambda pr} - e^{-\lambda p\bar{r}}}{\lambda p}.$$

Let us find the probability of service at time $t_e > 0$ given that on the interval $(0, t_e)$ the requests arrive in the system with zero probability. This probability is defined by

$$1 - rP(X_{pr} \geq 1)e^{-\mu_1 t} - \bar{r}P(X_{p\bar{r}} \geq 1)e^{-\mu_2 t}$$

$$= 1 - r\left(1 - P(X_{pr} = 0)\right)e^{-\mu_1 t} - \bar{r}\left(1 - P(X_{p\bar{r}} = 0)\right)e^{-\mu_2 t}$$

$$= 1 - r\left(1 - e^{-\lambda} \sum_{N=0}^{\infty} \frac{\lambda^N}{N!}(1 - pr)^N\right)e^{-\mu_1 t}$$

$$- \bar{r}\left(1 - e^{-\lambda} \sum_{N=0}^{\infty} \frac{\lambda^N}{N!}(1 - p\bar{r})^N\right)e^{-\mu_2 t}$$

$$= 1 - r\left(1 - e^{-\lambda pr}\right)e^{-\mu_1 t} - \bar{r}\left(1 - e^{-\lambda p\bar{r}}\right)e^{-\mu_2 t}.$$

For the Poisson number of players, Eq. (10.28) takes the form

$$\frac{2 - e^{-\lambda p_e r} - e^{-\lambda p_e \bar{r}}}{\lambda p_e} = 1 - r\left(1 - e^{-\lambda p_e r}\right)e^{-\mu_1 t_e} - \bar{r}\left(1 - e^{-\lambda p_e \bar{r}}\right)e^{-\mu_2 t_e}. \quad (10.41)$$

If $t_e(1) \geq T$, then the equilibrium strategy is pure, that is, sends the requests to the system at the time $t = 0$ with probability 1. We further assume that $t_e(1) < T$.

It is necessary to find the equilibrium density function $f(t)$ of the arrival times in the system on the interval $[t_e, T]$. Define a Markov process with system states (i, j) at each time $t \in [t_e, T]$, where $i, j \in \{0, 1\}$ are the states of the first and second servers, respectively (0 – free, 1 – busy). At each time t, the request rate in the system is $\lambda f(t)$. The Kolmogorov equations for the system state probabilities p_{ij} are given by

$$\begin{aligned}
p'_{00}(t) &= -\lambda f(t)p_{00}(t) + \mu_1 p_{10}(t) + \mu_2 p_{01}(t), \\
p'_{10}(t) &= r\lambda f(t)p_{00}(t) - (\bar{r}\lambda f(t) + \mu_1)p_{10}(t) + \mu_2 p_{11}(t), \\
p'_{01}(t) &= \bar{r}\lambda f(t)p_{00}(t) - (r\lambda f(t) + \mu_2)p_{01}(t) + \mu_1 p_{11}(t), \\
p'_{11}(t) &= \lambda f(t)(rp_{01}(t) + \bar{r}p_{10}(t)) - (\mu_1 + \mu_2)p_{11}(t).
\end{aligned} \quad (10.42)$$

In the equilibrium the probability of service at any fixed time $t \in [t_e, T]$ is constant and makes up $p_{00}(t) + rp_{01}(t) + \bar{r}p_{10}(t) = C(p_e)$. Then the sum of the corresponding derivatives must be zero. Substituting the derivatives of the system state probabilities from the Kolmogorov equations (10.42) into the above sums, we obtain the equilibrium density function

$$f(t) = \frac{r\mu_1(p_{10}(t) + p_{11}(t)) + \bar{r}\mu_2(p_{01}(t) + p_{11}(t))}{\lambda(r^2(p_{00}(t) + p_{01}(t)) + \bar{r}^2(p_{00}(t) + p_{10}(t)))} \tag{10.43}$$

for $t \in [t_e, T]$.

Note that, for the one-server system, the equilibrium strategy on the interval $[t_e, T]$ is the uniform distribution. Now, we will show that in the general case this is not true, even in the case of identical servers, due to the terms r^2 and $\bar{r}^2$ in the denominator.

Let us define the initial conditions for the system, that is, the state probabilities at time t_e given that there are no request arrivals on the interval $(0, t_e)$. For each state (i, j), the corresponding probability can be calculated by

$$p_{ij}(t_e) = e^{-\lambda} \sum_{N=0}^{\infty} \frac{\lambda^N}{N!} \sum_{k=0}^{N} p_{ijk}^N(t_e),$$

where $p_{ijk}^N(t_e)$ means the probability of state (i, j, k) at time t_e in the case of N players. Consequently,

$$p_{00}(t_e) = e^{-\lambda} \sum_{N=0}^{\infty} \frac{\lambda^N}{N!}$$

$$\times \sum_{k=0}^{N} C_N^k p_e^k (1 - p_e)^{N-k} \left[\mathbb{1}_{k=0} + \mathbb{1}_{k>0} \left(r^k (1 - e^{-\mu_1 t_e}) + \bar{r}^k (1 - e^{-\mu_2 t_e}) \right) \right.$$
$$\left. + \mathbb{1}_{k>1} (1 - r^k - \bar{r}^k)(1 - e^{-\mu_1 t_e})(1 - e^{-\mu_2 t_e}) \right].$$

Transform the inner sum in the following way:

$$\sum_{k=0}^{N} C_N^k p_e^k (1 - p_e)^{N-k} \left[\mathbb{1}_{k=0} + \mathbb{1}_{k>0} \left(r^k (1 - e^{-\mu_1 t_e}) + \bar{r}^k (1 - e^{-\mu_2 t_e}) \right) \right.$$
$$\left. + \mathbb{1}_{k>1} (1 - r^k - \bar{r}^k)(1 - e^{-\mu_1 t_e})(1 - e^{-\mu_2 t_e}) \right]$$
$$= \sum_{k=0}^{N} C_N^k p_e^k (1 - p_e)^{N-k} \left[\left(r^k (1 - e^{-\mu_1 t_e}) + \bar{r}^k (1 - e^{-\mu_2 t_e}) \right) \right.$$
$$\left. + (1 - r^k - \bar{r}^k)(1 - e^{-\mu_1 t_e})(1 - e^{-\mu_2 t_e}) \right]$$
$$+ (1 - p_e)^N \left(1 - (1 - e^{-\mu_1 t_e}) - (1 - e^{-\mu_2 t_e}) - (1 - e^{-\mu_1 t_e})(1 - e^{-\mu_2 t_e}) \right)$$
$$= (1 - e^{-\mu_1 t_e})(1 - p_e)^N \sum_{k=0}^{N} C_N^k \left(\frac{p_e r}{1 - p_e} \right)^k$$

$$+(1 - e^{-\mu_2 t_e})(1 - p_e)^N \sum_{k=0}^{N} C_N^k \left(\frac{p_e \bar{r}}{1-p_e}\right)^k$$

$$+(1 - e^{-\mu_1 t_e})(1 - e^{-\mu_2 t_e})(1 - p_e)^N$$

$$\times \sum_{k=0}^{N} C_N^k \left[\left(\frac{p_e}{1-p_e}\right)^k - \left(\frac{p_e r}{1-p_e}\right)^k - \left(\frac{p_e \bar{r}}{1-p_e}\right)^k\right]$$

$$+(1 - p_e)^N \left(1 - (1 - e^{-\mu_1 t_e}) - (1 - e^{-\mu_2 t_e}) - (1 - e^{-\mu_1 t_e})(1 - e^{-\mu_2 t_e})\right)$$

$$= (1 - e^{-\mu_1 t_e})(1 - p_e \bar{r})^N + (1 - e^{-\mu_2 t_e})(1 - p_e r)^N$$

$$+(1 - e^{-\mu_1 t_e})(1 - e^{-\mu_2 t_e})\left[1 - (1 - p_e \bar{r})^N - (1 - p_e r)^N\right]$$

$$+(1 - p_e)^N \left(1 - (1 - e^{-\mu_1 t_e}) - (1 - e^{-\mu_2 t_e}) - (1 - e^{-\mu_1 t_e})(1 - e^{-\mu_2 t_e})\right)$$

$$= (1 - e^{-\mu_1 t_e})(1 - e^{-\mu_2 t_e})$$

$$+(1 - p_e r)^N((1 - e^{-\mu_2 t_e}) - (1 - e^{-\mu_1 t_e})(1 - e^{-\mu_2 t_e}))$$

$$+(1 - p_e \bar{r})^N((1 - e^{-\mu_1 t_e}) - (1 - e^{-\mu_1 t_e})(1 - e^{-\mu_2 t_e}))$$

$$+(1 - p_e)^N \left(1 - (1 - e^{-\mu_1 t_e}) - (1 - e^{-\mu_2 t_e}) - (1 - e^{-\mu_1 t_e})(1 - e^{-\mu_2 t_e})\right).$$

Then

$$p_{00}(t_e) = (1 - e^{-\mu_1 t_e})(1 - e^{-\mu_2 t_e})$$

$$+e^{-\lambda p_e r}((1 - e^{-\mu_2 t_e}) - (1 - e^{-\mu_1 t_e})(1 - e^{-\mu_2 t_e}))$$

$$+e^{-\lambda p_e \bar{r}}((1 - e^{-\mu_1 t_e}) - (1 - e^{-\mu_1 t_e})(1 - e^{-\mu_2 t_e}))$$

$$+e^{-\lambda p_e} \left(1 - (1 - e^{-\mu_1 t_e}) - (1 - e^{-\mu_2 t_e}) - (1 - e^{-\mu_1 t_e})(1 - e^{-\mu_2 t_e})\right).$$

Using the same transformation, we obtain the following expressions for all state probabilities at time t_e:

$$p_{00}(t_e) = (1 - e^{-r\lambda p_e})(1 - e^{-\mu_1 t_e})e^{-\bar{r}\lambda p_e} + e^{-r\lambda p_e}(1 - e^{-\bar{r}\lambda p_e})(1 - e^{-\mu_2 t_e})$$

$$+(1 - e^{-r\lambda p_e})(1 - e^{-\mu_1 t_e})(1 - e^{-\bar{r}\lambda p_e})(1 - e^{-\mu_2 t_e}) + e^{-\lambda p_e},$$

$$p_{10}(t_e) = (1 - e^{-r\lambda p_e})e^{-\mu_1 t_e}(e^{-\bar{r}\lambda p_e} + (1 - e^{-\bar{r}\lambda p_e})(1 - e^{-\mu_2 t_e})),$$

$$p_{01}(t_e) = (1 - e^{-\bar{r}\lambda p_e})e^{-\mu_2 t_e}(e^{-r\lambda p_e} + (1 - e^{-r\lambda p_e})(1 - e^{-\mu_1 t_e})),$$

$$p_{11}(t_e) = (1 - e^{-r\lambda p_e})e^{-\mu_1 t_e}(1 - e^{-\bar{r}\lambda p_e})e^{-\mu_2 t_e}.$$

$$(10.44)$$

Therefore, we have the Cauchy problem for the combined differential equations (10.42) and the initial conditions (10.44). The solution of this problem yields the state probabilities $p_{ij}(t)$ that depend on the parameter p_e. Expression (10.43) with the known state probabilities defines the equilibrium density function $f(t)$ on the interval $[t_e, T]$, which also depends on the parameter p_e. It is required that the density function of the arrival times takes its last positive value exactly at time T; to this effect, the parameter p_e

is chosen so that

$$p_e + \int\limits_{t_e}^{T} f(t)dt = 1. \tag{10.45}$$

Our analysis naturally leads to the following result.

Theorem 63. *Any symmetric Nash equilibrium distribution of the arrival times in the two-server random-access system with loss described by the distribution function $F(t)$ on the interval $[0, T]$ has the following properties.*

1. *There exists a strictly positive probability $p_e = F(0) > 0$ of request arrival in the system at the zero time.*
2. *The players send their requests to the system with zero probability on the interval $(0, t_e)$, where t_e satisfies Eq. (10.41).*
3. *If for $p_e = 1$, Eq. (10.41) yields a solution $t_e > T$, then the equilibrium strategy is the pure strategy in which all players send their requests to the system at the zero time.*
4. *Otherwise, if $p_e < 1$, then on the interval $[t_e, T]$, there exists a continuous positive density function $f(t)$ of the arrival times in the system that is defined by formula (10.43).*
5. *The equilibrium probability of request arrival at the zero time is found from Eq. (10.45).*
6. *The value $C(p_e) = \frac{2 - e^{-\lambda p_e} - e^{-\lambda p_e}}{\lambda p_e}$ gives the probability of service on the whole strategy carrier.*

Lemma 47. *The distribution function $F(t)$ representing the solution of (10.41) and (10.43) with the initial condition $F(0) = p$ increases in p at any point of the interval $[0, T]$.*

Proof. The proof coincides with that of Lemma 46 for the deterministic number of players. ☐

Then, just like in the case of the deterministic number of players, we obtain the following result.

Theorem 64. *The symmetric equilibrium distribution F of the arrival times that is defined by Theorem 63 actually exists and is unique.*

Computing experiments

To find the equilibria in the problem with $\lambda > 0$, we adopt a numerical algorithm that integrates the dichotomy methods for the equations in one unknown with the Euler method for the combined first-order ordinary

Table 10.4 Equilibrium characteristics

λ	$r = 0.1$			$r = 0.9$		
	p_e	t_e	$C(p_e)$	p_e	t_e	$C(p_e)$
1	0.181	0.068	0.929	0.802	0.566	0.737
5	0.17	0.059	0.725	0.656	0.312	0.374
20	0.15	0.037	0.396	0.48	0.105	0.168
100	0.155	0.011	0.115	0.279	0.039	0.069
200	0.16	0.066	0.061	0.224	0.024	0.044
300	0.1598	0.004	0.042	0.202	0.018	0.033

differential equations. First, the algorithm verifies the inequality $t_e(1) < T$ (otherwise, the equilibrium strategy represents the pure strategy in which all players send their requests to the system at the zero time). The next step is to choose an initial value p_e and find the corresponding time t_e as the solution of Eq. (10.41). Then at point t_e we calculate the initial values for system (10.42) and also the value $f(t_e)$. For each successive point of division of the interval $[t_e, T]$, it is necessary to solve both systems by the Euler method, that is, $p_{ij}(t + \delta) \approx p_{ij}(t) + \delta p'_{ij}(t)$, and then formula (10.43) yields the successive value of $f(t)$. Next, we calculate $F(T)$ and compare this value with 1. If the equality $F(T) = 1$ holds with a sufficiently small error ε, then the algorithm ends. If the above value exceeds 1, then p_e is reduced (otherwise, increased), and the algorithm continues to obtain the new value p_e.

Table 10.4 illustrates the resulting equilibria constructed by the algorithm under specific values of the system parameters. Here the system operates on the time interval $[0, 1]$. The first server has a considerably smaller performance than the second one, $\mu_1 = 1$ versus $\mu_2 = 10$. We compare the equilibria for different numbers of the players under high ($r = 0.1$) and low ($r = 0.9$) probabilities of request arrival to the fast server. The graphs in Figs. 10.13 and 10.14 are the corresponding equilibrium density functions of the arrival times in the system. In addition, Fig. 10.15 shows how the equilibrium densities change their graphs as we vary the parameter r (the probability that the player's request is redirected to the first server).

10.2.8 Comparison of random-access schemes in terms of efficiency

Deterministic number of players

In this subsection, we compare the efficiency of different random-access schemes for (1) the one-server system and (2) the random-access two-server

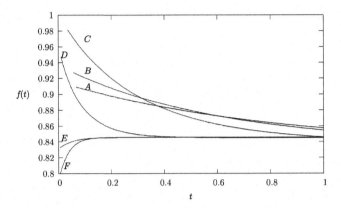

Figure 10.13 Equilibrium densities $f(t)$ for $T = 1, \mu_1 = 1, \mu_2 = 10, r = 0.1$, and (A) $\lambda = 1$, (B) $\lambda = 5$, (C) $\lambda = 20$, (D) $\lambda = 100$, (E) $\lambda = 200$, (F) $\lambda = 300$

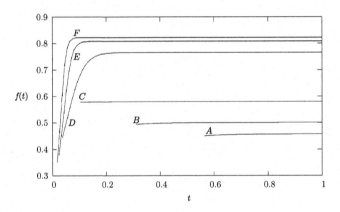

Figure 10.14 Equilibrium densities $f(t)$ for $T = 1, \mu_1 = 1, \mu_2 = 10, r = 0.9$, and (A) $\lambda = 1$, (B) $\lambda = 5$, (C) $\lambda = 20$, (D) $\lambda = 100$, (E) $\lambda = 200$, (F) $\lambda = 300$

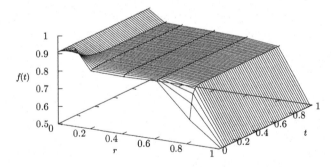

Figure 10.15 Equilibrium densities for $T = 1, \mu_1 = 1, \mu_2 = 10, \lambda = 100$ under variation of r

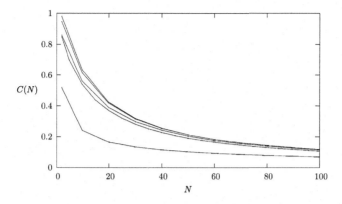

Figure 10.16 Efficiencies of different systems depending on the number of players

system that redirects user requests to servers without any information about their states (free or busy). Our aim is to answer the following question: which option is better, using two servers or one server with the same performance as the two servers have in total. Consider the two-server model with service rates $\mu_1 = 1$ and $\mu_2 = 10$. The service rate of the one-server model is $\mu = \mu_1 + \mu_2 = 11$. Both systems operate on the time interval $[0, 1]$. As an efficiency criterion, we choose the equilibrium payoff of a player, that is, the equilibrium probability of service in the system, which is directly proportional to the expected number of requests served by the system. The graphs in Fig. 10.16 show the efficiency of both systems under different numbers of players N. The graphs are arranged one above the other without intersections and correspond to the following cases in the descending order of efficiency:

1. the two-server system with the rational random-access scheme and high probability of request arrival to the fast server ($r = 0.1$);
2. the two-server system with the rational random-access scheme and low probability of request arrival to the fast server ($r = 0.9$);
3. the two-server system with the pure random-access scheme and high probability of request arrival to the fast server ($r = 0.1$);
4. the one-server system;
5. the two-server system with the pure random-access scheme and low probability of request arrival to the fast server ($r = 0.9$).

Poisson number of players

By analogy with the deterministic number of players, here we compare the efficiency of different random-access schemes for the same systems as before. Again, the problem is to find a better option, using two servers

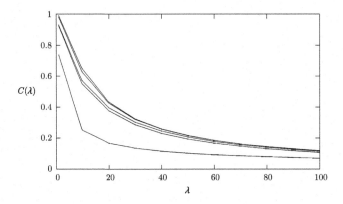

Figure 10.17 Efficiencies of different systems depending on request rate λ

or one server with the same performance as the two servers have in total. Consider the two-server model with service rates $\mu_1 = 1$ and $\mu_2 = 10$. The service rate of the one-server model is $\mu = \mu_1 + \mu_2 = 11$. Both systems operate on the time interval $[0, 1]$. As an efficiency criterion, we also choose the equilibrium probability of service in the system, which is directly proportional to the expected number of requests served by the system. The graphs in Fig. 10.17 demonstrate the efficiency of both systems under different request rates λ. Like in the previous case, the graphs are arranged one above the other without intersections and correspond to the following cases in the descending order of efficiency:

1. the two-server system with the rational random-access scheme and high probability of request arrival to the fast server ($r = 0.1$);
2. the two-server system with the rational random-access scheme and high probability of request arrival to the fast server ($r = 0.1$);
3. the two-server system with the rational random-access scheme and low probability of request arrival to the fast server ($r = 0.9$);
4. the two-server system with the pure random-access scheme and high probability of request arrival to the fast server ($r = 0.1$);
5. the one-server system;
6. the two-server system with the pure random-access scheme and low probability of request arrival to the fast server ($r = 0.9$).

CHAPTER 11

Cloud Operator Games

Contents

Modern information transfer tools such as the Internet and mobile communication has led to a new–type market with virtual agents distributed in space. We are observing the formation of new market structures differing in the scale of their resources and tasks, the price and quality of services, and other parameters. With the course of years, the separation of network and services has increased the competition among the past monopolies of communication technologies. The markets in these industries are now more efficient due to the growing functional compatibility and decreasing reconfiguration cost. As a result, cloud technologies have been developed, and cloud (or virtual) operators have appeared, which suggest various services using their own platforms and interfaces and also the ones leased from large companies. Owing to such a strategy, virtual operators manage without capital investments required for creating and maintaining a high-capacity infrastructure (e.g., a mobile communication network, computing clusters and networks, etc.).

The public cloud computing market is dominated by the services based on proprietary platforms and customer interfaces. Under such circumstances, the customers expose switching costs and lock in to the cloud service provider. Other significant observed problem, which hinders the proliferation of cloud computing, is related to trust issues between service providers and their customers. Software as a Service (*SaaS*) providers can easily lose their reputation if the underlying Infrastructure as a Ser-

Copyright © 2019 Elsevier Inc.
All rights reserved.

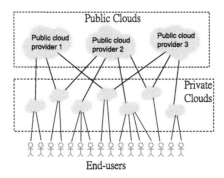

Figure 11.1 Three-level cloud market model

vice (*IaaS*) infrastructure creates Quality of Service (*QoS*) or privacy-related problems.

A hybrid or federated cloud is a promising architecture to the market-oriented cloud ecosystems. In this context, a public cloud with unlimited capacity provides a solution to handle unexpected traffic peaks of variable Internet traffic and private cloud capacity for typical load. It has been discovered that an optimal cost structure occurs in certain IaaS applications when 40 percent computation is in a private cloud and 60 percent in a public cloud. Additionally, the hosting of a private cloud can be outsourced to a broker, who is connected with the public clouds.

Currently, there are significant efforts to standardize customer interfaces of public clouds in order to realize better interoperability between various clouds. In this chapter, we introduce a game-theoretical model, which describes the behavior of a hybrid cloud market. Additionally, based on simulation, we explore the effect of interoperability to the market efficiency. In particular, we concentrate on the effect of the number market players, switching cost, and pricing.

11.1 CLOUD COMPUTING MARKET

First, we formulate a market model corresponding to a cloud computing service [56]. For that, let us introduce three main roles that are present in the cloud market today, namely, (i) *end-users*, (ii) *broker cloud service providers*, and (iii) *public cloud service providers* (see Fig. 11.1). Public cloud service providers (*CSPs*) are big companies that sell their cloud capacity to individual clients or other CSPs. See http://searchcloudprovider.techtarget.com/definition/cloud-broker for a broader definition of broker CSPs. Conventionally, they are assumed to have large enough amount of resources provisioned for high-demand peaks.

Broker CSPs are small or medium-sized cloud providers that have limited resources. They do not provision high capacity, and in case of higher-demand peaks, they buy resources from public CSPs. These broker CSPs may be pure virtual (without any internal resources), thus functioning as resellers, or they can provide some base of internal resource, thus, functioning as private clouds.

Finally, there are end-users. End-users may buy resources from both broker CSPs and public CSPs. Those buying resources from public CSPs are considered to be more advanced. We take them out of our consideration as they are normally adjusted to one public CSP and influence only load levels of that CSP. Other end-users are connected to broker CSPs (Fig. 11.1). They buy resources from a set of local brokers. Our game-theoretical model uses a logistic function for definition of locality. A logistic function defines locality through the corresponding parameter.

Using the definition above, we construct a hierarchical market structure (Fig. 11.1), where public CSP are on the top. They are selling resources to everyone interested. Public CSPs have known pricing models, which are defined in this work as the resource price per unit based on the current load of the public CSPs. Broker CSPs in the middle compete with each other and sell resources to end-users on the bottom. If the limited internal resources of the brokers are not sufficient enough to serve their clients, then the brokers buy resources from the public CSPs. Brokers can set the prices for own services directly. However, if the price is too high, then the end-users start to prefer other brokers. On the other hand, if the price is too low, then brokers reduce their own profit and have losses in case of excess of clients and insufficiency of own resources. Thus, the price that the brokers announce is defined by the competitiveness on the market and own resource availability. End-users select the most appropriate broker CSP from whom they buy the resources. The selection criteria for end-user include the price the broker defines, the brokers locality, trustworthiness, and the amount of own resources at the broker.

Evidence of such a market is already observed in the computational clouds; as examples of such brokers, there can be:

Rackspace – www.rackspace.com,

Cloudswitch – www.cloudswitch.com,

Spotcloud – www.spotcloud.com.

11.2 GAME-THEORETICAL MODEL

We consider a strategic noncooperative game $\Gamma = < N, \{P_i\}_{i=1}^n, u_i(p) >$ with player set $N = \{1, 2, \ldots, n\}$, strategy sets $P_1 \times P_2 \times \cdots \times P_n$, and utility functions $u_i(p)$, $i = 1, \ldots, n$.

Here the players are Private Clouds (PrCs). The resources of the clouds are r_i, $i = 1, 2, \ldots, n$. Each PrC chooses a price p_i for the resource. There is a demand R in the market. The customers observing the profile of the prices $p = (p_1, \ldots, p_n)$ are distributed among the PrCs in logistic manner [60].

So, the portion

$$\gamma_i(p, r) = \frac{\exp\{-\alpha_i \cdot p_i + \beta_i \cdot r_i\}}{\sum_{k=1}^n \exp\{-\alpha_k \cdot p_k + \beta_k \cdot r_k\}}$$

of the customers' demand is attracted by the ith PrC, $i = 1, \ldots, n$. Let the costs for ith PrC to serve the customers be c_i, $i = 1, \ldots, n$. Thus the net revenue of the PrC_i depending of the demand R is equal to

$$R \cdot \gamma_i(p, r) \cdot (p_i - c_i).$$

If the demand R becomes larger than the summarized resources of the PrC $r_1 + \cdots + r_n$, then the PrCs have to apply to Public Clouds (PuCs) and buy additional resources in PuCs. The price for the resource of the PuC is described by some function $p = F(L)$ in dependence of the current load L of the PuC. The function $F(L)$ is nondecreasing and continuous.

We suppose that the customers' demand is a random variable distributed with CDF $G(R)$, so it is possible for the demand to be sufficiently large ($R \gg r_1 + \cdots + r_n$). Suppose also that there are m PuCs $PuC_1, \ldots, PuC_m$, which have some initial loads $L_1, \ldots, L_m$. Without loss of generality, suppose that $L_1 \le \cdots \le L_m \le L_{m+1} = \infty$. So, the PrCs apply at the beginning to the first cheapest PuC and, after the load of PuC_1, reach the value L_2, then they apply to both PuC_1 and PuC_2, etc.

The use of price-filling algorithm we utilize in this model is dictated by the fact that each of the private cloud in optimal way buys the cheapest resources from a public cloud. This reflects the way in which the market-clearing price is found. Although there could be multiple ways to organize market for selling public resources, that is, in a form of flat prices or auctions, the principle of finding the market-clearing price remains the same. We, however, omit the study of defining the exact selling mechanism of public resources and process of determining the market-clearing price. Instead, we mimic the existence of the latter and parameterize the general selling mechanism using the function $F(l)$. This is the reason we utilize "water-filling algorithms." This principle does not require any coordination between public cloud operators. Furthermore, the pricing mechanisms at different clouds may be different. The market itself through the search of market-clearing price makes the distribution of the PrC demands the way we described.

Now we can write the utility function of the PrC_i:

$$u_i(p) = \int_0^\infty R \cdot \gamma_i(p, r) \cdot (p_i - c_i) dG(R)$$

$$- \int_{r_1 + \cdots + r_n}^\infty \gamma_i(p, r) \cdot \left[\sum_{j=1}^k \left(j \cdot \int_{L_j}^{L_{j+1}} F(l) dl \right) \right.$$

$$\left. + (k+1) \cdot \int_{L_{k+1}}^{L_{k+1} + \frac{\delta}{k+1}} F(l) dl \right] dG(R),$$

where $\delta = R - (r_1 + \cdots + r_n) - \sum_{j=1}^k (L_{j+1} - L_j) \cdot j$, and k is the number of PuCs the resources of which will be asked in the cloud market. The value of k is determined as the minimum k satisfying the conditions

$$\sum_{j=1}^k (L_{j+1} - L_j) \cdot j \le R - (r_1 + \cdots + r_n) < \sum_{j=1}^{k+1} (L_{j+1} - L_j) \cdot j.$$

Simplifying,

$$u_i(p) = \gamma_i(p, r) \cdot (\overline{R} \cdot p_i - C_i) = \overline{R} \cdot \gamma_i(p, r) \cdot (p_i - C_i/\overline{R}),$$

where $\overline{R} = \int_0^\infty R dG(R)$ is the expected value of the demand, and C_i are the general costs of the PrC_i, $i = 1, \ldots, n$.

Let us find the Nash equilibrium, that is, the stable profile p^* such that

$$u_i(p^*) \ge u_i(p_i, p_{-i}^*)$$

for any player i and his strategy p_i. In Chapter 2, it was shown that in potential games the Nash equilibrium coincides with the maximum of a potential function. We further show that our cloud game is a potential game. A difference with Chapter 2 is that in the cloud operator game we determine an ordinal potential function $P(p)$ such that $\frac{\partial u_i}{p_i} \ge 0$ if and only if $\frac{\partial P}{p_i} \ge 0$. In that case the solution of the cloud operator game is the Nash equilibrium in the potential game.

Let $k_j = \exp\{\beta_j \cdot r_j\} > 0$.

Theorem 65. *Let* $\Gamma = < N, \{P_i\}_{i=1}^n, u_i(p) >$ *be the noncooperative game with payoffs*

$$u_i(p) = (p_i - C_i) \cdot \frac{\exp\{-\alpha_i \cdot p_i\}}{\sum_{j=1}^n k_j \cdot \exp\{-\alpha_j \cdot p_j\}}, \quad i = 1, \ldots, n.$$

Then the game Γ *is an ordinal potential game, and the function*

$$P(p) = P(p_1, \ldots, p_n) = \prod_{i=1}^n (p_i - C_i) \cdot \frac{\exp\{-\sum_{j=1}^n \alpha_j \cdot p_j\}}{\sum_{j=1}^n k_j \cdot \exp\{-\alpha_j \cdot p_j\}}$$

is an ordinal potential.

Proof. Denote, for convenience,

$$E(p) = \sum_{j=1}^n k_j \cdot \exp\{-\alpha_j \cdot p_j\}.$$

Notice that

$$\frac{\partial P(p)}{\partial p_i} = \frac{1}{E^2(p)} \cdot \left[\left(\prod_{j \neq i} (p_j - C_j) \cdot \exp\{-\sum_{j=1}^n \alpha_j \cdot p_j\} \right. \right.$$
$$\left. - \alpha_i \cdot \prod_{j=1}^n (p_j - C_j) \cdot \exp\{-\sum_{j=1}^n \alpha_j \cdot p_j\} \right) \cdot E(p)$$
$$\left. + \alpha_i \cdot k_i \cdot \exp\{-\alpha_i \cdot p_i\} \cdot \prod_{j=1}^n (p_j - C_j) \cdot \exp\{-\sum_{j=1}^n \alpha_j \cdot p_j\} \right]. \quad (11.1)$$

Simplifying we have

$$\frac{\partial P(p)}{\partial p_i} = \frac{1}{E^2(p)} \cdot \prod_{j \neq i} (p_j - C_j) \cdot \exp\{-\sum_{j=1}^n \alpha_j \cdot p_j\} \cdot [E(p) \cdot (1 - \alpha_i \cdot (p_i - C_i))$$
$$+ \alpha_i \cdot k_i \cdot (p_i - C_i) \cdot \exp\{-\alpha_i \cdot p_i\}]. \quad (11.2)$$

It is not difficult to check that

$$\frac{\partial P(p)}{\partial p_i} = \prod_{j \neq i} (p_j - C_j) \cdot \exp\{-\sum_{j=1}^n \alpha_j \cdot p_j\} \cdot \frac{\partial u_i(p)}{\partial p_i}, \quad i = 1, \ldots, n.$$

So, we see that in the region $p_i \geq C_i, i = 1, \ldots, n$, $\frac{\partial P(p)}{\partial p_i} \geq 0$ if and only if $\frac{\partial u_i(p)}{\partial p_i} \geq 0$ for any $i = 1, \ldots, n$. From here it follows that the game Γ is an ordinal potential game. $\square$

The potential games with compact strategy spaces are known to possess at least one Nash equilibrium in pure strategies, and if the profile p^* maximizes the potential $P(p)$, then it is a Nash equilibrium.

Remark. The potential $P(p)$ is a continuous differentiable function. To find the maximum of $P(p)$, we can form the system of equations $\frac{\partial P(p)}{\partial p_i} = 0$, $i = 1, \ldots, n$. From (11.2) we obtain

$$E(p) \cdot (1 - \alpha_i \cdot (p_i - C_i)) + \alpha_i \cdot k_i \cdot (p_i - C_i) \cdot \exp\{-\alpha_i \cdot p_i\} = 0, \qquad (11.3)$$

$i = 1, \ldots, n$. From (11.2) it follows that, for any profile p_{-i} (except $p_j = C_j, j \neq i$), if $p_i = C_i$, then $\frac{\partial P(p)}{\partial p_i} > 0$. However, for large p_i, $\frac{\partial P(p)}{\partial p_i}$ becomes negative. Consequently, system (11.3) has a nontrivial solution.

Moreover, the sign of the derivative $\frac{\partial P(p)}{\partial p_i}$ is changing at this point from plus to minus. So, in this point the potential achieves the maximum value.

Notice also that, at the point $p_i = C_i + 1/\alpha_i$, the derivative $\frac{\partial P(p)}{\partial p_i}$ is positive. So, the function $P(p)$ is increasing in p_i. This means that in equilibrium $p_i^* \geq C_i + 1/\alpha_i$, $i = 1, \ldots, n$.

11.3 TWO-PLAYER GAME

Suppose we have two private clouds. In this case the potential function has the following form:

$$P(p) = P(p_1, p_2) = \frac{(p_1 - \frac{C_1}{R}) \cdot (p_2 - \frac{C_2}{R}) \cdot e^{-\alpha_1 \cdot p_1 - \alpha_2 \cdot p_2}}{k_1 \cdot e^{-\alpha_1 \cdot p_1} + k_2 \cdot e^{-\alpha_2 \cdot p_2}}.$$

From the first-order conditions for the maximum of the potential $\partial P/\partial p_i = 0$, $i = 1, 2$, we obtain the system of equations

$$\begin{cases} \alpha_1 \cdot (p_1 - \frac{C_1}{R}) - 1 = \frac{k_1}{k_2} e^{-\alpha_1 \cdot p_1 + \alpha_2 \cdot p_2}, \\ \alpha_2 \cdot (p_2 - \frac{C_2}{R}) - 1 = \frac{k_2}{k_1} e^{-\alpha_2 \cdot p_2 + \alpha_1 \cdot p_1}. \end{cases} \qquad (11.4)$$

Multiplying the equations, we get the following hyperbola equation:

$$\left(\alpha_1 \cdot (p_1 - \frac{C_1}{R}) - 1\right) \cdot \left(\alpha_2 \cdot (p_2 - \frac{C_2}{R}) - 1\right) = 1; \qquad (11.5)$$

see Fig. 11.2. The Nash equilibrium lies on the curve.

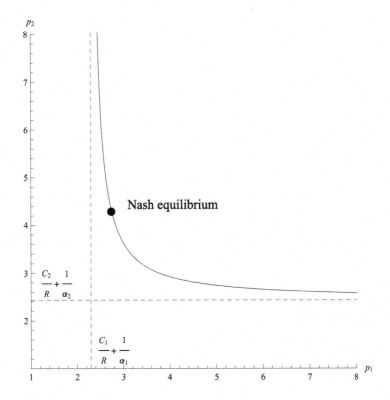

Figure 11.2 Two-player game

Let us prove the following extra theorem on the uniqueness of the Nash equilibrium.

Theorem 66 (Uniqueness of equilibrium). *For the two-player game, there is only one Nash equilibrium.*

Proof. From Eq. (11.4) we know that the points of Nash equilibrium lie on a hyperbola, but we do not know how many of them. Thus we can prove the uniqueness if we prove that one (any) of the equations in the system is nondecreasing. Let we have a function $p_2(p_1)$ and consider the first equation. Let us produce the derivative of it for p_1, and thus

$$\alpha_1 = \frac{k_1}{k_2} \cdot (-\alpha_1 + \alpha_2 \cdot p_2') \cdot e^{-\alpha_1 \cdot p_1 + \alpha_2 \cdot p_2}.$$

Then we have that

$$p_2' = \frac{\alpha_1 \cdot \left(\frac{k_2}{k_1} \cdot e^{\alpha_1 \cdot p_1 - \alpha_2 \cdot p_2} + 1 \right)}{\alpha_2} > 0.$$

The latter means that the derivative is positive, which means that it intersects the hyperbola only at a single point, the Nash equilibrium. This concludes the proof of the uniqueness of the Nash equilibrium.   □

In the symmetric case ($\alpha_1 = \alpha_2 = \alpha$, $C_1 = C_2 = C$), from Eq. (11.5) we obtain the explicit form for the equilibrium

$$p_1^* = p_2^* = \frac{C}{R} + \frac{2}{\alpha}.$$

11.4 SYMMETRIC CASE FOR n-PLAYER GAME

Suppose that the resources and the costs of PrCs are equal, so that $r_1 = \cdots = r_n$ and $C_1 = \cdots = C_n$. This corresponds to the symmetric case, and the equilibrium must be symmetric, that is, $p_1^* = \cdots = p_n^* = p^*$. From Eq. (11.3) we obtain

$$n \cdot k \cdot \exp\{-\alpha \cdot p^*\} \cdot (1 - \alpha(p^* - \frac{C}{R})) + \alpha \cdot k \cdot (p^* - \frac{C}{R}) \cdot \exp\{-\alpha \cdot p^*\} = 0.$$

Consequently,

$$p^* = \frac{C}{R} + \frac{n}{n-1} \cdot \frac{1}{\alpha}.$$

We see that, for large number of PrC (strong competition in the market), the equilibrium is close to the value $C/R + 1/\alpha$. In fact, the prices in equilibrium are determined mainly by the expected costs for applying to PuC per demand unit and the inverse of α, which reflects the influence of prices for the demand.

11.5 NUMERICAL SIMULATIONS

We compute the market with three PrCs and two PuCs. Suppose that demand on the market follows the exponential law $\lambda e^{-\lambda R}$. The resources of PrCs are respectively r_1, r_2, r_3. The initial costs are equal. We suppose that the price in public clouds is a function of load (L) and it is a linear function with minimal value p_{min} and maximum p_{max}.

The values for the parameters we use in numerical simulation can be found in Table 11.1.

Table 11.1 Parameters

Variable	Description	Initial value
α	Weight of price in log-function	1
β	Weight of resource in log-function	0.01
p_{min}	Price for minimally loaded PuC	0.1
p_{max}	Price for maximally loaded PuC	1
L_{max}	Maximal possible load at PuC	1000
L_1	Initial load of the 1st PuC	100
L_2	Initial load of the 2nd PuC	0; 70; 110; or 150
λ	Exponential law parameter	0.004
$\bar{p}$	Average market price	n/a

Table 11.2 Numerical results

r_1	r_2	r_3	p_1	p_2	p_3	U_1	U_2	U_3	$\bar{p}$
					1 pub. cloud				
100	100	100	1.529	1.529	1.529	113.553	113.553	113.553	1.529
100	80	50	1.649	1.555	1.435	137.244	116.536	90.091	1.556
100	50	10	1.786	1.549	1.392	163.542	109.783	77.617	1.607
				2 pub. clouds ($L_2 = 150$)					
100	100	100	1.524	1.524	1.524	113.553	113.553	113.553	1.524
100	80	50	1.641	1.548	1.428	137.339	116.554	90.017	1.549
100	50	10	1.775	1.532	1.382	163.857	109.793	77.471	1.596
				2 pub. clouds ($L_2 = 110$)					
100	100	100	1.523	1.523	1.523	113.553	113.553	113.553	1.523
100	80	50	1.639	1.546	1.426	137.363	116.558	89.999	1.547
100	50	10	1.773	1.529	1.380	163.93	109.796	77.437	1.594
				2 pub. clouds ($L_2 = 70$)					
100	100	100	1.521	1.521	1.521	113.553	113.553	113.553	1.521
100	80	50	1.637	1.544	1.424	137.391	116.564	89.976	1.545
100	50	10	1.770	1.526	1.377	164.019	109.799	77.395	1.591

Based on these parameters, we run 12 different scenarios. The four main classes of scenario include (i) a setup with only one PuC, (ii) a setup with two PuCs ($L_2 = 150$), (iii) a setup with two PuCs ($L_2 = 110$), and (ii) a setup with two PuCs ($L_2 = 70$). Each of these main classes of scenario is a same way divided into three scenario subclasses, based on the PrC resources available (r_1, r_2, r_3). The numerical results can be found in Table 11.2.

The first thing we observe is that introduction of a new PuC reduces the overall average market price for the resources ($\bar{p}$). The same holds if the load at second PuC (L_2) is reduced. The market can reduce prices for the resources, as they buy excess cheaper. However, we observe that utilities of individual PrCs do not correlate with average market price. It happens due to competition on the market. If a new PuC is introduced to the system, then big PrCs can reduce the price as the costs for them are reduced. After that, small PrCs start to be less attractive to customers, and in order to compete, they have to reduce own prices, but at the same time the accumulative costs at PuCs do not reduce proportionally for them, as they do not use much of PuCs. The numerical results show that the reduction in utility does affect highly the small PrCs. For $r_1 = 100, r_2 = 50$, and $r_3 = 10$, comparing the case $L_2 = 150$ with the case $L_2 = 70$, we notice that u_3 changes from 77.471 to 77.395, which is 0.1% in relative value.

Our main observation is that, in the hybrid cloud infrastructure we study, high competition does not allow us to manipulate prices, and introduction of new resources does not necessary lead to increase in revenue. However, we clearly observe that this market structure does benefit endusers, as the new resources at higher layers transparently reduce their costs for the resources at the PrC level.

11.6 TWO-SIDED TELECOMMUNICATION MARKET

Here we apply the game-theoretic approach to the virtual mobile operator market. In previous consideration, we supposed that the cloud services lease computational resources from large companies and gain income from a comfortable provision of their resources. For example, the cloud firms solving large-scale computational problems may contract for the resources of Google or Amazon. Federal-level communication operators (Rostelecom, Transtelecom) grant their trunk lines on lease to the providers. On a commercial basis, large mobile operators (MTS, Megafon, Beeline) grant access to the infrastructure of their communication networks to virtual mobile operators (NetbyNet, Svyaznoi Mobile, etc.) by selling services under their trademark. In addition, mobile communication networks can be used to transfer data in different cloud services, for example, the operation of cloud short messaging centers.

We present a game-theoretic model in the form of the following twostep game [80]. At the first step, the players (virtual operators, i.e., the owners of cloud services) distribute themselves between the large companies (i.e., the owners of resources for communication, computations, etc.). Then the virtual operators assign the prices for their services. The clients are the users (target population) who choose a certain service via the Internet or mobile devices according to their personal preferences.

An important feature of the model consists in the partition of company's clients choosing the services of a given operator. By our assumption the clients are partitioned in accordance with the Hotelling specification [2], that is, the clients compare their utilities from choosing the services of certain virtual operators. After defining the clients partition, we calculate the payoffs of all cloud operators and find a Nash equilibrium for this model of competition. The Nash equilibrium is constructed as a sequence of the best responses of the players to the opponents' strategies.

Consider a market where several large companies provide services to the population through smaller "cloud" virtual operators buying companies' services and reselling them to clients. Here and further, the term operator means a virtual operator, whereas the term companies applies to large real operators whose resources are resold by virtual operators to clients.

Each company i allocates some resource $r_i > 0$ and grants access to it for operators with a wholesale rate $p_i > 0$ per unit of the resource. Company i has its own client base (subscribers) of size n_i. The resource $r_i > 0$ characterizes the amount and quality of services provided by this company (and hence its attractiveness for the clients).

Each operator needs to choose a company whose services he is going to sell and also to define a price for the services to be sold to clients. Operator j enters into a business agreement with company i with probability x_{ij}. In particular, $x_{ij} = 1$ means that operator j contracts with company i and $x_{ij} = 0$ otherwise. Then each operator j establishes a price q_j for his services.

Depending on these characteristics, the clients choose a virtual operator for their services. While making his choice, a client is interested in the minimum price for the services of a given operator and also in the maximum attractiveness of the services and the highest probability that this operator provides the services of the contracted company. Denote by $h_{ij} = S + r_i x_{ij} - q_j$ the utility of the clients of company i from choosing operator j. Buying a unit of service of utility S from an operator, a client pays q_j for it and obtains a resource r_i (e.g., an improved quality of services, an additional functionality, a discount) if this operator contracts with his company. Choosing between operators j and l, a client compares their utility.

Each operator j seeks to maximize his total profit $u_j(x, q) + C_j$, where the payoff $u_j(x, q)$ depends on the strategies x and q and is defined by *revenue_per_client* ⋆ *clients_count* − *leasing_costs* (possibly, negative); C_j is a utility from leased resources, a large enough quantity to guarantee a nonnegativity of the total profit of operator j. Note that C_j may also include additional funds of operator j (e.g., a grant for business setup). We further consider only the payoff $u_j(x, q)$ of operator j instead of his total profit, assuming that the total profit is positive.

11.7 GENERALIZED HOTELLING SPECIFICATION FOR TWO OPERATORS

Let two operators $(j = 1, 2)$ compete in the market. Then the partition of company i clients choosing operator j is given by $\frac{1}{2} + \frac{h_{ij} - h_{i(3-j)}}{2k_{ij}}$. The coefficient k_{ij} describes their preferences, measuring the degree of dissatisfaction that the clients of company i feel toward operator j. This coefficient can be related to the difficult-to-access maintenance points and transport cost, low-level service, and so on. Unlike the standard Hotelling specification with $k_{ij} = k_i$ for all j, where the whole set of clients is strictly partitioned into two groups by the operators, in the generalized case, these groups may intersect (i.e., a certain part of clients can be served by both operators), and their union may include not all the clients (i.e., some clients can be served directly by companies without intermediary of operators). By assumption the problem parameters are adjusted so that the partition of company i clients choosing operator j does not exceed 1 for all i, j. This can be achieved, for example, by specifying sufficiently large values k_{ij}. In addition, we suppose that $(k_{ij} - ki(3 - j))(h_{ij} - h_{i(3-j)}) \geq 0$ to ensure that the number of clients of company i using the services of operator 1 or operator 2 is not greater than n_i.

The payoff function of each operator $j = 1, 2$ under the known strategies x and q has the form

$$u_j(x, q) = q_j \sum_i n_i \left(\frac{1}{2} + \frac{h_{ij} - h_{i(3-j)}}{2k_{ij}} \right) - \sum_i \frac{x_{ij}}{x_{i1} + x_{i2}} p_i r_i.$$

At the beginning of the game, the initial prices q used by the operators for selling their services to clients are given. The system moves to a new state through a repetition of two steps as follows. At the first step, each operator j chooses his strategy x under fixed prices q, that is, the companies to contract with. At the second step, each operator j assigns an optimal price q for his service under fixed x. Then the game repeats: the distributions of the operators between the companies are corrected under the new prices q, and the optimal prices are calculated for the new distributions. After several iterations, the system may reach a stationary state, which is a Nash equilibrium for the game in which the operators choose companies to contract with and simultaneously a Nash equilibrium in the optimal pricing game of the services sold. Note that, at any step, there may exist two or more equilibria, and we will discriminate between the notions of "stationary" and "equilibrium" states.

Suppose that there are two large companies in the market and the operators choose between them. Denote by x_j the probability to contract with the first company for operator j. Then the opposite probability $1 - x_j$ is the probability that operator j chooses the second company. With such notations, the payoff functions are written as

$$u_1(x, q) = \frac{q_1}{2}\left((n_1 + n_2) - (q_1 - q_2)\left(\frac{n_1}{k_{11}} + \frac{n_2}{k_{21}}\right) + \left(\frac{n_1 r_1}{k_{11}} - \frac{n_2 r_2}{k_{21}}\right)(x_1 - x_2)\right)$$
$$- \frac{x_1}{x_1 + x_2}p_1 r_1 - \frac{1 - x_1}{2 - x_1 - x_2}p_2 r_2,$$

$$u_2(x, q) = \frac{q_2}{2}\left((n_1 + n_2) + (q_1 - q_2)\left(\frac{n_1}{k_{12}} + \frac{n_2}{k_{22}}\right) - \left(\frac{n_1 r_1}{k_{12}} - \frac{n_2 r_2}{k_{22}}\right)(x_1 - x_2)\right)$$
$$- \frac{x_2}{x_1 + x_2}p_1 r_1 - \frac{1 - x_2}{2 - x_1 - x_2}p_2 r_2.$$

The payoff functions $u_j(x, q)$ are convex in x_j. Hence the optimal values x_j lie at one of the limits of the interval $[0, 1]$, which means that the optimal strategies at this step are pure strategies.

Consider the first step of the game where the operators choose their distribution between the companies. Find the best response of the first player to the opponent's strategy $x_2 = 1$, that is, the choice of the first company. In this case, the payoff of the first player is given by

$$u_1(x_1|x_2 = 1, q) = \frac{q_1}{2}\left((n_1 + n_2) - (q_1 - q_2)\left(\frac{n_1}{k_{11}} + \frac{n_2}{k_{21}}\right)\right.$$
$$+ \left.\left(\frac{n_1 r_1}{k_{11}} - \frac{n_2 r_2}{k_{21}}\right)(x_1 - 1)\right) - \frac{x_1}{x_1 + 1}p_1 r_1 - \frac{1 - x_1}{1 - x_1}p_2 r_2$$
$$= \alpha(q) + \frac{q_1 x_1}{2}\left(\frac{n_1 r_1}{k_{11}} - \frac{n_2 r_2}{k_{21}}\right) - \frac{x_1}{x_1 + 1}p_1 r_1,$$

where $\alpha(q)$ indicates a term independent of x_1. The payoff function is convex in x_1 and thus achieves the maximum at one of the limits of the interval $[0, 1]$.

For compactness, introduce the notation $R_j = \frac{n_1 r_1}{k_{1j}} - \frac{n_2 r_2}{k_{2j}}, j = 1, 2$. Then the best response of the first player to the opponent's strategy $x_2 = 1$ is

$$x_1 = \begin{cases} 1 \text{ if } \frac{q_1}{2}R_1 - \frac{p_1 r_1}{2} \geq 0, \\ 0 \text{ if } \frac{q_1}{2}R_1 - \frac{p_1 r_1}{2} \leq 0. \end{cases}$$ Note that the best response belongs to the

two-element set $\{0, 1\}$ in the case $\frac{q_1}{2}R_1 - \frac{p_1 r_1}{2} = 0$. Similarly, the best response of the first player to the opponent's strategy $x_2 = 0$ is $x_1 =$
$$\begin{cases} 1 \text{ if } \frac{q_1}{2}R_1 + \frac{p_2 r_2}{2} \geq 0, \\ 0 \text{ if } \frac{q_1}{2}R_1 + \frac{p_2 r_2}{2} \leq 0. \end{cases}$$

By analogy we calculate the best response of the second player to

the opponent's strategy $x_1 = 0$ as $x_2 = \begin{cases} 1 \text{ if } \frac{q_2}{2}R_2 + \frac{p_2 r_2}{2} \geq 0, \\ 0 \text{ if } \frac{q_2}{2}R_2 + \frac{p_2 r_2}{2} \leq 0, \end{cases}$ and the

best response of the second player to the opponent's strategy $x_1 = 1$ as

$$x_2 = \begin{cases} 1 \text{ if } \frac{q_2}{2}R_2 - \frac{p_1 r_1}{2} \geq 0, \\ 0 \text{ if } \frac{q_2}{2}R_2 - \frac{p_1 r_1}{2} \leq 0. \end{cases}$$

Consequently, we obtain the following equilibria under the current prices q:

$$x^*(q) = (x_1^*(q), x_2^*(q)) = \begin{cases} (0, 0) \text{ if } \begin{cases} q_1 R_1 \leq -p_2 r_2, \\ q_2 R_2 \leq -p_2 r_2, \end{cases} \\ (0, 1) \text{ if } \begin{cases} q_1 R_1 \leq p_1 r_1, \\ q_2 R_2 \geq -p_2 r_2, \end{cases} \\ (1, 0) \text{ if } \begin{cases} q_1 R_1 \geq -p_2 r_2, \\ q_2 R_2 \leq p_1 r_1, \end{cases} \\ (1, 1) \text{ if } \begin{cases} q_1 R_1 \geq p_1 r_1, \\ q_2 R_2 \geq p_1 r_1. \end{cases} \end{cases} \qquad (11.6)$$

In these cases, each strategy of a player is the best response to the opponent's strategy, and hence nobody benefits by a unilateral deviation. In fact, if any of the players unilaterally deviates from his strategy, then the opponent changes his strategy accordingly by choosing the best response to the new strategy of the former. Note also that at the first step a pure strategy equilibrium does not always exist. If R_1 and R_2 are both greater or smaller than zero simultaneously, then a pure strategy equilibrium exists (in some cases, even two or three equilibria). If they have different signs, then for q, there are ranges without pure strategy equilibria. For example, under $R_1 < 0$ and $R_2 > 0$, no pure strategy equilibria can be found within the ranges $\frac{p_1 r_1}{R_1} < q_1 < -\frac{p_2 r_2}{R_1}$ and $-\frac{p_2 r_2}{R_2} < q_2 < \frac{p_1 r_1}{R_2}$.

Consider the second step at which the players assign their prices for services under a given distribution x. Let negative prices q be also admissible and interpret this scenario as operator's investments in some promotion actions for costs minimization. Each of the functions u_j is concave in q_j, representing a parabola with descending branches. This means that the optimal strategy to assign the price q_j is the maximum of u_j in q_j.

The best response of the first player to the opponent's strategy q_2 makes up

$$q_1 = \frac{n_1 + n_2 + q_2 \left(\frac{n_1}{k_{11}} + \frac{n_2}{k_{21}} \right) + R_1(x_1 - x_2)}{2 \left(\frac{n_1}{k_{11}} + \frac{n_2}{k_{21}} \right)},$$

and the best response of the second player to the strategy q_1 is given by

$$q_2 = \frac{n_1 + n_2 + q_1 \left(\frac{n_1}{k_{12}} + \frac{n_2}{k_{22}} \right) - R_2(x_1 - x_2)}{2 \left(\frac{n_1}{k_{12}} + \frac{n_2}{k_{22}} \right)}.$$

Hence the equilibrium prices are

$$q^*(x) = (q_1^*(x), q_2^*(x)) = \left(\frac{n_1 + n_2}{3} \left(\frac{2}{K_1} + \frac{1}{K_2} \right) + \frac{x_1 - x_2}{3} \left(\frac{2R_1}{K_1} - \frac{R_2}{K_2} \right), \right.$$

$$\frac{n_1 + n_2}{3} \left(\frac{2}{K_2} + \frac{1}{K_1} \right) - \frac{x_1 - x_2}{3} \left(\frac{2R_2}{K_2} - \frac{R_1}{K_1} \right) \right)$$

$$= \left(\frac{(n_1 + n_2)(K_1 + 2K_2) + (x_1 - x_2)(2R_1 K_2 - R_2 K_1)}{3K_1 K_2}, \right.$$

$$\left. \frac{(n_1 + n_2)(2K_1 + K_2) - (x_1 - x_2)(2R_2 K_1 - R_1 K_2)}{3K_1 K_2} \right), \quad (11.7)$$

where $K_j = \frac{n_1}{k_{1j}} + \frac{n_2}{k_{2j}}, j = 1, 2$.

Consequently, evolving optimally, the system changes its states in the following way. Denote by $x^{(s)} = (x_1^{(s)}, x_2^{(s)})$ the system state before the first transition step s when the players distribute themselves between the companies. This state corresponds to the optimal prices $q^{(s)} = (q_1^*(x^{(s)}), q_2^*(x^{(s)}))$ defined by (11.7). Then the next state (see (11.6)) is calculated as $(x_1^*(q^{(s)}), x_2^*(q^{(s)}))$.

Before the transition $s > 1$, when the equilibrium distribution of the operators and the prices for services were defined at least once, we have four possible states of the system, namely:

1) $(0, 0)$ with the prices $\left(\frac{(n_1+n_2)(K_1+2K_2)}{3K_1K_2}, \frac{(n_1+n_2)(2K_1+K_2)}{3K_1K_2} \right)$,

2) $(0, 1)$ with the prices

$$\left(\frac{(n_1+n_2)(K_1+2K_2)-(2R_1K_2-R_2K_1)}{3K_1K_2}, \frac{(n_1+n_2)(2K_1+K_2)+(2R_2K_1-R_1K_2)}{3K_1K_2} \right),$$

3) $(1, 0)$ with the prices

$$\left(\frac{(n_1+n_2)(K_1+2K_2)+(2R_1K_2-R_2K_1)}{3K_1K_2}, \frac{(n_1+n_2)(2K_1+K_2)-(2R_2K_1-R_1K_2)}{3K_1K_2} \right),$$

4) $(1, 1)$ with the prices $\left(\frac{(n_1+n_2)(K_1+2K_2)}{3K_1K_2}, \frac{(n_1+n_2)(2K_1+K_2)}{3K_1K_2} \right)$.

11.8 TWO OPERATORS AND COMPANY-DEPENDENT CLIENT PREFERENCES

As before, consider the market with two operators ($j = 1, 2$) competing with each other. Let the partition of company i clients choosing operator j makes up $\frac{1}{2} + \frac{h_{ij}-h_{i(3-j)}}{2k_i}$, in accordance with the Hotelling specification; for the clients of company i, the coefficient k_i measures their conservatism, inconveniences of changing operators, and unwillingness to do it. In this case, the total number of clients of company i who choose the first or second operator is n_i.

The payoff functions take the form

$$u_1(x, q) = \frac{q_1}{2}\left((n_1 + n_2) - (q_1 - q_2)\left(\frac{n_1}{k_1} + \frac{n_2}{k_2} \right) + (x_1 - x_2)\left(\frac{n_1 r_1}{k_1} - \frac{n_2 r_2}{k_2} \right) \right)$$
$$- \frac{x_1}{x_1 + x_2}p_1 r_1 - \frac{(1-x_1)}{2 - x_1 - x_2}p_2 r_2,$$

$$u_2(x, q) = \frac{q_2}{2}\left((n_1 + n_2) + (q_1 - q_2)\left(\frac{n_1}{k_1} + \frac{n_2}{k_2} \right) - (x_1 - x_2)\left(\frac{n_1 r_1}{k_1} - \frac{n_2 r_2}{k_2} \right) \right)$$
$$- \frac{x_2}{x_1 + x_2}p_1 r_1 - \frac{(1-x_2)}{2 - x_1 - x_2}p_2 r_2.$$

For definiteness, assume without loss of generality that $\frac{n_1 r_1}{k_1} - \frac{n_2 r_2}{k_2} \geq 0$ (otherwise, simply renumber the companies). Denote this difference by $R = \frac{n_1 r_1}{k_1} - \frac{n_2 r_2}{k_2}$.

The following equilibria are then possible for the distributions of the operators between the companies:

$$x^*(q) = (x_1^*(q), x_2^*(q)) = \begin{cases} (0,0) \text{ if } \begin{cases} q_1 R \leq -p_2 r_2, \\ q_2 R \leq -p_2 r_2, \end{cases} \\[2ex] (0,1) \text{ if } \begin{cases} q_1 R \leq p_1 r_1, \\ q_2 R \geq -p_2 r_2, \end{cases} \\[2ex] (1,0) \text{ if } \begin{cases} q_1 R \geq -p_2 r_2, \\ q_2 R \leq p_1 r_1, \end{cases} \\[2ex] (1,1) \text{ if } \begin{cases} q_1 R \geq p_1 r_1, \\ q_2 R \geq p_1 r_1. \end{cases} \end{cases} \tag{11.8}$$

In these cases, the strategy of each player is the best response to the opponent's strategy, and hence nobody benefits by a unilateral deviation.

The equilibrium prices for services are

$$q^*(x) = (q_1^*(x), q_2^*(x)) = \left(\frac{k_1 k_2 (n_1 + n_2)}{n_1 k_2 + n_2 k_1} + \frac{(x_1 - x_2)(n_1 r_1 k_2 - n_2 r_2 k_1)}{3(n_1 k_2 + n_2 k_1)}, \right.$$
$$\left. \frac{k_1 k_2 (n_1 + n_2)}{n_1 k_2 + n_2 k_1} - \frac{(x_1 - x_2)(n_1 r_1 k_2 - n_2 r_2 k_1)}{3(n_1 k_2 + n_2 k_1)} \right). \tag{11.9}$$

Now, there is an important question: Does the system come to a stationary state or to a cycle of states under a multiple repetition of the two-step game?

Before the transition $s > 1$, when the equilibrium distribution of the operators between the companies and the prices for services were defined at least once, we have four possible states of the system:

1) $(0,0)$ with the prices $\left(\frac{k_1 k_2 (n_1 + n_2)}{n_1 k_2 + n_2 k_1}, \frac{k_1 k_2 (n_1 + n_2)}{n_1 k_2 + n_2 k_1} \right)$,

2) $(0,1)$ with the prices

$$\left(\frac{k_1 k_2 (n_1 + n_2)}{n_1 k_2 + n_2 k_1} - \frac{(n_1 r_1 k_2 - n_2 r_2 k_1)}{3(n_1 k_2 + n_2 k_1)}, \frac{k_1 k_2 (n_1 + n_2)}{n_1 k_2 + n_2 k_1} + \frac{(n_1 r_1 k_2 - n_2 r_2 k_1)}{3(n_1 k_2 + n_2 k_1)} \right),$$

3) $(1,0)$ with the prices

$$\left(\frac{k_1 k_2 (n_1 + n_2)}{n_1 k_2 + n_2 k_1} + \frac{(n_1 r_1 k_2 - n_2 r_2 k_1)}{3(n_1 k_2 + n_2 k_1)}, \frac{k_1 k_2 (n_1 + n_2)}{n_1 k_2 + n_2 k_1} - \frac{(n_1 r_1 k_2 - n_2 r_2 k_1)}{3(n_1 k_2 + n_2 k_1)} \right),$$

4) $(1,1)$ with the prices $\left(\frac{k_1 k_2 (n_1 + n_2)}{n_1 k_2 + n_2 k_1}, \frac{k_1 k_2 (n_1 + n_2)}{n_1 k_2 + n_2 k_1} \right)$.

a) The state $(0,0)$ cannot be stationary, since the equilibrium conditions (11.8) fail for it. As a result, from this state the system moves to one of the three remaining states.

b) Consider the fourth state $(1,1)$ of the system. Here we have the equality $q_1^{(s)} = q_2^{(s)}$. If the equilibrium conditions (11.8) hold for $(1,1)$, then the system comes to a stationary state. Otherwise, both conditions fail, and the system moves to $(0, 1)$ or $(1, 0)$. Note that the operator choosing the first company increases his price, whereas the one choosing the second company decreases his price, which guarantees satisfaction of the equilibrium conditions and the stationarity of the new state.

c) Let the system be in the second state $(0, 1)$. The second condition of (11.8) holds for this state since $q_2^{(s)} > 0$. If this also applies to the first condition, then the system is in a stationary state. Otherwise, the system moves to the stationary state $(1, 1)$, since $q_1^{(s+1)} = q_2^{(s+1)}$ increases in comparison with $q_1^{(s)}$ and both conditions are valid in it.

d) Suppose the system is the third state $(1, 0)$. The first condition of (11.8) holds for this state because $q_1^{(s)} > 0$. If the second condition is also valid, then the system is in a stationary state. Otherwise, by analogy with item c), the system moves to the stationary state $(1, 1)$.

Summarizing the results of this analysis, we draw a series of conclusions for the system with $\frac{n_1 r_1}{k_1} \geq \frac{n_2 r_2}{k_2}$.

1. The system comes to a stationary state at most after three transitions. After the first transition, the system moves to one of the four states described. Then the longest path to a stationary state (two transitions) is possible if after the first transition the system moves to the state $(0, 0)$.

2. The admissible stationary states of the system are defined by the model parameters. The system can come to the stationary states $(0, 1)$ and $(1, 0)$ if

$$\left(\frac{k_1 k_2 (n_1 + n_2)}{n_1 k_2 + n_2 k_1} - \frac{(n_1 r_1 k_2 - n_2 r_2 k_1)}{3(n_1 k_2 + n_2 k_1)} \right) R \leq p_1 r_1$$

and to the state $(1, 1)$ if

$$\frac{k_1 k_2 (n_1 + n_2)}{n_1 k_2 + n_2 k_1} R \geq p_1 r_1.$$

Note that when the second condition fails, the first one is valid. However, under

$$\frac{k_1 k_2 (n_1 + n_2)}{n_1 k_2 + n_2 k_1} - \frac{(n_1 r_1 k_2 - n_2 r_2 k_1)}{3(n_1 k_2 + n_2 k_1)} \leq \frac{p_1 r_1}{R} \leq \frac{k_1 k_2 (n_1 + n_2)}{n_1 k_2 + n_2 k_1},$$

both conditions hold, and any of the three states is stationary.

3. The equilibrium and stationary states of the system are independent of the price for services of the second company.

Example 38. The companies have the same number of clients $n_1 = n_2 = 10$. The first company provides a larger resource ($r_1 = 1$, $r_2 = 0.5$) than the second but with higher prices ($p_1 = 5$, $p_2 = 1$). In addition, the degree of dissatisfaction with the former is smaller in comparison with the latter ($k_1 = 1$, $k_2 = 2$). The initial prices for services assigned by the operators are $q_1 = 1$ and $q_2 = 0.5$. For these prices, formula (11.8) yields the equilibrium distribution $x^{(1)} = (1, 0)$ in the market. Using (11.9), we easily calculate the new prices $q^{(1)} \approx (1.5, 1.667)$. For the new prices, the distribution is $x^{(2)} = (1, 1)$; see (11.8). For the distribution $x^{(2)}$, the new prices are $q^{(2)} = (1.333, 1.333)$, which lead to $x^{(3)} = x^{(2)} = (1, 1)$. In other words, the system comes to a stationary state after two transitions.

11.9 TWO OPERATORS AND OPERATOR-DEPENDENT CLIENT PREFERENCES

Now, suppose that the partition of company i clients choosing operator j makes up $\frac{1}{2} + \frac{h_{ij} - h_{i(3-j)}}{2k_j}$ and the coefficient k_j measures the degree of dissatisfaction of the clients served by operator j, for example, due to the difficult-to-access maintenance points and transport cost, low-level service, and so on.

The payoff functions take the form

$$u_1(x, q) = \frac{q_1}{2k_1} \left((n_1 + n_2)(k_1 - q_1 + q_2) + (n_1 r_1 - n_2 r_2)(x_1 - x_2) \right)$$
$$- \frac{x_1}{x_1 + x_2} p_1 r_1 - \frac{(1 - x_1)}{2 - x_1 - x_2} p_2 r_2,$$

$$u_2(x, q) = \frac{q_2}{2k_2} \left((n_1 + n_2)(k_2 + q_1 - q_2) - (n_1 r_1 - n_2 r_2)(x_1 - x_2) \right)$$
$$- \frac{x_2}{x_1 + x_2} p_1 r_1 - \frac{(1 - x_2)}{2 - x_1 - x_2} p_2 r_2.$$

The following equilibria are then possible for the distributions of the operators between the companies:

$$x^*(q) = (x_1^*(q), x_2^*(q)) = \begin{cases} (0, 0) \text{ if } \begin{cases} q_1(n_1 r_1 - n_2 r_2) \leq -p_2 r_2 k_1, \\ q_2(n_1 r_1 - n_2 r_2) \leq -p_2 r_2 k_2, \end{cases} \\[2mm] (0, 1) \text{ if } \begin{cases} q_1(n_1 r_1 - n_2 r_2) \leq p_1 r_1 k_1, \\ q_2(n_1 r_1 - n_2 r_2) \geq -p_2 r_2 k_2, \end{cases} \\[2mm] (1, 0) \text{ if } \begin{cases} q_1(n_1 r_1 - n_2 r_2) \geq -p_2 r_2 k_1, \\ q_2(n_1 r_1 - n_2 r_2) \leq p_1 r_1 k_2, \end{cases} \\[2mm] (1, 1) \text{ if } \begin{cases} q_1(n_1 r_1 - n_2 r_2) \geq p_1 r_1 k_1, \\ q_2(n_1 r_1 - n_2 r_2) \geq p_1 r_1 k_2. \end{cases} \end{cases} \quad (11.10)$$

The equilibrium prices for services are

$$q^*(x) = (q_1^*(x), q_2^*(x)) = \left(\frac{2k_1 + k_2}{3} + \frac{(x_1 - x_2)(n_1 r_1 - n_2 r_2)}{3(n_1 + n_2)}, \right.$$

$$\left. \frac{2k_2 + k_1}{3} - \frac{(x_1 - x_2)(n_1 r_1 - n_2 r_2)}{3(n_1 + n_2)} \right). \quad (11.11)$$

Like in the previous case, let us find out whether the system comes to a stationary state or to a cycle of states under a multiple repetition of the two-step game. For definiteness, assume that $n_1 r_1 \geq n_2 r_2$ (otherwise, simply renumber the companies).

Before the transition $s > 1$, when the equilibrium distribution of the operators between the companies and the prices for services were defined at least once, we have four possible states of the system:

1) $(0, 0)$ with the prices $(\frac{2k_1 + k_2}{3}, \frac{2k_2 + k_1}{3})$,
2) $(0, 1)$ with the prices $(\frac{2k_1 + k_2}{3} - \frac{(n_1 r_1 - n_2 r_2)}{3(n_1 + n_2)}, \frac{2k_2 + k_1}{3} + \frac{(n_1 r_1 - n_2 r_2)}{3(n_1 + n_2)})$,
3) $(1, 0)$ with the prices $(\frac{2k_1 + k_2}{3} + \frac{(n_1 r_1 - n_2 r_2)}{3(n_1 + n_2)}, \frac{2k_2 + k_1}{3} - \frac{(n_1 r_1 - n_2 r_2)}{3(n_1 + n_2)})$,
4) $(1, 1)$ with the prices $(\frac{2k_1 + k_2}{3}, \frac{2k_2 + k_1}{3})$.

a) For the first state, the system moves to one of the three other states $(0, 1)$, $(1, 0)$, or $(1, 1)$.

b) Consider the fourth state $(1, 1)$ of the system. If the equilibrium conditions (11.10) hold for $(1, 1)$, then the system comes to a stationary state. If the first condition fails, then the system moves to $(0, 1)$. In addition, $q_1^{(s+1)}$ decreases in comparison with $q_1^{(s)}$, whereas $q_2^{(s+1)}$ increases in comparison with $q_2^{(s)}$, that is, the equilibrium conditions hold for this state at the next transition $s + 1$, and the state under consideration becomes stationary for the system. By analogy, if the second condition is not valid, then the system moves to $(1, 0)$, which also leads to a stationary state. Finally, whenever both conditions take no place, the system moves to $(0, 1)$ or $(1, 0)$, which becomes stationary.

c) Let the system be in the second state $(0, 1)$. The second condition of (11.10) holds for this state since $q_2^{(s)} > 0$. If this also applies to the first condition, then the system is in a stationary state. Otherwise, the system moves to the state $(1, 1)$ or $(1, 0)$. If both conditions are valid for the state $(1, 1)$, then the system moves to this state, new prices are assigned for it, and, in accordance with item b), the system comes to a stationary state at most after one transition. If the second condition fails for $(1, 1)$, then the system moves to the state $(1, 0)$. In this state, $q_1^{(s+1)}$ increases in comparison with $q_1^{(s)}$, whereas $q_2^{(s+1)}$ decreases in comparison with $q_2^{(s)}$, that is, the equilibrium conditions hold for this state at the next transition $s+1$, and the state under consideration becomes stationary for the system.

d) Suppose the system is in the third state $(1, 0)$. The first condition of (11.10) holds for this state because $q_1^{(s)} > 0$. If the second condition is also valid, then the system is in a stationary state. Otherwise, by analogy with item c), the system moves to the state $(1, 1)$ or $(0, 1)$. If both conditions are valid for the state $(1, 1)$, then the system moves to this state, new prices are assigned for it, and, in accordance with item b), the system comes to a stationary state at most after one transition. If the first condition fails for $(1, 1)$, then the system moves to the state $(0, 1)$. In this state, $q_1^{(s+1)}$ decreases in comparison with $q_1^{(s)}$, whereas $q_2^{(s+1)}$ increases in comparison with $q_2^{(s)}$, that is, the equilibrium conditions hold for this state at the next transition $s+1$, and the state under consideration becomes stationary for the system.

Summarizing the results of this analysis, we draw a series of conclusions for the system with $n_1 r_1 \geq n_2 r_2$.

1. Like in the previous case, the system comes to a stationary state at most after three transitions.

2. The system comes to the following stationary states (x_1, x_2) only under the following conditions imposed on its parameters:

$$(x_1, x_2) = \begin{cases} (0, 1) \text{ if } \left(\frac{2k_1+k_2}{3} - \frac{(n_1 r_1 - n_2 r_2)}{3(n_1+n_2)}\right)(n_1 r_1 - n_2 r_2) \leq p_1 r_1 k_1, \\ (1, 0) \text{ if } \left(\frac{2k_2+k_1}{3} - \frac{(n_1 r_1 - n_2 r_2)}{3(n_1+n_2)}\right)(n_1 r_1 - n_2 r_2) \leq p_1 r_1 k_2, \\ (1, 1) \text{ if } \begin{cases} \frac{2k_1+k_2}{3}(n_1 r_1 - n_2 r_2) \geq p_1 r_1 k_1, \\ \frac{2k_2+k_1}{3}(n_1 r_1 - n_2 r_2) \geq p_1 r_1 k_2. \end{cases} \end{cases}$$

3. The equilibrium and stationary states of the system are independent of the price for services of the second company.

Example 39. The companies have the same number of clients $n_1 = n_2 = 10$. The first company provides a larger resource ($r_1 = 1$, $r_2 = 0.5$) than the second but with higher prices ($p_1 = 5$, $p_2 = 1$). In addition, the degree of dissatisfaction with the first operator is greater in comparison with the second ($k_1 = 4$, $k_2 = 2$). The initial prices for services assigned by the operators are $q_1 = 1$ and $q_2 = 2$. For these prices, formula (11.10) yields the equilibrium distribution $x^{(1)} = (0, 1)$ in the market. Using (11.11), we easily calculate the new prices $q^{(1)} = (3.25, 2.75)$. For the new prices, the distribution is $x^{(2)} = x^{(1)} = (0, 1)$; see (11.10). In other words, the system comes to a stationary state after one transition.

Example 40. The companies have the same number of clients $n_1 = n_2 = 10$. The first company provides a larger resource ($r_1 = 0.5$, $r_2 = 0.25$) than the second but with higher prices ($p_1 = 5$, $p_2 = 1$). In addition, the degree of dissatisfaction with the first operator is smaller in comparison with the second ($k_1 = 2$, $k_2 = 4$). The initial prices for services assigned by the operators are $q_1 = 1$ and $q_2 = 2$. For these prices, formula (11.10) yields the equilibrium distribution $x^{(1)} = (0, 1)$ in the market. Using (11.11), we easily calculate the new prices $q^{(1)} = (2.625, 3.375)$. For the new prices, the distribution is $x^{(2)} = (1, 0)$; see (11.10). For the distribution $x^{(2)}$, the new prices are $q^{(2)} \approx (2.708, 3.292)$, which give $x^{(3)} = x^{(2)} = (1, 0)$. In other words, the system comes to a stationary state after two transitions.

11.10 M OPERATORS AND COMPANY-DEPENDENT CLIENT PREFERENCES

Now, consider the market where $M \geq 3$ operators distribute themselves between two companies. In this case, the partition of company i clients choosing operator j is defined as $\frac{1}{M} + \sum_{l \neq j} \frac{h_{ij} - h_{il}}{Mk_i}$.

The payoff function of each operator j under the known strategies x and q has the form

$$u_j(x, q) = q_j \sum_i n_i \left(\frac{1}{M} + \sum_{l \neq j} \frac{h_{ij} - h_{il}}{Mk_i} \right) - \sum_i \frac{x_{ij}}{\sum_l x_{il}} p_i r_i.$$

The operators choose between two large companies operating in the market. As in the case of two operators, we use the notation x_j to represent the probability that operator j contracts with the first company. Then $1 - x_j$ is the probability that operator j contracts with the second company. With this notation, the payoff function of operator $j = 1, \ldots, M$ can be written as

$$u_j(x, q) = \frac{q_j}{M} \left((n_1 + n_2) - ((M - 1)q_j - \sum_{l \neq j} q_l) \left(\frac{n_1}{k_1} + \frac{n_2}{k_2} \right) \right.$$

$$+ ((M - 1)x_j - \sum_{l \neq j} x_l) \left(\frac{n_1 r_1}{k_1} - \frac{n_2 r_2}{k_2} \right) \Bigg)$$

$$- \frac{x_j}{\sum_l x_l} p_1 r_1 - \frac{(1 - x_j)}{M - \sum_l x_l} p_2 r_2$$

$$= \alpha_j(q) + \frac{\left(\frac{n_1 r_1}{k_1} - \frac{n_2 r_2}{k_2}\right) q_j}{M} \left((M-1)x_j - \sum_{l \neq j} x_l\right)$$

$$- \frac{x_j}{\sum_l x_l} p_1 r_1 - \frac{(1-x_j)}{M - \sum_l x_l} p_2 r_2,$$

where $\alpha_j(q)$ is a value independent of x. Here we let $\frac{0}{0} = 1$.

The payoff functions $u_j(x, q)$ are convex in x_j. Hence the optimal values x_j lie at one of the limits of the interval $[0, 1]$, which means that the optimal strategies are pure strategies.

For definiteness, assume that $\frac{n_1 r_1}{k_1} \geq \frac{n_2 r_2}{k_2}$ (if this inequality fails, just renumber the companies). Denote this difference by $R = \frac{n_1 r_1}{k_1} - \frac{n_2 r_2}{k_2} \geq 0$.

For the given prices q, the equilibrium distribution of the operators between the companies is a distribution $x^*(q) = \{x_j^*(q)\}_{j=1}^M$, where all $x_j^*(q) \in \{0, 1\}$, so that the inequality $u_j(x, q)|_{x=x^*(q)} \geq u_j(x, q)|_{x_j=1-x_j^*(q), x_{l\neq j}=x_l^*(q)}$ holds for all $j = 1, \ldots, M$. In other words, the choice $x_j^*(q)$ of each operator j is the best response to the choice of all other operators. Denote by $K^{-j} = \sum_{l \neq j} x_l^*(q)$ the number of operators choosing the first company minus operator j.

Consider a scenario in which all operators except operator j chose the second company, that is, $K^{-j} = 0$ for any j. Then the choice $x_j = 0$ of each operator j is the best response if $-\frac{0}{0}p_1 r_1 - \frac{1}{M}p_2 r_2 \geq \frac{Rq_j}{M}(M-1) - \frac{1}{1}p_1 r_1$ or $\frac{(M-1)Rq_j}{M} \leq -\frac{p_2 r_2}{M}$. Conversely, under the condition $\frac{(M-1)Rq_j}{M} \geq -\frac{p_2 r_2}{M}$, the best choice is $x_j = 1$.

Consider a scenario in which all operators except operator j chose the first company, that is, $K^{-j} = M - 1$ for any j. Then the choice $x_j = 1$ of each operator j is the best response if $\frac{1}{M}p_1 r_1 - \frac{0}{0}p_2 r_2 \geq -\frac{Rq_j}{M}(M-1) - \frac{1}{1}p_2 r_2$ or $\frac{(M-1)Rq_j}{M} \geq \frac{p_1 r_1}{M}$. Conversely, under the condition $\frac{(M-1)Rq_j}{M} \leq \frac{p_1 r_1}{M}$, the best choice is $x_j = 0$.

For the scenarios $0 < K^{-j} < M - 1$, the choice $x_j = 1$ of each operator j is the best if $\frac{Rq_j}{M}(M - 1 - K^{-j}) - \frac{1}{K^{-j}+1}p_1 r_1 \geq -\frac{Rq_j}{M}K^{-j} - \frac{1}{M-K^{-j}}p_2 r_2$ or $\frac{(M-1)Rq_j}{M} \geq \frac{p_1 r_1}{K^{-j}+1} - \frac{p_2 r_2}{M-K^{-j}}$. Conversely, under the condition $\frac{(M-1)Rq_j}{M} \leq \frac{p_1 r_1}{K^{-j}+1} - \frac{p_2 r_2}{M-K^{-j}}$, the best choice is $x_j = 0$.

In the general case, the best response of operator j to the choice of the first company by the group of K^{-j} operators is $x_j = 0$ if $\frac{(M-1)Rq_j}{M} \leq \frac{p_1 r_1 \mathbb{I}_{K^{-j}>0}}{K^{-j}+1} - \frac{p_2 r_2 \mathbb{I}_{K^{-j}<M-1}}{M-K^{-j}}$ and $x_j = 1$ if $\frac{(M-1)Rq_j}{M} \geq \frac{p_1 r_1 \mathbb{I}_{K^{-j}>0}}{K^{-j}+1} - \frac{p_2 r_2 \mathbb{I}_{K^{-j}<M-1}}{M-K^{-j}}$.

Hence we obtain the following equilibria $x^*(q) = \{x_j^*(q)\}_{j=1}^M$, where all $x_j^*(q) \in \{0, 1\}$ and $K = \sum_l x_l^*(q)$, under the following conditions:

$$\begin{cases} \frac{(M-1)Rq_j}{M} \geq \frac{p_1r_1\mathbb{I}_{K>1}}{K} - \frac{p_2r_2\mathbb{I}_{K<M}}{M-K+1} & \text{for } x_j^*(q) = 1, \\ \frac{(M-1)Rq_j}{M} \leq \frac{p_1r_1\mathbb{I}_{K>0}}{K+1} - \frac{p_2r_2\mathbb{I}_{K<M-1}}{M-K} & \text{for } x_j^*(q) = 0. \end{cases} \quad (11.12)$$

Consider the second step at which the operators assign their prices for services. Each of the functions u_j is concave in q_j, representing a parabola with descending branches. This means that the optimal strategy to assign the price q_j is the maximum of u_j in q_j.

The best response of each player j to the strategies of the other players is q_j that satisfies the equation

$$2(M-1)\left(\frac{n_1}{k_1} + \frac{n_2}{k_2}\right)q_j = n_1 + n_2 + \left(\sum_l q_l - q_j\right)\left(\frac{n_1}{k_1} + \frac{n_2}{k_2}\right)$$

$$+ R\left(Mx_j - \sum_l x_l\right).$$

Summing up the equations and expressing q_j, we calculate the equilibrium $q^*(x) = \{q_j^*(x)\}_{j=1}^M$, where

$$q_j^*(x) = \frac{k_1 k_2 (n_1 + n_2)}{(M-1)(n_1 k_2 + n_2 k_1)} + \frac{k_1 k_2 R\left(Mx_j - \sum_l x_l\right)}{(2M-1)(n_1 k_2 + n_2 k_1)}. \quad (11.13)$$

Consequently, evolving optimally, the system changes its states in the following way. Denote by $x^{(s)} = (x_j^{(s)}, j = 1, \ldots, M)$ the system state before the first transition step s when the companies are redistributed among the players. This state corresponds to the optimal prices $q^{(s)} = (q_j^*(x^{(s)}), j = 1, \ldots, M)$ defined by (11.13). Then the next state (see (11.12)) is calculated as $x^*(q^{(s)})$.

Consider the system state before the transition $s > 1$ when the equilibrium distribution of the companies and the prices for services were defined at least once. Denote by $x^{(s)}$ the current state of the system before the transition s. Note that the operators are symmetric and can vary only in their strategies. Hence it is possible to simplify the notations by dividing operators into two groups as follows.

The group A consists of the operators j contracting with the first company, that is, $x_j = 1$, and the group B contains the remaining operators who choose the second company. Note that the prices $q_j^{(s)}$ defined by (11.13) are identical for all players from the same group. Hence, the equilibrium conditions hold or do not hold for all of them simultaneously. Denote by

$q_A(K)$ and $q_B(K)$ the prices of operators that belong to the groups A and B, respectively. Then the equilibrium condition (11.12) in the case where the group A contains K operators can be written as

$$\begin{cases} \frac{(M-1)Rq_A(K)}{M} \geq \frac{p_1 r_1 \mathbb{I}_{K>1}}{K} - \frac{p_2 r_2 \mathbb{I}_{K<M}}{M-K+1}, \\ \frac{(M-1)Rq_B(K)}{M} \leq \frac{p_1 r_1 \mathbb{I}_{K>0}}{K+1} - \frac{p_2 r_2 \mathbb{I}_{K<M-1}}{M-K}. \end{cases} \tag{11.14}$$

Clearly, if $K = 0$, then the first condition disappears, and if $K = M$, then the second.

Before any iteration $s > 1$ of the game, the system state can be described as the number of players in the group A. The states are the following:

0) all the players chose the second company and have the same prices $q_B(0) = Q = \frac{k_1 k_2 (n_1 + n_2)}{(M-1)(n_1 k_2 + n_2 k_1)}$, $1 \leq K \leq M-1$ players chose the first company, and their prices are $q_A(K) = Q + \frac{k_1 k_2 R(M-K)}{(2M-1)(n_1 k_2 + n_2 k_1)}$, whereas the other players have the prices $q_B(K) = Q - \frac{k_1 k_2 RK}{(2M-1)(n_1 k_2 + n_2 k_1)}$, all M players chose the first company and have the same prices $q_A(M) = Q$.

1) Consider the system states 0 and M. All the prices are identical and equal Q. The state 0 cannot be stationary, since the second condition of (11.14) fails, $(M-1)Rq_B(0) \leq -p_2 r_2$ due to $Rq_B(0) = Q > 0$, and so the system moves to one of the remaining states. The system is in the stationary state M only if the first equilibrium condition of (11.14) $(M-1)RQ \geq p_1 r_1$ holds in this state and the system was in the state M before or moved there from the state 0. Otherwise, from the state 0 or M the system moves to the state $K < M$, in which it is required that

$$\begin{cases} \frac{(M-1)RQ}{M} \geq \frac{p_1 r_1 \mathbb{I}_{K>1}}{K} - \frac{p_2 r_2 \mathbb{I}_{K<M}}{M-K+1}, \\ \frac{(M-1)RQ}{M} \leq \frac{p_1 r_1 \mathbb{I}_{K>0}}{K+1} - \frac{p_2 r_2 \mathbb{I}_{K<M-1}}{M-K}. \end{cases}$$

These conditions take place only for $K \in \{1, M-1\}$. The value K can be 1 under both conditions, that is,

$$\begin{cases} \frac{(M-1)RQ}{M} \geq -\frac{p_2 r_2}{M}, \\ \frac{(M-1)RQ}{M} \leq \frac{p_1 r_1}{2} - \frac{p_2 r_2}{M-1}. \end{cases}$$

The first condition obviously holds. If the second condition is also valid, then in this state, we have $q_A(1) > Q > 0$, $q_B(1) < Q$; after assignment of the new prices, the equilibrium conditions remain valid, and the state $K = 1$ becomes stationary.

If the second condition fails, that is, $\frac{(M-1)RQ}{M} < \frac{p_1 r_1}{2} - \frac{p_2 r_2}{M-1}$, then the only option is $K = M - 1$. Check the conditions

$$
\begin{cases}
\frac{(M-1)RQ}{M} \geq \frac{p_1 r_1}{M-1} - \frac{p_2 r_2}{2}, \\
\frac{(M-1)RQ}{M} \leq \frac{p_1 r_1}{M}.
\end{cases}
$$

The second condition holds because of the nonstationary state $K = M$. The first condition is valid, since $\frac{(M-1)RQ}{M} > \frac{p_1 r_2}{2} - \frac{p_2 r_2}{M-1} \geq \frac{p_1 r_1}{M-1} - \frac{p_2 r_2}{2}$ under $M \geq 3$. For the new prices $q_A(M - 1) > Q$ and $q_B(M - 1) < Q$, the conditions still hold, and the state $K = M - 1$ becomes stationary.

In other words, from the state 0 the system comes to a stationary state from the set $\{1, M - 1, M\}$. Then either state M is stationary, or from this state the system moves to a stationary state from the set $\{1, M - 1\}$.

2) Let the system be in the state K, where $1 \leq K \leq M - 1$. If the equilibrium conditions (11.14) hold, then the system arrives at a stationary state. Otherwise, a new state K' is formed. If $K' = M$ and this state is not stationary, then in accordance with item 1), the system moves from this state to a stationary state from the set $\{1, M - 1\}$. In the case $K' = 0$ (which applies to the negative prices $q_B(K)$), by item 1) the system moves from this state to a stationary state from the set $\{1, M - 1, M\}$.

Otherwise, the state K' is such that $1 \leq K' \leq M - 1$ and

$$
\begin{cases}
\frac{(M-1)Rq_A(K)}{M} \geq \frac{p_1 r_1 \mathbb{I}_{K'>1}}{K'} - \frac{p_2 r_2}{M-K'+1} \text{ for the players staying in the group } A, \\
\frac{(M-1)Rq_B(K)}{M} \leq \frac{p_1 r_1}{K'+1} - \frac{p_2 r_2 \mathbb{I}_{K'<M-1}}{M-K'} \text{ for the players staying in the group } B, \\
\frac{(M-1)Rq_B(K)}{M} \geq \frac{p_1 r_1 \mathbb{I}_{K'>1}}{K'} - \frac{p_2 r_2}{M-K'+1} \text{ for the players moving from} \\
\text{the group } B \text{ to } A, \\
\frac{(M-1)Rq_A(K)}{M} \leq \frac{p_1 r_1}{K'+1} - \frac{p_2 r_2 \mathbb{I}_{K'<M-1}}{M-K'} \text{ for the players moving from} \\
\text{the group } A \text{ to } B.
\end{cases}
$$

Next, new prices $q_A(K')$ and $q_B(K')$ are assigned for the state K'. Note that the prices increase for the players moving from the group B to A and decrease for the players moving from the group A to B regardless of K', since $q_A(K) > Q \geq q_B(K')$ and $q_B(K) < Q \leq q_A(K')$ under $1 \leq K \leq M - 1$. Subsequently, the equilibrium conditions (11.14) hold for them given the new prices. Therefore, in the case where all operators changed their group, the new state is stationary.

a) If $1 \leq K < K' \leq M - 1$, then there exist operators who moved from the group B to A, that is,

$$\frac{(M-1)Rq_B(K)}{M} \geq \frac{p_1r_1}{K'} - \frac{p_2r_2}{M-K'+1}.$$

Since $K' \leq M - 1$, some player either stayed in the group B or joined it by moving from the group A. In the former case, we have

$$\frac{(M-1)Rq_B(K)}{M} \leq \frac{p_1r_1}{K'+1} - \frac{p_2r_2\mathbb{I}_{K'<M-1}}{M-K'};$$

in the latter,

$$\frac{(M-1)Rq_B(K)}{M} < \frac{(M-1)Rq_A(K)}{M} \leq \frac{p_1r_1}{K'+1} - \frac{p_2r_2\mathbb{I}_{K'<M-1}}{M-K'},$$

and then

$$\frac{p_1r_1}{K'} - \frac{p_2r_2}{M-K'+1} \leq \frac{p_1r_1}{K'+1} - \frac{p_2r_2\mathbb{I}_{K'<M-1}}{M-K'},$$

which is possible only if $K' = M - 1$.

As a result, for $K' = M - 1$ and hence for $K < M$, we have

$$\begin{cases} \frac{(M-1)Rq_A(K)}{M} > \frac{(M-1)Rq_B(K)}{M} \geq \frac{p_1r_1}{M-1} - \frac{p_2r_2}{2}, \\ \frac{(M-1)Rq_B(K)}{M} \leq \frac{p_1r_1}{M}. \end{cases}$$

After assignment of the new prices, the second condition of (11.14) remains valid, since $q_B(M-1) < q_B(K)$ for $K < M - 1$. The first inequality holds, since

$$\frac{(M-1)Rq_A(M-1)}{M} > \frac{(M-1)Rq_B(K)}{M} \geq \frac{p_1r_1}{M-1} - \frac{p_2r_2}{2}$$

under $1 < K < M - 2$. In other words, the state $K' = M - 1$ is stationary.

b) If $1 \leq K' < K \leq M - 1$, then there exist operators who moved from the group A to B, that is,

$$\frac{(M-1)Rq_A(K)}{M} \leq \frac{p_1r_1}{K'+1} - \frac{p_2r_2}{M-K'}.$$

Since $K' \geq 1$, some player either stayed in the group A or joined it by moving from the group B. In the former case, we have

$$\frac{(M-1)Rq_A(K)}{M} \geq \frac{p_1r_1\mathbb{I}_{K'>1}}{K'} - \frac{p_2r_2}{M-K'+1};$$

in the latter,

$$\frac{(M-1)Rq_A(K)}{M} > \frac{(M-1)Rq_B(K)}{M} \geq \frac{p_1r_1\mathbb{I}_{K'>1}}{K'} - \frac{p_2r_2}{M-K'+1},$$

and then

$$\frac{p_1r_1\mathbb{I}_{K'>1}}{K'} - \frac{p_2r_2}{M-K'+1} \leq \frac{p_1r_1}{K'+1} - \frac{p_2r_2}{M-K'},$$

which is possible only if $K' = 1$.

As a result, for $K' = 1$ and hence for $K > 1$, we have

$$\begin{cases} \frac{(M-1)Rq_A(K)}{M} \geq -\frac{p_2r_2}{M}, \\ \frac{(M-1)Rq_B(K)}{M} < \frac{(M-1)Rq_A(K)}{M} \leq \frac{p_1r_1}{2} - \frac{p_2r_2}{M-1}. \end{cases}$$

After assignment of the new prices, the first condition of (11.14) remains valid, since $q_A(1) > q_A(K)$ for $K > 1$. The second inequality holds, since

$$\frac{(M-1)Rq_B(1)}{M} < \frac{(M-1)Rq_A(K)}{M} \leq \frac{p_1r_1}{2} - \frac{p_2r_2}{M-1}$$

under $2 < K < M - 1$. In other words, the state $K' = 1$ is stationary.

Consequently, we obtain the following results for the system with stepwise choice of optimal states: the system comes to a stationary state at most after three transitions, which is one of the states $\{1, M-1, M\}$; other stationary states from the residual set $\{2, \ldots, M-2\}$ are not excluded but can be achieved after one transition if the system by chance has suitable initial prices q.

Example 41. Consider the system with two companies as follows. The first company has been in the market for a long time and has more subscribers ($n_1 = 25$, $n_2 = 10$), but its resources are more expensive ($p_1 = 10$, $p_2 = 5$). To catch the market opportunities, the second company assigns low prices, implements an aggressive advertising policy ($k_1 = 1$, $k_2 = 2$), and allocates more resources for accessibility ($r_1 = 0.5$, $r_2 = 0.6$). There are $M = 10$ virtual operators reselling the services of these companies. Depending on initial prices q, the system arrives at one of the states presented in Table 11.3 and then changes its state until coming to one of the stationary states (typed in boldface). Clearly, in the states $K = 8$ and $K = 9$, the operators choosing the second company have negative prices, but this does not interfere with the fact that the state $K = 9$ is stationary. Besides, note that the stationary states $K = 2, 3$ are isolated and the system can arrive at them only by chance with suitable initial prices.

Table 11.3 Transitions between system states

State K	q_A	q_B	Possible transitions
0	–	0.13	1, 10
1	0.28	0.112	
2	0.26	0.096	
3	0.246	0.08	
4	0.23	0.063	1, 10
5	0.213	0.046	1, 9
6	0.196	0.03	1, 9
7	0.18	0.013	1, 9
8	0.163	−0.004	1, 9
9	0.146	−0.02	
10	0.13	–	

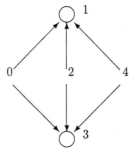

Figure 11.3 Transitions between states

Example 42. Consider the previous example with a smaller number of clients and operators ($n_1 = 10$, $n_2 = 4$, $M = 4$). Depending on the initial prices q, the system moves to one of the states illustrated in Fig. 11.3, in the final analysis arriving at one of the stationary states 1 or 3.

REFERENCES

[1] E. Altman, N. Shimkin, Individually optimal dynamic routing in a processor sharing system, Operations Research 46 (6) (1998) 776–784.

[2] M. Armstrong, Competition in two-sided markets, The RAND Journal of Economics 37 (3) (2006) 668–691.

[3] R. Aumann, R. Myerson, Endogenous formation of links between players and coalitions: an application of the Shapley value, in: The Shapley Value, Cambridge University Press, 1988, pp. 175–191.

[4] K. Avrachenkov, N. Litvak, V. Medyanikov, M. Sokol, Alpha current flow betweenness centrality, in: Proceedings of WAW 2013, in: Lecture Notes in Computer Science, vol. 8305, 2013, pp. 106–117.

[5] K. Avrachenkov, N. Litvak, D. Nemirovsky, E. Smirnova, M. Sokol, Quick detection of top-k personalized pagerank lists, in: Proceedings of WAW 2011, in: Lecture Notes in Computer Science, vol. 6732, 2011, pp. 50–61.

[6] K.E. Avrachenkov, V.V. Mazalov, B.T. Tsinguev, Beta current flow centrality for weighted networks, in: Proceedings of Computational Social Network, in: Lecture Notes in Computer Science, vol. 9197, 2015, pp. 216–227.

[7] B. Awerbuch, Y. Azar, A. Epstein, The price of routing unsplittable flow, in: Proceedings of the 37th Annual ACM Symposium on Theory of Computing, STOC 2005, 2005, pp. 331–337.

[8] S. Berry, J. Levinsohn, A. Pakes, Automobile prices in market equilibrium, Econometrica 63 (4) (1995) 841–890.

[9] A. Bogomolnaia, O.M. Jackson, The stability of hedonic coalition structures, Games and Economic Behavior 38 (2) (2002) 201–230.

[10] S.P. Borgatti, M.G. Everett, L.C. Freeman, UCINET for Windows: Software for Social Network Analysis, Harvard, 2002.

[11] P. Borm, A. van den Nouweland, S. Tijs, Cooperation and communication restrictions: a survey, in: Imperfections and Behavior in Economic Organizations, 1994.

[12] P.E.M. Borm, G. Owen, S.H. Tijs, On the position value for communication situation, SIAM Journal on Discrete Mathematics 5 (3) (1992) 305–320.

[13] D. Braess, Über ein paradoxon aus der verkehrsplanung, Unternehmensforschung 12 (1) (1968) 258–268.

[14] U. Brandes, A faster algorithm for betweenness centrality, Journal of Mathematical Sociology 25 (2001) 163–177.

[15] U. Brandes, D. Fleischer, Centrality measures based on current flow, in: Proceedings of the 22nd Annual Conference on Theoretical Aspects of Computer Science, STACS 2005, 2005, pp. 533–544.

[16] L.A. Breyer, G.O. Roberts, Catalytic perfect simulation, Methodology and Computing in Applied Probability 3 (2) (2001) 161–177.

[17] S. Brin, L. Page, The anatomy of a large-scale hypertextual web search engine, Computer Networks and ISDN Systems 30 (17) (1998) 107–117.

[18] E. Calvo, J. Lasaga, A. van den Nouweland, Values of games with probabilistic graphs, Mathematical Social Sciences 37 (1999) 79–95.

[19] Yu.V. Chirkova, Routing problem with splittable traffic and incomplete information, Large-Scale Systems Control 26 (1) (2009) 164–176 (in Russian).

[20] Yu.V. Chirkova, Price of anarchy in machine load balancing game, Automation and Remote Control 76 (10) (2015) 1849–1864.

[21] Yu.V. Chirkova, Optimal arrivals in a two-server rationally random access system with loss, Matematicheskaya Teoriya Igr i ee Prilozheniya 8 (3) (2016) 67–99 (in Russian).

[22] Yu.V. Chirkova, Price of anarchy in minimum machine delay maximization problem for queueing system, Large-Scale Systems Control 62 (2016) 30–59 (in Russian).

[23] Yu.V. Chirkova, Optimal arrivals in a two-server random access system with loss, Automation and Remote Control 78 (3) (2017) 557–580.

[24] G. Christodoulou, E. Koutsoupias, On the price of anarchy and stability of correlated equilibria of linear congestion games, in: Algorithms – ESA 2005, in: Lecture Notes in Computer Science, vol. 3669, 2005, pp. 59–70.

[25] G. Christodoulou, E. Koutsoupias, The price of anarchy of finite congestion games, in: Proceedings of the 37th Annual ACM Symposium on Theory of Computing, STOC 2005, 2005, pp. 67–73.

[26] L. Epstein, Equilibria for two parallel links: the strong price of anarchy versus the price of anarchy, Acta Informatica 47 (7) (2010) 375–389.

[27] L. Epstein, E. Kleiman, R. van Stee, Maximizing the minimum load: the cost of selfishness, in: Proceedings of the 5th International Workshop on Internet and Network Economics, in: Lecture Notes in Computer Science, vol. 5929, 2009, pp. 232–243.

[28] R. Feldmann, M. Gairing, T. Lücking, B. Monien, M. Rode, Selfish routing in non-cooperative networks: a survey, in: Proceedings of the 28th International Symposium on Mathematical Foundations of Computer Science 2003, in: Lecture Notes in Computer Science, vol. 2747, 2003, pp. 21–45.

[29] D. Fotakis, S.C. Kontogiannis, E. Koutsoupias, M. Mavronicolas, P.G. Spirakis, The structure and complexity of Nash equilibria for a selfish routing game, in: Proceedings of the 29th International Colloquium on Automata, Languages and Programming, ICALP2002, 2002, pp. 123–134.

[30] L.C. Freeman, A set of measures of centrality based on betweenness, Sociometry 40 (1977) 35–41.

[31] L.C. Freeman, Centrality in social networks conceptual clarification, Social Networks 1 (1979) 215–239.

[32] L.C. Freeman, S.P. Borgatti, D.R. White, Centrality in valued graphs: a measure of betweenness based on network flow, Social Networks 13 (1991) 141–154.

[33] M. Gairing, B. Monien, K. Tiemann, Routing (un-) splittable flow in games with player-specific linear latency functions, in: Proceedings of the 33rd International Colloquium on Automata Languages and Programming, ICALP 2006, 2006, pp. 501–512.

[34] M. Gairing, B. Monien, K. Tiemann, Selfish routing with incomplete information, Theory of Computing Systems (2008) 91–130.

[35] H. Gao, J. Hu, V. Mazalov, A. Shchiptsova, L. Song, J. Tokareva, Location-price competition in airline networks, Journal of Applied Mathematics 2014 (2014) 494103.

[36] A.V. Gasnikov, E.V. Gasnikova, M.A. Mendel, K.V. Chepurchenko, Evolutionary methods to construct entropy-based model of correspondence matrix calculation, Mathematical Modeling 28 (4) (2016) 111–124 (in Russian).

[37] A.V. Gasnikov, S.L. Klenov, E.A. Nurminskii, Ya.A. Kholodov, N.B. Shamrai, Introduction to Mathematical Modeling of Transport Flows, Moscow Center for Continuous Mathematical Education, 2013 (in Russian).

[38] M. Girvan, M.E.J. Newman, Community structure in social and biological networks, Proceedings of the National Academy of Sciences of USA 99 (12) (2002) 7821–7826.

[39] A. Glazer, R. Hassin, ?/m/1: on the equilibrium distribution of customer arrivals, European Journal of Operational Research 13 (2) (1983) 146–150.

[40] P. Hines, S. Blumsack, A centrality measure for electrical networks, in: Proceedings of the 41st Hawaii International Conference on System Sciences, 2008, p. 185.

[41] I.C.F. Ipsen, S. Kirkland, Convergence Analysis of an Improved Pagerank Algorithm, Technical Report CRSC-TR04-02, North Carolina State University, 2004.

[42] M.O. Jackson, Allocation rules for network games, Games and Economic Behavior 51 (1) (2005) 128–154.

[43] M.O. Jackson, Social and Economic Networks, Princeton University Press, 2008.

[44] M.O. Jackson, J. Wolinsky, A strategic model of social and economic networks, Journal of Economic Theory 71 (1) (1996) 44–74.

[45] R.E. Jamison, Alternating Whitney sums and matchings in trees, part 1, Discrete Mathematics 67 (2) (1987) 177–189.

[46] O. Johnson, C. Goldschmidt, Preservation of log-concavity on summation, ESAIM: Probability and Statistics 10 (2006) 206–215.

[47] S. Kamvar, T. Haveliwala, G. Golub, Adaptive methods for the computation of pagerank, Linear Algebra and Its Applications 386 (2004) 51–65, Special Issue on the Conference on the Numerical Solution of Markov Chains 2003.

[48] Y.A. Korillis, A.A. Lazar, A. Orda, Avoiding the Braess's paradox for traffic networks, Journal of Applied Probability 36 (1999) 211–222.

[49] M.E. Koryagin, Competition of transport flows, Automation and Remote Control 67 (3) (2006) 472–479.

[50] E. Koutsoupias, C. Papadimitriou, Worst-case equilibria, in: STACS 99, in: Lecture Notes in Computer Science, vol. 1563, 1999, pp. 404–413.

[51] A.N. Langville, C.D. Meyer, Deeper inside pagerank, Internet Mathematics 1 (3) (2004) 335–400.

[52] A.N. Langville, C.D. Meyer, Updating pagerank with iterative aggregation, in: Proceedings of the 13th World Wide Web Conference, 2004.

[53] H. Lin, T. Roughgarden, E. Tardos, On Braess's paradox, in: Proceedings of the 15th Annual ACM-SIAM Symp. on Discrete Algorithms, SODA04, 2018, pp. 333–334.

[54] M. Mavronicolas, P. Spirakis, The price of selfish routing, in: Proceedings of the 33th Annual ACM STOC, 2001, pp. 510–519.

[55] V. Mazalov, Mathematical Game Theory and Applications, Wiley, 2014.

[56] V. Mazalov, A. Lukyanenko, S. Luukkainen, Equilibrium in cloud computing market, Performance Evaluation 92 (2015) 40–50.

[57] V.V. Mazalov, Yu.V. Chuiko, Non-cooperative Nash equilibrium in an optimal arrival time problem for a queueing system, Computational Technologies 11 (6) (2006) 60–71 (in Russian).

[58] V.V. Mazalov, A.V. Melnik, Equilibrium prices and flows in the passenger traffic problem, International Game Theory Review 18 (1) (2016).

[59] V.V. Mazalov, L.I. Trukhina, Generating functions and the Myerson vector in communication networks, Discrete Mathematics and Applications 24 (5) (2014) 295–303.

[60] D. McFadden, Conditional logit analysis of qualitative choice behaviour, in: P. Zarembka (Ed.), Frontiers in Econometrics, Academic Press, New York, 1973, pp. 105–142.

[61] I. Milchtaich, Congestion games with player-specific payoff functions, Games and Economic Behavior 13 (1996) 111–124.

[62] D. Monderer, L.S. Shapley, Potential games, Games and Economic Behavior 14 (1) (1996) 124–143.

[63] R.B. Myerson, Graphs and cooperation in games, Mathematics of Operations Research 2 (1977) 225–229.

[64] J. Nash, Non-cooperative games, The Annals of Mathematics 54 (2) (1951) 286–295.

[65] M.E.J. Newman, A measure of betweenness centrality based on random walks, Social Networks 27 (2005) 39–54.

[66] M.E.J. Newman, Modularity and community structure in networks, Proceedings of the National Academy of Sciences of USA 103 (23) (2006) 8577–8582.

[67] T. Opsahl, F. Agneessens, J. Skvoretz, Node centrality in weighted networks: generalizing degree and shortest paths, Social Networks 32 (2010) 245–251.

[68] C.H. Papadimitriou, Algorithms, games, and the internet, in: Proceedings of the 33th Annual ACM STOC, 2001, pp. 749–753.

[69] L.A. Petrosjan, A.A. Sedakov, Multistage networking games with full information, Matematicheskaya Teoriya Igr i ee Prilozheniya 1 (2) (2009) 66–81.

[70] L. Ravner, M. Haviv, Equilibrium and socially optimal arrivals to a single server loss system, in: International Conference on NETwork Games COntrol and OPtimization, NetGCoop'14, Trento, Italy, 2014, 2014.

[71] L. Ravner, M. Haviv, Strategic timing of arrivals to a finite queue multi-server loss system, Queueing Systems 81 (1) (2015) 71–96.

[72] R.W. Rosenthal, A class of games possessing pure-strategy Nash equilibria, International Journal of Game Theory 2 (1973) 65–67.

[73] T. Roughgarden, The price of anarchy is independent of the network topology, Journal of Computer and System Sciences 67 (2003) 341–364.

[74] T. Roughgarden, É. Tardos, How bad is selfish routing?, Journal of the ACM 49 (2) (Mar 2002) 236–259.

[75] M. Shaked, J.G. Shanthikumar, Stochastic Orders, Springer Series in Statistics, Springer, 2007.

[76] M. Slikker, Link monotonic allocation schemes, International Game Theory Review 7 (4) (2005) 473–489.

[77] M. Slikker, R.P. Gilles, H. Norde, S. Tijs, Directed networks, allocation properties and hierarchy formation, Mathematical Social Sciences 49 (1) (2005) 55–80.

[78] D. Talman, Y. Yamamoto, Average tree solutions and subcore for acyclic graph games, Journal of the Operations Research Society of Japan 51 (3) (2008) 187–201.

[79] Z. Tan, L. Wan, Q. Zhang, W. Ren, Inefficiency of equilibria for the machine covering game on uniform machines, Acta Informatica 49 (6) (2012) 361–379.

[80] V.V. Mazalov, Yu.V. Chirkova, J. Zheng, J.W. Lien, A game-theoretic model of virtual operators competition in a two-sided telecommunication market, Automation and Remote Control 79 (4) (2018) 737–756.

[81] H. Wang, H. Hua, D. Wang, Cacti with minimum, second-minimum, and third-minimum Kirchhoff indices, Mathematical Communications 15 (2010) 347–358.

[82] Z. Wang, A. Scaglione, R. Thomas, Electrical centrality measures for electric power grid vulnerability analysis, in: Proceedings of the 49th IEEE Conference on Decision and Control, CDC, 2010, pp. 5792–5797.

[83] J.G. Wardrop, Road paper. Some theoretical aspects of road research, Proceedings of the Institution of Civil Engineers 1 (3) (1952) 325–362.

[84] W.W. Zachary, An information flow model for conflict and fission in small groups, Journal of Anthropological Research 33 (1977) 452–473.

[85] A.B. Zhizhchenko, A.D. Izaak, The information system Math-Net.Ru. Application of contemporary technologies in the scientific work of mathematicians, Russian Math. Surveys 62 (5) (2007) 943–966.

INDEX

Printed in the United States
By Bookmasters